OZARK FOLKSONGS, Volume II

D1568064

OZARK FOLKSONGS

Collected and Edited by
VANCE RANDOLPH

(Revised Edition)
Introduction by W. K. McNeil

In Four Volumes
Volume II
Songs of the South and West

University of Missouri Press
Columbia & London, 1980

Library of Congress Cataloging in Publication Data

Randolph, Vance, 1892–
    Ozark Folksongs.

    Unacc. melodies.
    Reprint of the 1946–50 ed. published by the State
Historical Society of Missouri.
    Includes bibliographies.
    CONTENTS: v. 1.   British ballads and songs.—
v. 2.   Songs of the South and West.—v. 3.   Humorous
and play-party songs. [etc.]
        1.   Folk-songs, American—Ozark Mountains.
I. Title.
M1629.6.09R3   1980   784.4'06   79-3611
ISBN 0-8262-0297-7 (v. 1) ISBN 0-8262-0298-5 (v. 2)
ISBN 0-8262-0299-3 (v. 3) ISBN 0-8262-0300-0 (v. 4)

Grateful acknowledgments are given to Shapiro, Bernstein and Co.
for allowing to reprint "The Little Black Mustache," copyrighted
© 1926, copyright renewed and used by permission only, "Putting
on Airs," copyrighted © 1926, copyright renewed and used by
permission only, "The Wreck of the Southern Old 97," copyrighted
© 1924, copyright renewed and used by permission only, "The
Two Lanterns," copyrighted © 1926, copyright renewed and used
by permission only, "The Dream of the Miner's Child," copyrighted
© 1926, copyright renewed and used by permission only; and to
Mrs. Carson J. Robison for "The Wreck of Old Number Nine."

To H. M. Belden

Publisher's Foreword

The four volumes of *Ozark Folksongs* were originally published by The State Historical Society of Missouri from 1946 until 1950. With them, Vance Randolph compiled one of the most comprehensive regional collections of folksongs ever published. The collection was well received and is the standard reference work in its field, but it has been out of print for many years.

The University of Missouri Press is now reissuing the volumes, very much as they first appeared. All of the peculiarities that Randolph originally recorded in the texts of the songs have been left intact. We have taken the liberty of making a few improvements—an introduction by W. K. McNeil to underline the contemporary significance of the collection, additions to the bibliography, and a few typographical corrections. The Frank C. Brown Collection, which Randolph cites frequently, was just that—an unedited collection of papers—when *Ozark Folksongs* was first published. In 1964, the seventh and final volume of *The Frank C. Brown Collection of North Carolina Folklore* was published by Duke University Press.

Unfortunately, a few of the 883 songs that appeared originally have had to be eliminated. They are indicated in the contents pages by an asterisk and a note. However, most of them are readily available in other sources. In Volume II, they are "Moonlight and Skies," "Turnip Greens," and "Beautiful, Beautiful Brown Eyes"; in Volume III, "He Kept A-Kissin' On"; and in Volume IV, "I Have No Loving Mother Now," "The Spelling Song," "Why Do You Bob Your Hair, Girls?" "The Ship That Is Sailing By," "Motherless Children," "Once I Had a Sweetheart," "If I Was on Some Foggy Mountain Top," "How Sadly My Heart Yearns Toward You," "A Distant Land to Roam," and "Mother, the Queen of My Heart."

Except for these few deletions, this publication makes Vance Randolph's comprehensive collection, made unique by his wide-ranging knowledge of American folklore and his genuine identification with the people who have sung these songs, available to the public once again.

Contents

* Songs indicated by an asterisk were deleted from this edition; see first edition.

CONTENTS—*Continued*

CONTENTS—*Continued*

Page

CHAPTER VII. NEGRO AND PSEUDO-NEGRO SONGS

CONTENTS—*Continued*

CONTENTS—*Continued*

OZARK FOLKSONGS, Volume II

Chapter IV

SONGS ABOUT MURDERERS AND OUTLAWS

Songs of crime and criminals are popular among primitive people everywhere, and it is not surprising that many of the Ozark favorites are of this type. The hillman is an indomitable individualist, with an open contempt for some generally accepted forms of legal restraint; he has always been accustomed to settle his personal difficulties in his own way, and frequently chooses to do it with firearms and cutlery. When a man felt himself seriously affronted, in the old days, he often sent a messenger to give the other party "fa'r warnin'," and some shooting affrays were arranged with a certain degree of formality—a rustic survival of the old duelling code.

The mountain minstrel never ventures to glorify wickedness per se, and he seldom fails to point out that the way of the transgressor is hard indeed. In many cases a sort of homiletic epilogue is delivered from the scaffold by the hero-criminal himself, or shouted out just after the execution by one of his relatives. With all this, there is no denying that even the most moral and religious of the hill people have a singular antipathy for the restraints of the regularly constituted authority, and they still feel a certain admiration for anybody who has the courage to defy the vague power of the "Guv'ment."

The hillman has a particular weakness for the light-hearted rascality of bank-robbers and the like—a reaction which comes easily to a man who has no money and does not believe much in banks anyhow. I have observed that this tolerance does not extend to horse-thieves or petty grafters whose operations do affect the mountaineer's personal fortunes. It must be remembered that the outlaws with whom the hillman is aquainted do not come into the Ozarks on business bent, but merely to recuperate and "lay low" for a time — they do their robbing elsewhere. In any case the native has nothing to fear from these gentry, since he does not possess anything worth stealing. Not only this, but a successful bank-robber on vacation is singularly open-handed, much more generous than the tourists and summer-resort people who have invaded the Ozarks in recent years.

There are many old people in the Ozarks who knew the James and Younger boys very well indeed, and stories of their gallant deeds and unparalleled generosity are still current in our best hill-country families. Of Frank James in particular it is said that he never left a mountain cabin without placing a gold-piece on the "fire-board" to pay for his night's lodging, and some of his colleagues in derring-do were equally liberal. It is no wonder that the poverty-ridden hill-folk welcomed such men, concealed them when concealment was necessary, and helped them in every possible way.

There are no Jameses or Youngers in the Ozarks now, but something of the same attitude toward the highwayman still persists, and real outlaws are not altogether lacking even today. I remember a quiet, hard-faced young fellow whom one of my best friends introduced as his "cousin from out West," but it was not until several years later, when I had become more intimately associated with the family, that I learned his true identity. The fact that this man was a notorious criminal was kept from me at the time only because I was still regarded as a "furriner," and I discovered later that at least a dozen people in the neighborhood knew all about him.

There is no ballad about this man as yet, but one has only to talk with any of the local gossips to hear thrilling tales of his courage, generosity, kindness to women and children, and loyalty to those whom he regarded as his friends. Doubtless there is a grain of truth in every one of these narratives, but the touch of the troubadour is upon them all, and they are not reliable sources of definite information. So it is that Jesse James and Sam Bass and Cole Younger have already become semi-mythical heroes, and the material of the songs and stories about them is even now more legendary than historical.

131

COLE YOUNGER

Cole Younger was a Missourian who rode with Quantrill's guerillas, and became a captain in Shelby's Missouri Cavalry toward the end of the Civil War. He and his brothers turned outlaw, and robbed trains and banks with the James boys. Captured while trying to loot a bank at Northfield, Minn., in 1876, Cole was sent to prison for murder. Pardoned in 1903, he joined his old comrade Frank James in a Wild West Show venture. I saw him in Joplin, Mo., about 1904, a shabby fat man, looking more like a rural preacher than a dashing bandit. Compare the photograph in Emmett Dalton's book *When the Daltons Rode* (Garden City, N. Y., 1931, p. 18). He died at Lee's Summit, Mo., in 1916. See Emerson Hough (*The Story of the Outlaw*, 1907, pp. 340-370) and Robertus Love (*The Rise and Fall of Jesse James*, 1926) for information about his life and times. Lomax (*Cowboy Songs*, 1910, p. 106; *American Ballads and Folk Songs*, 1934, pp. 128-131) prints two texts of this song, which is an adaptation of the "Patrick Powers" ballad recorded by Gordon (*New York Times Magazine*, June 5, 1927). Finger (*Frontier Ballads*, 1927, p. 87) mentions "Cole Younger" as a widely known range ballad, "full of dash and spirit," but does not quote the text. A Missouri variant is reported in the *Kansas City Times*, Feb. 27, 1934.

A

Sung by Miss Ethel Rodney, Jane, Mo., May 20, 1927.

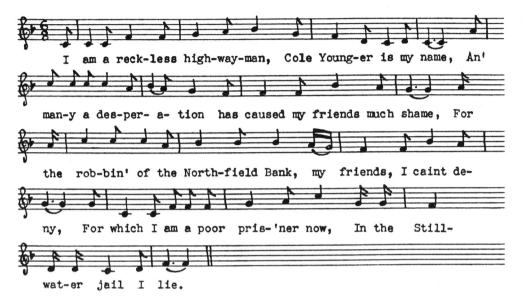

I am a reck-less high-way-man, Cole Young-er is my name, An'
man-y a des-per-a-tion has caused my friends much shame, For
the rob-bin' of the North-field Bank, my friends, I caint de-
ny, For which I am a poor pris-'ner now, In the Still-
wat-er jail I lie.

Of all my darin' bold robberies a story to you I'll tell,
Of a California miner on whom my eyes befell,
I robbed him of his money an' told him to go his way,
For which I will be sorry of until my dyin' day.

An' then we started for Texas, where brother Bob did say
That on fast horses we must ride in revenge of our father's day,
On them fast horses we did go to try to win the prize,
An' we'll fight them anti-guerillas until our dyin' day.

An' the next we surprised was the Union Pacific train,
The crimes we done that bloody day brings tears into my eyes,
The engineer an' fireman killed, the conductor escaped alive,
An' now their bodies lie moulderin' beneath the Nebraska skies.

Then again we started for Texas, that good old Lone Star state,
A-crossin' the Nebraska prairies the James boys we did meet,
With guns an' knives an' revolvers we all sat down to play,
While drinkin' a lot of bad whiskey to pass the time away.

An' again we saddled our horses back up north for to go,
To that God-forsaken country that they call Minnesoto,
I had my eye on the Northfield Bank when brother Bob did say,
Oh Cole, if you undertake that job you sure will rue the day.

Although we stationed our pickets an' up to the bank did go,
It was there behind the counter, boys, I struck my fatal blow,
Then hand us out your money, an' give us no delay,
For we are the noted Younger boys an' have no time to play.

An' while the cashier was ponderin' I heard poor Jesse say,
It's gettin' pretty warm out here, we'd better be gettin' away!

B

Mr. Jack Seidler, Joplin, Mo., heard an almost identical ballad sung to a different tune. Seidler had been a peace officer at Galena, Kan., in the 80's, when Bruce Younger was living with Belle Starr at the Evans Hotel. Bruce was a cousin of Cole Younger, and Seidler watched him closely when this song was sung in his presence, in a honkytonk on Redhot Street. "What did Bruce do?" I asked. "Aw, he just laughed," said Mr. Seidler. Follows the first stanza of the "Cole Younger" ballad as remembered by Mr. Jack Seidler, Joplin, Mo., Nov. 4, 1921.

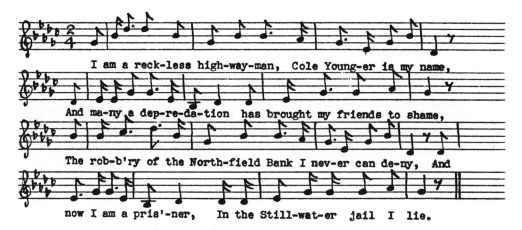

I am a reck-less high-way-man, Cole Young-er is my name,
And ma-ny a dep-re-da-tion has brought my friends to shame,
The rob-b'ry of the North-field Bank I nev-er can de-ny, And
now I am a pris'-ner, In the Still-wat-er jail I lie.

C

Contributed by Miss Nancy Clemens, Springfield, Mo., Feb. 2, 1934. Miss Clemens obtained this text from Mr. Ben Rice, also of Springfield.

I am a bandit highwayman
Cole Younger is my name,
For many a depredation
I have brought my friends to shame,
By the robbing of the Northfield Bank,
For which I can't deny,
Oh now I am a poor prisoner,
In the Stillwater jail I lie.

Of all my bold robberies
The stories to you I'll tell,
A California miner
Upon him I fell.
I robbed him of his money, boys,
And bid him go his way,
For which I will be sorry of
Until my dying day.

Oh now we'll buy fast horses,
As brother Bob did say,
Oh now we'll buy fast horses
On which to ride away.
We'll strive for our father's revenge
And seek to win the prize,
We'll fight those anti-guerillas
Until the day we die.

We started out for Texas
That good old Lone Star state,
And on the Nebraska prairies
The James boys we did meet.
With our guns, knives and pistols
We all sat down to play,
With a bottle of good whiskey, boys,
To pass the time away.

The Union Pacific railway
Oh then we next surprised,
The fears of our bloody hands
Brought tears into their eyes.
The engineerman, fireman killed,
Conductor escaped his life,
Oh now their bodies are lying
Beneath Nebraska's burning skies.

We saddled up our horses
And northward we did go,
To the God-forsaken country
Called Minnesot-e-o,
We had our eyes on the Caddo Bank
When Brother Bob did say,
Cole, if you undertake this job
You will always curse the day.

We then took our stations
And to the bank did go,
'Twas as I crossed the counter
I hit my fatal blow.
It's hand us over your money, boys,
And don't make no delay,
For we're the noted Younger boys,
And spare no time to pray.

D

Fragment recalled by Mr. Wythe Bishop, Fayetteville, Ark., Dec. 9, 1941.   Mr. Bishop
is seventy-five years old, and says that he heard this song when it was new, in the early 80's.

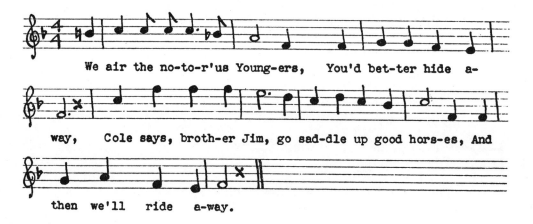

We air the no-to-r'us Young-ers,   You'd bet-ter hide a-

way,   Cole says, broth-er Jim, go sad-dle up good hors-es, And

then we'll ride a-way.

Oh brother Cole, you'll rue the day
You turned the horses' heads.
Go saddle up good horses
And then we'll ride away.

Oh hand me up your money, boys,
We've not got long to stay,
We air the notor'us Youngers,
We're going to ride away.

It was in the state of Texas
I met Frank and Jesse James,
It was drinking and gambling
To pass the time away.

132

JESSE JAMES

The "Jesse James" ballads are widely known, and full references to the literature are found in Tolman (*JAFL* 29, 1916, p. 178) and Cox (*Folk-Songs of the South*, 1925, p. 216). See also Lomax (*Cowboy Songs*, 1910, p. 27), Pound (*American Ballads and Songs*, 1922, p. 251), Combs (*Folk-Songs du Midi des Etats-Unis*, 1925, pp. 182-185), Sandburg (*American Songbag*, 1927, pp. 374, 420), Finger (*Frontier Ballads*, 1927, p. 57), Milburn (*Hobo's Horn-book*, 1930, p. 191 *n.*), Larkin (*Singing Cowboy*, 1931, pp. 155-159), Chappell (*Folk-Songs of Roanoke and the Albemarle*, 1939, p. 192), Gardner (*Ballads and Songs of Southern Michigan*, 1939, pp. 339-340), Belden (*Ballads and Songs*, 1940, pp. 401-404), and the Brown (North Carolina Folk-Lore Society) collection.

The name "Thomas Howard" mentioned in many of the songs was merely a *nom de guerre* used by Jesse when he lived on Lafayette Street, St. Joseph, Mo., where he was shot down by Robert Ford on Apr. 4, 1882. The song swept the whole Middle West like wildfire. Mr. Robert L. Kennedy, in the Springfield (Mo.) *Leader*, October 18, 1933, reminisces as follows:

> Soon after the killing of James a ten-foot poem, set to music, came out and was sung on the streets of Springfield quite frequently. It told how Jesse James had a wife and she warned him all her life and the children they were brave and the dirty little coward who shot Mr. Howard and they laid poor Jesse in the grave. It caused tears to be shed; it was the Mark Antony eulogy at the bier of Caesar. An old blind woman used to stand in front of the court house in Springfield and sing it by the hour; mourners would drop coins in her tin can. She went up to Richmond, Mo., and was singing her sad song with tears in her voice when she found herself slapped and kicked into the middle of the street. Bob Ford's sister happened to be passing that way.

A

Sung by Mr. Lee Herrick, Sulphur Springs, Ark., May 15, 1920. Mr. Herrick learned the song from his father-in-law, who had often entertained the James and Younger boys in his cabin.

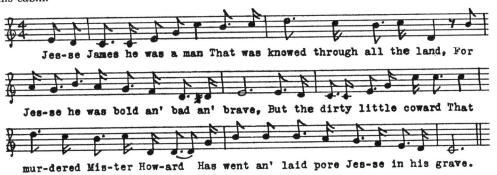

Jes-se James he was a man That was knowed through all the land, For Jes-se he was bold an' bad an' brave, But the dirty little coward That mur-dered Mis-ter How-ard Has went an' laid pore Jes-se in his grave.

Hit was on a Friday night,
An' the moon a-shinin' bright,
An' Bob Ford had been hidin' in a cave,
He had ate of Jesse's bread,
He had slept in Jesse's bed,
But he went an' laid pore Jesse in his grave.

B

Sung by Mrs. Lee Stephens, White Rock, Mo., Aug. 18, 1928.

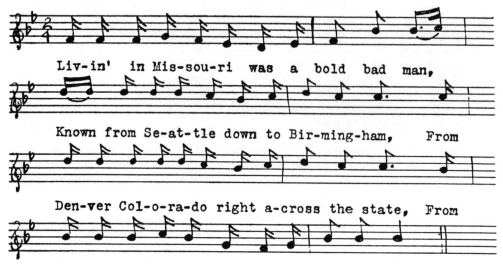

Liv-in' in Mis-sou-ri was a bold bad man,

Known from Se-at-tle down to Bir-ming-ham, From

Den-ver Col-o-ra-do right a-cross the state, From

Bos-ton Mas-sa-chu-setts to the Gol-den Gate.

Some people will forget a lot of famous names,
But in every nick an' corner was a Jesse James,
We used to read about him in our home at night,
When the wind blew down the chimney we would shake with fright.

Jesse James said boys, some money we need,
Stepped out an' got his rifle an' his trusty steed,
An' then he galloped over for to see his brother Frank,
Says boys, we'll git the money from the Smithfield Bank.

Next mornin' when they arrived about ten o'clock,
The cashier of the bank he got an awful shock,
For Jesse had him covered with his forty-four,
An' he counted out half-a-million bonds or more.

Jesse he sat at home one day all alone,
His wife had left him there for to straighten out their home,
While scrubbin' out the kitchen the doorbell rang,
An' in stepped the leader of an outlaw gang.

Jesse says tonight before we make our haul
I'll just hang my dear wife's picture on the wall,
But a forty-four bullet went through Jesse's head,
An' the news went round the country that Jesse was dead.

Next week upon the tombstone was the words that ran,
If you want to be an outlaw be a single man,
For we all know Jesse wouldn't of lost his life,
If it hadn't been the picture of his darlin' wife.

C

The words of Mrs. Stephens' version fit the tune of "Casey Jones," and I have heard soldiers of the 334th Field Artillery (Camp Pike, Ark., Dec. 20, 1917), sing it with a refrain improvised from the verses, in the traditional "Casey Jones" fashion. Thus, after the fourth stanza, they sang the chorus:

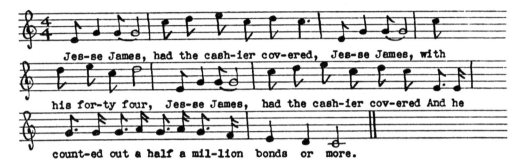

Jes-se James, had the cash-ier cov-ered, Jes-se James, with
his for-ty four, Jes-se James, had the cash-ier cov-ered And he
count-ed out a half a mil-lion bonds or more.

D

Sung by Mr. Ed Stephens, Jane, Mo., 18, 1928.

Jes-se James was a lad that killed many a man, He robbed the Dan-ville
train, But the dir-ty lit-tle cow-ard that killed Mis-ter How-ard, Has
laid poor Jes-se in his grave.

It was Robert Ford, that dirty little coward,
I wonder how he could feel,
For he ate up Jesse's bread an' he slept in Jesse's bed,
Then he laid poor Jesse in his grave.

Poor Jesse left a wife to mourn for his life,
His children they was brave,
But the dirty little coward that shot Mister Howard,
Has laid poor Jesse in his grave.

Now Jesse was a man, a friend to the poor,
He never would see a man in pain,
But with his brother Frank he robbed the Chicago bank
An' he stopped the Glendale train.

It was Jesse's brother Frank that robbed the Galopean bank,
An' carried the money from the town,
It was in this very place that they had a little race,
For they shot Captain Sheets to the ground.

It was on a Saturday night an' Jesse was at home,
A-talkin' with his family so brave,
Robert Ford came along like a thief in the night
An' he laid poor Jesse in his grave.

The people held their breath when they heard of Jesse's death,
An' they wondered how he come to die,
It was one of the gang called little Robert Ford
That shot poor Jesse in the back.

                              E

From a manuscript sent me by Mrs. F. M. Warren, Jane, Mo., Feb. 25, 1927.   Mrs. Warren writes: "We have had this ballet in the family for about forty years.   I suppose it was written soon after Jessie was killed."

                    I suppose you all have heard
                    Of Bob and Charley Ford,
                    The slayers of pore Jessie James,
                    And how he was betrayed
                    Upon one April day
                    By the murders of Bob and Charley Ford.

                    Yes, Jessie leaves a wife
                    To mourn all her life,
                    A mother and two children so brave.
                    'Twas a dirty little coward
                    That shot Mister Howard
                    And laid Jessie James in his grave.

                    Saint Joe it was excited
                    As it never was before,
                    On hearing of pore Jessie's death.
                    And Bob and Charley Ford,
                    For the deeds they had did,
                    For protection to the citizens they fled.

The detectives held their breath
When they heard of Jessie's death,
And they wondered how he ever come to die.
For to get the big reward
It was Bob and Charley Ford
Shot pore Jessie James on the sly.

Jessie always was a friend
To all of the pore,
Although he had never suffered pain,
He and his brother Frank
They robbed the Northfield Bank,
And stopped the Glendale train.

Jessie he has gone down
To the Old Man's town,
Intending for to do as he pleased;
But he will rebel
In the city of Hell,
And maybe put old Satan to his knees.

Jessie James has gone to rest
With his hands upon his breast,
And there are many who never saw his face;
He was born one day in the county of Clay
And he came from the good old human race.

So it's now in the end
When cheated by a friend,
Just think of the days gone by;
And when you all drink
I hope you'll stop and think
How pore Jessie James come to die.

Pore Jessie leaves a wife
To mourn all her life,
And Frank is in the Independence jail,
But his friends stood by his side,
And they saw him through all right,
And give him any amount of bail.

F

Sung by Dr. George Hastings, Fayetteville, Ark., Dec. 16, 1941.

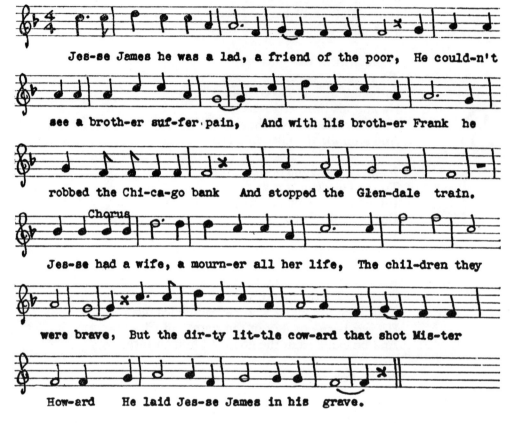

Jes-se James he was a lad, a friend of the poor, He could-n't see a broth-er suf-fer pain, And with his broth-er Frank he robbed the Chi-ca-go bank And stopped the Glen-dale train.

Chorus Jes-se had a wife, a mourn-er all her life, The chil-dren they were brave, But the dir-ty lit-tle cow-ard that shot Mis-ter How-ard He laid Jes-se James in his grave.

It was on a Friday night when the moon was shining bright,
They robbed the Glendale train,
The express messenger on his knees delivered up the keys
To Frank and to Jesse James.

It was on a Saturday night when Jesse was at home,
A-talkin' to his family so brave,
Robert Ford he came along like a thief in the night,
And he laid Jesse James in his grave.

Oh the people of the West they go where you request,
You needn't ever be afraid to die,
But little Robert Ford for the great reward,
He shot Jesse James on the sly.

Oh the people held their breath when they heard of Jesse's death,
They wondered how on earth he came to die,
'Twas little Robert Ford who for the great reward,
He shot Jesse James on the sly.

When Robert Ford he saw that Jesse James was dead,
I wonder if he thought that he was brave,
For he ate of Jesse's bread and he slept in Jesse's bed,
And he laid poor Jesse in his grave.

G

Sung by Mrs. Lillian Short, Galena, Mo., June 17, 1942. She learned it from Mr. Lonnie Gentry, also of Galena, in 1931.

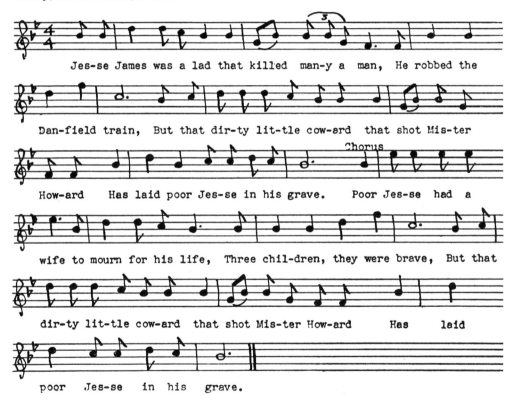

Jes-se James was a lad that killed man-y a man, He robbed the Dan-field train, But that dir-ty lit-tle cow-ard that shot Mis-ter How-ard Has laid poor Jes-se in his grave. Poor Jes-se had a wife to mourn for his life, Three chil-dren, they were brave, But that dir-ty lit-tle cow-ard that shot Mis-ter How-ard Has laid poor Jes-se in his grave.

It was Robert Ford, that dirty little coward,
I wonder how he does feel,
For he ate of Jesse's bread and he slept in Jesse's bed,
Then laid poor Jesse in his grave.

Now Jesse was a man of brilliance to the core,
He never would see a man in pain,
And with his brother Frank he robbed the Chicago bank
And stopped the Glendale train.

It was Jesse's brother Frank that robbed the Galatin bank,
And carried the money from the town,
It was in this very place that they had a little race
For they shot Captain Sheets to the ground.

It was on a Saturday night and Jesse was home,
Talking with his family brave,
Robert Ford came along like a thief in the night
And laid poor Jesse in his grave.

The people held their breath when they heard of Jesse's death,
And wondered how he came to die,
It was one of the gang, called little Robert Ford,
That shot poor Jesse on the sly.

133

McFEE'S CONFESSION

The old singers tell me that this is the record of a murder which occurred "back East some'rs" before the Civil War. Tolman (*JAFL* 29, 1916, p. 168) mentions an Indiana woman who said that her mother knew Hattie Stout personally. Belden (*Song-Ballads and Other Popular Poetry*, 1910, No. 24) found the song in Missouri; Shearin and Combs (*Syllabus of Kentucky Folk-Songs*, 1911, p. 26) report a text from Kentucky; Pound (*American Ballads and Songs*, 1922, p. 153) publishes a good one from Iowa; Cox (*Folk-Songs of the South*, 1925, p. 192) has six West Virginia variants, one of which is regarded as descriptive of a crime committed in Magoffin County, Kentucky; Finger (*Frontier Ballads*, 1927, p. 40) found this piece in Arizona, but confuses some of the stanzas with those usually attributed to another old song known as "Gambling on the Sabbath Day"; in this he probably follows Lomax (*Cowboy Songs*, 1910, p. 166) who earlier reported a similar mixture. Sharp (*English Folk Songs from the Southern Appalachians*, 1932, II, pp. 15-16) prints a text in which the charming "other woman" is called "Miss Harry Gray." Belden (*Ballads and Songs*, 1940, pp. 317-321) connects the song with John McAfee who was hanged at Dayton, Ohio, in 1825, for the murder of his wife. See also Eddy (*Ballads and Songs from Ohio*, 1939, pp. 289-291) and Gardner (*Ballads and Songs of Southern Michigan*, 1939, pp. 337-338). The song is mentioned by McCollum and Porter (*JAFL* 56, 1943, pp. 106-107).

A

Sung by Mrs. Anna Hadenfeldt, Anderson, Mo., July 12, 1928.

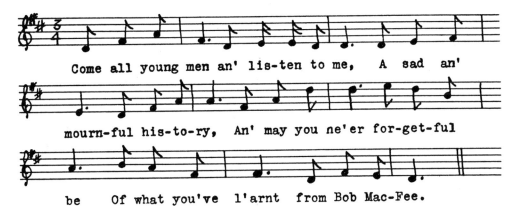

Come all young men an' lis-ten to me, A sad an'

mourn-ful his-to-ry, An' may you ne'er for-get-ful

be   Of what you've l'arnt from Bob Mac-Fee.

My woman she was good to me,
As any woman needs to be,
An' she'd be a-livin' without no doubt
If I had not met Miss Hattie Stout.

'Twas on a balmy summer night,
All things were still, the stars bright,
My wife was a-layin' on the bed,
When I approached her an' said,

Dear wife, here's medicine I've brought,
For you this day that I have bought,
Of them wild fits it will cure you,
Oh take it dear, oh darlin' do.

Ten thousand pounds I'd freely give
To bring her back with me to live,
To bring her back again to life,
My dear, my darlin' murdered wife.

Her body lies beneath the sod,
Her soul I trust is with its God,
An' soon into eternity
My guilty soul must also be.

Young men, young men, be warned by me,
Keep away from all bad company,
An' walk in ways of righteousness,
An' God your souls will surely bless.

B

Miss Elizabeth Waddell, Ash Grove, Mo., Dec. 10, 1929, contributes a longer text which tells of McFee's childhood in the following stanzas:

> Before I reached my fifteenth year
> My father an' my mother dear,
> Was both laid in the silent grave
> Beside them who their bein' gave.
>
> No more a mother's voice I heard,
> No more a father's love I shared,
> No more was I a mother's joy,
> But a poor helpless orphan boy.
>
> Beneath an uncle's kindly roof,
> From want an' danger an' reproof,
> Nine years was I most kindly served
> An' good advice I often heard.
>
> But I was thoughtless, young an' gay,
> An' often broke the sabbath day,
> In wickedness I took delight
> An' oft-times done what was not right.
>
> At length my uncle did me chide,
> An' I turned from home dissatisfied,
> I joined again in wickedness
> An' Satan served with eagerness.
>
> Full well I know the very day,
> When I was from my home away,
> Unto my sorrow-distressed life
> I took unto myself a wife.

The part of this version which deals with the murder and its consequences is very much like the foregoing text, except for the final stanza in which McFee cries out from the gallows:

> On Canaan's bright an' happy plain
> I hope to meet you-all again!

'Twas on a splendid summer's night
When all was still, the stars shone bright,
My wife was laying on the bed
When I approach-ed her and said:
Here is some medicine I brought,
This very day for you I bought,
The doctor says it will cure you
Of those vile fits, pray take it, do.

She gave to me a tender look
And in her mouth the poison took,
Down on her bed beside her babe
To one long lasting sleep she laid.
Fearing that she might not be dead,
My hand upon her throat I laid,
And there such deep impressions made
Her soul soon from her body fled.

And now my heart was filled with woe,
I cried oh whither shall I go?
How can I leave this mournful place,
The world again how can I face?
I'd freely give up all my store,
Had I ten thousand pounds or more,
If I could only bring to life
My dear, my darling murdered wife.

Her baby's now beneath the sod,
Her spirit with its maker, God,
And soon to all eternity
My guilty soul will also be.
The moments are a-drawing nigh
When from this world my soul will fly,
And meet Jehovah at his bar
And there my final sentence hear.

Young men, young men, be warned by me
And always shun bad company,
Walk in the ways of righteousness
And God, I'm sure, your soul will bless.
Adieu, adieu, dear friends adieu,
If I on earth no more see you,
I hope on Heaven's flowery plane
We all some day will meet again.

C

Text from Mr. J. A. Dethrow, Springfield, Mo., Jur
script copy inscribed "written in 1858 by Ellen West."

Draw near, young men, and
My sad and mournful history
And may you ne'er forgetful
Of what this day I tell to th
I had not reached my fifth y
My father and my mother d
Were both laid in their silen
By Him who their souls will

No more a father's voice I h
No more a mother's love I sl
No more was I a mother's jo
I was a helpless orphan boy.
But Providence, the orphan'
A quick relief did quickly se
And snatched from want and
Poor little orphan McAfee.

Under my uncle's tender roo
From want and danger was a
Nine years was I most kindl
His kind advice I often hear
But I was young, thoughtles
And often broke the Sabbatl
Often I did what was not rig
In wickedness I took delight

But when my uncle would n
I turned from him dissatisfie
And joined again in wickedn
I Satan served with eagernes
Well do I mind the very day
When from my home I ran a
And to my sorrow since in li
I took unto myself a wife.

And she was good and kind
As any woman need to be,
And always would have beer
Had I not met Miss Hattie S
Well do I mind the very day
When Hattie stole my heart
'Twas love for her controlled
And . . . . me my wife to k

134

CHARLES GUITEAU

The origin of this piece is unknown, according to Pound (*American Ballads and Songs*, 1922, pp. 146, 251), who suggests that it may be an adaptation of "My Name It is John T. Williams," a song widely current in the decade preceding the assassination of President Garfield in 1881. Compare the West Virginia text reported by Combs (*Folk-Songs du Midi des Etats-Unis*, 1925, p. 218), and the versions given by Chappell (*Folk-Songs of Roanoke and the Albemarle*, 1939, p. 188), Eddy (*Ballads and Songs from Ohio*, 1939, pp. 288-289), Belden (*Ballads and Songs*, 1940, pp. 412-413), who prints a text from Missouri and gives further references, Brewster (*Southern Folklore Quarterly* 4, 1940, p. 191), and in the Brown (North Carolina Folk-Lore Society) collection. Annemarie Ewing and Morris Bishop (*The New Yorker*, Mar. 18, 1939, p. 35) print three stanzas with the note: "It is alleged to be the work of the murderer Guiteau himself, who supposedly sang the song proudly to visitors in his cell." There is a phonograph record by Kelly Harrell (*Victor* 20797).

A

Sung by Mrs. E. E. Hinds, Ketchum, Okla., June 18, 1922. Mrs. Hinds learned the song from some country people in northwestern Arkansas.

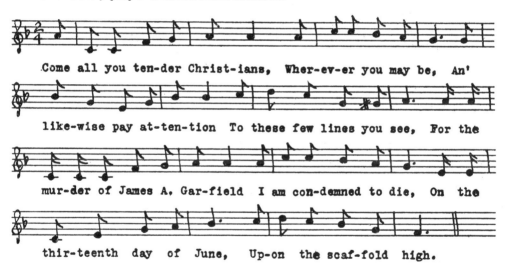

Come all you ten-der Christ-ians, Wher-ev-er you may be, An'
like-wise pay at-ten-tion To these few lines you see, For the
mur-der of James A. Gar-field I am con-demned to die, On the
thir-teenth day of June, Up-on the scaf-fold high.

My name is Charles Guiteau,
My name I'll never deny,
I left my aged parents
In sorrow for to die,
But little did they think
When in my youthful bloom,
I'd ever climb the gallows high
To meet my fatal doom.

'Twas down by the depot
I tried to make my escape,
But providence was against me
An' I found it was too late.
I tried to offer insane
But found it would not go,
The people was all against me
An' I did not get no show.

My sister come to see me,
To bid her last farewell,
She threw her arms around my neck
An' wept most bitterly.
She says my darlin' brother,
You're surely goin' to die,
On the thirteenth day of June,
Upon the scaffold high.

B

Mrs. Marie Wilbur, Pineville, Mo., July 7, 1929, supplies a text containing the following
stanza:

Judge Cox he read the sentence,
The clerk he wrote it down,
And on the thirtieth day of June
I must meet my fatal doom.

C

From Mrs. Maggie Morgan, Springdale, Ark., Jan. 30, 1942.

I tried to play off insane, but found that never would do,
The people being against me, it proved to be untrue,
Judge Colway passed the sentence, the clerk he wrote it down,
On the thirtieth day of June I'll meet my fatal doom.

D

Sung by Dr. George Hastings, Fayetteville, Ark., Dec. 16, 1941.

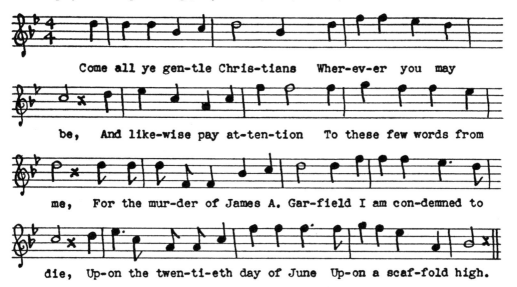

Come all ye gen-tle Chris-tians Wher-ev-er you may

be, And like-wise pay at-ten-tion To these few words from

me, For the mur-der of James A. Gar-field I am con-demned to

die, Up-on the twen-ti-eth day of June Up-on a scaf-fold high.

My name it is Charles Guiteau,
It's a name I'll never deny,
I left my aged parents
In sorrow they must die.
Oh little did they think
While in my youthful bloom,
That I'd be led to a scaffold high
To meet a fatal doom.

It was down by the railroad
I tried to make my escape,
But providence was against me,
It proved to be too late.
So they took me to the jail-house
All in my youthful bloom,
And I'll be led to a scaffold high
To meet a fatal doom.

I tried to prove insane
But it proved to be no use,
For the people were against me,
To escape there was no clews.
So Judge Cox read the sentence,
And the clerk he took it down,
And I'll be led to a scaffold high
To meet my fatal doom.

My sister came to see me,
To bid me a last goodbye,
She threw both arms around my neck
And wept most bitterly.
She said, my darling brother,
Today you must surely die
For the murder of James A. Garfield,
Upon a scaffold high.

E

Some people use the second stanza of "Charles Guiteau" as a chorus, and sing it to a different tune. Here is this chorus as sung by Mrs. May Kennedy McCord, Springfield, Mo., Nov. 12, 1941.

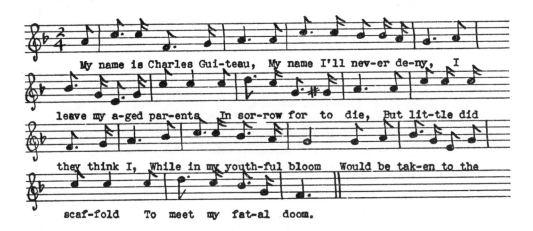

My name is Charles Gui-teau, My name I'll nev-er de-ny, I leave my a-ged par-ents In sor-row for to die, But lit-tle did they think I, While in my youth-ful bloom Would be tak-en to the scaf-fold To meet my fat-al doom.

135

THE DALLAS COUNTY JAIL

This seems to be an adaptation of "The Logan County Court House" reported by Cox (*Folk-Songs of the South*, 1925, p. 212) from West Virginia. Lomax (*Cowboy Songs*, 1910, pp. 254, 310) has two cowboy pieces which contain almost identical stanzas. The third verse is paralleled in the "Bob Sims" ballad recovered by Combs (*Folk-Songs du Midi des Etats-Unis*, 1925, pp. 216-217), also in a British convict song known as "Van Dieman's Land" (Mackenzie, *Ballads and Sea Songs from Nova Scotia*, 1928, pp. 304-305). See also Henry (*Folk-Songs from the Southern Highlands*, 1938, p. 329) for a similar piece from North Carolina.

A

Sung by Mrs. W. E. Jones, Pineville, Mo., Nov. 3, 1928.

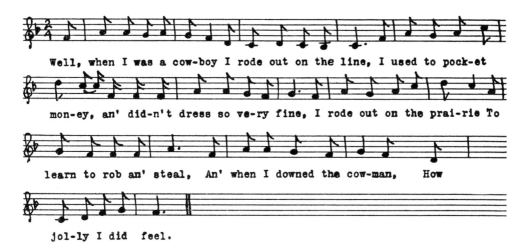

Well, when I was a cow-boy I rode out on the line, I used to pock-et
mon-ey, an' did-n't dress so ve-ry fine, I rode out on the prai-rie To
learn to rob an' steal, An' when I downed the cow-man, How
jol-ly I did feel.

I wore a broad-brimmed white hat, rode a horse an' saddle fine,
I used to court a pretty girl, you bet I called her mine,
I courted her for beauty, an' for love that was in vain,
She sent me down to Huntsville to wear the ball an' chain.

One night when I was in prison I dreampt a happy dream,
I dreampt I was in old Missouri down by some flowin' stream,
With my darlin' girl beside me, she had come to go my bail,
But I woke up broken-hearted in the Dallas county jail.

An' then in come the jailor next day at twelve o'clock,
With a bunch of keys all in his hand my cell for to unlock,
Sayin' I'll chain you up, my prisoner, for I heard the jury say,
You're bound to go to Huntsville, for ten long years to stay.

In come my darlin' girl, ten dollars in her hand,
Sayin' give this to my Willie, it's all that I demand,
Give this to my young cowboy, to think of olden times,
An' don't forget the darlin' girl you left so far behind.

While I was in the prison, my father says to me,
May heaven look down upon you, wherever you may be,
May heaven look down upon you, wherever you may go.
An' I could snatch the jury that sent my boy below.

B

Miss Mabel Buhler, Joplin, Mo., Jan. 21, 1930, showed me an old manuscript copy very similar to the above, save for the first stanza:

> I was a jolly cowboy, I rode the Kansas line,
> I always made good money, didn't dress so very fine,
> I rode the Kansas prairies along with Robert Steele,
> And when we robbed a rich man, how happy we would feel.

C

From a manuscript book belonging to Mrs. Linnie Boraker Stevens, Notch, Mo., Sept. 12, 1934.

> When I was a cowboy I learnt to rob and steal,
> And when I robbed a ritch man how jolly I would feel,
> I'd rob him of his money and bid him go his way,
> Of whom I will be sorrow for until my dying day.
>
> When I was a cowboy I rode out on the line,
> I always coined the money but I didn't dress very fine,
> I wore a broad brim white hat, rode horses and saddle fine,
> And when I seen a pretty girl I always called her mine.
>
> Oh when I meet a poor girl I treat her very kind,
> And when I meet a ritch girl I ask her to be mine,
> In courting her for money her love it was obtained,
> But they taken me down to Hot Springs to wear the ball and chain.
>
> Last night as I was sleeping I dreampt a pleasant dream,
> I dreampt I was in Texas, down by some flowing stream,
> My Annie was there beside me, she had come to go my bail
> But I woke up broken hearted in the Hot Springs county jail.
>
> In come my little Annie with ten dollars in her hand,
> Saying give this to my Willie, it's all that I command,
> And heaven may shine over him wherever he may be,
> And hell fire burn the jury that parted you and me.

D

Sung by Mr. Charles Ingenthron, Walnut Shade, Mo., Sept. 6, 1941. He calls it "When I Was a Cowboy," and says he learned it in the 90's.

When I was a cow-boy I rode up-on the line, I al-ways coined the mon-ey But did-n't dress so fine.

I wore a broad-brimmed white hat,
Rode a horse and saddle fine,
And when I'd court a pretty girl
You bet I'd call her mine.

I courted them for beauty,
For love it was all in vain,
Till they took me down to Huntsville
To wear the ball and chain.

In stepped the jailer
About eleven o'clock,
A bunch of keys a-carrying
My cell door to unlock.

Cheer up, down-hearted cowboy,
I heard the judges say
That you would go to Huntsville
For ten long years to stay.

Up stepped my true love,
Ten dollars in her hand,
Saying give this to my Willie,
It's all that I command.

Saying take this, darling Willie,
And think of olden times,
And don't forget the pretty girl
You left so far behind.

The heavens may smile upon you
Wherever you may go,
And Satan burn the jury
That sentenced you below.

E

Sung by Mr. Fred Woodruff, Lincoln, Ark., Dec. 12, 1941. Woodruff called it "The
Logan County Jail," and learned it near Lincoln about 1905.

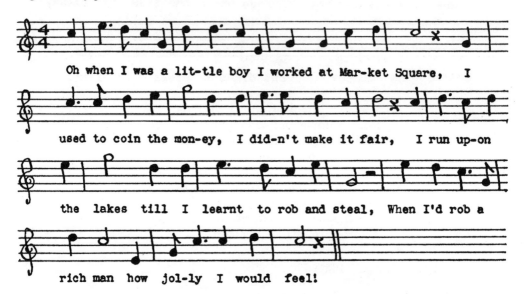

Oh when I was a lit-tle boy I worked at Mar-ket Square,   I
used to coin the mon-ey, I did-n't make it fair,   I run up-on
the lakes till I learnt to rob and steal, When I'd rob a
rich man how jol-ly I would feel!

Last night as I lie sleeping I had a pleasant dream,
I dreamt I was a merchant all down a golden stream,
But I woke up broken-hearted in the Logan County jail
My friends was all around me, but no one to go my bail.

Oh down came my true love, ten dollars in her hand,
Saying take this, my dearest lover, doin' all for you I can,
May God protect and guide you wherever you may go,
And Satan burn the jury for sending you so low.

Oh down come the jailer about eleven o'clock,
A bunch of keys all in his hands to shove against the lock,
Cheer up, my down-hearted prisoner, I heerd the jury say
It's twenty-one years in Nashburg they said you're bound to stay.

I love my father's children, but I love myself the best,
And them that don't pervide for me will never see no rest,
A pocket full of money, a pocket full of rye,
A dram of good old whiskey would pass my troubles by.

My father is a gambler, he learned me how to play,
He learned me how to stack my cards all on the ace and trey,
The gambler swore he'd beat me, but likely* I did know,
Ace and deuce all in my hand I'm bound to play high low.

136

THE LOUISVILLE BURGLAR

The "Louisville Burglar" song is evidently a Southern variant of the well-known "Boston Burglar" piece, once copyrighted by Edwin B. Marks and credited to M. J. Fitzpatrick, but derived directly from the old English ballad of "Botany Bay" (Barrett, *English Folk-Songs*, London, 1891, p. 90). See Lomax (*Cowboy Songs*, 1910, p. 147), Pound (*American Ballads and Songs*, 1922, p. 57), Cox (*Folk-Songs of the South*, 1925, p. 296), Spaeth (*Read 'Em and Weep*, 1927, p. 178), also the phonograph records by Vernon Dalhart (*Edison 51608-L*) and Carl T. Sprague (*Victor 20534*). Some of the stanzas are reminiscent of "The Sheffield Apprentice" as reported by Sharp (*English Folk Songs from the Southern Appalachians*, 1932, II, pp. 66-69). I have not found the regular "Boston Burglar" song in the Ozarks, but Finger (*Frontier Ballads*, 1927, p. 88) heard it sung by a native workman near Fayetteville, Ark. Further texts are reported by Chappell (*Folk-Songs of Roanoke and the Albemarle*, 1939, pp. 100-101), Eddy (*Ballads and Songs from Ohio*, 1939, pp. 204-206), Gardner (*Ballads and Songs of Southern Michigan*, 1939, pp. 335-336), and Brewster (*Ballads and Songs of Indiana*, 1940, pp. 223-225).

A

Sung by Mrs. Ora Pace, Anderson, Mo., Aug. 7, 1928.

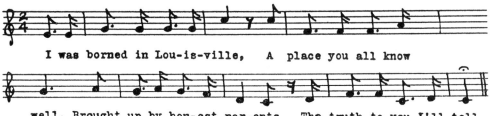

I was borned in Lou-is-ville, A place you all know well, Brought up by hon-est par-ents, The truth to you I'll tell.

Brought up by honest parents,
An' raised most tenderly,
Till I became a roguish lad
At the age of twenty-three.

An' then I was arrested,
Placed in the Louisville jail,
My friends they tried to git me out
But I could not give no bail.

*luckily?

The jury found me guilty,
The clerk he wrote it down,
The judge pronounced the sentence,
You're bound for Frankfort town.

I saw my aged father
Stand pleadin' at the bar,
Likewise my aged mother
A-tearin' at her hair.

A-tearin' at those old gray locks
Till the tears come rollin' down,
My son, my son, what have you done
That you're bound for Frankfort town?

They started me on a east-bound train
One cold an' snowy day,
An' every station we passed through
I heard the people say:

Yonder goes a noted burglar,
In iron chains bound down,
For some great crime or another
He's bound for Frankfort town.

I loved a girl in Louisville,
A place you all know well,
An' if I ever gain sweet liberty
Together we will dwell.

Together we will spend our days,
An' shun bad company.
Quit drinkin' of cheap whiskey, boys,
While out upon a spree.

B

Contributed by Mrs. C. P. Mahnkey, Mincy, Mo., Aug. 12, 1939. She says the song was always known as "The Springfield Burglar," and that nobody ever doubted that Jefferson Town was identical with Jefferson City, where the Missouri State Penitentiary is located.

I was born an' raised in Springfield,
A town you all know well,
Brought up by honest parents,
An' the truth to you I'll tell.

Brought up by honest parents
An' raised most tenderly,
Till I became a roving lad,
At the age of twenty-three.

My friends an' I did rob a bank
An' I was sent to jail,
My folks their efforts did put forth
To get me out on bail.

The jury found me guilty,
The clerk he wrote it down,
An' rose an' read it in the court,
Six years in Jefferson Town!

I saw my aged father
A-pleading at the bar,
I saw my aged mother
A-tearing out her hair.

A-tearing out those old white locks
While tears her cheeks rolled down,
Crying son, oh son, what have you done
To be bound for Jefferson Town?

I stepped on board an east-bound train,
One cold December day,
An' every station that we stopped
I could hear the people say:

There goes that noted burglar,
With arms he is bound down,
For robbing of the National Bank
He's bound for Jefferson Town.

I have a girl in Springfield,
A girl that I love well,
If ever I gain my liberty
At home with her I'll dwell.

At home with her I'll dwell, boys,
An' live most honorably,
In a simple little cottage
How happy we will be!

137

GAMBLING ON THE SABBATH DAY

Finger (*Frontier Ballads*, 1927, pp. 42-43) prints three stanzas of this piece, attributing them to another old song called "McFee's Confession." Lomax (*Cowboy Songs*, 1910, pp. 164-165) also reported a confusion of these two songs. See also the variant from Mrs. Coral Almy Wilson, Zinc, Ark. (*Ozark Life*, Kingston, Ark., Feb., 1930, p. 12).

There is a persistent legend in the Ozark country that this song was written by Bill Walker, one of a group of night-riders known as Bald Knobbers, who was hanged at Ozark, Mo., May 10, 1889. It seems that Walker sang the song in jail while awaiting his execution, and told many people that he had written the words and "made up" the tune. Mrs. Sarah Davis Couts (or Crouch), Springfield, Mo., was employed as a cook for the prisoners, and obtained a copy of the "ballet" from Walker himself. Mrs. May Kennedy McCord, folksong enthusiast of Springfield, accepts the story of Walker's authorship, and prints an account of the whole affair in her newspaper column (Springfield, Mo., *News and Leader*, Jan. 31, 1937; Springfield, Mo., *News*, Nov. 14, 1940). Mr. William L. Vandeventer, Springfield, Mo., has studied the history of the Bald Knobbers for many years, and has collected a vast amount of valuable material. He writes me (Mar. 7, 1938) that "Gambling on the Sabbath Day" was well known in the Ozarks before 1889, and points out that the murder described in the song has nothing in common with the killing of which Walker was convicted. "Since Walker was the only young man to be hanged in this section of Missouri, when the song was popular, it naturally led to thoughts of Walker, and in my opinion that is why there is a fanciful connection between the song and Walker . . . Will Walker was only sixteen years old, and was practically illiterate . . . He might have sung this ballad while in jail, which is very likely, but I am reasonably certain that he did not compose it." Miss Lucile Morris, Springfield, Mo., whose *The Bald Knobbers* (Caxton Printers, 1939) is the best book on the subject, tells me that she finds no evidence that Walker wrote the song.

A

Contributed by Mrs. Martha Duckworth, Springfield, Mo., Oct. 12, 1933. Mrs. Duckworth is a sister of Mrs. Sarah Davis Couts, who learned the song from Bill Walker in the jail
at Ozark, Mo., in 1889.

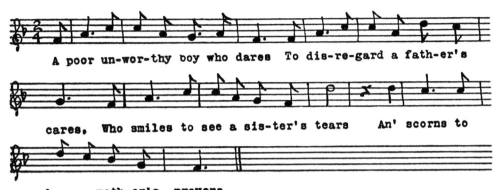

A poor un-wor-thy boy who dares To dis-re-gard a fath-er's cares, Who smiles to see a sis-ter's tears An' scorns to hear a moth-er's prayers.

From their advice he turned away,
At dice an' cards he learnt to play,
An' then a comrade he did slay
While gamblin' on the Sabbath day.

His father, sixty years in age,
The best of counsel did engage,
To see if something could be done
To save his disobedient son.

But nothin' could the counsel do,
The testimony was too true,
'Twas he the bloody weapon drew
An' pierced his comrade's body through.

His weepin' mother standin' by,
To hear them tell the reason why,
Her son in prison had to lie
Till on the scaffold he must die.

Don't weep for me, my mother dear,
When I am safely laid away,
For on the scaffold I must pay
For gamblin' on the Sabbath day.

The sheriff cut the slender cord,
His soul has went to meet his Lord,
The doctor cried the wretch is dead.
The soul has from the body fled.

His weepin' mother cried aloud,
God save and pity this gazin' crowd,
That they may all be turned away
From gamblin' on the Sabbath day.

B

Sung by Mrs. May Kennedy McCord, Springfield, Mo., Nov. 12, 1941. She learned it from Mrs. Sarah Davis Couts, also of Springfield.

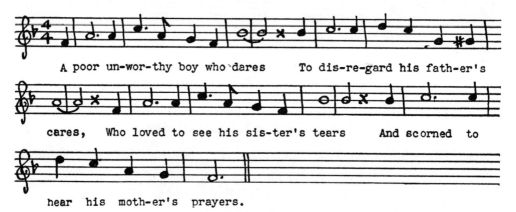

A poor un-wor-thy boy who dares   To dis-re-gard his fath-er's

cares,   Who loved to see his sis-ter's tears   And scorned to

hear his moth-er's prayers.

From their advice he turned away,
'Twas cards and dice he learned to play,
Till he the bloody dagger drew
While gambling on the Sabbath day.

His weeping mother cried aloud,
Oh God forgive this gazing crowd,
That they may never cast away
By gambling on the Sabbath day.

C

Sung by Mr. and Mrs. Arlie Freeman, Natural Dam, Ark., Dec. 14, 1941.

A father sixty years of age,
Who now as counsel was engaged
To see if something could be done
To save his boy, his only son.

But nothing could the counsel do
By witnesses they all proved true,
They proved it was too plain for him
He never could be free again.

Oh darling sister, fare you well,
My soul is filled with redeeming dwell,
My soul is filled with burning hell,
Oh darling sister, fare you well.

Oh yonder stands my darling wife
Who has prayed for me all through her life,
But from her side I've strayed away
And gambled on the Sabbath day.

Oh wife, come lay your head right here,
And let me see those falling tears,
In one short hour I must die,
It breaks my heart to hear you cry.

These cruel men's going to take my life,
And take me from my darling wife,
I'll leave with her one precious joy,
And that's my darling baby boy.

Oh God, a father to him be,
Teach him, oh to remember me,
Teach him not to lead astray
And gamble on the Sabbath day.

Teach him, oh, to follow thee,
On earth wherever he may be,
Teach him at night to kneel and pray
That we might meet in heaven some day.

The sheriff then cut the tender cord,
My soul has gone to its reward,
The spirit from the body fled,
The doctor says the wretch is dead.

The gray-haired mother prayed aloud
For God to save all gambling crowds,
That they might never go astray
And gamble on the Sabbath day.

D

Mrs. Mildred Tuttle, Farmington, Ark., Dec. 31, 1941, sings an almost identical "Gambling on the Sabbath Day," except for the first stanza:

Oh who can tell a mother's thought
When first to her the news was brought,
The sheriff knew her son was lost
When unto prison he was brought.

E

Compare a similar verse from Mrs. Emmaline Crabtree, Chester, Ark., Jan. 12, 1942.

Oh who could tell a mother's thought,
Since this sad news to her was brought,
That her dear boy had been caught
And back to prison had been brought.

138

THE JEALOUS LOVER

Barry (*JAFL* 22, 1909, p. 370) once claimed this as a native American ballad, but later (*American Speech* 3, Aug. 1928, pp. 441-444) pointed out its relation to "The Murder of Betsy Smith," published in England early in the nineteenth century. Pound (*American Ballads and Songs*, 1922, p. 248) describes this as one of the "most wide spread of American ballads," and remarks upon the uncertainty of its origin. Cox (*Folk-Songs of the South*, 1925, p. 197) thinks that some variants are based upon the murder of Pearl Bryan, a Greencastle, Ind., girl who was decapitated by two medical students near Fort Thomas, Ky., in 1896. Some texts refer to "Pearl" or "Pearl Bryan," but other names are also used, and several of the Ozark ballad-singers insist that they knew the song long before 1896. The piece has been adapted to describe numerous recent crimes; as late as 1929 a woman named Drew confessed a murder by mailing an adaptation of "The Jealous Lover" to Governor T. G. Bilbo of Mississippi (*Time* 15, Feb. 24, 1930, p. 17). For other texts and references see Kittredge (*JAFL* 30, 1917, p. 344), Shoemaker (*North Pennsylvania Minstrelsy*, 1919, p. 49), Richardson (*American Mountain Songs*, 1927, p. 30), Spaeth (*Weep Some More, My Lady*, 1927, p. 122), Finger (*Frontier Ballads*, 1927, p. 80), Combs (*Folk-Songs du Midi des Etats-Unis*, 1925, pp. 203-204), and Bradley Kincaid (*My Favorite Mountain Ballads*, 1928, p. 17). Lilith Shell (*Ozark Life*, Kingston, Ark., Oct. 1929, p. 14) reports a text from the Arkansas Ozarks, later reprinted by Allsopp (*Folklore of Romantic Arkansas*, 1931, II, p. 204). Add Greenleaf (*Ballads and Sea Songs from Newfoundland*, 1933, pp. 365-366), who recovered a lengthy text in Newfoundland, Combs (*Folk-Songs from the Kentucky Highlands*, 1939, pp. 38-40), Eddy (*Ballads and Songs from Ohio*, 1939, pp. 236-241), Gardner (*Ballads and Songs of Southern Michigan*, 1939, pp. 83-85), Belden (*Ballads and Songs*, 1940, pp. 324-330) of Missouri, and Brewster (*Ballads and Songs of Indiana*, 1940, pp. 248-252 and 283-289). See also the Nell Cropsey songs in Chappell (*Folk-Songs of Roanoke and the Albemarle*, 1939, pp. 108-116). This piece is in the Brown (North Carolina Folk-Lore Society) collection. Rayburn (*Ozark Country*, 1941, pp. 230 - 231) prints eleven stanzas from "the Big Springs Country of the Missouri Ozarks," by which he probably means Shannon County, Mo.

A

Sung by Mrs. Warren Durbin and Mrs. Sissie Pierce, Pineville, Mo., June 12, 1929.

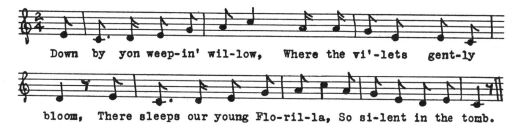

Down by yon weep-in' wil-low, Where the vi'-lets gent-ly
bloom, There sleeps our young Flo-ril-la, So si-lent in the tomb.

She died not broken hearted,
Nor in sickness did she fail,
But in one moment parted
From those she loved so well.

One evenin' as the moon shone brightly
An' soft o'er hill an' dale,
Unto this maiden's cottage
A jealous lover came.

Florilla, let us wander
Down by yon meadow gay,
There we will sit an' ponder
Upon our weddin' day.

The way was cold an' dreary
An' the night was comin' on,
As into this lonesome valley
He led the maiden on.

Oh Edward, I am tired,
Of wanderin' here along,
The night is cold an' dreary,
I beg you take me home.

You have not the wings of an eagle,
Nor from me can you fly,
No earthly soul can hear you,
You instantly must die.

Down on her knees she bended,
An' begged him for her life,
But into that snowy bosom
He plunged a gleamin' knife.

Oh Edward, I'll forgive you
With my last an' dyin' breath,
I never have deceived you,
As I close my eyes in death.

Here's adieu to my fond parents,
An' to my friends adieu,
An' you, my dearest Edward,
May all your words prove true.

Down on his knees he bended,
Sayin' oh, what have I done,
I've murdered my Florilla,
True as the risin' sun.

Down in that lonely valley,
Where the willows weep o'er her grave,
Florilla lies forgotten
Where the merry sunbeams play.

B

Mrs. Lucy White, Sulphur Springs, Ark., Aug. 12, 1928, has a "Jealous Lover" song in which the principals' names are Nellie and Elmer. Here is the final stanza:

Oh Elmer, I'll forgive you,
Was her last words as she lie,
An' down there by the droopin willows
He left her there to die.

C

Miss Myrtle Lain, Linn Creek, Mo., Mar. 14, 1930, contributes a version called "Fair Emily," with the following stanza directly after the one telling of the fatal knife-thrust:

She sighed not when he pressed her
To his young an' jealous heart,
She smiled not when he pressed her,
For she knew that they must part.

D

Sung by Mrs. Bessie Anderson, Jane, Mo., Aug. 11, 1929.

One night when the moon shone brightly
The stars was shin-in too,
Up to a lonely cottage
A jealous lover drew.

He says, my love, let us wander
Down in the meadow gay,
An' there we'll set an' ponder
Upon our weddin' day.

Oh Edward, I am weary,
I care not for to roam,
Oh Edward, I am weary,
I pray you take me home.

Up rose the jealous lover,
He made one solemn vow,
No human hand can save you,
In a moment you shall die.

Down, down she knelt before him
An' humbly begged for life,
But into her snow white bosom
He plunged the fatal knife.

Oh mother, dearest mother,
You'll never see me no more,
An' you will miss my comin'
Up to the cottage door.

Oh Edward, I forgive you,
This bein' my dyin' breath,
I never did deceive you,
An' she closed her eyes in death.

Down beneath the lonely willow,
Where the daisies grow an' bloom,
There lies my darlin' Nola,
So silent in the tomb.

E

Contributed by Mrs. Coral Almy Wilson, Zinc, Ark., Dec. 17, 1928. Mrs. Wilson calls it the "Pearl Bright" ballad. The Scott Jackson mentioned in the first stanza is one of the medical students who murdered the Pearl Bryan mentioned in the headnote, and this version probably dates back only to the late 90's.

Last night as the moon was shinin',
An' the stars was shinin' too,
Up to her cottage window
Scott Jackson, her lover, drew.

Dear Pearly, let's take a ramble
Out over the meadows gay,
There is no one to disturb us,
We will name our weddin' day.

Scott Jackson, I am so weary,
That I do not care to roam,
For roamin' is so dreary,
I pray you take me home.

Down in this valley I have you,
From me you cannot fly,
No human hand can save you,
In a moment you must die.

What have I done, Scott Jackson,
That you should take my life?
You know I've always loved you,
An' would have been your wife.

Down on her knees before him
She was prayin' to God for her life,
When into her snowy white bosom
He plunged th' fatal knife.

There's room for my picture in my album,
There's room for my love in your heart,
There's room for us both in heaven
Where lovers never part.

Down in that lonesome valley,
Where the flowers fade an' bloom
There lies my own sweet Pearly
In the cold an' silent tomb.

F

Contributed by Miss Maudeva McCord, Springfield, Mo., May 16, 1938. Local title
"The Jewish Lover."

> One eve when the moon shone brightly,
> And gently fell the dew,
> Up to a maiden's cottage
> A Jewish lover flew.
>
> Come love, and let us wander
> Through the fields and meadows gay,
> Come love, and let us ponder,
> Until our wedding day.
>
> No Edgar, I feel dreary,
> And do not care to roam,
> For roaming makes me weary,
> I pray you take me home.
>
> Down on her knees before him,
> She humbly begged for life,
> Into her snowy bosom
> He pierced a dagger knife.
>
> Oh Edgar, I forgive you,
> Though this be my last breath,
> Whene'er have I deceived you?
> And she closed her eyes in death.
>
> 'Neath yonder drooping willows,
> Where the flowers sweetly bloom,
> There lies our sweet Flo Ellen
> In a cold and silent tomb.
>
> We know not how she suffered,
> We know not how she moaned,
> We only know her last words was
> Please, Edgar, take me home.

G

Mrs. Olga Trail, Farmington, Ark., Dec. 10, 1938, showed me a manuscript "ballet" entitled "The Jealous Lover of Lone Green Valley."

> Way down in Lone Green Valley
> Where roses bloom and fade,
> There was a jealous lover
> In love with a beautiful maid.

One night the stars shone brightly,
The moon shone brightly too,
Into the maiden's cottage
This jealous lover drew.

Come love, and we will wander
Down where the woods are green,
While strolling we will ponder
Upon our wedding day.

So arm in arm they wandered,
The night birds sang above,
The jealous lover grew angry
With the beautiful girl he loved.

The night grew cold and dreary,
Said she, I'm afraid to stay,
It is so cold and dreary
I want to retrace my way.

Retrace your way, no never,
For you have met your doom,
So bid farewell forever
To parents, friends and home.

Oh, Willie, my poor darling,
I know there's something wrong,
You must not harm me, Willie,
For we've been friends too long.

Down on her knees before him
She pleaded for her life,
But deep into her bosom
He plunged a dagger knife.

Oh Willie, my poor darling,
Why have you taken my life?
You know I've always loved you
And wanted to be your wife.

I never have deceived you,
And with my dying breath
I will forgive you, Willie,
She closed her eyes in death.

H

Sung by Miss Callista O'Neill, Day, Mo., Sept. 2, 1941. Learned near Day in the late 90's. She thinks the word *jealant* in the 5th stanza may be a combination of *jealous* and *gallant;* several of Miss O'Neill's neighbors sing the song, and they all say *jealant* instead of *jealous*. Miss O'Neill calls the song "The Weeping Willow."

Down by the weep-ing wil-low Where the vio-lets are in bloom, There lies a fair young maid-en. All si-lent in the tomb.

She died not broken-hearted,
Nor sickness e'er befell,
But all in an instant parted
From the one she loved so well.

Come love, and let us wander
Out over the meadows gay,
Come love, and let us ponder
All over our wedding day.

Oh Edward, I am weary,
And do not care to roam,
For roaming is so dreary,
I pray you take me home.

Up stepped that jealant lover,
And with a silent cry,
No mortal one shall love you,
In an instant you shall die.

Down, down, she sank before him
And humbly begged for life,
But into her snow-white bosom
He plunged the fatal knife.

Oh Edward, I forgive you,
Though this is my last breath,
I never did deceive you,
She closed her eyes in death.

Down by the weeping willow
Where the violets are in bloom,
There lies a fair young maiden
All silent in the tomb.

I

Dr. George E. Hastings, Fayetteville, Ark., Jan. 6, 1942, showed me a manuscript text with the final stanza:

How cold was the morning,
How shrill was the bugle sound,
The hunters then they found her
Cold and lifeless on the ground.

J

Sung by Mrs. Ray Oxford, Fayetteville, Ark., Dec. 13, 1941.

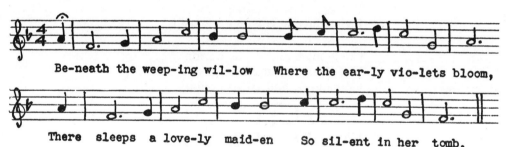

Be-neath the weep-ing wil-low   Where the ear-ly vio-lets bloom,

There sleeps a love-ly maid-en   So sil-ent in her tomb.

She died not broken-hearted,
Nor sickness e'er befell,
But in one moment parted
From the one she loved so well.

One night the moon shone brightly
And lightly fell the dew,
When to young Edna's cottage
Her jealous lover drew.

Come, Edna, let us wander
Over the fields so fresh and gay,
Come Edna, let us ponder
Upon our wedding day.

Oh Edward, I'm so weary,
I do not care to roam,
For roaming is so dreary
I'd rather stay at home.

Down on her knees before him
She sweetly prayed for life,
But in her snow-white bossom
He plunged a fatal knife.

Oh Edward, I'll forgive you,
This may be my last pleading breath
For in one moment surely
I shall close my eyes in death.

Oh God in Heaven pity
My sad and mournful life,
For heaven knows I loved her
If she would a been my wife.

And now I am tired of living,
For my love and I must part,
And with the same bloody dagger
He pierced his jealous heart.

Come all you girls, take warning,
And listen now to me,
If you have a loving sweetheart,
Beware of jealousy.

139

THE SILVER DAGGER

For other texts and references see *JAFL* (20, 1907, p. 267), Pound (*American Ballads and Songs*, 1922, No. 52), Cox (*Folk-Songs of the South*, 1925, No. 109), Lilith Shell (*Ozark Life*, Kingston, Ark., Oct., 1929, p. 13), Allsopp (*Folklore of Romantic Arkansas*, 1931, II, p. 202), Thomas (*Devil's Ditties*, 1931, p. 110), and Sharp (*English Folk Songs from the Southern Appalachians*, 1932, II, pp. 229-230). As Belden (*JAFL* 30, 1917, p. 388) points out, this piece has been more or less confused with "The Drowsy Sleeper." Belden (*Ballads and Songs*, 1940, pp. 123-126) reports one tune and several texts from Missouri. See also Eddy (*Ballads and Songs from Ohio*, 1939, pp. 227-229), Gardner (*Ballads and Songs of Southern Michigan*, 1939, pp. 89-90), Brewster (*Ballads and Songs of Indiana*, 1940, pp. 211-214), and Morris (*Southern Folklore Quarterly* 8, 1944, pp. 185-186). The piece is in the Brown (North Carolina Folk-Lore Society) collection.

A

Sung by Miss Leone Duvall, Pineville, Mo., June 6, 1923.

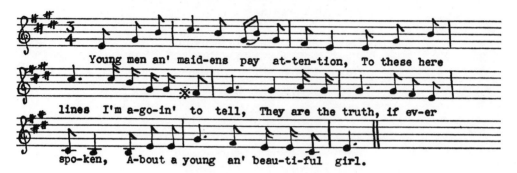

Young men an' maid-ens pay at-ten-tion, To these here lines I'm a-go-in' to tell, They are the truth, if ev-er spo-ken, A-bout a young an' beau-ti-ful girl.

A young man courted a handsome lady,
He loved her more than he loved his life,
He oft-times made her the solemn promise
That she should be his lawful wife.

But when his parents come to know this,
They strove to part them night an' day,
O son, oh son, don't be so foolish,
She is too pore, they would oft-times say.

He fell upon his knees before them,
Sayin' father, mother, pity me,
Don't take from me my precious jewel,
For she is all the world to me.

An' when the lady come to know this,
She quick resolved what she would do,
She wandered forth from the busy city,
Its love an' pleasure she no more knew.

She wandered down by the flowin' river,
For three long days in a deep despair,
She told her friends farewell forever,
An' then for death she did prepare.

She gazed a moment up to heaven,
Wherein her soul should find its rest,
She then drawed out the silver dagger
An' pierced it through her snow white breast.

The young man at the roadside near her,
He thought he heard his true love cry,
He run around as one distracted
Oh love, I fear you're a-goin' to die.

He then picked up the bloody weapon,
An' pierced it through his own true heart,
Oh let this be a woeful warnin',
To all that would true lovers part.

A double coffin was directed,
Their hands placed on each others' breast,
An' now the lovers lie a-sleepin'
Together in eternal rest.

B

Contributed by Mrs. Charles L. Mosier, Pineville, Mo., Feb. 24, 1927.

Both young and old, come pay attention
To these few lines I'm a-going to write,
They're just as true as ever was mentioned
Concerning a fair and beautiful bride.

He courted a fair and handsome lady,
He loved her as he loved his life,
He oft-times vowed while in her presence
That he would make her his lawful wife.

But when his parents came to know it,
They strove to part them night and day,
Saying son, oh son, why be so foolish?
She is too poor, they would oft-times say.

Then down before his father kneeling,
Cried father, father pity me,
Don't deprive me of my whole heart's treasure,
For she is all the world to me.

But when this lady came to know it,
She soon resolved what she would do,
She wandered forth and left the city,
No more her loving friends to view.

She wandered forth by the flowing river,
For three long days in deep despair,
Saying must I stand here a woeful warning,
And must I sink in deep despair.

She then picked up the silver dagger
And pierced it through her snow white breast,
At first she reeled and then she staggered,
Saying goodbye vain world, I'm a-going to rest.

As he came near the lonely thicket,
He thought he heard his true love's voice,
He ran, he ran like one distracted,
Crying love, oh love, I'm afraid you're lost.

She opened her eyes like shining diamonds,
Saying love, oh love, you've come too late,
Prepare to meet me on Mount Zion,
Where all true lovers never part.

He then picked up the bloody dagger,
And pierced it through his own true heart,
Saying let this be a woeful warning
To all who would true lovers part.

C

Two variant stanzas from Mrs. Bessie Anderson, Powell, Mo., May 6, 1927.

The son got down on his knees a-begging,
Saying father, father pity me,
Don't keep me from my dearest Julia,
For she is all this world to me.

. . . . . .

Then he picked up the bloody body,
And turned it over on his arm,
Saying neither gold nor love can save you,
And you must die in all your charm.

D

Contributed by Miss Esther Davidson, Rocky Comfort, Mo., Mar. 9, 1927.

Both young and old, pray lend your attention,
To these few words I'm a-going to impress,
They are just as true as was ever mentioned,
Concerning a fair and beautiful miss.

. . . .
. . . .
He often went to her a-vowing
He would make her his lawful and wedded wife.

. . . .

. . . .

Saying here I am in youth and mourning,
And I have sank in deep despair.

Her coal black eyes like stars did open,
Saying love, oh love, you have come too late,
Prepare to meet me on Mount Zion
Where all our joys will be complete.

Some day they'll meet upon Mount Zion,
There to walk down the golden street,
And there to live in that beautiful city
Where all their joys will be complete.

E

Mrs. W. E. Jones, Pineville, Mo., Sept. 14, 1928, sings the final stanza as follows:

Come all ye friends and mourn around,
For they are dead and in the ground,
And o'er their graves flew a turtle dove
To show the world that they died for love.

F

Sung by Mrs. Sula Hudson, Crane, Mo., Sept. 15, 1941. She calls it "Young William."

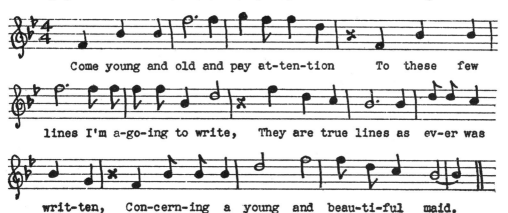

Come young and old and pay at-ten-tion   To these few
lines I'm a-go-ing to write,   They are true lines as ev-er was
writ-ten,   Con-cern-ing a young and beau-ti-ful maid.

Young William courted a handsome lady,
He loved her dear as he loved his life,
Oft-times he made his vowings to her
To make her his own . . . . wife.

And when his parents came to know this
They tried to part them day and night,
Saying son, oh son, don't be so foolish,
For she's too poor to be your bride.

Young William on his knees a-praying,
Saying father, father, pity me,
Don't part me from my darling Julie,
For she is all this world to me.

He then fell down on the roadside near her,
He thought he heard her wailing voice,
He ran, he ran like someone distracted,
Saying love, oh love, I hear your voice.

She then drew out the silver dagger,
And sank it in her snow-white breast,
At first she reeled and then she staggered,
Saying fare you well, I'm going to rest.

Her coal-black eyes like stars were shining,
Saying love, oh love, you've come too late,
Prepare to meet your darling Julie
Where all our joys would be complete.

He then picked up the bleeding body,
And rolled it o'er and in his arms,
Saying neither gold nor silver can buy you,
For you are worthless all their charms.

He then drew out the silver dagger
And sank it in his manly heart,
Saying this should be an awful warning
That all true lovers should never part.

140

YOUNG EDMOND DELL

This piece seems to have borrowed its most effective lines from the "Lowlands Low" song reported by Belden (*Songs-Ballads and Other Popular Poetry*, 1910, No. 97) and from the "Young Edward" ballad which Kittredge (*JAFL* 20, 1907, p. 274) found in Kentucky. See also Tolman and Eddy (*JAFL* 35, 1922, p. 421) and Cox (*Folk-Songs of the South*, 1925, p. 345). Mackenzie (*Quest of the Ballad*, 1919, p. 155) reported a related piece from Nova Scotia under the title "Young Emily," which is reprinted in his *Ballads and Sea Songs from Nova Scotia* (1928, pp. 92-93). See also "Edwin in the Lowlands Low" which Belden (*Ballads and Songs*, 1940, pp. 127-128) found in Missouri, and the versions in Chappell (*Folk-Songs of Roanoke and the Albemarle*, 1939, pp. 63-65), Treat (*JAFL* 52, 1939, pp. 25-26), Gardner (*Ballads and Songs of Southern Michigan*, 1939, pp. 62-63), and Brewster (*Ballads and Songs of Indiana*, 1940, pp. 202-203).·

A

Sung by Mrs. Lee Stephens, White Rock, Mo., Feb. 13, 1929.

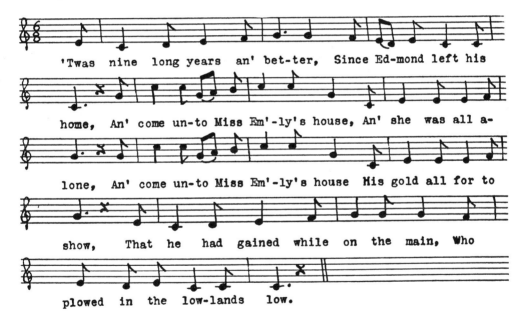

My father keeps a public house
Down yonder by the sea,
Go there, go there, my own true lover
An' spend the night with me.
Go there, go there, my own true lover,
Don't let my parents know
Your name it is young Edmond Dell
Who plowed the lowlands low.

Miss Emily passes a sleepless night,
She had a turrible dream,
She dreampt she saw her true lover's blood
A-flowin' in a stream.
Next mornin' she rose up early
An' straightway she did go,
For she dearly loved young Edmond Dell
Who plowed in the lowlands low.

Oh father, where is that young man
Who came here last night to dwell?
He's dead an' gone to his father's house,
No news for you to tell.
Oh father, cruel father,
You'll die of shame you know,
For the murderin' of young Edmond Dell
Who plowed in the lowlands low.

She went unto her counsel
Her story to make known,
Her father he was sent for,
An' soon his trial come on,
Her father he was sentenced
An' he was hung also,
For the murderin' of young Edmond Dell
Who plowed in the lowlands low.

I'll go away down yonder,
Down yonder by the sea,
To see my own true lover's blood
A-flowin' in a stream,
The ships sail o'er the ocean,
The tide waves to an' fro,
It reminds me of young Edmond Dell
Who plowed in the lowlands low.

B

Sung by Mr. Fred Woodruff, Lincoln, Ark., Dec. 12, 1941. He calls it "Young Edward in the Lowlands Low," and says he learned it near Lincoln about 1910.

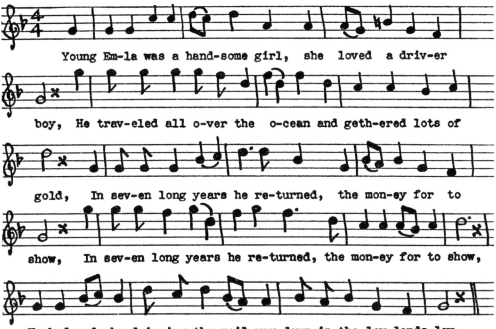

Young Em-la was a hand-some girl, she loved a driv-er boy, He trav-eled all o-ver the o-cean and geth-ered lots of gold, In sev-en long years he re-turned, the mon-ey for to show, In sev-en long years he re-turned, the mon-ey for to show, He had made by driv-ing the mail way down in the low-lands low.

My father runs a boarding-house down by the waterside,
It's you can go there and enter in and also be obliged,
I'll meet you there in the morning, don't let my parents know
I'll meet you there in the morning, don't let my parents know,
Your name might be young Edward who drove in the lowlands low.

Young Edward tuck a drink that night before he went to bed,
He little knew of the trouble that prowled around his head,
Young Henry said to his father, his money will make us a show,
Let's send his body a-sinking way down in the lowlands low.

Young Emla went to bed that night, she dreampt a frightful dream,
She dreampt her Edward were bleeding, the blood run down in a stream,
So early the next morning she arose and to her neighbors did go,
A-hunting for her driver boy who drove in the lowlands low.

Straightway to her mother, and to her did say,
Oh where is the stranger that stopped last night to stay?
Oh where is the stranger that stopped last night to stay?
He's gone to dwell, no tongue can tell, way down in the lowlands low.

Father, cruel father, you'll die a public show,
Father, cruel father, you'll die a public show,
For murdering of my driver boy who drove in the lowlands low.

The ships all over the ocean sails over my true love's breast,
His body is in a motion, I hope his soul's at rest,
The trees all over the mountains a-tosting to and fro,
The trees all over the mountains a-tosting to and fro,
Reminds me of my driver boy who drove in the lowlands low.

Mr. Wythe Bishop, Fayetteville, Ark., Dec. 15, 1941, said that he heard this song as a boy, but remembers only that it is about "Young Edwin in the lowlands low . . . he carried the mail *from Ging to Golden.*"

C

Sung by Mrs. Laura Wasson, Elm Springs, Ark., Jan. 28, 1942. She calls it "Young Emma," and says that she learned it at Elm Springs in the 80's.

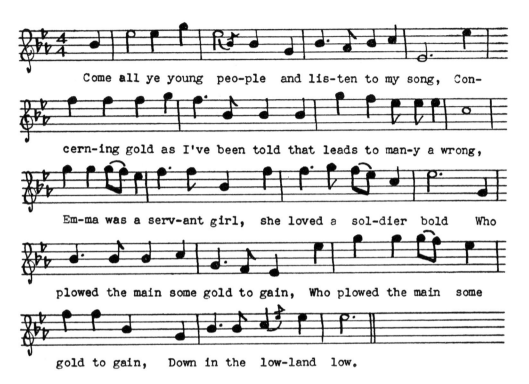

Come all ye young peo-ple and lis-ten to my song, Con-cern-ing gold as I've been told that leads to man-y a wrong, Em-ma was a serv-ant girl, she loved a sol-dier bold Who plowed the main some gold to gain, Who plowed the main some gold to gain, Down in the low-land low.

Young Emma she had daily mourned since Edward first left home,
Seven long years had passed and gone since Edward had been home,
He returned to Emma's home again, his gold for to show,
That he had gained upon the main,
That he had gained upon the main,
Down in the lowland low.

Young Edward sat a-smoking till time to go to bed,
For little was he thinking of the sorrow that crowned his head,
Said Emma's cruel parents, his gold will make a show,
And we'll send his body a-floating,
And we'll send his body a-floating,
Down in the lowland low.

Young Edward had gone to bed and scarcely fell asleep
When Emma's cruel parents into his room did creep,
They beat him, they dragged him, and to the beach did go
And they sent his body a-floating,
And they sent his body a-floating,
Down in the lowland low.

Young Emma lay sleeping, she dreamed a dreadful dream,
She dreamed her love was murdered, the blood appeared in streams,
She arose at the break of daylight, and to his room did go,
'Twas because she loved him dearly,
'Twas because she loved him dearly,
Who plowed the lowland low.

Oh father, where's that stranger came here last night to lie?
He's dead and gone, no tongue can tell, the father did reply,
Oh father, oh father, you'll die a public show,
For murdering my poor Edward,
For murdering my poor Edward
Who plowed the lowland low.

Says Emma I'll go and wander down by yon stormy wave,
When my true love is buried all in the sea so brave,
The fish are in the ocean, swimming o'er my true love's breast,
While his body lies there moldering,
While his body lies there moldering,
I know his soul's at rest.

141

FAIR FANNY MOORE

This is a British song, according to Pound (*Poetic Origins and the Ballad*, 1921, p. 226), but many variants have been popular in the United States. See Belden (*Song-Ballads and Other Popular Poetry*, 1910, No. 25; *JAFL* 25, 1912, p. 12), Shoemaker (*North Pennsylvania Minstrelsy*, 1919, p. 59), Pound (*American Ballads and Songs*, 1922, p. 206), Cox (*Folk-Songs of the South*, 1925, p. 441). Also W. H. Fawcett (*Captain Billy's Smokehouse Poetry*, Minneapolis, 1929, p. 81), who prints a garbled text entitled "Sweet Marceline Lamoore." Belden (*Ballads and Songs*, 1940, pp. 139-141) reports two good ones from Missouri, remarking that the song is "undoubtedly a product of the ballad press, but I have not found any stall print of it. Nor have I found that it is known in the British Isles." It appears in the Brown (North Carolina Folk-Lore Society) collection.

A

Sung by Mrs. Dan Pierce, Jane, Mo., Oct. 22, 1928.

There's a cot in Yon-ders val-ley, 'Tis de-ser-ted an' a-

lone, It has late-ly been ne-glect-ed, An' is green-ly o-ver-grown.

As you enter the door,
See the red stain on the floor,
Oh that is the blood
Of the fair Fanny Moore.

Young Fanny was a-bloomin',
Her two lovers came,
One offered young Fanny
His wealth an' his fame.

But all of his riches
It could not allure,
The fair burnin' bosom
Of the fair Fanny Moore.

Young Henry the shepherd
Was of lowly degree,
But he won her fond heart
An' accepted was he.

Then quick to the altar
He there did secure,
The hand an' the heart
Of the fair Fanny Moore.

As Fanny was a-settin'
In her cottage one day,
When business had called
Her fond husband away,

Young Randall the haughty,
Come in at the door,
An' clasped in his strong arms
The fair Fanny Moore.

Oh spare me, oh spare me,
Oh spare me, she cried,
Oh spare me in mercy
For now I'm a bride.

Oh no, said young Randall,
You go to your rest,
An' he buried his knife
In her snowy white breast.

Young Randall the haughty
Was taken an' tried,
Young Fanny a-bloomin'
In her beauty had died.

Young Randall was hung
On a tree by the door,
For takin' the life
Of the fair Fanny Moore.

Young Henry the shepherd
Went distracted an' wild,
He wandered away from
His lonely defile.

At length he died
An' was carried from the door,
An' laid by the side
Of his fair Fanny Moore.

B

Sung by Mrs. J. F. Trail, Farmington, Ark., Oct. 7, 1941. She learned it in Sebastian County, Ark., about 1890.

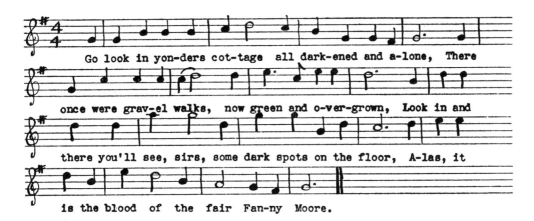

Go look in yon-ders cot-tage all dark-ened and a-lone, There once were grav-el walks, now green and o-ver-grown, Look in and there you'll see, sirs, some dark spots on the floor, A-las, it is the blood of the fair Fan-ny Moore.

Young Fanny, all blooming, two lovers they came,
They offered her their gold, their riches and their fame,
Their gold and their riches failed to allure
The long burning bosom of the fair Fanny Moore.

The first was young Randolph, all haughty with pride,
He offered his gold, his riches beside,
His gold and his riches failed to allure
The long burning bosom of the fair Fanny Moore.

The next was young Edward of lowly degree,
He offered her his heart, enraptured was she,
So quickly to the altar, so for to secure,
The heart and the hand of the fair Fanny Moore.

As Fanny was sitting in her cottage one day,
Business having called her fond husband away,
Young Randolph the haughty stepped in at the door
And clasped to his bosom the fair Fanny Moore.

Oh Fanny, dearest Fanny, beware of your fate,
Accept of my offer before it's too late,
For one thing is certain, I'm determined to secure
The life or the love of the fair Fanny Moore.

Oh spare me, oh spare me, young Fanny she cried,
Oh spare me, oh spare me for mercy's sake, she sighed,
Then go ye, go ye, to the land of the blest,
He buried his dagger in her snowy white breast.

Young Fanny all blooming in bloodstains she died,
Young Randolph the haughty was taken and tried,
He was hung in his chains on a tree before the door,
For taking the life of the fair Fanny Moore.

Young Edward the shepherd, distracted and wild,
Roamed far . . . . on his own native isle,
Till at length he was carried from his own cottage door,
And laid by the side of the fair Fanny Moore.

C

Manuscript copy from Mrs. W. R. Carlisle, Farmington, Ark., Jan. 6, 1942.

Go down to yonder cottage all dark and alone,
The walks once were gravel, but now are o'ergrown.
Go there and you will find one dark spot on the floor,
Alas, 'tis the blood of the fair Fanny Moore.

As Fanny was blooming two lovers there came,
One offered his riches, the other his fame,
But their fame and their riches they failed to secure
The heart and the hand of the fair Fanny Moore.

Then came young Edward of a lowly degree,
Offered his heart and accepted was he,
And straightway to the altar and quickly did secure
The heart and the hand of the fair Fanny Moore.

As Fanny was setting in her cottage one day,
Some business had called young Edward away,
Up halted young Randall and opened the door,
And clasped to his bosom the fair Fanny Moore.

Oh Fanny, oh Fanny, oh Fanny, cried he,
Though you've wedded another my heart's all for thee,
Come mount on behind me, to a faraway shore,
I safely will carry the fair Fanny Moore.

I beg you to leave me, and cause no disgrace,
The wife of young Edward in another's embrace!
My hand it is given, my love it is pure,
None ever shall name me the false Fanny Moore.

He drew out his long knife both bladed and keen,
Into her snow-white bosom he plunged the blade in.
Young Edward returning, did raise from the floor
All cold in her life blood the fair Fanny Moore.

Young Randall was taken straightway and tried,
His crime did repent, on the gallows he died
To be an example the wide world o'er,
For shedding the blood of the fair Fanny Moore.

Young Edward the shepherd grew straightway and wild,
He wandered all round his own cottage isle,
Till at last he was taken from his own cottage door
And laid by the side of his fair Fanny Moore.

142

YOUNG SAM BASS

Sam Bass the train-robber was killed at Round Rock, Texas, in 1878. For information about the historical Sam Bass see Emerson Hough (*The Story of the Outlaw*, 1907, p. 338), and W. P. Webb (*Texas Folk-Lore Society Publications* 3, 1924, pp. 226-230), also Allen Johnson's *Dictionary of American Biography* (II, 1929, pp. 35-36). Emmett Dalton (*When the Daltons Rode*, 1931, p. 195) has an excellent photograph of Bass and the traitorous Murphy mentioned in the song. Thorp (*Songs of the Cowboys*, 1921, p. 135) thinks that the ballad was written by one John Denton, Gainesville, Texas, in 1878. Wayne Gard, in his biography *Sam Bass* (New York, 1936), prints a text of the song (pp. 237-239), and remarks that "the ballad has been attributed to a John Denton, of Gainesville, Texas, but apparently it was the work of more than one hand." For other texts and references see Pound (*American Ballads and Songs*, 1922, p. 149), Finger (*Frontier Ballads*, 1927, pp. 65-71), Sandburg (*American Songbag*, 1927, p. 422), Larkin (*Singing Cowboy*, 1931, pp. 161-164), Lomax (*American Ballads and Folk Songs*, 1934, pp. 126-128), and Belden (*Ballads and Songs*, 1940, pp. 399-400).

A

Sung by Mr. William Lewis, Anderson, Mo., Mar. 4, 1928.

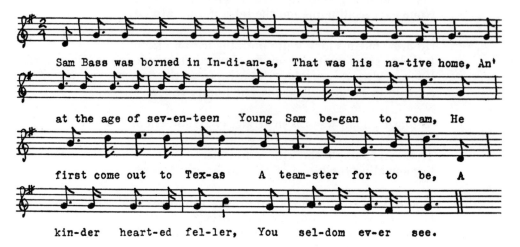

Sam Bass was borned in In-di-an-a, That was his na-tive home, An'
at the age of sev-en-teen Young Sam be-gan to roam, He
first come out to Tex-as A team-ster for to be, A
kin-der heart-ed fel-ler, You sel-dom ev-er see.

Young Sam he dealt in race stock,
One called the Denton mare,
He matched her in scrub races
An' took her to the Fair.
Sam always coined money,
An' spent it just as free,
He always drunk good liquor
Wherever he might be.

Sam he left the Collins ranch
In the merry month of May,
With a herd of Texas cattle
The Black Hills for to see,
Sold out in Custer City
An' all went on a spree,
A harder set of cowboys
You'll seldom ever see.

On their way back to Texas
They robbed the U.P. train,
They busted up in couples
An' started on again,
Joe Collins an' his partner
Was overtaken soon,
An' with all their hard-earned money
They had to meet their doom.

Sam Bass come back to Texas
All right side up with care,
Rode into the town of Denton
With all his friends to share.
Sam's time was short in Texas,
Three robberies did he do,
He took an' robbed the passengers,
An' mail an' express too.

Sam had four brave companions,
Four brave an' darin' lads,
There was Richardson an' Jackson,
Joe Collins an' old Dad,
As brave an' darin' cowboys
As Texas ever knew,
They whipped the Texas Rangers
An' run the boys in blue.

Sam had another companion,
Called Arkansaw for short,
He was shot by a Texas ranger
By the name of Thomas Floyd.
Tom is a big six-footer
An' he thinks he's mighty fly,
But I can tell you his racket,
He's a dead-beat on the sly.

Jim Murphy was arrested
An' then released on bail,
He jumped his bond at Taylor
An' took the train for Trail*
Old Major Jones had posted Jim,
An' that was all a sell,
It was all a plan to capture Sam
Before the comin' Fall.

Sam met his fate at Round Rock
On July twenty-first,
They pierced pore Sam with rifle balls
An' emptied out his purse.
Sand within the valley,
Pepper in the quay,
An' Jackson in the bushes
A-tryin' to git away.

*Terrell.

Jim Murphy borrowed gold from Sam
Their robberies to pay,
The only way he saw to win
Was to give pore Sam away.
He sold out Sam an' Barnes,
An' left their friends to mourn,
Oh what a scorchin' he will git
When Gabriel blows his horn!

B

Mrs. Lee Stephens, Jane, Mo., Apr. 3, 1927, contributes a long text with several slightly different stanzas:

Sam had four bold companions,
Four bold and daring lads,
Frank Jackson, Henry Underwood,
Joe Collins and Old Dad.

.   .   .   .   .

Poor Sam a corpse now lies,
They pitched him in the bay,
While Jackson's on the border
Still trying to get away.

.   .   .   .   .

Jim Murphy borrowed Sam's good gold
And did not want to pay,
And all the way he saw to win
Was to give poor Sam away.

He sold both Sam and Barney,
And left their friends to mourn,
Oh what a scorching Jim will get
When Gabriel blows his horn.

143

FULLER AND WARREN

Amasa Fuller killed Palmer Warren at Lawrenceburg, Indiana, in January, 1820. The circumstances of the crime and the provenience of the ballad are discussed at length by Barry (*Bulletin of the Folk-Song Society of the Northeast* 8, 1934, pp. 12-13; 9, 1935, pp. 14-17). Pound (*American Ballads and Songs*, 1922, p. 116) has a variant sung in Nebraska in 1874; Finger (*Frontier Ballads*, 1927, p. 168) prints a text obtained from a Texas cowpuncher in the Argentine. In the "Fuller and Warren" song reported by Lomax (*Cowboy Songs*, 1910, p. 126) there is an additional stanza, to the effect that the rope broke when Fuller was hanged, and that he was strangled by two physicians who were in attendance; compare Larkin (*Singing Cowboy*, 1931, pp. 123-127). "Ye sons of Columbia" was the opening line of a song entitled "Adams and Liberty" which Robert Treat Paine, Jr., wrote for John Adams' presidential campaign, and set to the tune of "The Star-Spangled Banner." Belden (*Ballads and Songs*, 1940, pp. 302-307) reports one tune and four texts from Missouri. Brewster (*Ballads and Songs of Indiana*, 1940, pp. 363-368) has seven texts of this genuine Indiana product.

A

Sung by Mrs. L. A. Thomas, Anderson, Mo., Dec. 16, 1927.

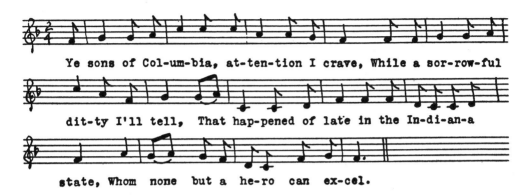

Ye sons of Col-um-bia, at-ten-tion I crave, While a sor-row-ful
dit-ty I'll tell, That hap-pened of late in the In-di-an-a
state, Whom none but a he-ro can ex-cel.

Like Sampson he courted his choice of the fair,
Intending to make her his bride,
But like Delilah fair she did his heart ensnare,
And robbed him of his honor and his life.

A gold ring he gave her in token of his love,
On the posey was the image of a dove,
They assentingly agreed to be married with speed,
And they promised by the powers above.

But this fickle-minded maid she avowed again to wed
With young Warren, a liver in the place,
And it was a fatal blow, causing his overthrow
And proved to be her shame and disgrace.

Now when Fuller come to know he was deprived of his dear
Who he had vowed by the powers to wed,
Unto Warren he did go, with his heart so full of woe,
And thus unto Warren he said:

Now Warren, you have wronged me to gratify your cause
By reporting I had left a prudent wife,
Now Warren, you acknowledge it before I break the law,
Or Warren, I'll deprive you of your life.

Then Warren he replied, your wish must be denied,
Since my heart to your darling is bound,
And further I must say that this is my wedding day,
In spite of all the heroes in this town!

Then Fuller in a passion of honor and love,
Which after caused many for to cry,
With one fatal shot he killed Warren on the spot,
Saying Lord, I am ready now to die.

Then Fuller was condemmed by the courts of Lawrenceburg,
Sentenced to die the ignominious death,
To swing above the earth or hang on the gallows high,
When the time arrives when Fuller is to die.

The time at length arrived when Fuller was to die,
He smiled and bade the audience adieu,
Like an angel he did stand for he was a handsome man,
On his breast he wore a ribbon of blue.

B

Mrs. Kate Stubblefield, Crane, Mo., Sept. 9, 1928, supplies two concluding stanzas:

Come all who have wives that are prudent and true,
Pray crown them with honor and love,
For my great opinion is that they are very hard to find,
They are blessings from the powers above.

For marriage is a lottery and few that gains a prize,
That is pleasing to the heart and to the eye,
And he that never married may well be known as wise,
So ladies and gentlemen, goodbye.

C

A slightly different version communicated by Professor F. M. Goodhue, Mena, Ark., Sept. 4, 1930, tells us that Fuller was hanged at a place called Davenport, and concludes with the following reflection:

All the ancient histories, we do understand,
And the Bible that we have to believe,
That woman is a sensual, and the downfall of man,
Just as Adam was beguiled by old Eve.

144

LOCKED IN THE WALLS OF PRISON

The repetition of the "poor boy" line is found in many Negro and "nigger minstrel" songs; see Scarborough (*On the Trail of Negro Folk-Songs*, 1925, pp. 87-89, 243-244), Cox (*Folk-Songs of the South*, 1925, pp. 179-185), Finger (*Frontier Ballads*, 1927, p. 175) and Sandburg (*American Songbag*, 1927, p. 310).

Sung by Mrs. W. E. Jones, Pineville, Mo., Jan. 8, 1929.

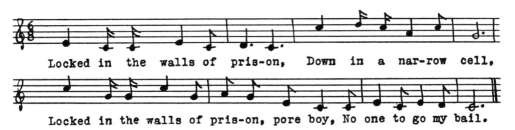

Locked in the walls of pris-on, Down in a nar-row cell,
Locked in the walls of pris-on, pore boy, No one to go my bail.

If I was worth ten thousand
I'd bury it away in my trunk,
Or else I'd surely gamble, pore boy,
Besides I might git drunk.

One foot upon the platform,
T'other foot on the train,
Oh take me back to Nashville, pore boy,
To wear the ball an' chain.

145

THE LILY OF THE WEST

Tolman and Eddy (*JAFL* 35, 1922, pp. 368-369) cite many British texts and references, and report a variant from rural Ohio entitled "Flora, the Lily of the West." The song was published in *The Dime Songster No. 3* (Indianapolis, 1859, p. 8), also in *Beadle's Dime Song Book* (New York, 1860, p. 48). Bradley Kincaid (*My Favorite Mountain Ballads*, 1928, p. 46) prints a fragment, while Sharp (*English Folk Songs from the Southern Appalachians*, 1932, II, p. 199) has a fine text from the Kentucky mountains. Eddy (*Ballads and Songs from Ohio*, 1939, pp. 147-149) gives two texts and a tune. See also two stanzas in Chappell (*Folk-Songs of Roanoke and the Albemarle*, 1939, p. 192) and a stanza from "The Lover's Lament" (*ibid.*, pp. 130-131). Belden (*Ballads and Songs*, 1940, pp. 132-133) gives numerous references, and six stanzas from Jefferson City, Mo. The piece appears in the Brown (North Carolina Folk-Lore Society) collection.

A

Sung by Mr. A. L. Hardy, Fayetteville, Ark., Dec. 7, 1920.

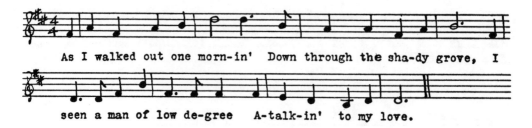

As I walked out one morn-in' Down through the sha-dy grove, I

seen a man of low de-gree   A-talk-in'   to my love.

I steps up to him boldly,
With my rifle in my hand,
I caught him by the collar
An' boldly bade him stand.

I drawed my penknife out
An' pierced it in his breast,
Here lies a lifeless corpse, says I,
For the Lily of the West.

For five long years at Frankfort
A prisoner I was sent,
For all my misbehavior
I shorely did repent.

An' then when I am free again,
An' I am set to rest,
I'll ramble this wide world over
For the Lily of the West.

B

Supplied by Mrs. O. A. Loomis, Pea Ridge, Ark., Oct. 18, 1925. Mrs. Loomis took it from an old manuscript book in the possession of her family.

I just come down from Louisville
Some pleasures for to find,
A handsome girl from Michigan
So pleasing to my mind.
Her rosy cheeks and rolling eyes
Like arrows pierced my breast,
They call her handsome Mary,
The Lily of the West.

I courted her for many a day,
Her love I thought to gain,
Too soon, too soon, she slighted me
Which caused me grief and pain,
She robbed me of my liberty,
Deprived me of my rest,
They call her handsome Mary,
The Lily of the West.

One evening as I rambled
Down by yonder shady grove,
I saw a lord of high degree
Conversing with my love,
He sang, he sang so merrily
That I was sore oppressed,
He sang for handsome Mary,
The Lily of the West.

I rushed up to my rival,
A dagger in my hand,
I tore him from my own true love
And boldly bade him stand.
Being mad to desperation
My dagger pierced his breast,
I was betrayed by Mary,
The Lily of the West.

And now my trial has come up,
And sentenced I'll soon be,
They put me in the criminal box
And there convicted me.
She so deceived the jury,
So modestly did dress,
She far outshone bright Venus,
The Lily of the West.

Since then I've gained my liberty,
I'll rove the country through,
I'll travel the city over
To find my loved one true,
The girl who stole my liberty,
And deprived me of my rest,
I must find handsome Mary,
The Lily of the West.

C

Contributed by Professor George E. Hastings, Fayetteville, Ark., Nov. 14, 1938. Dr. Hastings had it from Miss Grace Sadler, of Van Buren, Ark. Miss Sadler could not quote any more of the song, but wrote that "Flora has the typical love affair, and meets death by way of the dagger in a shady grove."

> I come down from Louisville
> Some pleasure for to find,
> An' spied a handsome lady
> Most suiting to my mind.
> She had rings on her fingers,
> An' she was richly dressed,
> They call her Handsome Flora,
> The Lily of the West.

Sung by Mr. Charles Ingenthron, Walnut Shade, Mo., Sept. 4, 1941. Mr. Ingenthron sings it to the same air he uses for "Joe Bowers" and "Caroline of Edinborough Town."

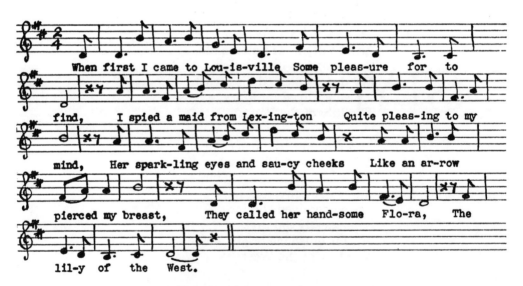

> Her curly locks of yellow hair
> In ringlets shone like gold,
> . . . . ,
> . . . .
> She had a ring on every finger,
> So handsome was she dressed,
> They called her handsome Flora,
> The lily of the West.

One evening as I walked out
Down by yon shady grove,
I spied a man of low degree
Conversing with my love.
He sang her a song of melody
Which so enraged my breast,
He called her handsome Flora,
The lily of the West.

I stepped up to my rival,
My dagger in my hand,
I took him by the collar
And boldly bid him stand.
I was mad to desperation,
I swore I'd pierce his breast,
Saying go, false-hearted Flora,
The lily of the West.

In due time come my trial,
I boldly made my plea,
A flaw in the indictment
They said would set me free.
But she turned both judge and jury,
So handsome was she dressed,
They smiled on handsome Flora,
The lily of the West.

But now I am convicted,
To prison I must go,
For five long years in Frankfort,
Which fills my heart with woe.
She's robbed me of my liberty,
Deprived me of my rest,
I never can forgive her,
The lily of the West.

146

MY FATHER WAS A GAMBLER

Mr. Billy Laws, Argenta, Ark., Dec. 12, 1917, told me that this piece was part of a very long ballad about a murderer who was hanged at Fort Smith, Ark., in the 70's; the letter mentioned in the song, according to Mr. Laws, was a decoy sent by the sheriff in order to effect the fugitive's capture. Pound (*American Ballads and Songs*, 1922, p. 130) prints a shorter version which was "secured for H. M. Belden by Miss Frances Barbour, Washington University, from the singing of Minnie Doge at Arlington, Phelps County, Missouri, in 1917." In Pound's text the gambler received his letter "in old Fort Smith"—presumably Fort Smith, Ark.—instead of at some undesignated point in Missouri. The third stanza of the following piece has a parallel in "Moonlight," which Sandburg (*American Songbag*, 1927, p. 216) regards as the original of the famous "Prisoner's Song," also in the sixth stanza of "Wild Bill Jones" as reported from the Southern mountains by Spaeth (*Weep Some More, My Lady*, 1927, p. 134). Some verses of "My Father Was a Gambler" are often introduced into another old song "The Roving Gambler," which has a very different melody and which has been recorded phonographically by Al Craver (*Columbia* 15034-D). In his *Ballads and Songs* (1940, pp. 472-473) Belden reprints the text cited by Pound in 1922, adding some further references in a headnote.

A

Sung by Mrs. W. E. Jones, Pineville, Mo., Jan. 8, 1929.

My fath-er was a gam-bler, he l'arnt me how to play, My fath-er was a gam-bler, he l'arnt me how to play, Say-in' son, don't go a-beg-gin' while you got the ace an' trey.

Chorus

Hang me, oh hang me, an' I'll be dead an' gone, Hang me, oh hang me, an' I'll be dead an' gone, I would-n't mind the hang-in', but to lay in my grave so long, To lay in my grave so long!

Down in old Missouri, as sick as I could be,
Down in old Missouri, as sick as I could be,
Along comes a letter sayin'
Son, come home to me.

If I had of minded mamma, I wouldn't be here today,
If I had of minded mamma, I wouldn't be here today,
But I was young an' foolish,
An' easy persuaded away.

Father an' mother an' little sister makes three,
Father an' mother an' little sister makes three,
A-marchin' to th' gallows
For to see the last of me.

They put the rope around my neck an' drawed me very high,
They put the rope around my neck an' drawed me very high,
The last words that I heerd 'em say
Was it won't be long till he'll die.

B

Sung by Mr. Wythe Bishop, Fayetteville, Ark., Dec. 9, 1941. He calls the song "Blue-Stone Mountain," but says that it is sometimes known as "Tommy's Hangin' Day."

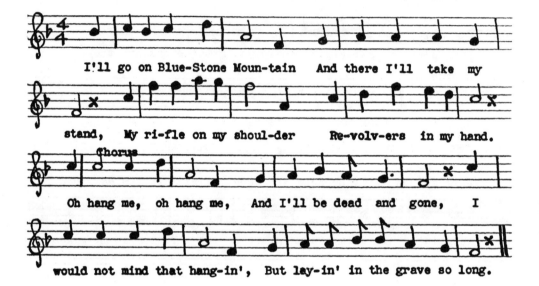

I'll go on Blue-Stone Moun-tain   And there I'll take my
stand, My ri-fle on my shoul-der   Re-volv-ers in my hand.
Oh hang me, oh hang me, And I'll be dead and gone, I
would not mind that hang-in', But lay-in' in the grave so long.

I have one little brother
And two little sisters makes three,
To follow me down to the gallows tree
And see the last of me.

I've been all around this world,
But never was in jail before,
Oh send for my two babies to come and see me die,
Oh send for my two babies to wring their hands and cry.

147

THE CASSVILLE PRISONER

This a fragment of a long ballad about some forgotten Missouri criminal; Cassville is the county seat of Barry County, and the Missouri State Penitentiary is located at Jefferson City. The first part of the tune is reminiscent of several other old songs; compare "Early, Early in the Spring" as recorded elsewhere in this book, also Carl Sprague's phonograph record of "Following the Cow Trail" (*Victor* 20067).

Sung by Mrs. Carrie Baber, Pineville, Mo., Mar. 6, 1921. Mrs. Baber recalls only two stanzas, but says that there were seven or eight in the song as she first heard it near Pineville in 1885. The first stanza, she says, was always sung to a different tune than that which served the other verses.

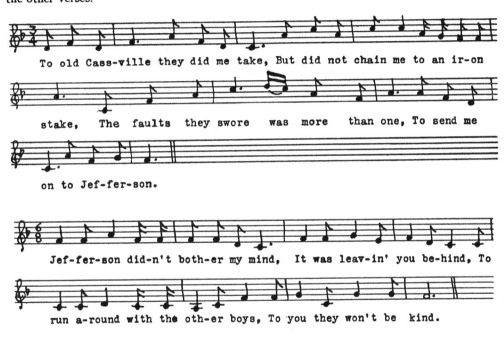

148

THE RAMBLING BOY

Evidently of British origin, this piece is related to songs reported from the Kentucky mountains by Shearin and Combs (*Syllabus of Kentucky Folk-Songs*, 1911, p. 17) and by Combs (*Folk-Songs du Midi des Etats-Unis*, 1925, pp. 215-216). Mr. David Rice, Springfield, Mo., sings a very similar version which he calls "I Robbed Old Nelse." James Still (*River of Earth*, 1940, pp. 143-144) quotes one stanza of a similar piece entitled "Rich and Rambling Boy." See Belden (*Ballads and Songs*, 1940, pp. 136-137) for several British and American references, and one good Missouri text. The piece appears in the Brown (North Carolina Folk-Lore Society) collection.

A

Sung by Mrs. Lee Stephens and Miss Ethel Rodney, White Rock, Mo., Feb. 17, 1929.

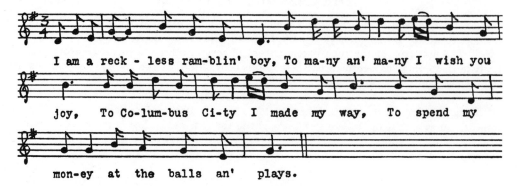

I am a reck - less ram-blin' boy, To ma-ny an' ma-ny I wish you
joy, To Co-lum-bus Ci-ty I made my way, To spend my
mon-ey at the balls an' plays.

An' on my way I found me a wife,
I loved her dear as I loved my life,
To dress her up in silks so gay
She caused me to rob on the road highway.

I robbed them all, I do declare,
I robbed them all, says James so fair,
I robbed them all ten thousand times,
One night while I was a-ramblin' around.

With well-loaded guns to bear my way,
A pretty bright sword an' a pistol gay,
A neat young lad to wear the bow
Of her pink silk ribbon or her silver an' gold.

I bought me a ticket to Gainesville town,
Got on the train and there set down,
The wheels did roll an' the whistle did blow,
In about five days I rolled in home.

But now I am caught an' condemned to die,
A many a pretty girl will surely cry,
But tears of grief won't set me free
Or save me from the gallows tree.

My mother said she was left alone,
My sister said she would weep and mourn,
My sweetheart lays in her deep despair,
With her diamond ring an' her curly hair.

Oh when I am gone, go sing it to all,
Oh when I am gone go sing it afar,
Oh when I am gone, go sing it for joy,
For this is the last of the ramblin' boy.

B

Contributed by Mrs. Emma L. Dusenbury, Mena, Ark., Sept. 4, 1930. Mrs. Dusenbury says that the fourth word in the first line should be spelled "reek," and insists that it was always so pronounced.

I am a reek* an' a ramblin' one,
From Eastern shores I have lately come,
To learn my books an' to learn my trade,
Some call me the reek an' ramblin' blade.

I come here a-spendin' money free,
A-spendin' money at balls an' play,
At length my money did grow very low,
An' then to rovin' I did go.

I married me a handsome wife,
A girl I loved as dear as my life,
To keep her dressed so neat an' gay
Caused me to rob on this here highway.

I robbed old Nelson, I do declare,
I robbed him on St. James's square,
I robbed him of five thousand pounds,
Dividin' with my comrades round.

But now I am condemned to die,
An' many a lady will for me cry,
Pretty Nelly weeps, tears down her hair,
A lady alone, left in despair.

My father weeps, he makes his moan,
My mother cries my darlin' son,
But all their weepin' won't never save me,
Nor keep me from the gallows tree.

When I am dead, laid in my grave,
The final funeral preached over my head,
All round my grave play tunes of joy,
Away goes the reek an' ramblin' boy.

*rake?

149

POOR OMA WISE

This piece is very similar to the "Pretty Oma" song reported by Belden (*Song-Ballads and Other Popular Poetry*, 1910, No. 17) also to an item recovered by Campbell and Sharp (*English Folk Songs from the Southern Appalachians*, 1917, p. 228). Pound (*American Ballads and Songs*, 1922, pp. 119, 249) prints a text from Kentucky, and quotes one of Belden's correspondents, who locates the occurrence in Indiana. Lunsford (*30 and 1 Folk-Songs*, 1929, pp. ii, 28) says flatly that "Jonathan Lewis drowned his sweetheart, Naomi Wise, in Deep River, in 1808" in North Carolina. Miss Myrtle Lain, Linn Creek, Mo., showed me a text obtained from one of her neighbors; this neighbor told Miss Lain that he had lived at Adams' Spring near Springfield, Mo., where the murder of Naomi Wise took place. Mr. Otto Ernest Rayburn (*Arcadian Magazine*, April, 1931, p. 14) prints a text which he describes as "a true Ozark folksong, originating here and not carried from the Tennessee or Kentucky mountains as the majority of ballads were." For a discussion of the provenience of this piece see Belden's headnote (*Ballads and Songs*, 1940, pp. 322-324), giving some of the information cited by Pound in 1922. Further references are Eddy (*Ballads and Songs from Ohio*, 1939, pp. 217-218), Morris (*Southern Folklore Quarterly* 8, 1944, pp. 186-187), and Brown (the North Carolina Folk-Lore Society) collection. Compare also the phonograph records of "Naomi Wise" as sung by Al Craver (*Columbia* 15053-D) and Vernon Dalhart (*Victor* 19867-B).

A

Sung by Mrs. Judy Jane Whittaker, Anderson, Mo., May 16, 1928. Mrs. Whittaker learned the song in 1862.

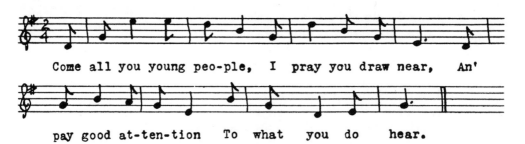

Come all you young peo-ple, I pray you draw near, An'
pay good at-ten-tion To what you do hear.

I'll sing you a ditty
Of pore Oma Wise,
How she was deluded
By Lewis's lies.

When he first come to see her
Fine stories he'd tell,
How when they got married
He'd use her so well.

He told her to meet him
At Adams's spring,
Some money he'd bring her,
An' other fine things.

He brought her no money,
But flatterin' the case,
He says we'll git married,
An' it aint no disgrace.

Come jump up behind me,
We'll ride down through town,
An' we will be married,
In union be bound.

She jumped up behind him
An' away they did go,
They went to Deep River
Where the waters overflow.

Oh, Oma, oh Oma,
I'll tell you my mind,
My mind is for to drownd you
An' leave you behind.

Oh pity, oh pity,
Oh pity, she cried,
Oh let me go mournin'
An' not be your bride.

No pity, no pity,
No pity, he cried,
My mind is for to drownd you
An' leave you behind.

He slipped up behind her
An' chok-ed her down,
An' throwed her in the water
Just below the mill dam.

He jumped on his geldin',
Rode off at great speed,
Sayin' now I'll see pleasure,
From Oma I'm freed.

The screams of pore Oma
They follered him nigh,
Oh I'm a pore rebel,
Not fittin' to die.

In come Oma's mother
An' these words did say:
George Lewis drownded Oma,
An' he's now run away.

He's gone to Elk River,
So I understand,
An' there put in prison
For killin' a man.

In prison, in prison,
In prison he's bound,
He made his confession
An' wrote it all down.

B

Mrs. Carrie Baber, Pineville, Mo., Oct. 10, 1921, contributes a single stanza, which she heard in McDonald County, Mo., in 1888.

Oh Loney, little Loney, I've made up mind,
My mind is for to drownd you, an' leave you behind,
He beat her an' cuffed her till she could scarce stand,
An' throwed her in the river below the mill dam.

C

Sung by Mrs. Lee Stephens, White Rock, Mo., Jan. 8, 1928. Mrs. Stephens calls it "John Hall."

John Hall he is a prisoner an' sentenced to be hung,
He wrote out his confession all gallantly sung,
Sayin' hang me, oh hang me, for I waylaid a man,
An' I drownded poor Neoma just below the mill dam.

Sayin' git down from behind him, an' go along with me,
For you shall not be his wedded bride, with either him or me,
So poor Neoma she got down from behind her own true love,
An' went with John Hall down below the old mill dam.

Now poor Neoma is drownded just below the mill dam,
Her spirit is a-floatin' just below the old mill dam,
John Hall he is a-hangin', John Hall is a-hangin' high,
John Hall is a-hangin' between the earth an' sky.

D

Sung by Mr. Lewis Kelley, Cyclone, Mo., Aug. 2, 1931.   Mr. Kelley knows the song as "Little Ona."

It's raining an' hailing,
It's a cold stormy night,
Let's go in the parlor
An' stay there all night.

You promised to meet me
At Adams' Gum springs,
With a pocket of money
An' other fine things.

You've brought me no money
To flatter my case,
An' if you an' I get married
It will be no disgrace.

Come get up behind me,
An' away we will ride,
To yonder fair city
I'll make you my bride.

She got up behind him,
An' away they did go,
To the banks of deep waters
Where the island overflows.

Little Ona, little Ona,
Let me tell you my mind,
My mind is to drown you
An' leave you behind.

Oh pity, oh pity,
An' spare me my life,
An' let me go beggin'
If I can't be your wife.

No pity, no pity,
No pity, says he,
In yonders deep water
Your body must be.

Little Ona was missin'
An' nowhere to be found,
Her friends they all gathered
An' hunted the ground.

Her dearest old mother
Just come for to hear,
Jim Lewis drownded Ona
An' is runnin' away.

He's down on Off Rivers,
As we all understand,
They have got him in prison
For killin' a man.

He wrote his confessions
To the friends all around,
To the friends of little Ona,
Though she may be found.

Come kill me, come hang me,
For I am the man
Who drownded little Ona
Below the mill dam.

E

Sung by Miss Faye Baker and her brother Bill, St. Paul, Ark., Apr. 17, 1934.

Oh come all you young people, a story I will tell,
About a girl they called Naomi Wise,
Her face was fair an' handsome, she was loved by every one,
In old Deep River now her body lies.

They say she had a lover, young Lewis was his name,
They say that he was heartless to the core,
So in the stream he throwed her, below the old mill dam,
An' sweet Naomi's smile was seen no more.

. . . .
. . . .

An' now they say her spirit still hovers round the place,
To save the young girls from some villain's lies.

F

Sung by Mrs. Irene Carlisle, Fayetteville, Ark., Sept. 30, 1941. Part of a long ballad
called "Little Omie," learned from her grandmother about 1912.

So hop on be-hind me and a-way we will ride, To some
dis-tant ci-ty where I'll make you my bride, She hopped on behind him and a-way they did ride, Till they came to   the
mill stream so deep and so wide.

Omie, my little Omie, I'll tell you my mind,
My mind is to drownd you and leave you behind,
Oh William, sweet William, oh spare me my life,
And I'll always go a-begging if I can't be your wife.

. . . . .

He rode on across and he reached the far side,
And he thought on little Omie and how she had died,
And he wrote his confession and sent it around
To the friends of little Omie that she might be found.

Saying shoot me or hang me, for I am no man,
I drownded little Omie below the mill dam.

G

Mrs. Olga Trail, Farmington, Ark., Oct. 13, 1941, says that the "Little Omie" song begins:

He promised to meet me at Higgins's spring
And bring me some money and other fine things,
No money I've brought you, you can argue the case,
Come let us get married, it is no disgrace.

So hop on behind me and away we will ride
To some distant city, I'll make you my bride,
She hopped on behind him and away they did ride
Till they come to the wide water where the bullfrogs do glide.

H

A text from Mrs. Mary Hall, Fayetteville, Ark., Mar. 14, 1942, has the following lines:

He whipped her and he beat her till she scarcely could stand,
And threw her in the water below the mill dam.

Up stepped Omie's mother, these words she did say:
Jim Lulers killed Omie, and he has run away.

They've got him in island, bound down to the ground,
He has written his confessions and sent them around.

You can hang me or drownd me, for I am the man
That drownded little Omie below the mill dam.

150

THE NOEL GIRL

Many people in McDonald County, Mo., remember this song, and insist that it refers to the fate of Lula Noel, whose body was found in the Cowskin River near Lanagan, Mo., Dec. 10, 1892. William Simmons, Joplin, Mo., was convicted of the murder and sentenced to the penitentiary. See Sturgis (*History of McDonald County, Missouri*, 1897, pp. 106-111). The words of the "Noel Girl" song, however, are almost identical with those of "The Wexford Girl," derived from an English piece about a "Cruel Miller" who was hanged in Berkshire in 1744 (Cox, *Folk-Songs of the South*, 1925, p. 311). For other texts and references see Belden (*JAFL* 25, 1912, p. 11), Shearin and Combs (*Syllabus of Kentucky Folk-Songs*, 1911, pp. 13, 28), Mackenzie (*Ballads and Sea Songs from Nova Scotia*, 1928, pp. 293-294), Eddy (*Ballads and Songs from Ohio*, 1939, pp. 231-232), Gardner (*Ballads and Songs of Southern Michigan*, 1939, pp. 77-79), and Brewster (*Ballads and Songs of Indiana*, 1940, pp. 204-205). Compare the phonograph records of "The Knoxville Girl," sung by Arthur Tanner (*Columbia* 15145-D). Belden (*Ballads and Songs*, 1940, pp. 133-136) reports a Missouri variant entitled "The Oxford Girl."

A

Sung by Mrs. Lee Stephens, White Rock, Mo., Aug. 10, 1927.

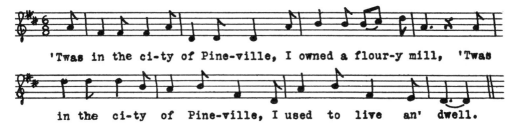

'Twas in the ci-ty of Pine-ville, I owned a flour-y mill, 'Twas
in the ci-ty of Pine-ville, I used to live an' dwell.

One day I saw a pretty fair maid,
On her I cast an eye,
I told her I would marry her
An' she believed a lie.

I went unto her sister's house
At eight o'clock that night,
I ask her if she'd walk with me
A little ways away.

So arm in arm we walked along
Till we come to a lonely place,
Then I took a rail from off the fence
An' struck her in the face.

She fell down on her bended knees,
An' loud for mercy cried,
For heaven's sake don't murder me
For I'm not prepared to die.

I paid no attention to what she said,
But kept on strikin' her more,
Until I saw the innocent looks
That I never could restore.

I run my fingers through her coal black hair,
To cover up my sin,
I drug her to the river side
An' there I plunged her in.

When I returned unto my mill
I met my servant John,
He ask me why I looked so pale
An' yet so very warm.

An' what occasion so much blood
Upon my hands an' clothes?
The sad an' only answer was
A bleedin' from the nose.

I lit my candle an' went to bed
Expectin' to take some rest,
But it seemed to me the fires of hell
Was a-burnin' in my breast.

Come all young men an' warnin' take,
That to your lovers prove true,
An' never let the devil get
The upper hand of you.

B

Mrs. Eva Shockley, Noel, Mo., Aug. 12, 1928, sings a very similar version of this song except for the first stanza, which runs as follows:

My tender parents brought me up,
Provided for me well,
'Twas in the city of Lexton Town
They placed me in a mill.

Mrs. Shockley insists that this piece is called "The Noel Girl," and has never doubted that it referred to the murder of Lula Noel. When asked what "the city of Lexton Town" had to do with this murder she said that perhaps Lexton was an old name for the village now called Pineville, and cited several cases in which the names of nearby settlements had been changed within her own memory.

C

Sung by Miss Laura Thornton, Pineville, Mo., Oct. 4, 1926.

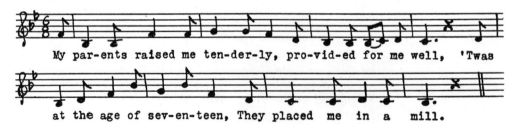

My par-ents raised me ten-der-ly, pro-vid-ed for me well, 'Twas
at the age of sev-en-teen, They placed me in a mill.

Three weeks ago last Saturday night,
An' cursed be the day,
The devil put it in my heart
To take her life away.

. . . . .

I paid but little attention to her,
But only beat her more,
Until the ground was all around
In a awful bloody gore.

. . . . .

Come all young men an' warnin' take.
Prove true to your lovers true,
An' never let the devil get
The upper hand of you.

A very similar "Noel Girl" song contributed by Mr. Lewis Kelley, Cyclone, Mo., July 6, 1931, includes the following local reference:

I throwed her in old Cowskin River
Below the Rutledge dam.

The Cowskin River is the stream in which the body of the Noel girl was found, and Rutledge is the old name for the village now called Elk Springs, near the scene of the crime. Mr. Kelley is a "singin'-teacher," and has given some thought to the matter. He told me that, in his opinion, the song was "made up" from a still older piece called "The Expert Girl," about a lady who was murdered back in Tennessee.

None of my neighbors knew anything about "The Expert Girl," but a couple of years later the Springfield (Mo.) *Leader* (Feb. 18, 1933) described an amateur stunt at a local theater:

"Two little boys sang a blood-curdling song called 'My Expert Girl'—all about a man who murdered his sweetheart and threw her in the river because he didn't want to marry her."

The two little boys could not be located next morning, but I found several other persons in Springfield who were familiar with the song.

D

The following text of "The Expert Girl" was contributed by Miss Lucile Morris, Springfield, Mo., Feb. 22, 1933.

'Twas in the town of Echo, was where I used to dwell,
But in the town of Expert I owned a flouring mill,
I fell in love with an Expert girl, and rolling was her eyes,
I fell in love with another girl, and loved her just as nice.

. . . .
. . . .
My father he persuaded me to make this girl my wife,
The devil he persuaded me to take away her life.

I called up to her sister's house, was eight o'clock at night,
And little did this poor girl think that I owed her a spite,
I called on her to take a walk out over the meadow so gay,
Perhaps we'd have a private talk to point the wedding day.

Together we walked and together we talked till we come to level ground,
And picking up a stick of hedge I knocked this poor girl down,
She fell upon her bended knees, for mercy's sake she cried,
Sweet Willie, do not murder me here, I'm not prepared to die.

But little attention did I pay and only beat her more,
Until the ground we stood upon was in a bloody gore,
I picked her up by her long yellow hair and slung her round and round,
I drug her to the river and throwed her in to drowned.

Lie there, lie there, you Expert girl, you ne'er shall be my bride,
Lie there, lie there, you Expert girl, to me you'll ne'er be tied.
I called up to my mother's house, was twelve o'clock at night,
My mother being restless, she woke up in a fright.

My God, my son, what have you done to bloody your hands and clothes?
The answer that she got from me was bleeding at the nose,
I called to her for a handkerchief to bind my aching head,
And also for a candlestick to light my way to bed.

. . . .
. . . .
I kicked and tossed and rolled around, no comfort could I find,
The flames of hell around my bed and in my eyes did shine.

In just about three weeks or four this poor girl she was found,
A-floating down the river that runs through Expert town.
They took me on suspicion, locked me in the Expert jail,
There was no one a friend to me, no one to go my bail.

. . . .
. . . .
Her sister swore my life away, without a bit of doubt,
She swore I was the same young man that called her sister out.

E

Another text, also supplied by Miss Lucile Morris, Springfield, Mo., Feb. 22, 1933, concluded with the following stanza:

Come all you false-hearted lovers, take warning now by me,
And never treat your own true love in any severity,
For if you do you sure will rue the day until you die,
And hanged you'll be upon the tree, a murderer's death you'll die.

F

Mr. Clarence G. O'Neill, Day, Mo., July 28, 1941, recalls a fragment he heard near Day in 1900:

. . . .
. . . .
He bound me to a miller boy
That I might learn his trade.

. . . . .

. . . .
. . . .
My father he persuaded me
To take this dear girl's life.

. . . . .

Her father then he questioned me
Whence came my bloody clothes,
I answered him untruthfully
From bleeding at the nose.

. . . . .

. . . .
. . . .
. . . . take no night walks,
And shun bad company.

G

Sung by Mr. J. Will Short, Galena, Mo., Aug. 15, 1941. He learned the song from his
mother, near Galena, about 1890.

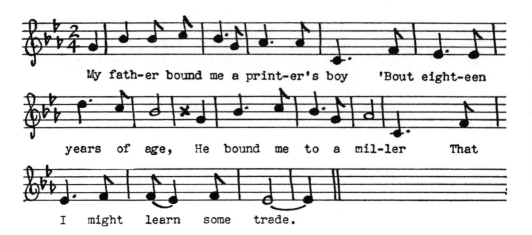

My fath-er bound me a print-er's boy   'Bout eight-een
years of age, He bound me to a mil-ler   That
I might learn some trade.

And there I fell in love with an orphan girl
With dark and sparkling eyes,
I thought that I would marry her
If she did not deny.

I went into this lady's house
About eight o'clock at night,
But little did the lady know
I owed her in despite.

I asked her to take a walk with me
To some far distant place,
Where we might have some private talk
And name the wedding date.

She agreed to take a walk with me
To some far distant place,
Where we might have some private talk
And name the wedding date.

I took her by the lily-white hand
And led her to the place,
And from the fence I drew a stake
And smoothed her down the face.

She fell upon her bended knees,
Oh Lord, have mercy on me, she cried,
Oh John, my dear, don't murder me here
For I'm not prepared to die.

The second time I drew my stake
Just as I did before,
And out of her eyes and nose and mouth
The gushing blood did flow.

I took her by the lily-white hand
And swung her round and round,
And drug her down to the river's side
And plunged her in to drown.

I went into the miller's house
About twelve o'clock at night,
But little did the miller know
As he gazed upon my sight.

Oh Johnny dear, how came that blood
Upon your hands, likewise your clothes?
The only reply I gave the miller
Was bleeding at the nose.

I snatched the candle out of his hand
And to my bed I ran,
And there I lie a-trembling
For the murder I had done.

And there I lie a-trembling,
No peace, no comfort, no rest,
I felt the guilty pains of hell
A-rushing through my breast.

They took me down to Washington,
And there my life to try,
And by my own confession
I was condemned to die.

H

Part of a text from Mrs. Georgia Dunaway, Fayetteville, Ark., Jan. 30, 1942. She calls
it "The Rexford Girl."

Side by side together we strolled
Till we come to a silent place,
I taken a stick from off'n the fence
And hit her in the face.

. . . . .

It was three weeks, three weeks or more
Before that maid was found,
She was found a-floating down the stream
That flows through Rexford town.

I

Sung by Mr. Fred Painter, Galena, Mo., Sept. 26, 1941. He calls it "The Knoxville Girl."

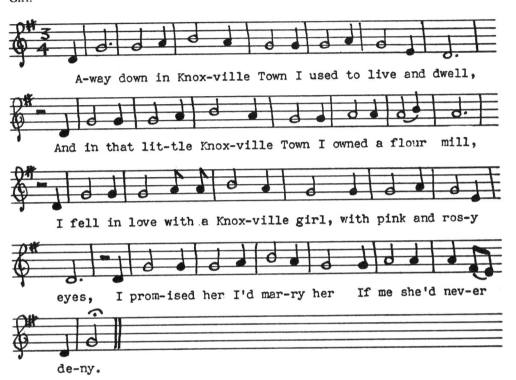

A-way down in Knox-ville Town I used to live and dwell,

And in that lit-tle Knox-ville Town I owned a flour mill,

I fell in love with a Knox-ville girl, with pink and ros-y

eyes, I prom-ised her I'd mar-ry her If me she'd nev-er

de-ny.

We walked along and talked along
Till we come to a level ground,
And I picked up a heavy stick
And knocked this pretty girl down.
She fell upon her bending knees,
Oh Willie, have mercy, she cried,
Oh Willie, my dear, don't murder me here
For I'm not prepared to die.

I laughed at every word she said,
I beat her more and more,
I beat her till the ground around
To . . . . a bloody . . . .
I tuck her by her lily-white hair,
I drug her round and round,
I drug her down to the stillwater deep
That flows to Knoxville Town.

A dreadful trick we played her,
This Knoxville girl was found,
A-floating' down the still water deep
That flows to Knoxville Town.

Her sister swore my life away,
She swore without a doubt,
She swore I was the very man
That layed her sister out.
And now they're going to hang me,
A dreadful death to die,
And now they're going to hang me
Between the earth and sky.

J

Sung by Mrs. Mildred Tuttle, Farmington, Ark., Dec. 31, 1941. Learned years ago from her parents.

I fell in love with a nice young girl,
Dark rolling was her hair,
I told her that I'd marry her
If me she'd never deny.
I fell in love with another girl,
I loved her just as well,
The devil put it in my mind
My first true lover to kill.

K

Sung by Mr. and Mrs. Arlie Freeman, Natural Dam, Ark., Dec. 14, 1941. Mrs. Freeman calls it "that song about the *edward stick*," but has no idea what the term means.

I fell in love with an Expert girl
To see if she'd be my bride,
I ask her if she'd marry me,
'Twas me she did deny.

They walked along, they talked along
Till they come to level ground,
And there he picked up an edward stick
And knocked that fair maid down.

He picked her up by her yellow hair
And slung her round and round,
He picked her up by her yellow hair
And slung her in to drownd.

Lie there, lie there, you Expert girl,
You'll never be my bride,
Lie there, lie there, you Expert girl,
To me you'll never be tied.

He went into his mother's room
And found her sick in bed,
And she was worried in her sleep
And waked up in a fright.

Oh Willie, my son, what have you done?
There's blood all over your clothes.
The only answer he could give
Was bleeding at the nose.

He called for a handkerchief
To bind his aching head,
He also called for a candlestick
To light himself in bed.

He rolled and he tumbled,
No comfort could he find,
For the flames of hell were round him so,
Oh how his eyes did shine.

L

Sung by Mrs. Sula Hudson, Crane, Mo., Sept. 15, 1941.

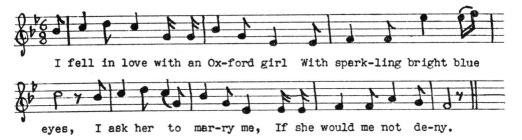

I fell in love with an Ox-ford girl With sperk-ling bright blue

eyes,   I ask her to mar-ry me, If she would me not de-ny.

I ask her to take a walk with me
To some far and distant place,
And there we'd have some private talk
And appoint our wedding day.

She went and took a walk with me
To the far and distant place,
And there we had some private talk
And appointed our wedding day.

I drew a stake that was standing by
And smoothed her down the face,
. . . .
. . . .

I drew the stake . . . .
Just as I did before,
And out of her eyes, her nose and mouth
The gushing blood did pour.

She fell upon her bended knees,
Oh Lord have mercy, she cried,
Oh Johnny dear, don't murder me here,
I'm not prepared to die.

I heeded not the words she said,
But still went on the more,
Till all the ground around her
Was all a bloody yoe.

I took her by the lily-white hand
And slung her round and round,
And plunged her in the river
Down in Oxford town.

151

WILD BILL JONES

For other versions of the "Wild Bill Jones" song see Richardson (*American Mountain Songs*, 1927, p. 36), Spaeth (*Weep Some More, My Lady*, 1927, pp. 134-135), Lunsford (*30 and 1 Folk Songs*, 1929, p. 6), Sharp (*English Folk Songs from the Southern Appalachians*, 1932, II, p. 74), Hudson (*Folksongs of Mississippi*, 1936, pp. 239-240), Chappell (*Folk-Songs of Roanoke and the Albemarle*, 1939, p. 193), and Combs (*Folk-Songs from the Kentucky Highlands*, 1939, pp. 24-25).

Sung by Mrs. Isabel Spradley, Van Buren, Ark., June 17, 1929. Mrs. Spradley learned the song from her neighbors in the hills north of Van Buren.

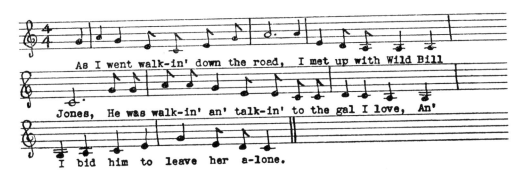

As I went walkin' down the road, I met up with Wild Bill
Jones, He was walkin' an' talkin' to the gal I love, An'
I bid him to leave her a-lone.

He says my age it is of twenty-one,
Too old for to be controlled,
I drawed my revolver from my side
An' I shattered that pore boy's soul.

He reeled, he rocked, he staggered,
He gave one dyin' groan,
He threwed his arms round my woman's neck
Sayin' baby, you're left all alone.

One dollar in my pocket,
My six-shooter in my hand,
With friends an' relations all around me
We'll make old Wild Bill stand.

One dollar in my pocket,
A-layin' in this here jail,
I sure am sad an' lonesome,
Nobody to go my bail.

I wrote my mother a letter
To tell her I was in jail,
She wrote me back a answer
Sayin' son, I'll go your bail.

I got a letter from Luly,
An' this is the way it read:
Daddy, if you ever git in trouble,
Don't never hang down your head.

Come on all you wild cowboys,
Let's all get on a spree,
Today was the last of Wild Bill Jones
An' tomorrow 'll be the last of me.

152

THE MEEKS MURDER

This song is concerned with a real crime which occurred May 11, 1894, in Linn County, some four miles southeast of Browning, Mo. The following account is condensed from the *Encyclopedia of the History of Missouri* edited by Howard L. Conard, (1901, IV, p. 320), supplemented by a letter from Mr. Floyd C. Shoemaker, Secretary of the State Historical Society of Missouri, Columbia, Mo.

The Taylor brothers, William P. and George E., were prosperous and influential citizens, but were nevertheless suspected of cattle-stealing. One Gus Meeks, who lived on a farm owned by the Taylors, knew something of his landlords' affairs, and he and his family were murdered to dispose of their testimony. The killing was done with an ax, and the bodies hidden in a straw-stack. Little Nellie (or Sadie, according to the Jefferson City *Tribune*, June 27, 1894, p. 4) was left for dead, but revived and made her way to a neighbor's cabin where she told of the crime. Both Taylors were convicted of murder, and William Taylor was hanged, but George broke jail and was never recaptured. The Columbia *Missourian* (July 12, 1926, p. 1) reported that a hermit who died near Tulsa, Okla., July 8, 1926, was identified as George Taylor. Nellie Meeks recovered and lived for many years, but it is said that she had a conspicuous "dint" in her forehead.

This piece was once well known in the Ozark country. I heard it sung by a blind pencil-peddler in Joplin, Mo., about 1913. Belden (*Ballads and Songs*, 1940, pp. 404-412) gives a full account of the murder, and several texts and tunes. For a fairly detailed study of this affair see "A Study in Contemporary Balladry" in the *Midwest Quarterly* (Jan. 1914, V, 2, pp. 162-172).

Many people have told me that the song was sung by Nellie Meeks herself, as she traveled about with a carnival company in the late 90's; Belden (*Ballads and Songs*, 1940, p. 408) repeats this story. Mrs. Nora Page Irwin, Galena, Mo., who says that she and Nellie Meeks were cousins, denies that Nellie ever had anything to do with carnivals (Springfield, Mo., *News*, April, 5, 1941). "Nellie lived with her grandmother Page until she was sixteen," says Mrs.

Irwin, "and then she married Albert Spray. When she was eighteen she gave birth to a baby and died."

A man named Childers, near Farmington, Ark., tells me that Gus Meeks's brother George, a blind singer with a hand-organ, used to follow the county fairs and picnics in southern Missouri and northern Arkansas. This Meeks sold a little paper-back songbook for ten cents; one of the songs in the book was "The Meeks Murder." George Meeks always claimed to have written this song himself, and always sang it with tears running down his cheeks . . . There is some mention of George Meeks, and a photograph of him, in an account of the crime called "Bodies Under the Straw" written from Sheriff James A. Niblo's diary (*Master Detective Magazine*, July 1937, pp. 16-21, 51-54).

A

Sung by Mr. Clyde Weems, Cardin, Okla., July 10, 1927. Mr. Weems learned the song at Mount Vernon, Mo., in 1915.

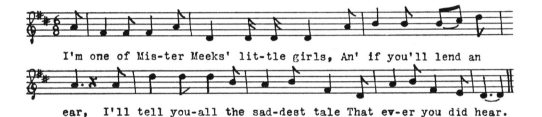

I'm one of Mis-ter Meeks' lit-tle girls, An' if you'll lend an ear, I'll tell you-all the sad-dest tale That ev-er you did hear.

We lived upon the Taylor's farm
Not many miles from town,
One night while we was all asleep
The Taylor boys come down.

They wanted to take my papa away,
My mamma answered no,
We could not be left here alone,
But the family all could go.

We got into the wagon then,
An' rode to Jenkins Hill,
An' all at once we knew not why
But the team was standin' still.

They murdered my mamma an' papa too,
An' knocked baby in the head,
They murdered my brothers an' sisters four
An' left me there as dead.

An' now my little song you've heard,
An' the rest you all know well,
I'm left an' orphaned here alone
In this wide world to dwell.

I want you all to pray for me,
That I may meet them there
In heaven above where all is love,
There'll be no murderin' there.

B

Contributed by Mr. George Parham, who set down the words as sung by Mrs. Nellie May Essick, Springfield, Mo., Apr. 20, 1934. Mr. Parham says that the local title is "Little Nellie Meeks."

About one mile from Brownington
At the foot of Jenkins' hill,
Took place this awful murder
By the Taylors George and Bill

They wrote Gus Meeks a letter,
Told him to be ready at ten,
They tried to leave the country
To save disgrace from them.

But then the hand of providence
Come to little Nellie's aid,
An' ere the break of mornin'
The safe escape she made.

She came out of her straw made grave,
To the Carter's house she came,
An' told this mournful story
That leads to a country shame.

She stood before the door
With that awful gash in her head,
She sobbed an' wept most bitterly
These were the words she said:

Some very cruel men last night
Come an' took us from our bed,
They shot my mamma an' papa
An' thought us young ones was dead.

They put us in a wagon
An' took us to our strawy grave,
How little did they think
That God's little Nellie was saved.

The mornin' after the murder
George was seen out in the field,
A–harrowin' up the wagon tracks
Their mischief to conceal.

But that was all in vain,
For nothin' could they say,
By Johnine South* was captured,
An' took to Carlton jail.

I once did have a mother,
A mother so good an' true,
Those wicked men they shot her,
They shot my papa too.

So now I am a orphan,
Nobody to care for me,
May God's blessing be with her,
Wherever she may be.

C

The following stanzas are recalled by Mr. Henry J. Childers, Arlington, Mo., Mar. 27, 1941. "I was borned at Cabool, Mo., in the year of 1892, and I knew little Nellie Meeks at a school near Mountain Grove, Mo., in the year of 1905. She had the print or scar of a hatchet in her forehead, and she was staying with the Carter family."

About one mile from Brownings
At the foot of the Jinkins Hill
Took place an awful murder
By the Taylors George and Bill.

They wrote Gus Meeks a letter,
Told him to be ready at ten,
To try and leave the country
To save disgrace for them.

---

*They were captured by Jerry C. South, at Buffalo, Ark., in June, 1894, and taken to the jail at Carrollton, Mo.

But little did he think
The Taylors George and Bill,
Last night would murder his family
At the foot of the Jinkins Hill.

But Providence was against them,
The righteous hand was there,
. . . . willed against them
Little Nellie's life did spare.

She came out of her strawy grave,
To Carter's house she came
To tell the mournful story
That adds to her country's shame.

She stood before the door
With an awful gash in her head,
She sobbed and wept most bitterly
While those worthy words she said.

Some very cruel men last night
Come took us from our bed,
They shot my papa and mamma
And they thought us children dead.

Next morning after the murder
George was seen out in the field,
A-harrowing out the wagon tracks
His mischief to conceal.

D

Sung by Mrs. Nora Page Irwin, near Reeds Spring, Mo., Aug. 1, 1942. She sang it to the
tune of "Home, Sweet Home," and said that it was written by Marion Anderson, Browning,
Mo., in the summer of 1894, a few weeks after the murder. She says that Mr. Anderson had
it printed on little slips of paper, which he sold for ten cents, and that people sang it in that
vicinity for many years afterward. The following song, says Mrs. Irwin, is called "The Mid-
night Murder of the Meeks Family."

'Twas in the lovely Springtime,
In the lovely month of May,
When Meeks, his wife, and children
Were induced to go away.

They were leaving, little dreaming
When they took their midnight flight,
They'd be murdered ere the morning,
In the darkness of the night.

About two miles from Browning
They crossed a little rill,
The team was slowly climbing
The fatal Jenkins Hill.

When springing from the roadway
Assassins fierce and wild,
They killed this helpless family
Except one little child.

A blinding flash of fire,
A groan of death and pain,
A bleeding human being
Was numbered with the slain.

The mother pled for mercy,
She sank upon her knees,
But also was foully murdered
Beneath the rustling trees.

They buried them 'neath the strawstack
Out on George Taylor's farm,
But Nellie did recover
And then she gave the alarm.

The neighbors quick responded
But found this family dead,
The Taylors had absconded
And from this country fled.

At last they were arrested
And for this murder tried.
The evidence was taken.
Their fate to thus decide.

The jury was selected
And the verdict written we (?)
The jury found them guilty
Of murder in the first degree.

153

PRETTY POLLY

"Pretty Polly" is a condensation of "The Gaspard Tragedy," a long British ballad that dates at least to the middle of the eighteenth century (Ebsworth, *Roxburghe Ballads*, 1899, VIII, pp. 143, 173). See Kittredge (*JAFL 20*, 1907, p. 261) for references. American texts have been reported by Campbell and Sharp (*English Folk Songs from the Southern Appalachians*, 1917, No. 39), Mackenzie (*Quest of the Ballad*, 1919, p. 55), Cox (*Folk-Songs of the South*, 1925, p. 308), Kincaid (*My Favorite Mountain Ballads*, 1928, p. 35), Niles (*More Songs of the Hill-Folk*, 1936, pp. 2-3), and Scarborough (*A Song Catcher in Southern Mountains*, 1937, pp. 128-134). Cox (*Traditional Ballads*, 1939, p. 62) reports a West Virginia text, with a reference to one Polly Aldridge, murdered by William Chapman near Warfield, Ky., about 1820. "The Gosport Tragedy" is given by Combs (*Folk-Songs from the Kentucky Highlands*, 1939, pp. 35-37), and "Pretty Polly" by Brewster (*Ballads and Songs of Indiana*, 1940, pp. 298-299). Compare also the phonograph records by Dock Boggs (*Brunswick* 132) and B. F. Shelton (*Victor* 35838).

A

Contributed by Miss Hannah Garren, Stella, Mo., Apr. 13, 1927.

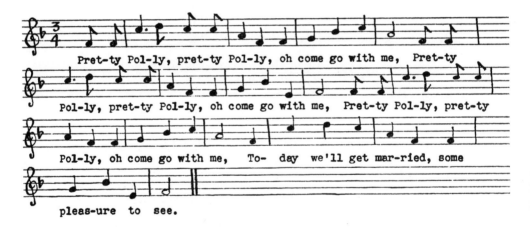

Pret-ty Pol-ly, pret-ty Pol-ly, oh come go with me, Pret-ty
Pol-ly, pret-ty Pol-ly, oh come go with me, Pret-ty Pol-ly, pret-ty
Pol-ly, oh come go with me, To- day we'll get mar-ried, some
pleas-ure to see.

They went on a piece further an' there they did stop,
They went on a piece further an' there they did stop,
They went on a piece further an' there she did sigh,
A grave bein' dug an' the pick lyin' by.

Dear Willie, dear Willie, I fear from your care,
Dear Willie, dear Willie, I fear from your care,
Dear Willie, dear Willie, I fear from your care,
I'm afraid you are goin' to lead me astray.

Pretty Polly, pretty Polly, you're guessin' just right,
Pretty Polly, pretty Polly, you're guessin' just right,
Pretty Polly, pretty Polly, you're guessin' just right,
For the whole of last night I was diggin' your grave.

His knife bein' drawn an' all in his right hand,
His knife bein' drawn an' all in his right hand,
His knife bein' drawn an' all in his right hand,
He stobbed her to the heart an' the blood it did flow.

The blood it did flow an' the blood it did flow,
The blood it did flow an' the blood it did flow,
The blood it did flow an' the blood it did flow,
He throwed her in the grave an' back home he did go.

B

Miss Elizabeth Waddell, Ash Grove, Mo., June 9, 1929, supplies two stanzas of another version:

He led her through hedges and ditches so deep,
At last this poor maiden began for to weep,
Saying I'm fearful, sweet Willie, you've led me astray,
On purpose my innocent life to betray.

Oh yes, pretty Polly, you've guessed it just right,
I was digging your grave the biggest part of last night.
The grave it is dug and the spade lying by,
Oh yes, pretty Polly, you're sure going to die.

C

From a manuscript copy supplied by Mrs. Charles Huntoon, St. Louis, Mo., May 2, 1934. Mrs. Huntoon called the song "The Ship's Carpenter," and had learned it from relatives living near Cotter, Ark.

In London a fair maid did dwell,
Her wealth and her beauty no one could compare,
A young man courted her for his lawful wedded wife,
He was by trade but a ship's carpenter.

With love and embraces they parted that night,
She arose next morning to meet him by light,
Oh come and go with me, before we are married,
Oh come and go with me, a friend for to see.

Over ridges and ditches and hollows so deep,
At last this fair maiden began for to weep,
I am fearful, dear Willie, you've led me astray,
And now for some purpose my life will betray.

Oh yes, pretty Polly, you are talking just right,
I was digging your grave all in order last night,
Poor innocent maiden . . . .
And the tears from her eyes in fair fountains did flow.

She looked to his side, and her grave was there to see,
Is this the bright home you have prepared for me?
Oh pity my soul, my sweet life is betrayed,
And I young and blooming am hurried to my grave!

This here is no time for to talk or to stand,
He immediately drew a long knife in his hand,
He pierced through her heart and the blood it did flow,
And into the grave her fair body he did throw.

He covered her up and returned back home,
He left nothing there but the small birds to mourn,
He mounted a steamer that very same day,
Pretty Polly a-blooming lay mouldering away.

154

THE BALD KNOBBER SONG

The Bald Knobbers were vigilantes organized in 1884, in Taney County, Mo., to defend
law and order in an outlaw-ridden settlement. They were so named because they held meetings on a certain "bald knob" between Branson and Kirbyville. Their leader was a Springfield saloon-keeper named Nat N. Kinney. The organization soon degenerated into a mob of
irresponsible night-riders; many were imprisoned, several were hanged for murder. For a
history of the movement see *Bald Knobbers* by Lucile Morris (Caxton Printers, 1939, 253 pp.).
The Bald Knobber dictatorship ended in 1889, but there are still many people in Taney
County who feel very strongly about the matter, and retain bitter memories of the persons
and incidents mentioned in the "Bald Knobber Song." I should not care to sing this song
publicly, even today, in either Forsyth or Kirbyville.

Mrs. Mary Elizabeth Mahnkey, Mincy, Mo., is a daughter of Col. A. S. Prather, a charter
member of the Bald Knobbers. She remembers all about the Bald Knobber trouble, and she
writes me (Jan. 15, 1938) that this song "was composed by young Andy Coggburn, an Anti-
Baldknobber who was killed by Capt. Kinney." It was sung, she adds, to the tune of "My
Name is Charles Guiteau."

Mr. William L. Vandeventer, an attorney in Springfield, Mo., who has studied the history
of the Bald Knobbers for many years, recently examined the text and tune of the song as
printed below. He writes me (Mar. 7, 1938) that "the Bald Knobber song is unquestionably

authentic, and was written by . . . a young desperado named Andrew Coggburn, who had because of his lawlessness been flogged by the Bald Knobbers . . . I have always understood, and the old-timers say, that Coggburn composed the song while he was dodging the law and the Bald Knobbers after the flogging. I heard the song many times when I was a child at Garrison, Mo." Mr. Vandeventer continues with a vivid account of the killing of young Coggburn by Nat N. Kinney, which occurred at the Oak Grove schoolhouse, near Bald Knob, Feb. 28, 1886.

The first stanza of the text below is identical with the sixth verse of "The Rebel Soldier" (Cox, *Folk-Songs of the South*, 1925, p. 280), except that in the latter piece it is "hard times and the Yankees" which have driven the singer away, and "forced him for to roam." In the "Blind Fiddler" song reported by Belden (*Ballads and Songs*, 1940, p. 446) the same stanza occurs, but here it is "hard times and misfortune" instead of "hard times and Bald Knobbers."

A

Contributed by Mr. B. F. Carney, Crane, Mo., June 20, 1932. Mr. Carney wishes it made clear that he does not approve of the song, which he describes as "doggerel."

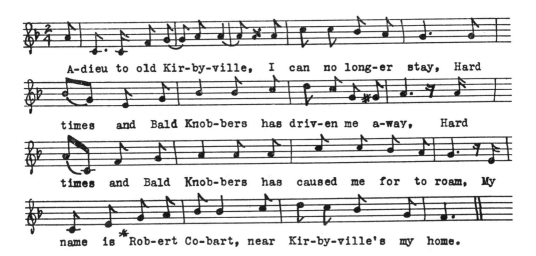

My friends and relations, it's much against my will
To leave my dear old mother and go from Kirbyville,
But for the sake of dear ones, who wants me for to go
I'll arm myself with weapons, and off to Mexico.

Bald Knobbers are no gentlemen, they're nothing more than hogs,
They tried to hunt me down, boys, and treat me like a dog,
With their guns and their horses they tried to hunt me down,
And treat me like the Taylor boys, who now lies in the ground.

---

*Some old-timers contend that the song was written by Robert Coggburn, who was either an uncle or a cousin of the Andrew Coggburn killed by Captain Kinney.

There's one big Bald Knobber who is a noted rogue,
He stole from Joseph Bookout some sixteen head of hogs,
Walked boldly in the courthouse and swore they was his own,
He stole them by the drove, boys, and horsed them over home.

There is another Bald Knobber who rides a pony blue,
He robbed old Nell Macully, and Mr. Thompson too,
He took from them their money, boys, and from them rode away,
And now the highway robbers is the big men of the day.

There is one big black rascal whose name I will expose,
His name is Nat MacKinny and he wears his Federal clothes,
He tries to boss the people and make them do his will,
There's some that does not fear him, but others mind him still.

To raise a Bald Knobber excitement I made a splendid hand,
I don't fear judge nor jury, I don't fear any man.
And if they want to try me, they've nothing else to do,
I'll take my old Colt's patent, and I'll make an opening through.

. . . .
. . . .
But there's a day a-coming, boys, when they will hunt their dens,
And if I'm not mistaken there is some will find their ends.

B

Mr. W. T. Moore, Hollister, Mo., Nov. 10, 1939, recalls a few fragments of this piece, which he says was "made up" by Andrew Coggburn. "I was in Kirbyville on the 9th of May, 1886," says he, "when Sam Snapp come a-ridin' into town, a-hummin' that song. He wasn't singin' the words, he was just a-hummin' the tune. Wash Middleton was standin' there, an' he told Sam not to sing no such a song as that. Sam he went right ahead with his hummin', an' pretty soon Wash shot Sam an' killed him." Sam Snapp was a friend of Andrew Coggburn, and was present when Coggburn was shot down by Captain Kinney.

Andrew Coggburn is my name,
Near Kirbyville my home,
An' it was the Bald Knobbers
That caused me to roam.

. . . . .

An' there is Sam King
Who rides a pony blue,
I'll take my forty-five
An' shoot a pathway through.

"I knowed Sam King, well," Mr. Moore told me. "He got drunk one time, an' fell off his blue horse, an' froze to death."

C

Here is a fragment of a related Anti-Baldknobber song as recalled by Mr. John Haworth, Forsyth, Mo., Nov. 20, 1939. Captain Nat N. Kinney was the "old blue gobbler," while the "General" is identified with Adjutant General J. C. Jamison, who came to Forsyth on Apr. 8, 1886.

> The old blue gobbler went a-struttin' around,
> But he didn't strut so big when the General come to town!

Mr. Haworth says that this song was "made up" by Aunt Matt Moore, who lived just south of Forsyth. It was this piece, Mr. Haworth adds, and not the "Andrew Coggburn" song, which Sam Snapp was singing when he was killed by Wash Middleton.

Mrs. Mary Elizabeth Mahnkey, Mincy, Mo. (Springfield *News*, July 12, 1940) says that "Aunt Matt Moore composed a very stirring song, in the Bald Knobber days." Aunt Matt was a sister to Uncle Jord Haworth, pioneer preacher.

155

BAD LEE BROWN

Scarborough (*On the Trail of Negro Folk-Songs*, 1925, pp. 87-89, 243) reports a very similar piece, and Sandburg (*American Songbag*, 1927, pp. 310-311) found a related item in Fort Smith, Ark. See also the "Bad Man Ballad" which Lomax (*American Ballads and Folk Songs*, 1934, pp. 89-91) "learned from a tongue-tied Negro convict at Parchman, Mississippi."

A

Sung by Miss Billie Freese, Joplin, Mo., Apr. 17, 1922. Miss Freese learned it from her boy-friend, a native of West Plains, Mo.

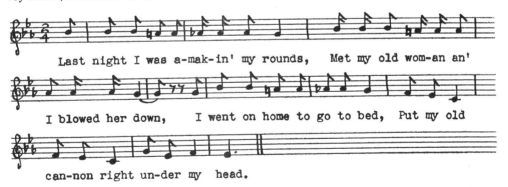

Last night I was a-mak-in' my rounds, Met my old wom-an an'
I blowed her down, I went on home to go to bed, Put my old
can-non right un-der my head.

> Jury says murder in the first degree,
> I says oh Lord, have mercy on me!
> Old Judge White picks up his pen,
> Says you'll never kill no woman ag'in.

B

Contributed by Mr. Robert L. Kennedy, Springfield, Mo., May 3, 1934. Mr. Kennedy
says that the song was popular in Springfield fifty years ago.

> Don't know whether to hang you or not,
> This killin' women jest nachelly's got to stop!

. . . . .

> Here I is bowed down with shame,
> Got a number instead of a name,
> Forty-nine years in prison for life,
> All I ever done was to kill my wife.

156

EWING BROOKS

This is one of the numerous adaptations of the "Charles Guiteau" song, which in turn
derived from a still older piece known as "My Name It is John T. Williams," according to
Pound (*American Ballads and Songs*, 1922, pp. 146, 251). Compare "The Death of Young
Bendall" (*ibid.*, p. 148) and "The Murder of F. C. Benwell" (Spaeth, *Weep Some More, My
Lady*, 1927, p. 135), said to have been written by the murderer himself, a genial chap named
Birchell. See also the "Johnny Runkins" ballad reported by Gordon (*Folk-Songs of America*,
1938, pp. 41-42). The "Ewing Brooks" mentioned in the song was really Hugh M. Brooks,
an Englishman who assumed the name of Walter Lennox Maxwell, and murdered Charles
Arthur Preller at the Southern Hotel, St. Louis, in 1885. Brooks fled to New Zealand, but was
brought back to Missouri and hanged Aug. 10, 1888. The "Marhouse" mentioned in the fifth
stanza is evidently A. P. Morehouse, governor of Missouri from 1887 to 1889. Belden (*Ballads
and Songs*, 1940, pp. 413-415) prints two texts under the title "Maxwell's Doom."

Contributed by Miss Myrtle Devore, Winslow, Ark., Jan. 2, 1930. Miss Devore says
that the murderer's name is usually spelled "Youen Brooks," but that it should be written
"Ewing Brooks."

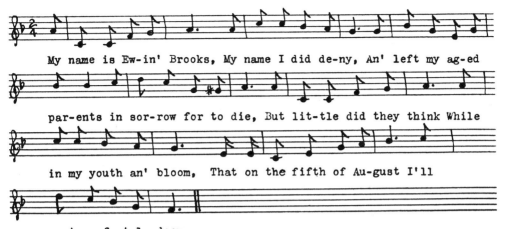

My name is Ew-in' Brooks, My name I did de-ny, An' left my ag-ed

par-ents in sor-row for to die, But lit-tle did they think While

in my youth an' bloom, That on the fifth of Au-gust I'll

meet my fa-tal doom.

I come to old America,
Old England I forsook,
I took the name of Maxwell,
Denied of Ewin' Brooks.
I bein' a very reckless man,
A spendthrift too was I,
I murdered Arthur Fralow
My wants to satisfy.

I went down to the old depot
An' boarded a Frisco train,
I knew that after such a crime
I could not there remain.
The speedin' of the train was fast,
An' I thought that I was free,
I did not know a telegram
Was on ahead of me.

I stepped aboard the old steamship,
Sayin' now I'm free I know,
The officers arrested me
Down on old Yeland Shore,
They took me back to old Saint Louis
An' placed me in a cell
For the crime that I committed
In the Southern Old Hotel.

I bid my friends farewell,
My mother an' sister so young,
Who pled with Governor Marhouse
That I might not be hung.
He would not even grant them time
To send my father word,
To cross the brinery water
To say farewell, my son.

I place my treasures all in heaven,
My earthly hopes are fled,
I know my friends will grieve for me
Long after I am dead.
An' when I'm dead an' laid away
Within my grave to rest,
I know we'll meet in heaven there
To be forever blest.

157

HENRY GREEN

Compare the "Mary Wyatt and Henry Green" song reported by Flanders and Brown (*Vermont Folk-Songs and Ballads*, 1931, p. 65). "Young Henry Green" is recorded by Gardner (*Ballads and Songs of Southern Michigan*, 1939, pp. 346-348). Belden (*Ballads and Songs*, 1940, p. 321) prints three stanzas of this piece, which he associates with "McAfee's Confession." Belden's text was obtained in 1922 indirectly from "Mrs. Charles Dillard of Crane, Stone County"—the same woman who sang the song for me in 1938. For detailed particulars and texts see "Folk-Songs of Mary Wyatt and Henry Green" by Louis C. Jones and comments by Phillips Barry (The Folk-Song Society of the Northeast, *Bulletin* 12, 1937, pp. 14-18).

A

Sung by Mrs. Lucy Short Dillard, Crane, Mo., Aug. 20, 1938. Mrs. Dillard learned it
from Mr. Frank Payne, Galena, Mo., about 1900.

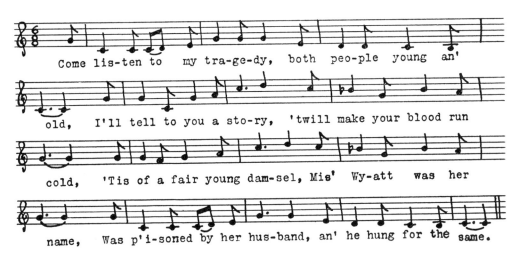

They hadn't been married scarce three weeks when she was taken ill,
Great doctors they were sent for to try their power an' skill,
Great doctors they were sent for to try her life to save,
But 'twas pronounced by many that she must go to her grave.

Her brother hearing of these strange news straightway to her did go,
Says sister dear, you're dyin', the doctors tell me so,
Says sister dear, you're dyin', your life is at a end,
An' have you not been p'isoned by him you called your friend?

I now lie on my death bed, an' I know that I must die,
I go to meet a just God, the truth I'll never deny,
I know my Henry's deceived me, oh brother, for him send,
I love him just as dearly as when he was my friend.

B

Here is a text from Mrs. May Kennedy McCord, Springfield, Mo., June 23, 1939. Mrs. McCord learned the song from Mrs. Lena Todd, Lockwood, Mo.

Come listen to my tragedy
Both people young and old,
I'll tell to you a story,
'Twill make your blood run cold.
'Tis of a fair young damsel,
Mis' Wyatt was her name,
She was poisoned by her husband
And he died for the same.

This lady she was beautiful
And of a high degree,
Young Henry Green was wealthy
As you can plainly see.
Says he my darling Mary,
If you will be my wife,
I'll guard you and protect you
Throughout this weary life.

Young Mary, believing all was well
Straightway became his wife,
Little did she think, poor girl,
That he would take her life.
Little did she think, poor girl,
Nor little did suspect
That he would take the life from her
He had sworn to protect.

They hadn't been married scarce three weeks
Till she was taken ill,
Great doctors they were sent for
To try their power and skill.
Great doctors they were sent for
To try her life to save,
It was pronounced by many
She must go to her grave.

Her father, a-hearing these strange things,
Straightway to her did go,
Saying daughter dear, you're dying,
The doctors tell me so.
Saying daughter dear, you're dying,
Your life they cannot save,
It is pronounced by many
You must go to your grave.

Young Henry was apprehended
And put into the jail,
There to await his trial
For none would go his bail.
There to await his trial
For the murder of his wife,
And on the cruel scaffold
They took young Henry's life.

C

Manuscript copy contributed by Dr. George Hastings, University of Arkansas, Jan. 6, 1942. He got it from Miss Gwendolyn Guinn, of Fayetteville, Ark., and she had it from Felix McMurray, Huntsville, Ark.

Come listen to my tragedy, you people young and old,
I'll tell you of a story will make your blood run cold,
'Tis of a fair young lady, Miss Wyat was her name,
Was poisoned by her husband and he hangs for the same.

Miss Wyat was a lady, not of high degree,
While Henry Green was wealthy as you can plainly see,
Says he Mary, dearest Mary, if you will be my wife,
I'll guard you as a parent all through your gloomy life.

To be your wife, dear Henry, I feel I might consent,
But before we would be married long, I feel you would repent,
Before we would be married long you would think me a disgrace,
For you are rich and I am poor, which oft-times is the case.

I'll swear by all that's innocent that I'll prove true to you,
And if you do reject me most sure it will end my life,
For I no longer wish to live unless you'll be my wife,
Now believing all that Henry said she soon became his wife.

Little did she think, poor girl, or little did she expect,
He had taken away her sacred life just for one true respect,
Now they had not been married long before she was taken ill,
Great doctors they were sent for to prove their perfect skill.

Great doctors they were sent for but none of them could save,
It had been pronounced by all of them she was bound to meet her grave,
Her brother heard the sad tidings, straightway to his sister did go,
Saying sister, dear, you're dying, the doctors tell me so.

Saying sister dear, you're dying, your life is at an end,
Pray haven't you been deceived by the one you called your friend?

Now lying on my death bed and knowing I must die,
And going to meet a just God, the truth I'll never deny.
I know my Henry has poisoned me, oh brother, for him send,
For I love him just as dearly as when he was my friend.

Her husband heard the tidings, straightway to his wife went he,
Saying Mary dear, dear Mary, was you ever deceived by me?
Three times she cried oh Henry, and then he left the room,
. . . .

Oh how my husband deceived me, oh how my heart is wrung,
And when I am gone, dear brother, don't have my Henry hung,
For I freely will forgive him, she turned upon her side,
In Heaven meet me, Henry, she sweetly smiled and died.

158

FRANKIE SILVER

Charles Silver was murdered Dec. 22, 1831, at Deyton Bend of Toe River, in the Blue Ridge Mountains of western North Carolina. His wife Frankie was convicted of the crime and hanged at Morganton, N.C., July 12, 1833. Muriel Earley Sheppard (*Cabins in the Laurel*, 1935, pp. 25-29) tells the whole story and prints two songs about the murder, one of them credited to Frankie herself. Robert Menzies and Edmond Smith (*True Detective Mysteries*, 24, July 1935, pp. 14-19, 72-73) repeat the tale at great length, including six stanzas of the song which Frankie is said to have sung on the gallows. "Many persons believe," according to Menzies and Smith, "that Frankie's doleful ballad became the origin of the now universally sung 'Frankie and Johnnie,' the song having gone through many changes before coming to its present form." Barry (*Bulletin of the Folk-Song Society of the Northeast* 10, 1935, p. 24) thinks that "Frankie and Johnnie" is based upon the killing of Charles Silver. Henry (*JAFL* 45, 1932, pp. 63-65) reports a long text of "Frankie Silvers" from the Appalachians, and apparently regards it as a comparatively recent song, remarking that Frankie was supposedly hanged in 1908. Barry (*JAFL* 45, 1932, p. 62) points out that the first line of Henry's text is from a song still current in Vermont about a British soldier in the Revolution, of which a broadside text was printed about 1800. I heard a phonograph record of a similar "Frankie Silver" song in Kansas City, Mo., about 1932, but have been unable to find it in the catalogues of the phonograph companies. The piece appears in the Brown (North Carolina Folk-Lore Society) collection.

Sung by Mrs. Marie Wilbur, Pineville, Mo., Apr. 11, 1934. Mrs. Wilbur heard the song near Pineville about 1910.

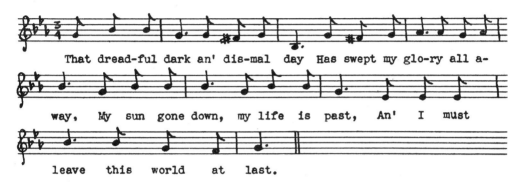

That dread-ful dark an' dis-mal day Has swept my glo-ry all a-
way, My sun gone down, my life is past, An' I must
leave this world at last.

> Jedge Daniels* has my sentence passed,
> These prison walls I'll leave at last,
> Nothin' to cheer my droopin' head
> Until I'm numbered with the dead.
>
> Oh dreadful thought for any wife,
> To try to take my husband's life,
> By weeks an' months was all my time
> For me to do this awful crime.
>
> Come you young folks an' on me gaze,
> Take warnin' how you spend your days,
> My sun gone down, my life is past,
> I leave this wicked world at last.

159

FRANKIE AND JOHNNY

The origin and history of this piece, formerly known as "Frankie and Albert," is still subject to debate. Spaeth (*Life* 102, June 1935, pp. 21-22) says that Shapiro & Bernstein copyrighted "Frankie and Johnny" in 1912, crediting the words to the Leighton Brothers (a vaudeville team) and the music to Ren Shields. Frank Crumit once claimed the "complete authorship" of the song, according to Spaeth, and Irving Berlin used the traditional tune for the verse of his "She's My Baby" song.

*The judge's name was John R. Donnell.

John Huston, author of the play *Frankie and Johnny* (New York, 1930) thinks that the song refers to the killing of Allen Britt by Frankie Baker, which occurred at St. Louis in 1899. Al Britt was an 18-year-old black boy who lived with mulatto Frankie at 212 Targee Street—where the Municipal Auditorium now stands. The shooting took place Oct. 15, 1899, and Britt died four days later. Frankie testified that he had threatened her with a knife, and that she fired one shot in self-defense. Frankie Baker is still living, some sixty-odd years old, the proprietor of a shoe-shine place in Portland, Ore. In 1939 she brought a $200,000 damage suit against Republic Pictures for defamation of character and invasion of her privacy. This company had produced a picture called *Frankie and Johnny*, based on the old song, starring Helen Morgan. Frankie Baker alleges that the ballad refers to her life in St. Louis, and that there never was any "Frankie and Johnny" song until after she killed Britt in 1899. The case was dismissed in 1942, and Frankie got nothing.

Thomas Beer (*The Mauve Decade*, 1926, p. 120) says that the song "was known on the Mississippi in the 50's, and chanted by Federal troops besieging Vicksburg in 1863; a copy of twelve stanzas was made by a young officer and is preserved . . . Mr. Emerson Hough dated this song from a murder at Natchez in the 40's." A number of eminent scholars have written to Beer about this matter, but he failed to answer their questions, or to divulge the whereabouts of the so-called "Beer manuscript." Professor Belden (*Ballads and Songs*, 1940, p. 330) says mildly that he has "not been able to get any documentation of Beer's claims."

Sandburg (*American Songbag*, 1927, p. 75) remarks that the song "was common along the Mississippi River and among railroad men as early as 1888." John J. Niles (*Mentor*, Mar. 1930, p. 15) stated flatly that the ballad was nearly a hundred years old, and was the record of a real crime. Orrick Johns (*Time of Our Lives*, 1937, p. 98) repeats a tradition that "Frankie and Johnny" originated with Mammy Lou, a blues singer at Babe Connors' high-brown bawdy-house in St. Louis, probably in the early 90's. Mammy Lou sang it for Paderewski and "was one of the first to sing the Negro spirituals and field songs to white men."

Professor Tyrrel Williams (*Missouri Historical Review* 34 Jan. 1940, pp. 292-293) has collected some evidence to show that "Frankie and Johnny" is pretty old—at least antedates the Civil War. He refers it to a crime committed in St. Louis by a Negro "crib man."

George Milburn, Pineville, Mo., is a "Frankie and Johnny" enthusiast, and showed me a large collection of texts, and the material he has assembled for a book on the subject. Milburn says that he doesn't know how old the song is—some verses are much older than others. "I do not deny," he writes me (Jan. 22, 1941) "that the Frankie song may have been applied to Frankie Baker's case, but there is ample evidence that the ballad was being sung in widely separated sections of the country long before 1899 . . . I have collected at least a hundred versions of the song that do not use the names Frankie and Albert . . . The Leighton Brothers vaudeville team changed 'Albert' to 'Johnny' in 1911—that seems to be well established . . . Courtney Riley Cooper remembered a version from his boyhood in Denver. Roark Bradford is positive that the song originated in Little Rock, Ark., because the version he knew had a reference to 'the corner of Third and Bird,' and there is such a corner in Little Rock! . . . Neither can the song be identified as purely a Negro composition, although there are many Negro 'pop ups' in it . . . A real folksong is the result of long accretion, and is not at all like a topical song. The Frankie ballad is a genuine folksong."

Barry (*Bulletin of the Folk-Song Society of the Northeast* 10, 1935, p. 24) thinks that the song is based upon the doings of Frankie Silver, a white woman who killed her husband at Toe River, N. C., in 1831. For information about this, see the "Frankie Silver" ballad elsewhere in this book.

Other texts of "Frankie and Johnny," including many from oral tradition, are reported by Cox (*Folk-Songs of the South*, 1925, pp. 216-220), Scarborough (*On the Trail of Negro Folk-*

Songs, 1925, pp. 79-80), Hudson (*Folksongs of Mississippi*, 1936, pp. 189-191), Richardson (*American Mountain Songs*, 1927, pp. 28-29), Spaeth (*Read 'Em and Weep*, 1927, pp. 34-39), White (*American Negro Folk-Songs*, 1928, p. 214), Louis Utermeyer (*American Poetry from the Beginning to Whitman*, 1931, pp. 799-801), Lomax (*American Ballads and Folk Songs*, 1934, pp. 106-110), Henry (*Folk-Songs from the Southern Highlands*, 1938, pp. 341-348), Chappell (*Folk-Songs of Roanoke and the Albemarle*, 1939, pp. 189-191), Eddy (*Ballads and Songs from Ohio*, 1939, pp. 245-247), and Belden (*Ballads and Songs*, 1940, pp. 330-333). The piece appears in the Brown (North Carolina Folk-Lore Society) collection.

See "The 'Frankie and Johnny' Episode of 1899" in the *Missouri Historical Review* 36, Oct. 1941, pp. 75-77.

A

Contributed by Mrs. John F. Smith, Elkins, Ark., Feb. 21, 1930. Mrs. Smith says that this version was known to her great-grandmother. I published this text in *Ozark Life*, July, 1930, p. 35.

Frankie was a good girl, Ev-'ry bo-dy knows, She paid a half a hund-red, For Al-bert a suit of clothes, He is my man, but he won't come home.

Way down in some dark alley
I heard a bulldog bark,
I believe to my soul my honey
Is lost out in the dark,
He is my man, but he won't come home.

Frankie went uptown this morning,
She did not go for fun,
Under her apron she carried
Albert's forty-one,
He is my man, but he won't come home.

Frankie went to the bartender,
Called for a bottle of beer,
Ask the bartender my loving Albert,
Has he been here?
He is my man, but he won't come home.

Bartender said to Frankie
I can't tell you a lie,
He left here about an hour ago
With a girl called Alice Bly,
He is your man, but he's doing you wrong.

Frankie went up Fourth Street,
Come back down on Main,
Looking up on the second floor
Saw Albert in another girl's arms
Saying he's my man, but he's doing me wrong.

Frankie says to Albert
Baby, don't you run!
If you don't come to the one you love
I'll shoot you with your own gun,
You are my man, but you're doing me wrong.

Frankie she shot Albert,
He fell upon the floor,
Says turn me over easy,
And turn me over slow,
I'm your man, but you shot me down.

Early the next morning
Just about half past four,
Eighteen inches of black crape
Was hanging on Frankie's door,
Saying he was my man, but he wouldn't come home.

Frankie went over to Mis' Moodie's,
Fell upon her knees,
Says forgive me, Mis' Moodie,
Forgive me, oh do please.
How can I, when he's my only son?

Frankie went down to the graveyard,
Police by her side,
When she saw the one she loved
She hollered and she cried,
He was my man, but he wouldn't come home.

Police said to Frankie
No use to holler and cry,
When you shot the one you loved
You meant for him to die,
He's your man, but he's dead and gone.

Rubber-tired buggy,
Silver-mounted hack,
Took Albert to the graveyard
But couldn't bring him back,
He was my man, but he wouldn't come **home**.

B

Sung by Mr. Homer F. Walker, Joplin, Mo., July 4, 1923.

Frankie went into the barroom,
She ordered up her beer,
Tell me, Mister Bartender,
Has my darlin' man been here?
He's my man, he wouldn't do me **wrong**.

Listen to me, little Frankie,
I'll tell you the truth,
He left here 'bout an hour ago
With a gal he call Miss Ruth,
He's your man, but he's doin' you wrong.

Frankie went down to the pawnshop,
She laid down a ten-dollar bill,
Give me a blue steel forty-four
That son-of-a-bitch to kill,
He was my man, but he done me wrong.

Frankie went to the ballroom,
Walked in the ballroom door,
There she seen her darlin' man
A-dancin' with a whore,
He was her man, but he done her wrong.

Then was a mighty rumble
There was a mighty roar,
And yonder laid pore Albert
Dead on the ballroom floor,
He was her man, but he done her **wrong**.

Walkin' down the Avenue
About the hour of four,
Fourteen inches of black crape
A-hangin' on Albert's door.
He was her man, but he done her wrong.

Rubber-tired hearses,
Easy-ridin' hacks,
Took Albert to the graveyard
And never brought him back,
He was her man, but she done him wrong.

The last time I seen Frankie
Was on a railroad train,
Goin' to the penitentiary
To wear the ball and chain,
He was her man, but he done her wrong.

C

Text from Mrs. Dottie Fall Parks, Winslow, Ark., Dec. 3, 1929.

Frankie was a good little girl,
That everybody knows,
She spent a hundred dollars
For Albert a suit of clothes,
Oh he's her man, and he wouldn't come home.

Frankie went down the back walk,
She did not go for fun,
For under her little white apron
She carried a smokeless gun,
To kill her man, cause he wouldn't come home.

Frankie went down to the first saloon,
She called for a glass of beer,
She asked the boy attending
Have you seen old Albert in here?
Oh he's my man, and he wouldn't come home.

Frankie went down to the next saloon,
Come take a drink on me,
I've got a pack of troubles,
Gonna get out on a spree,
All over my man, he did me wrong.

Frankie went down the back walk,
She didn't go for harm,
Looked up in a two-story building,
Saw Albert in Alice's arms,
Oh you're my man, and you'd better come home.

Albert, I called you once, I call you twice,
Aint gonna call you no more,
Next time I have to call you
It'll be with your forty-four,
Oh you're my man, and you'd better come home.

Bang, bang, bang went Albert's
Trusty old forty-four,
Next time I saw old Albert
He was layin' on the floor,
Oh he's her man, and he wouldn't come home.

Frankie went running home,
She fell acrost the bed,
Saying mamma, oh mamma,
I've killed old Albert dead,
Oh he's my man, and he done me wrong.

I'll silver seat my buggy,
I'll decorate my hack,
I'll take old Albert to the cemetery
But I'll never bring him back,
Oh he was my man, and he done me wrong.

The next time I saw old Frankie,
A terrible sight to see,
She was sitting in her silver-seated buggy
As drunk as a woman can be,
All over her man, that done her wrong.

D

Copied from a manuscript book belonging to Miss Miriam Lynch, Notch, Mo., July 20,
1932. The song was written down in 1924 by one of Miss Lynch's neighbors.

Frankie was a good girl
Most everbody nose,
She paid one hundred dollars
For Albert suit of close
He's her man but he done her rong.

Frankie went to the sloon keeper
She ordered one bottle of bear,
She ask the sloon keeper
Has my man been around here?
Oh he's my man but he done me rong.

I aint going to tell you no stories,
I aint going tell you no lies,
Your man past here about an hour ago
With gal name Alice Flies,
Well he's your man but he done you rong.

Frankie went a walking
She did not go for fun,
Under her blue apearn
She carried a forty one
To kill her man, he wouldn't come home.

Frankie went down allie
With a razor in her hand,
Saying stand around you rounders
I am looking for my man,
I'll kill a man, he wouldn't come home.

Frankie shot poor Albert
He fell on barbern floor,
Saying turn me over Frankie,
Oh turn me over slow,
I am your man, but I done you rong.

Frankie met Albert's mother
She fell upon her knees
I've murdered my loving Albert
I've murdered with a great release,
Well he's your man, but he done you rong.

Frankie, oh Frankie,
You know what you have done,
You murdered my loving Albert
For this crime you must be hung,
Oh he's your man, but he done you rong.

Oh rubber tire your buggie,
And nickle seated hack,
Take Albert to the grave yard
And bringing Frankie back,
He's the man that done her rong.

Frankie went to the enquest
With the shurf by her side,
When she seen the one she loved
She hollard and she cried
Oh he's my man, but he done me rong.

The judge wants to see you Frankie,
He wants to see you bad,
Wants you for to dentyfie
That forty-one gun you had
To kill your man, he done you rong.

They led Frankie to the gallice,
These words to them she said,
I've murdered my loving Albert
I want you to hang me dead,
He's my man, but he done me rong.

The shurf nocked the trigger,
They thought they herd her say,
I'll meat my loving Albert,
I'll meat him on the Judgment Day,
I'll meat the man, he done me rong.

E

From Miss Lucile Morris, Springfield, Mo., Oct. 29, 1934. Miss Morris had it from Miss Cassie Morrison, Zanoni, Mo.

Frankie and Johnnie were lovers,
Oh Lordy how they could love,
They swore to be true to each other
Just as true as the stars up above,
He was her man, but he done her wrong.

Frankie and Johnnie went walking,
Johnnie had on a brand new suit,
Frankie paid a hundred dollars
Just to make her man look cute,
He was her man, but he done her wrong.

Johnnie says I've got to leave you,
But I won't be very long,
Don't you wait for me honey,
Or worry while I'm gone,
He was her man, but he done her wrong.

Frankie went down to the station,
Stopped in to buy her some beer,
Says to the fat bartender
Has my lovin' Johnnie been here?
He was her man, but he done her wrong.

Now I aint going to tell you no story,
Aint going to tell you no lie,
I saw him pass about an hour ago
With a gal named Nellie Bly,
He was her man, but he done her wrong.

Frankie took a cab at the corner,
Says driver step on this can,
She was just a desperate woman
Getting two-timed by her man,
He was her man, but he done her wrong.

Frankie got off on South Clark street,
Looked in at a window so high,
Saw her Johnnie man a-lovin' up
That gay haired Nellie Bly,
He was her man, but he done her wrong.

Johnnie saw Frankie a-coming,
Out the back door he did scoot,
But Frankie took aim with her pistol
And the gun went root-a-toot-toot,
He was her man, but he done her wrong.

Oh roll me over so easy,
Roll me over so slow,
Roll me over easy, boys,
Cause my wounds they hurt me so,
I was her man, but I done her wrong.

Bring out the long black coffin,
Bring out the funeral clothes,
Johnnie's gone and cashed his checks,
To the graveyard Johnnie goes,
He was her man, but he done her wrong.

Drive out the rubber-tired carriage,
Drive out the rubber-tired hack,
There's twelve men going to the graveyard
And eleven men coming back,
He was her man, but he done her wrong.

The sheriff arrested poor Frankie,
Took her to jail the same day,
He locked her up in the dungeon cell
And threw the key away,
She shot her man, but he done her wrong.

This story has no moral,
This story has no end,
It only goes to show you
That there aint no good in men,
He was her man, but he done her wrong.

F

Sung by Mr. Tommy Davis, Galena, Mo., Sept. 21, 1941.

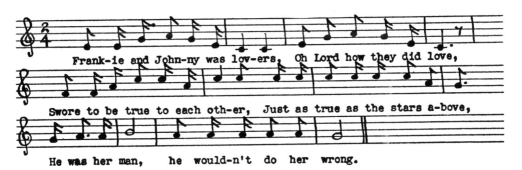

Frank-ie and John-ny was lov-ers, Oh Lord how they did love,

Swore to be true to each oth-er, Just as true as the stars a-bove,

He was her man,   he would-n't do her wrong.

Frankie went down to the corner
Just for a bucket of beer,
She says Mister Bartender
Has my lovin' Johnny been here?
He's my man, but he's doin' me wrong.

Says I aint a-goin' to cause you no trouble,
I aint a-goin' to tell you no lies,
I saw your lover 'bout an hour ago
Makin' love to Nelly Bly,
He's your man, but he's doin' you wrong.

Frankie looked over the transom,
There she saw to her surprise,
There on the couch sat Johnny
Makin' love to Nelly Bly,
He's my man, but he's doin' me wrong.

Frankie drew back her kimona,
Pulled out her little forty-four,
Rooty-toot-toot, three times she shot
Right through that hardwood door,
Shot her man, he was doin' her wrong.

Bring on your rubber-tired buggies,
Bring on your rubber-tired hacks,
I'm takin' my man to the grave-yard
And I aint a-goin' to bring him back,
He's my man, but he done me wrong.

This story has no moral,
This story has no end,
This story just goes to show
That there aint no good in men,
He was her man, but he done her wrong.

160

DOWN ON THE BANKS OF THE OHIO

This piece is reported from North Carolina by Henry (*Folk-Songs from the Southern High-lands*, 1938, pp. 220-221). Belden (*Ballads and Songs*, 1940, p. 322) mentions it in his head-note to "Oma Wise," but did not find the song in Missouri. Compare "On the Banks of the Ohio" in *Songs of the Rivers of America*, by Carl Carmer, New York, 1942, p. 168. Sigmund Spaeth (*California Folklore Quarterly* 2, July, 1943, p. 228) notes that it is "reminiscent" of the Cornish "Butcher Boy" song, also of "The Jealous Lover" and "Poor Omie."

A

Sung by Miss Louise McDowell, Galena, Mo., Aug. 18, 1941. Learned from her parents near Reeds Spring, Mo. She uses the second stanza as a refrain, repeating it after each of the other verses.

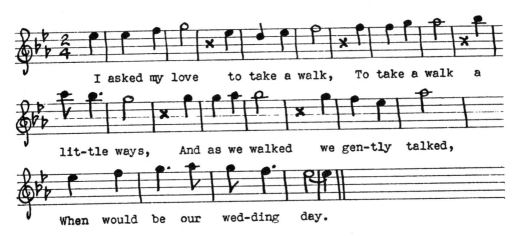

I asked my love to take a walk, To take a walk a
lit-tle ways, And as we walked we gen-tly talked,
When would be our wed-ding day.

Now say, my love, say you'll be mine,
And in my home you'll happy be,
Down where the water swiftly flows,
Down on the banks of the Ohio.

I drug her by her curly hair,
And took her to the river side,
I plunged her in and watched her drown,
Then watched her until she floated down.

I started home between twelve and one,
Just thinking of the deed I'd done,
For I'd murdered the one I loved,
Just because she would not wed.

B

Mr. Arlie Freeman, Natural Dam, Ark., Dec. 10, 1941, sings a garbled version he calls "I'll Never Be Yours" with a chorus as follows:

Then only say that you'll be mine,
And in your arms no other shall find,
Down beside where the water flows
Far on the banks of the Ohio.

C

Sung by Mrs. Gladys McCarty, Farmington, Ark., Oct. 24, 1941.

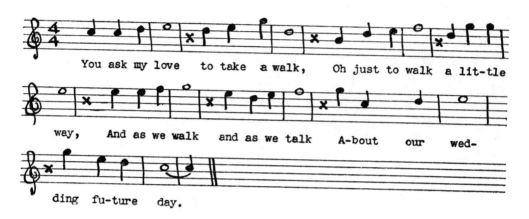

You ask my love to take a walk, Oh just to walk a lit-tle
way, And as we walk and as we talk A-bout our wedding fu-ture day.

And the only time that you'll be mine,
And in your heart no other will twine,
Down beside where the water flows,
Down on the banks of the Ohio.

He drew his knife acrost her breast
And in his arms as she did press,
Crying Willie, don't murder me,
For I am not prepared to die.

He took her by her little white hand
And led her down where the water flows,
Led her down where the water flows,
Down on the banks of the Ohio.

He shoved her in to drown
And watched her go a-floating down,
Then when he turned to go home,
He cried oh Lord, what have I done?

He cried oh Lord, what have I done,
I've killed the girl, the girl I love.

161

TANEY COUNTY

Evidently a local adaptation of "Bad Companions," a song I heard as long ago as 1918, and which has been sung by many radio "hill-billies" in recent years. "Bad Companions" is given in the Library of Congress *Check-list* (1942, I p. 14) as sung at Firebaugh, Calif., in 1940 and recorded by Charles L. Todd and Robert Sonkin. A text and tune of "Young Companions" is given by Lomax in *Cowboy Songs* (1938, pp. 212-214), the text alone in the 1910 edition (pp. 81-82).

A

Sung by Mr. Charles Ingenthron, Walnut Shade, Mo., Sept. 7, 1941. Mr. Ingenthron says that he first heard this song about 1910. He has no doubt that it was written about some local boy who went astray in the 90's. "We've had a plenty o' such fellers, right here in Taney county," he said soberly.

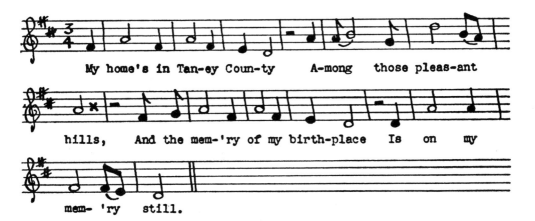

My home's in Tan-ey Coun-ty A-mong those pleas-ant hills, And the mem-'ry of my birth-place Is on my mem- 'ry still.

I landed in Chicago
In the merry midst of May,
And then I took to gambling
And sinned both night and day.

I courted a fair damsel,
Her name I will not tell,
For why should I disgrace her
When I am doomed to hell?

It was on one moonlight evening
When the stars were shining bright,
'Twas with an ugly dagger
I made her spirit's flight.

I now stand on the scaffold,
My name it will not be long,
You may forget the singer,
Pray don't forget the song.

B

Follows a text of "Bad Companions," contributed by Miss Pauline McCullough, Blue
Eye, Mo., June 6, 1938.

Come all you young companions
And listen unto me,
I'll tell you a sad story
Of some bad company,
I was born in Pennsylvania
Among the beautiful hills,
And the memory of my childhood
Is warm within me still.

I had a kind old mother,
Who oft would plead with me,
And the last words that she gave me
Was to pray to God in need.
I had two loving sisters
As fair as fair could be,
And oft beside me kneeling
They too would pray for me.

I did not like my fireside,
I did not like my home,
I had in view for rambling,
And far away did roam.
I bid adieu to loved ones,
To my home I said farewell,
And I landed in Chicago
In the very depths of hell.

It was there I took to drinking,
I sinned both night and day,
But still within my bosom
A feeble voice would say:
Oh fare you well, my loved one,
May God protect my boy,
May God forever bless him
Throughout his manhood joy.

I courted a fair young maiden,
Her name I will not tell,
For it would ever disgrace her,
Since I am doomed for hell.
It was on one fatal evening,
The stars were shining bright,
And with a fatal dagger
I took away her life.

So justice overtook me,
And you can plainly see
My soul is doomed forever
Through all eternity.
It's now I'm on the scaffold,
My moments are not long,
You may forget the singer,
But don't forget the song.

162

HARRISON TOWN

A

Sung by Mr. Arthur Trail, Farmington. Ark., Oct. 3, 1941. He learned it near Fayetteville about 1905, never heard any title for it.

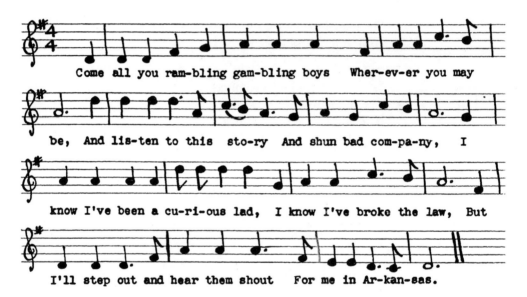

Come all you ram-bling gam-bling boys   Wher-ev-er you may
be, And lis-ten to this   sto-ry And shun bad com-pa-ny,   I
know I've been a cu-ri-ous lad, I know I've broke the law, But
I'll step out and hear them shout   For me in Ar-kan-sas.

       I traveled down to Harrison, boys,
       Stayed a couple of weeks or so,
       The crowd that followed after me
       They knew I'd have no doubt,
       That I would lay in the Federal jail
       Before the week went out.

       There's another thing that I left out
       In stating of my case,
       It was that noble horse of mine
       I rode upon a race.
       I hope that he'll be well cared for,
       His bed made out of straw,
       And live to see a right old age
       In the state of Arkansas.

B

Here is a text of "Harrison Town" contributed by Dr. George E. Hastings, Fayetteville, Ark., Nov. 14, 1941. Dr. Hastings had it from Miss Grace Bishop, Capps, Ark.

As I rode down to Harrison town
A couple of days ago,
I turned my face toward the west,
To Eureka I did go.

The people followed after me,
They said there would be no doubt,
But I would lie in the Berryville jail
Before the week was out.

They captured me on Kings River, boys,
I might have killed the crowd,
If it had not been for the ball and chain
That rang so clear and loud.

My mammy came and scorned for me,
She told me to shut my jaw,
. . . .
In the hills of Arkansas.

They took me down to Berryville, boys,
I went through the courts of law,
So I'll take a ride by the marshal's side
To Little Rock, Arkansas.

Oh there is one thing that I've left out
To you I'm going to tell,
And that is the girl, the pretty little girl,
The girl I loved so well.

Oh there is one thing that I've left out,
That is standing over my case,
And that is the horse, the noble horse,
The horse that rode on the race.

If ever I gain my liberty, boys,
Have bread and meat to chaw,
I'll stay at home with the blue-eyed girl
In Carroll county, Arkansas.

163

JOHN HARDY

This ballad, according to Cox (*Folk-Songs of the South*, 1925, p. 175), had its origin and development in West Virginia. Cox cites numerous references and gives nine variants. Compare the "John Hardy" piece reported by N. J. H. Smith (*Texas Folk-Lore Society Publications* 7, 1928, pp. 115-116). Some similar stanzas (about red and blue dresses) occur in "John Henry," a song about the steel-drivin' Negro with the 12-pound hammer, as reported by Sandburg (*American Songbag*, 1927, pp. 24-25). Two "John Henry" songs are given in Chappell (*Folk-Songs of Roanoke and the Albemarle*, 1939, pp. 179-181). See also the Brown (North Carolina Folk-Lore Society) collection.

A

Sung by Mr. Arthur Trail, Farmington, Ark., Oct. 11, 1941. Learned near Fayetteville, Ark., about 1910.

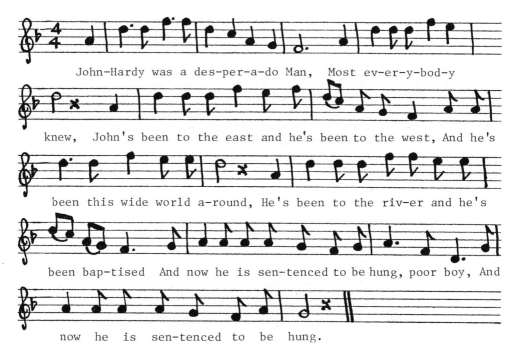

John-Hardy was a des-per-a-do Man, Most ev-er-y-bod-y knew, John's been to the east and he's been to the west, And he's been this wide world a-round, He's been to the riv-er and he's been bap-tised And now he is sen-tenced to be hung, poor boy, And now he is sen-tenced to be hung.

John Hardy standing in a dice-room door,
Not concerning a word in the game,
John threw down one bright silver dollar,
Says a half of this I'll play,
And the man that wins my pretty girl's money,
I'll blow him away, God knows, poor boy,
I'll blow him away, God knows.

John Hardy had a pretty little wife,
She dressed herself in blue,
She threw her arms around John Hardy's neck
Saying John Hardy, I've been true to you, poor boy,
Saying John Hardy, I've been true to you.

John's father and mother were standing around,
Saying son, what have you done?
I've killed a man in old Charleston Town,
And now I've met my fatal doom, poor boy,
And now I've met my fatal doom.

B

Sung by Mrs. Gladys McCarty, Farmington, Ark., Oct. 13, 1941.

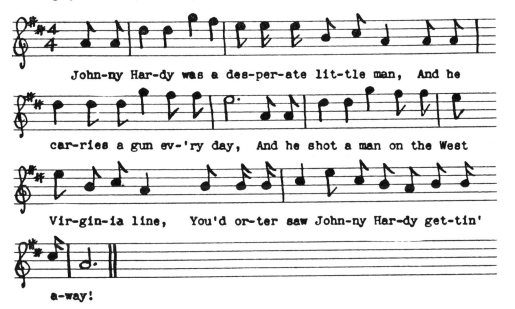

John-ny Har-dy was a des-per-ate lit-tle man, And he
car-ries a gun ev-'ry day, And he shot a man on the West
Vir-gin-ia line, You'd or-ter saw John-ny Har-dy get-tin'
a-way!

But 'long came a man and took him by the hand,
Saying march right along with me, Johnny.

He called his mother and he called his father
To come and go his bail,
But money won't go for the murderous case
And they locked poor Johnny Hardy back in jail.

Johnny Hardy had a pretty little girl,
The dress she wore was blue,
When she come a-skipping through the old jail hall,
Saying papa, I'd ruther be true.

Johnny Hardy had another little girl,
The dress she wore was red,
When she come a-skipping through the old jail hall,
Saying papa, I'd ruther be dead.

He's been to the east and he's been to the west,
And he's searched this wide world around,
And he's been to the river and he's been baptized,
And now he's on his hanging ground.

C

Text from Miss Aileen Rogers, Galena, Mo., May 10, 1942. She learned it from her mother.

John Hardy was a desperate little man,
He carried two guns every day,
He shot a man on the western city line
And you ought a seen John Hardy gettin' away.

He went to the end of the East Stone Bridge,
There he thought he would be free,
But up stepped a man and took him by the arm,
Saying Johnny, come and walk along with me.

They took John Hardy down to town
And locked him up in jail,
He asked for his mama and his papa
To come and go his bail.

But money would'nt do in a murdering case
So they kept John Hardy locked in jail.

John Hardy had a pretty little girl,
The dress that she wore was blue,
She came skipping through that old jail hall
Saying daddy, I will always be true.

John Hardy had another little girl,
The dress that she wore was red,
She followed John Hardy to his hanging ground,
Saying daddy, I would rather be dead.

Now I've been to the East and I've been to the West,
I've been this wide world around,
I've been to the river and I've been baptised
And now I'm on my hanging ground.

Then they raised John Hardy on the scaffold high,
His loving little wife by his side,
And the very last words that he heard her say,
Were I'll meet you in the sweet bye and bye.

164

A PRISONER FOR LIFE

Mrs. Lessie Stringfellow Read, editor of the *Northwest Arkansas Times*, Fayetteville, Ark., Dec. 12, 1941, told me that many Arkansas singers credit this song to William Alexander, convicted of murder at Fort Smith, Ark., Jan. 21, 1890. Judge Isaac Parker, the famous "hanging judge," sentenced him to death, but the sentence was changed to life imprisonment. It is said that he wrote this song in prison, about the middle of the year 1890. Several years later it appears that Alexander was pardoned, when the man he was convicted of murdering "showed up alive." Mrs. Read told me that she had checked the facts about Alexander's imprisonment, and saw no reason to doubt the local tradition that he was the author of this song. . . . There is a de Marsan broadside of "The Prisoner For Life" in the Los Angeles public library, with the note "tune of *Hunt the Buffalo.*" Several lines and stanzas occur in the "Dock Bishop" song reported by Perrow (*JAFL* 25, 1912, p. 151), also in the "Prisoner for Life" as published by Lomax (*Cowboy Songs*, 1910, pp. 200-203).

A

Sung by Mrs. Carrie Baber, Pineville, Mo., June 4, 1922.

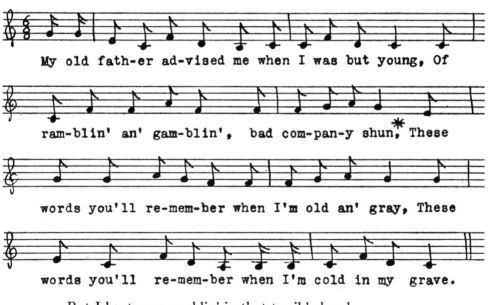

My old fath-er ad-vised me when I was but young, Of

ram-blin' an' gam-blin', bad com-pan-y shun,* These

words you'll re-mem-ber when I'm old an' gray, These

words you'll re-mem-ber when I'm cold in my grave.

But I kept on a-ramblin' in that terrible band,
Till I was attackted by the laws of the land,
Was tried an' convicted for mail robbery,
Nine years was transported across the salt sea.

*bad combination?

Then I met my old father a-leavin' the dock
He wrang his poor hands an' he tore his gray locks,
Sayin' son, they have ruint you, I've advised you before,
But now we are partin' to meet here no more.

If I was on ship board, pretty Molly by me,
Bound down in strong Ireland I'd feel myself free,
Bound down in strong Ireland an' kept like a slave,
'Twas in my own country I did not behave.

Farewell, little doogie, to an embel you fly,
You sing an' you sorrow your troubles all by,
Oh what would I give in such freedom to share,
To roam at my ease an' to breathe the fresh air.

Oh farewell, kind comrades, I'm willin' to own,
That such a wild outcast has never been known,
'Tis the cause of my ruin an' sudden downfall,
An' caused me to labor behind the stone wall.

B

Sung by Mr. Wythe Bishop, Fayetteville, Ark., Dec. 9, 1941. Bishop is 75 years old, and learned the song in the 90's. He says "it was wrote by Billy Alexander, who come mighty near bein' hung one time in Fort Smith."

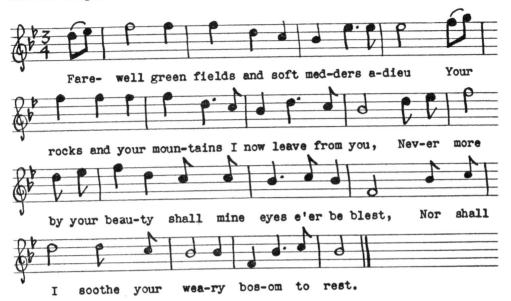

Fare- well green fields and soft med-ders a-dieu   Your
rocks and your moun-tains I now leave from you,   Nev-er more
by your beau-ty shall mine eyes e'er be blest,   Nor shall
I soothe your wea-ry bos-om to rest.

Farewell little birdies, how nimble you play,
Sing all of my sorrows and trouble away,
Oh what would I give sich freedom to share,
To roam as I please and to breathe the fresh air.

Farewell little fishes that glides through the stream,
Your life is all playful sunshine and gleam,
Never more do I witness . . . . . . still over the wave,
That parts all friends this side of the grave.

No change in my prison but a deep sigh,
My heart sinks in me, I wish I could die,
Nevermore do I see the pale shadder pass over the lawn,
Nevermore do I breathe the fresh air of the dawn.

Farewell kind friends, I'm willing to own
That such a wild outcast has never been known,
Adieu to my downfall to my dear little wife,
May God pity and pardon a prisoner for life.

C

A manuscript copy contributed by Dr. George E. Hastings, Fayetteville, Ark., Jan. 6, 1942, adds the following:

> Farewell, kind friends, I am willing to own
> That such a wild outcast never was known,
> The cause of my downfall is my own darling wife,
> God pity and pardon a prisoner for life.
>
> Farewell, little wife, I'll now bid you adieu,
> I would not have been here had it not been for you,
> You are the cause of my sorrow, my downfall and strife,
> God pity and pardon a prisoner for life.

D

Sung by Fred Woodruff, Lincoln, Ark., Dec. 12, 1941. He learned it from a wanderer in Mississippi, but thinks it was written by a prisoner at Fort Smith, Ark.

Fare you well to green fields and soft mead-ows a-dieu, Your rocks and your moun-tains I now part from you, Fare you well to lit-tle birdies so nim-ble can fly, You'll sing all your sor-rows and trou-bles all by.

> Rise up in the morning for to hear the birds sing,
> Rise up in the morning so early in Spring,
> It makes me so happy for to hear the calf bawl,
> To know that I'm free from a prisoner's stone wall.
>
> Fare you well to little fishes that glides through the stream,
> Your days are all numbered with sunshine and gleam,
> Fare you well to little woman, I now part from you,
> I wouldn't a been here if it hadn't been for you.

Sometimes I have wondered how women could love men,
More times have I wondered how men could love them,
They'll cause you some trouble, a sadder downfall,
And cause you to labor behind some stone wall.

165

SAINT LOUIS, BRIGHT CITY

Sung by Mr. Wythe Bishop, Fayetteville, Ark., Dec., 9, 1941. He calls it "Saint Louis,
Bright City," and says he learned it in the late 80's or early 90's.

In Saint Lou-is, bright ci-ty where I first saw the
light, I was raised by hon-est par-ents, the path-way of
right, At the age of ten years a orph-ern I was left, At the
grave of my moth-er I shed man-y a tear.

I scarcely reached manhood till I left my old home,
Me an' another young fellow o'er the West we did roam,
We tasted life's pleasure, we tasted sin and shame,
Lose all of our money, also our good name.

We searched for employment but none could we find,
And then we was drove unto steal.
Wc was arrested and tried and convicted and carried to the pen,
The gate was throwed open, says walk in, young men.

They give us a knife and an awl, to be a stone-cutter behind a stone wall,
It was there I swore to my Maker I'd never break the law.

166

THE HORSE-THIEF

Sung by Mr. Wythe Bishop, Fayetteville, Ark., Dec. 9, 1941. Mr. Bishop learned it in this vicinity in the late 80's or the early 90's.

I used to drink lager beer
But I was glad to get cold water,
But I'll be a good boy,
And I'll do so no more.

167

BONNIE BLACK BESS

This song celebrates the exploits of Dick Turpin (1706-1739), the notorious English highwayman. Turpin plied his trade in partnership with various smugglers and robbers, chiefly during the fourth decade of the eighteenth century. Finally sentenced for horse-stealing, he was hanged at York on the 7th of April, 1739. See the *Dictionary of National Biography* (XIX, pp. 1302-1303) for further details about this "very commonplace ruffian, who owes all his fame to the literary skill of Ainsworth."

William Harrison Ainsworth, whose boyhood was spent in the very countryside where some of Turpin's most famous robberies had been committed, presents in his romantic novel *Rookwood* (1834) the figure of Dick Turpin as hero and the famous, though apparently apocryphal, ride from London to York as central exploit (such a ride had formerly been associated with a highwayman known by the sobriquet of "Nicks," circa 1670.) The spot where the likewise famous but apocryphal black mare sank exhausted to the ground is still pointed out on York race course.

For a text discussion of the event and references see Mackenzie, *Ballads and Sea Songs from Nova Scotia* (1928, pp. 313-314). The version obtained from Mrs. Chadwick is paralleled in Pound (*American Ballads and Songs*, 1922, pp. 155-157). Lomax, whose 1910 edition of *Cowboy Songs* contains a text (pp. 194-196), notes in the 1938 edition (p. 217) that this was "said to have been the most popular song among the cowboys in the Indian Territory." Gardner (*Ballads and Songs of Southern Michigan*, 1939, pp. 320-322) has three texts and two tunes.

A

Sung by Mr. Fred Woodruff, Lincoln, Ark., Dec. 12, 1941. "A long piece about a road agent," he described it. But two stanzas were all that he could remember.

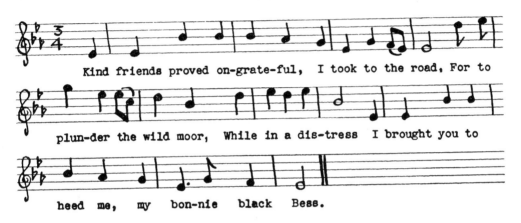

Kind friends proved on-grate-ful, I took to the road, For to plun-der the wild moor, While in a dis-tress I brought you to heed me, my bon-nie black Bess.

> The gold and the silver
> From the rich man did drop,
> No poor man we plundered
> Wherever we press,
> No widow nor orphant,
> My bonnie black Bess.

B

Sung by Mrs. Frances Oxford, Springdale, Ark., Dec. 28, 1941. She knew that the horse was owned by an outlaw named Turpin, although the name does not appear in the song as she sang it. She thinks Turpin was a recent American bandit, dating somewhere between the James boys and Pretty Boy Floyd. Says she read something about Turpin's robberies in the Little Rock newspaper.

> The gods of misfortune have led me abroad,
> Kind friends proved ungrateful, I took to the road,
> To plunder the wealthy and leave my distress
> I brought you to aid me, my bonnie black Bess.

When the dark clouds of midnight are mantled and thrown
O'er the face of green nature, how often we've gone
From the points to the low heath, though an unwelcome guest,
To plunder the wealthy, my bonnie black Bess.

Oh how gentle you stood when a mail coach I'd stop,
And the bright gold and silver from its inmates we got,
No poor man did we plunder, nor did we ever distress
The widow nor orphan, my bonnie black Bess.

When Augustus the justice had us pursued,
From London to Yorktown like lightning we flew,
No toll bars could stop us, wide rivers we'd breast,
In twelve hours I rode it, my bonnie black Bess.

Hark, hark, I hear the bloodhounds, they never shall have
A beast so noble, true and brave,
I must kill you, my bonnie, though it does me distress,
Oh there, I have shot you, my bonnie black Bess!

In age after ages when I'm dead and gone
My history'll be handed from father to son,
Some will pity while others confess,
And so I will die with my bonnie black Bess.

I'll die like a man and soon be at rest,
Farewell to my kind friends and bonnie black Bess.

C

A manuscript copy from Mrs. Maggie Chadwick, Springdale, Ark., Mar. 5, 1942.

Over highway and byway, in rough or smooth weather,
Some thousands of miles have we journeyed together;
Our couch the same straw, our meals the same mess,
No couple more constant than I and black Bess.

By moonlight, in darkness, by night or by day,
Her headlong career there is nothing can stay,
She cares not for distance, she knows not distress,
Can you show me a courser to match with black Bess?

Once it happened in Cheshire near Dunham, I popped
On a horseman alone, whom I suddenly stopped,
That I lightened his pockets you surely can guess,
Quick work makes Dick Turpin when mounted on Bess.

Now it seems the man knew me, Dick Turpin, says he,
You will swing for this job and I'll be there to see.
I laughed at his threats and his vows of redress,
I looked for my safety to bonny black Bess.

The road was a hollow, a sunken ravine,
O'er shadowed completely with woods like a screen,
I clambered the bank and I needs must confess
That one touch of the spur grazed the side of black Bess.

Brook, meadow and field black Bess fleetly bestrode,
As the crow wings his flight we selected our road,
We arrived at Hough Green in five minutes or less,
My neck it was saved by the speed of black Bess.

Stepping carelessly forward I lounged on the green,
Taking care that by all I am sighted and seen,
Some remarks on time's flight to the squires I address,
But I say not a word of the flight of black Bess.

I mention the hour, it is just about four,
Play a rubber at bowls, think the danger is o'er,
When amid my next game like a checkmate at chess
Comes the horseman in search of the rider of Bess.

No matter the chase, off in triumph I came,
He swears to the hour and the squires swear the same,
I had robbed him at four while at four they profess
I was quietly bowling, and thanks to black Bess.

Then a halloo, my boys, and a cheery halloo
For the swiftest of coursers, the gallant, the true,
Forever shall horsemen the memory bless
Of the horse of the highwayman, bonny black Bess.

168

TWENTY-ONE YEARS

A piece called "Twenty-One Summers" was recorded at Cumins state farm, Gould, Ark., by John A. Lomax in 1939 (*Check-List . . . Archives of American Folk Song*, 1942, p. 411).

A

Sung by Mrs. Lillian Short, Galena, Mo., June 17, 1942. She learned it from Dale and Lonnie Gentry, of Galena, in 1931.

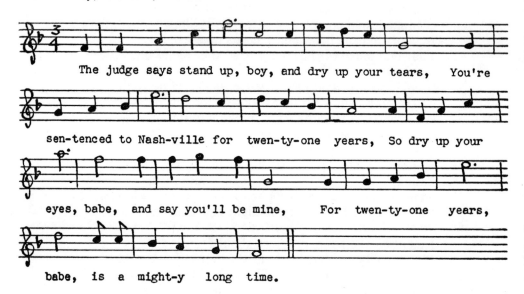

The judge says stand up, boy, and dry up your tears, You're sen-tenced to Nash-ville for twen-ty-one years, So dry up your eyes, babe, and say you'll be mine, For twen-ty-one years, babe, is a might-y long time.

I hear the train whistling, it'll be here on time,
To take me to Nashville to serve out my time,
The steam from the whistle, the smoke from the stack,
I know you'll be true blue, until I get back.

Go the governor, upon your sweet soul,
If you can't get a pardon, try to get a parole,
If I had the governor where the governor's got me,
Before Tuesday morning the governor'd be free.

Six months have gone by, babe, I wish I was dead,
This dirty old jail house, the floor for a bed,
It's raining, it's hailing, stars give me no light,
Darlin', please tell me why you never write.

I've counted the days, babe, I've counted the nights,
I've counted the footsteps, I've counted the lights,
I've counted the minutes, I've counted the stars,
I've counted a million of these prison bars.

I've counted on you, babe, to get me a break,
I guess you've forgot, babe, I'm here for your sake,
You know who is guilty, you know it too well,
But I'll rot in this jail house before I will tell.

Come all you young fellows, with a heart brave and true,
Don't believe any woman, you're doomed if you do,
Don't trust any woman, no matter what kind,
For twenty-one years, boys, is a mighty long time.

B

A text obtained from Mr. L. M. Bartley, Joplin, Mo., in 1933, is exactly like the above
except for two stanzas:

O hear that train blow, babe, she'll be here on time,
To take me to Nashville to serve out my time,
O look down that railroad as far as you can see,
And keep right on waving your farewell to me.

The smoke from the whistle, the smoke from the stack,
I know you'll be true blue until I come back,
So hold up your head, babe, and say you'll be mine,
For best friends must part, babe, so must you and I.

C

From Miss Lucile Morris, Springfield, Mo., Sept. 6, 1935. It is called "Answer to Twenty-
One Years," and is sung to the same tune.

She wrote him this letter all covered with tears,
And it was the answer to twenty-one years.

Six months have gone by, the good doctor said,
For six weary months, love, I've been sick in bed,
My poor hungry heart, love, was in agony,
The drugstore had nothin' could help what ailed me.

They say you are bitter 'cause I did not write,
But a brain that's in fever is dark as the night,
So you'll understand why I didn't write you,
The master in heaven knows what I've went through.

The judge made you stand up and dry up your tears,
They sent you to Nashville for twenty-one years,
They shackled your arms, love, they shackled your feet,
But they'll never shackle a love that is sweet.

As we stood embracin' they tore us apart,
But they'll never tear you out from my heart,
The angels all know, love, you'll always be mine,
And I'll still be waiting, though it's a mighty long time.

I went to the governor, got down on my knees,
Saying oh Mister Governor, won't you hear me please,
I begged for your pardon through hot burning tears,
But all I remember was twenty-one years.

Though you've been in prison behind all them bars,
When I get my strength back I'll come where you are,
I'll stand by them high walls and shout through my tears,
And I'll wait for you, love, for twenty-one years.

D

Sung by Miss Lee Morse, Springfield, Mo., Apr. 3, 1934. She calls it "Ninety-Nine Years," and sings it to the same tune as "Twenty-One Years."

The courtroom was crowded, the judges was there,
My mother was crying when I left my chair,
The sentence was sharp, folks, it cut like a knife,
For ninety-nine years, folks, is almost for life.

They said I was a criminal and to my despair
They sent me to Nashville and shaved off my hair,
So come hear my story, I'll tell you my fate,
I'm serving in Nashville for another man's sake.

I dreamed of the whistle, I heard the bell ring,
My sweetheart was coming some good news to bring,
I thought that she loved me, I thought she'd be true,
She said that she'd save me, for I'm guiltless as you.

She went for a pardon or a parole,
I know she'll come back for she's part of my soul,
If she ever fails me I'll be mighty blue,
I'll live in this jail house, I'll die in here too.

I've prayed to my mother, I've prayed to the stars,
To my heavenly father through these prison bars,
The storm clouds are heavy, the day gives no light,
For ninety-nine years, folks, is almost for life.

I got me a letter from old Nashville town,
And after I read it my spirit broke down,
It said that my sweetheart and the judge would be wed,
And here in this jail house I wish I was dead.

E

Sung by Mrs. Mildred Tuttle, Farmington, Ark., Dec. 15, 1941. She calls it "A Sequel to Nine-Nine Years." (The first four stanzas of this piece were printed in the Springfield, Mo., *News and Leader*, Jan. 6, 1935, by Miss Lucile Morris, who had the text from Miss Reva Caffey, of Springfield).   Mrs. Tuttle had never seen it in print, she said.

The old prison walls so cold and so gray,
The iron bars I've looked through for many a day,
The guards with their rifles who once guarded me
Are all left behind and again I am free.

I'm free but my old friends have all drifted on,
Even my dad and my mother are gone,
I still can see mother, her face wet with tears
When she heard me sentenced to ninety-nine years.

Though I was not guilty they sent me away,
Away from my loved ones in prison to stay,
The judge could have saved me but he closed the case,
And he sentenced me with a smile on his face.

He sent me to prison and ruint my life,
The girl that I trusted he took for his wife,
He led her to sorrow, he cheated and lied,
In less than a year he had cast her aside.

She wrote me a letter and told me goodbye,
She said she would go to some new town and try
To start life all over where no one would know,
Wherever she is, boys, that's where I will go.

With God's help I'll find her, I'll search till I do,
Then all our sorrows and cares will be through,
We'll both be so happy, forgetting the years,
That come with the sentence of ninety-nine years.

169

THE ROWAN COUNTY CREW

Compare the texts in Cox (*Folk-Songs of the South*, 1925, pp. 205-206), Thomas (*Ballad Makin' in the Mountains of Kentucky*, 1939, pp. 5-9), B. A. Botkin (*Treasury of American Folklore*, 1944, pp. 891-892).

Sung by Mr. Jim Cherry, Fayetteville, Ark., Jan. 30, 1942. Mr. Cherry learned it near Little Rock, Ark., in 1893, he says. The tune seems to be the same as the "Texas Rangers."

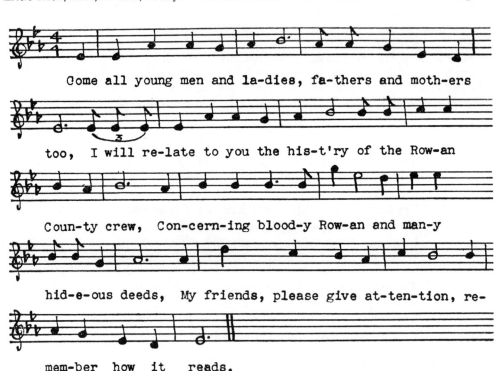

Come all young men and la-dies, fa-thers and moth-ers

too, I will re-late to you the his-t'ry of the Row-an

Coun-ty crew, Con-cern-ing blood-y Row-an and man-y

hid-e-ous deeds, My friends, please give at-ten-tion, re-

mem-ber   how   it   reads.

It was in the month of August, all on the election day,
Johnny Martin he was wounded, they say by Johnny Day,
But Martin could not believe it, he could not think it so,
He thought it was Floyd Tolliver that struck the fatal blow.

They shot and killed Saul Bradley, a sober and innocent man,
Left his wife and loving children to do the best they can,
They wounded young Ad Sizemore, although his life was saved,
He seems to shun the grog-shops since he stood so near t' his grave.

Now Martin did recover, some months had come and passed
All in the town of Morehead those men they met at last,
Tolliver and a friend or two about the streets did walk,
They seemed to be uneasy, with no one wished to talk.

They stepped into Judge Carey's grocery and stepped to the bar,
But little did they think, dear friends, they had met their fatal hour,
The sting of death was near him, Martin rushed in at the door,
A few words passed between them concerning the row before.

The people were soon all frightened, began to rush out of the room,
When a ball from Martin's pistol lay Tolliver in the tomb,
His friends did gather round him, his wife to weep and wail,
Then Martin was arrested and soon confined in jail.

He was put in the jail of Rowan, there to remain a little while,
In the hands of law and justice to bravely stand his trial,
The people talked of lynching him, at present they did fail,
The prisoner's friends soon moved him to the Winchester jail.

Some people forged an order, their names I do not know,
Their plan was soon agreed upon, for Martin they did go,
Martin seemed to be discouraged, he seemed to be in dread,
They've sought a plan to kill me, to the jailer Martin said.

They put the handcuffs on him, his heart was in distress,
They hurried to the station to get on the night express,
Along the line she lumbered at her usual speed,
There was only two in number to commit this dreadful deed.

Martin was in the smoking car, accompanied by his wife,
They did not want her present when they took her husband's life,
When they arrived at Farmer's they had no time to lose,
A band approached the engineer and told him not to move.

They stepped up to the prisoner with pistols in their hands,
In death he was soon sinking, he died in iron bands,
His wife she heard the horrid sound, she was in another car,
She cried oh Lord, they've killed him! when she heard the pistols fire.

Now the death of those two men have caused great trouble in our land,
Caused men to leave their families and take the parting hand,
Retaliating still at war, and it may never cease,
I would that I could only see our land once more in peace.

They shot the deputy sheriff, Bumgardner was his name,
They shot him from the bushes after taking deliberate aim,
The death of him was dreadful, it may never be forgot,
His body pierced and torn with thirty-three buckshot.

Now I've composed this as a warning, beware all you young men,
Your pistols will cause you trouble, on this you may depend,
In the bottom of the whiskey glass a lurking devil dwells,
It burns the breasts who drink it, and sends their souls to hell.

171

COTTON THE KID

From a manuscript copy contributed by Miss Lucile Morris, Springfield, Mo., Oct. 28, 1934. The name I. L. Shelton, and the address Eminence, Mo., is written in pencil on the margin.

Come all you young people, and listen while I tell
The story of a young man, a kid you all know well,
He was born in Shannon county, a nice young kid he seemed,
Until he became a rolling stone at the age of seventeen.

They say he stole some chickens, he only did that for fun,
They say he broke into a club-house and took away some guns,
Then the sheriff come got him and threw him in the jail,
The kid he had no money, no one to go his bail.

While sleeping in his cell the kid then took the blues,
Someone slipped him a hacksaw and he cut the bars in two,
While setting in a back cell escape was his greatest hope,
He tore up one of his blankets and made himself a rope.

He climbed up to the window twenty feet above the ground,
Tied his blanket to a bar and let himself slide down,
He left his rope a-hanging and then he left the town,
The sheriff with eight or nine deputies started to run him down.

I don't think you can catch him there is no use to try,
Because he always sets in the bushes and laughs as you go by.
It was on one rainy evening just at the close of day,
Two deputies they shot nine times, but Cotton got away.

Now there is Mister Summers, he is a lucky man,
He started after Cotton with a gun in each hand,
He swore that he would shoot him if he ever saw him again,
And now we know that sometime the kid's life will come to an end.

Now you have heard my story, but you bear this in mind,
The first one that shoots him had better go and resign.
I think if I was a sheriff, I believe I'd go back home,
Take off my star and six-guns and leave the kid alone.

172

THE FATE OF HARRY YOUNG

This piece has been printed in several Ozark newspapers (Springfield, Mo., *Leader and Press*, Dec. 28, 1935). The words are credited to Eugene Hilton, Spokane, Mo.

Harry Young and his brother Jennings were responsible for the massacre of six Springfield police officers in the yard of the Young farmhouse on Saturday afternoon, Jan. 2, 1932. Harry Young had long been wanted for murder, and his attempted capture led to the gun battle. The brothers escaped to Texas, where Harry had recently taken a bride, but were cornered in a small cottage in Houston on Jan. 5. Following the advice of their mother, then incarcerated in the Springfield jail, the desperadoes committed suicide rather than submit to capture.

A manuscript fragment from Mrs. Lillian Short, Cabool, Mo., Aug. 8, 1940.

It was down in old Republic, that old Missouri town,
Harry murdered the city marshal and for three years was not found,
Then at last way down in Texas the law got on his trail,
And they come back to Springfield for to tell this awful tale.

The sheriff says get ready men, and don't be very long,
We're going after the Young boys, and we've got a battle on,
A deputy and six policemen were ready at his call
And went out to the farmhouse where six of them did fall.

173

THE MURDER OF CHARLEY STACEY

This ballad is said to refer to a murder which occurred about 1900 at Grandin, Mo. I have never heard it sung. The text is from a manuscript copy sent me from Springfield, Mo., Dec. 19, 1935. The name "Hume Edgar Skaggs" was pencilled on the manuscript, but whether Mr. Skaggs was the author, the singer, or the collector I have no means of knowing. There is no Hume Edgar Skaggs in the Springfield *Directory*.

Come all you young people and listen while I tell
A story that was told me long ago,
About a tragic murder that happened near the spring
Where Little Black River's waters calmly flow.

It occurred one Sabbath morning, the birds were singing gay,
And everyone was happy as could be;
Poor Charlie never thought that morn, that e'er the sun went down
He would sleep so silent underneath the lea.

The fatal mob was drunk that night, they numbered three in all,
And one of them was hating Charley's heart
Because he'd won the virtuous love of a native maiden fair,
From which he vowed that he would never part.

They gathered round Black River spring to wait the boy's return,
For Charley and his sweetheart were at church,
When they saw him coming they assumed a dreadful frown
And from their lips came deadly peals of curses.

They quickly drew their pistols, we heard the loud reports,
Poor Charley fell, then staggered to his knees,
He swiftly drew his weapon, and one of them dropped down
While the white smoke floated on the spring-time breeze.

He's sleeping in the church-yard fair, where sunny violets bloom,
Where the wild rose creeps so silent o'er his grave,
I believe that God in Heaven will open wide the door
And bid poor Charley Stacey enter in.

174

THEY PUT ME UP TO KILL HIM

This song was written by Mr. Lloyd Robinson, Webster County, Mo., in June, 1935. Having murdered his father, Robert Robinson, on June 3, 1935, he "made up" the ballad while lying in jail at Marshfield, Mo. The piece enjoyed a brief local popularity, and is still sung occasionally in Robinson's old neighborhood to the tune of "The Boston Burglar." Robinson was sentenced to life imprisonment in the penitentiary at Jefferson City, Mo. An account of the crime, with photographs of Robinson and several stanzas of his song, was printed in the Springfield, Mo., *Leader and Press*, July 11, 1935. Two stanzas, evidently taken from the Springfield newspaper, appeared in the *New Yorker*, Oct. 26, 1935, p. 30.

Sung by Mr. Willie Baker, Springfield, Mo., Aug. 4, 1935.

They put me up to kill him,
My pore old white-haired dad,
I done it with a horseshoe rasp
The only thing I had.

I snuck right up behind him,
While he ate his supper cold,
I hit him once upon the head
Just like I was told.

He didn't make no holler,
All he did was groan,
My maw she grabbed him by the feet,
. . . .

And now I sure am sorry
I done this terrible crime,
For killin' my pore old daddy
I'll soon be doing time.

175

THE TENNESSEE KILLER

Manuscript copy from Dr. George E. Hastings, Fayetteville, Ark., Jan. 6, 1942. He had it from a man named Steele, who writes on the stationery of the Blackfriars Fraternity, University of Arkansas. Steele credits it to a Negro beggar in Conway, Ark.

Oh I've killed men in Georgia,
And men in Alabam'
But kill a man in Arkansas
And God your soul will damn!

I'd killed a man in Memphis
In the State of Tennessee,
And I rode straight through to Arkansas
With a posse after me.

I rode into the Ozarks
And there it did not fail,
The men that were a-following me
They soon did lose the trail.

They rode right back to Memphis
In the State of Tennessee,
While I stayed in the Ozarks,
Enjoyed my liberty.

But I went down to the city
For to get my gal a frock,
I killed a man in Conway
And two in Little Rock.

The sheriff saw me do it,
He got the drop on me,
I went up to the jail-house,
Give up my liberty.

So they'll hang me in the morning,
Ere this long night is done,
They'll hang me in the morning
And I'll never see the sun.

Beware, beware, you fellows,
If you must have your fun,
Go do it in a harmless way,
But do not touch a gun.

176

BRENNAN ON THE MOOR

There are eleven stanzas and a chorus of this piece in Wehman's *Irish Song Book*, New York, 1937, p. 106. Belden (*Ballads and Songs*, 1940, p. 284) gives several references and a text, accompanied by this note: "The highwayman William Brennan, who operated in County Cork and ended his career on the gallows in 1804, is the hero of the following ballad, which has something of the temper of the Robin Hood cycle and was frequently printed in the ballad press."

Sung by Mrs. Laura Wasson, Elm Springs, Ark., Jan. 28, 1942. She heard it in the late 80's.

It is of a fearless highwayman a story I will tell,
His name was Willie Brennan, in Ireland he did dwell,
It was high on Calvert Mountain he began his wild career,
And many a wealthy gentleman before him shook with fear.

Brennan on the moor, oh Brennan on the moor,
Bold and undaunted was Brennan on the moor.

Bold Brennan's wife she come in town provisions for to buy,
She saw her Willie captured, she begun to scream and cry,
He told her to cease her tempers, and as soon as Willie spoke,
She handed him a blunderbuss from underneath her coat.

. . . . .

In the county of Tipperary, near the place called Clonmore,
. . . .
The jury found him guilty, the judge passed his reply,
For robbing on the King's Highway you are condemned to die.

. . . . .

Farewell unto my loving wife and to my children three,
And to my aged father, he said many a prayer for me,
Likewise my aged mother tore her gray hair and cried,
Better if Willie Brennan in his cradle he had died.

Mr. and Mrs. J. E. Dethrow, Springfield, Mo.

Mr. and Mrs. Arlie Freeman, Natural Dam, Ark.

Mr. Arthur Trail, Farmington, Ark.

Mr. Doney Hammontree, Farmington, Ark.

MR. WYTHE BISHOP, Fayetteville, Ark.

Mr. Cass Little, Anderson, Mo.

Mr. Lum Bible, Rocky Comfort, Mo.

Mr. Fred Woodruff, Lincoln, Ark.

Chapter V

WESTERN SONGS AND BALLADS

Except for the Ozark country in which he lives, there are only two regions on earth which have any considerable interest for the Ozark backwoodsman. One of these places is the Southern Appalachian range, and the other is the cattle country of the West and Southwest. The hillman is familiar with the Appalachian region because this is the section from which his "fore-parents" came, and he has heard tall tales of grandpap's exploits in Virginia, or Kentucky, or Tennessee. And he is interested in the cattle country because he knows men who have been there.

Some of the more adventurous early settlers marched overland to California in the 50's, and a few drifted back later on to rear their families in the hill country. There were Western pilgrims also who started back to their old homes in Tennessee and Kentucky, but fell by the wayside when they reached the Ozarks, to say nothing of the horse-traders and gamblers and fugitives from justice who have wandered in from Texas and Oklahoma at various periods.

A genuine hillman seldom leaves his native hills unless forced to do so, but if he must go he almost invariably turns his face to the West, just as his ancestors did before him. Nearly every adult Ozarker can remember a "bad" season—when a late frost killed the fruit and a dry summer burned up the corn—and the almost insuperable difficulties of the following winter. There is always poverty in the hill country, but only one who has actually lived there can appreciate the heart-rending hardships of a "bad year." At the end of such a season of crop failures there are two or three families in every neighborhood who decide to sell out and go West. Usually they have only a cow and a pig and a few farm tools and a pitiful little pile of household goods, but these are sold to the highest bidder for cash, or traded for some more portable property. After this melancholy business is over the movers climb into their wagons and set out for Oklahoma, which many of the old-timers still refer to as the "Territory" or the "Nation."

Nowadays most of them find work in the Oklahoma oil fields or in California, but formerly large numbers wandered into Texas, Colorado, Arizona, and New Mexico. They worked on ranches and railroads and in mines, where they made contact with cowpunchers and migratory workers generally. A good many of these fellows returned to the Ozarks after a year or two, and they were probably responsible for the introduction of such comparatively recent Western songs as are now current in the hill country.

177

THE TEXAS RANGERS

Belden (*JAFL* 25, 1912, p. 14) thinks that this song is "surely an echo of the great fight at the Alamo on March 6, 1835. Certain resemblances suggest that it was modelled on the British ballad 'Nancy of Yarmouth.' " Pound (*American Ballads and Songs*, 1922, p. 163) prints a text which definitely labels the enemy as Indians, while Sharp (*English Folk Songs from the Southern Appalachians*, 1932, II, p. 253) has the Rangers fighting Yankees instead of Mexicans or Indians.

For other texts and references see Lomax (*Cowboy Songs*, 1910, p. 44), G. F. Will (*JAFL* 26, 1913, p. 186), B. L. Jones (*Folk-Lore in Michigan*, 1914, p. 4), Shoemaker (*North Pennsylvania Minstrelsy*, 1919, p. 78), Tolman and Eddy (*JAFL* 35, 1922, p. 417), Cox (*Folk-Songs of the South*, 1925, p. 262), Thomas (*Ballad Makin'*, 1939, p. 45), who prints five stanzas of a Kentucky variant; Eddy (*Ballads and Songs from Ohio*, 1939, pp. 291-293), Gardner (*Ballads and Songs of Southern Michigan*, 1939, pp. 239-240), Belden (*Ballads and Songs*, 1940, pp. 336-339), who gives one tune and several texts from Missouri; Brewster (*Ballads and Songs of Indiana*, 1940, pp. 316-317), Henry and Matteson (*Southern Folklore Quarterly* 5, 1941, pp. 141-142), and Doering (*JAFL* 57, 1944, pp. 72-73). Compare the phonograph record by Harry McClintock (*Victor* 21487). The piece is in the Brown (North Carolina Folk-Lore Society) collection.

A

Sung by Mrs. Judy Jane Whittaker, Anderson, Mo., Aug. 7, 1928.

Come all you Tex-as Ran-gers, Wher-ev-er you may be, I'll
tell you of some trou-bles That's hap-pened un-to me.

My name it is nothin' extra
An' it I will not tell,
But all you Texas Rangers
You know I wish you well.

'Twas at the age of sixteen
I j'ined the jolly band,
They marched us down to San Antone
So near the Rio Grande.

Our captain he informed us,
I'm sure he thought 'twas right,
Before we gained the station,
Says he, you'll have to fight.

I seen the smoke ascendin',
It seemed to reach the sky,
The first thought that struck me,
Now is my time to die.

We seen the enemy a-comin',
Our captain give command:
To arms, to arms, brave boys,
An' by your horses stand.

I seen the glitterin' lances,
An' bullets round me hailed,
My heart sunk low in trouble,
My courage almost failed.

I thought on my old mother,
In tears to me did say,
They are all strangers to you, son,
At home you better stay.

I thought she was old an' childish,
The best she did not know,
My mind was bent on rangin',
An' I was bound to go.

We fought 'em nine hours longer
Before th' strife was o'er,
The like of dead an' wounded
I never seen before.

Perhaps you have a mother,
Likewise a sister too,
An' maybe there's a sweetheart
To weep an' mourn for you.

If that's your situation,
Although you'd like to roam,
I tell you by experience
You better stay at home.

B

Mrs. W. E. Jones, Pineville, Mo., Nov. 7, 1928, sings the song with several slightly different stanzas.

I was the age of eighteen years
When I j'ined the jolly band,
I went from Western Texas
Into the Injun land.

.   .   .   .   .

I seen the smoke ascendin',
I heard 'em give the yell,
My feelin's at that moment
No tongue could ever tell.

. . . . .

The road was long an' lonesome,
The waters wide an' deep,
Oh think of me, dear mother,
When I aint here to sleep.

Oh take the lonely cowboy
Back to his native home,
An' from that hallowed fireside
I never more shall roam!

C

Sung by Mrs. Sula Hudson, Crane, Mo., Sept. 15, 1941. She learned it from her father, about 1901.

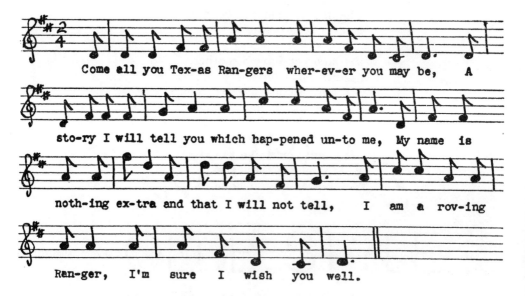

Come all you Tex-as Ran-gers wher-ev-er you may be, A
sto-ry I will tell you which hap-pened un-to me, My name is
noth-ing ex-tra and that I will not tell, I am a rov-ing
Ran-ger, I'm sure I wish you well.

All at the age of sixteen I joined this jolly band,
We marched from San Antonay down to the Rio Grande,
The captain he informed us, perhaps he thought it right,
Before you reach the station, brave boys, you'll have to fight.

I saw the Indians coming, I heard them give the yell,
My feelings at that moment no human tongue could tell,
I saw their glittering glancing arrows fall round us thick as hail,
My heart it sank within me, my courage almost failed.

We fought them for nine hours before the strive was o'er,
The likes that was killed and wounded I never saw before,
There was five of the gallant Rangers that ever served the West
Was buried by their comrades, sweet peace may be their rest.

I thought of my old mother in tears to me did say,
To you they are all strangers, at home you'd better stay,
I thought she was old and childish, the best she did not know,
My mind was bent on rambling and I was bound to go.

Perhaps you have a mother, likewise a sister too,
Perhaps you have a sweetheart that'll really mourn for you,
If this should be your condition, you have a mind to roam,
I advise you by experience you'd better stay at home.

D

Sung by Mr. Wythe Bishop, Fayetteville, Ark., Dec. 9, 1941.

We fought full nine hours before the strife was o'er,
The like of dead and wounded I never saw before,
'Twas fifteen braver rangers lay buried side by side,
'Twas fifteen braver rangers as ever ploughed the West.

E

Another stanza as sung by Mr. Doney Hammontree, Farmington, Ark., Dec. 28, 1941.

It lasted full nine hours before the battle was o'er,
The like of dead and wounded I never saw before,
Four of as noble rangers as ever roved the West
Was buried by their comrades with arrows in their breast.

178

LITTLE DOOGIE

Evidently a garbled fragment of the chorus to "Whoopee Ti Yi Yo, Git Along, Little Dogies," a cowboy song reported by Lomax (*Cowboy Songs*, 1910, p. 87), and reprinted by Pound (*American Ballads and Songs*, 1922, p. 174) and Sandburg (*American Songbag*, 1927, pp. 268-269). See also Gaines (*Texas Folk-Lore Society Publications* 7, 1928, p. 149) and Larkin (*Singing Cowboy*, 1931, pp. 91-97). Compare the phonograph record by Harry McClintock (*Victor* V-40016).

Sung by Mrs. Carrie Baber, Pineville, Mo., Oct. 16, 1922. Mrs. Baber learned this fragment from her parents about 1884. She has no idea that it is part of a cowboy song, and thinks that "Little Doogie" must be a girl's name.

Yip yip yap roll on, lit-tle Doo-gie, In old Wy-o-min' shall be your bright home, Such whoop-in' an' yel-lin' an' howl-in', lit-tle Doo-gie, A sad a mis-for-tune as ev-er was known.

179

THE OLD CHISHOLM TRAIL

For other texts and references see Lomax (*Cowboy Songs*, 1910, p. 58), Thorp (*Songs of the Cowboys*, 1921, p. 109), Pound (*American Ballads and Songs*, 1922, p. 167), Sandburg (*American Songbag*, 1927, p. 266), and Gaines (*Texas Folk-Lore Society Publications* 7, 1928, p. 150) who thinks that the tune is adapted from Stephen Foster's "Old Uncle Ned." Add Larkin (*Singing Cowboy*, 1931, pp. 1-8). Lomax in *American Ballads and Folk Songs* (1934, pp. 376-379) offers about forty verses which did not appear in his earlier book, and remarks in a footnote: "There remain hundreds of unprintable stanzas." Howard Thorp in *Frontier Times*, Bandera, Texas, 12, (Apr., 1935, p.302) says that the "Chisholm Trail song had a thousand verses to it—the more whiskey the more verses." Compare the phonograph records by Harry McClintock (*Victor* 21421-A) and the Cartwright Brothers (*Columbia* 15345-D).

Sung by Mr. E. J. Ferris, Camp Pike, Ark., Dec. 9, 1917. Mr. Ferris' grandfather heard the song in Little Rock, Ark., in 1881 or 1882.

Seat in the sad-dle an' a hand on the horn, Best damn cow-boy ev-er was born. Come a ti yi yoo-py, yip-py ay, yip-py ay, Come a ti yi yoo-py yip-py ay.

The wind it blowed an' the rain it fell,
An' the God damn' fools tore the wagon all to hell,
Come a ti yi yoopy, yippy ay, yippy ay,
Come a ti yi yoopy, yippy ay.

Stray in the shanty an' the boss says kill it,
So I shot him in the rump with the handle of the skillet,
Come a ti yi yoopy, yippy ay, yippy ay,
Come a ti yi yoopy, yippy ay.

I went to the house for to draw my roll,
But the boss had me figgered nine dollars in the hole,
Come a ti yi yoopy, yippy ay, yippy ay,
Come a ti yi yoopy, yippy ay.

180

COME ALL YE LONESOME COWBOYS

Similar lines are found in the "Jolly Cowboy" song which Hudson (*JAFL* 39, 1926, pp. 171-172) reported from Mississippi, also in a "Texas Ranger" piece listed by Lomax (*Cowboy Songs*, 1910, p. 46), and the "Rambling Cowboy" song which Henry (*Folk-Songs from the Southern Highlands*, 1938, pp. 356-357) found in Tennessee. Compare also Buell Kazee's phonograph record entitled "The Roving Cowboy" (*Brunswick* 156).

A

Sung by Mrs. Walter Harmon, Pineville, Mo., Mar. 6, 1927.

Oh come ye lone-some cow-boys, An' now a-round me stand, For
I am go-in' to leave you, An' take my part-in' hand, I
left my home an' coun-try On the wild an' drea-ry plain, But
now I'm go-in' to leave you, To nev-er re-turn a-gain.

My mother's voice did tremble,
Sayin' son, oh son, I fear
Some accident might happen
An' I'll never meet you here,
May God protect my darlin' boy
Wherever he may roam,
An' guide his wanderin' footsteps
Back to his native home.

A maid so fair an' lovely
Grew closely by my side,
An' promised me so faithfully
That she would be my bride,
I kissed her with a flowin' tear
That filled up my blue eye,
My heart has never grown colder,
My love has never died.

I've tried the trails of ramblin'
An' ramblin' I know well,
I've crossed the rocky mountains
Where many a brave boy fell,
I've seen the foreign country
Where many a angel grew wild,
But I never forgot the girl I loved,
Nor seen a sweeter smile.

B

Sung by Mr. Fred Woodruff, Lincoln, Ark., Dec. 12, 1941.

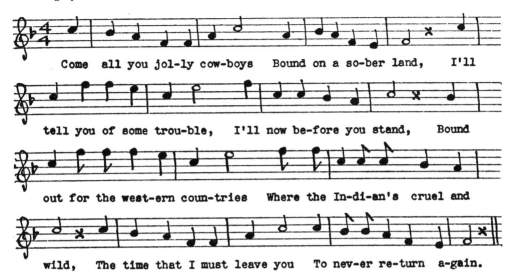

Come all you jol-ly cow-boys Bound on a so-ber land, I'll
tell you of some trou-ble, I'll now be-fore you stand, Bound
out for the west-ern coun-tries Where the In-di-an's cruel and
wild, The time that I must leave you To nev-er re-turn a-gain.

My mother stood beside me
Sayin' son, oh son, I fear,
I fear you're a-goin' to leave me
To never return again.
May God protect and guide you,
And leave you not alone,
Oh bring this wandering cowboy
Back to his native home.

A sweetheart fair and lovely
Drew closely by my side,
It's there she promised me fairly
To be my wife and bride.
I kissed away the flowing tears
That filled her bright blue eyes,
My heart shall never grow colder,
My love shall never die.

I've tried the streets of rambling,
I know them very well,
I crossed the Rocky Mountains
Where many a brave boy fell,
I've traveled the western countries
Where the Indian's cruel and wild,
I'll never forget the girl I left,
God bless her sweetest smile.

181

COME LIST TO A RANGER

This is a muddled fragment of the "Disheartened Ranger" song reported by Lomax (*Cowboy Songs*, 1910, p. 261), which doubtless goes back to print. Stuart Lake (*Saturday Evening Post* 203, Apr. 11, 1931, p. 145) gives part of a variant entitled "The Ranger's Lament," which he heard at a Ranger reunion in Eastland, Texas. According to J. Evetts Haley (*Charles Goodnight*, 1936, p. 97), two rangers, Tom Pollard and Alec McClosky, composed this "bit of doggerel" during Civil War times. One stanza, beginning "Oh pray for the Ranger," is reprinted in J. Frank Dobie's *Guide to Life and Literature of the Southwest* (Austin, Texas, 1943, p. 39). Several songs of similar content were once popular in Texas, praising the Rangers and calling upon the legislators to provide for them more generously. Two of these songs are printed in Lomax (*Cowboy Songs*, 1938, pp. 368 and 371), and one has been recorded phonographically by Carl T. Sprague (*Victor* V-40066).

Sung by Mrs. Lee Stephens, White Rock, Mo., Dec. 15, 1927.

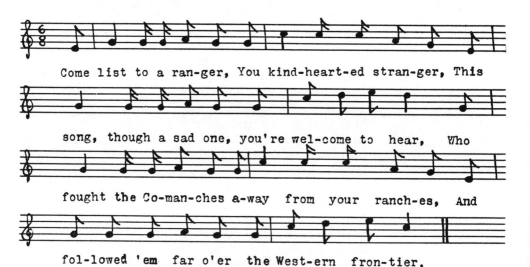

Come list to a ran-ger, You kind-heart-ed stran-ger, This song, though a sad one, you're wel-come to hear, Who fought the Co-man-ches a-way from your ranch-es, And fol-lowed 'em far o'er the West-ern fron-tier.

Though weary of routin' an' travellin' an' scoutin',
These bloodthirsty brutes over prairie an' woods,
The 'lection is a-comin' an' they will be drummin'
An' praisin' our value to purchase our food.

These big alligators an' stately legislators,
A-puffin' an' blowin' two-thirds of the time,
No rest for the sinner, no breakfast, no dinner,
We sleep in the mud an' we aint got a dime.

No corn, no potatoes, no beets, no tomatoes,
The jerked beef is dry as the sole of your shoe,
We fight in our blood an' we sleep in the mud,
An' what in the hell can a poor ranger do?

No glory, no payment, no victuals, no raiment,
No longer we'll fight on the Texas frontier;
So guard your own ranches, an' fight the Comanches
Yourself, or they'll scalp you in less'n a year.

182

THE COWBOY'S LAMENT

This piece, according to Belden (*Ballads and Songs*, 1940, p. 392) is a Western adaptation of a British stall ballad on the death of a soldier "disordered" by a woman; the "unfortunate lad" died for the lack of "salts and pills of white mercury." Barry (*JAFL* 24, 1911, p. 341) regards it as a communal re-creation of "The Unfortunate Rake," and traces its relation to an Irish ballad of 1790 (*JAFL* 25, 1912, p. 277). For other British references see Barrett (*English Folk-Songs*, 1891, No. 19), Baring-Gould and Sheppard (*A Garland of Country Song*, 1895, p. 39), and Sharp (*One Hundred English Folksongs*, 1916, No. 83). American texts are reported by Lomax (*Cowboy Songs*, 1910, p. 74), Belden (*Song-Ballads and Other Popular Poetry*, 1910, No. 68), Perrow (*JAFL* 25, 1912, p. 153), Shearin and Combs (*Syllabus of Kentucky Folk-Songs*, 1911, p. 15), Pound (*JAFL* 26, 1913, p. 356), Jones (*Folk-Lore in Michigan*, 1914, p. 4), Thorp (*Songs of the Cowboys*, 1921, p. 41), Combs (*Folk-Songs du Midi des Etats-Unis*, 1925, pp. 209-210), Cox (*Folk-Songs of the South*, 1925, p. 242), Sandburg (*American Songbag*, 1927, p. 263), Kincaid (*My Favorite Mountain Ballads*, 1928, p. 40), Larkin (*Singing Cowboy*, 1931, pp. 13-15), Eddy (*Ballads and Songs from Ohio*, 1939, pp. 283-284), and Gardner (*Ballads and Songs of Southern Michigan*, 1939, p. 252). Compare the phonograph records by Bradley Kincaid (*Supertone* 9404), Ewen Hall (*Brunswick* 141), and others (*Columbia* 15463-D).

A

Sung by Mr. Jim Fitzhugh, Sylamore, Ark., Sept. 9, 1919.

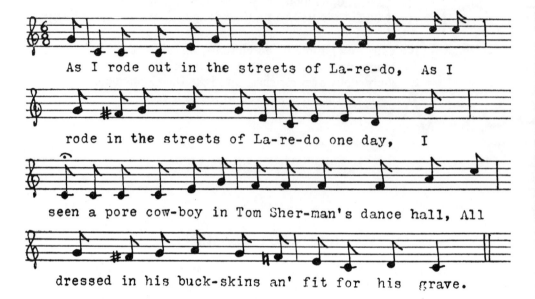

As I rode out in the streets of La-re-do,   As I
rode in the streets of La-re-do one day,   I
seen a pore cow-boy in Tom Sher-man's dance hall, All
dressed in his buck-skins an' fit for   his   grave.

Oh once in the saddle I used to go dashin',
An' once in the saddle I used to go gay,
But I first took to drinkin' an' then to card-playin',
An' then I got shot so I'm dyin' today.

I once had a mother, a gray-haired old mother,
She rocked me to sleep an' she sung me this song,
An' there was another more dear than a mother,
She never will know where her cowboy has gone.

Go gather around me a bunch of young cowboys,
An' tell 'em the tale of a cowboy's sad fate,
An' warn' em all gently to quit their wild rovin',
To quit their wild rovin' before it's too late.

My friends an' relations they live in the Nation,
They never will know where their cowboy has gone,
I first went to Texas an' . . . .
I'm just a pore cowboy, I know I done wrong.

Then beat your drum slowly an' play your fife lowly,
Get six of them gamblers to carry me along,
An' in the grave throw me an' roll some rocks o'er me,
I'm just a pore cowboy, I know I done wrong.

B

Contributed by Mrs. Albert King, Clarksville, Ark., July 12, 1927.

My lasso I used to throw to perfection,
A-ropin' wild cattle for me was great fun,
At punchin' I always have give satisfaction
With a bunch of wild cowboys, but now I am done.

Oh break the news softly to my gray-haired mother,
Break it as softly to my sister dear,
An' nary a word of this place do you mention
When they all gather round you my story to hear.

An' then there's another more dear than a sister,
Oh how she will weep when she hears I am gone,
But there'll be another to gain her affection,
I'm just a wild cowboy, an' I know I done wrong.

Oh go out an' get me a glass of cold water
To cool my hot temples, the cowboy he said,
But when I returned he had gone to his maker,
The once handsome cowboy lay senseless an' dead.

C

A text from Mrs. Joe Pointer, Cabool, Mo., Mar. 22, 1940, is identical except for the first stanza:

As I went a-riding by Tom Sherman's barroom,
By Tom Sherman's barroom one morning in May,
I spied a young cowboy dressed up in white garments,
Dressed up in white garments as though for the grave.

183

THE DYING CALIFORNIAN

This song was published by the Ditson Company of Boston, copyright 1855, and was evidently current several years earlier. It was circulated in many cheap songbooks (Kittredge, *JAFL* 35, 1922, p. 365), and H. A. Franz included it in his *American Popular Songs* (Berlin, 1867, p. 15). Pound (*American Ballads and Songs*, 1922, No. 90) prints a text which goes back to 1856, and remarks (*JAFL* 26, 1913, p. 359) that it is evidently modelled after William Haines Lytle's poem which begins "I am dying, Egypt, dying." Kittredge writes me (June 17, 1931) that "The Dying Californian" was printed in a newspaper (*The New England Diadem*, Providence, R. I., Feb. 9, 1850) as: "Lines suggested on hearing read an extract of a letter from Capt. Chase, concerning the dying words of Brown Owen, who recently died on his passage to California." Since the poem is headed "For the New England Diadem," Professor Kittredge supposes that this is its first publication. . . . An old manuscript copy owned by Mrs. O. A. Loomis, Pea Ridge, Ark., has this note pencilled upon the margin: "Written by Miss Kate Harris of Pascoag, R. I., now Mrs. Charles Plass of Napa City, Calif. It was suggested by hearing a letter which was dictated by Brown Owens, dying on his way to California. The song was sung at his funeral services at Chepaelet, R. I." For other texts and references see Tolman and Eddy (*JAFL* 35, 1922, p. 364), Hudson (*Specimens of Mississippi Folk-Lore,* 1928, No. 60), Greenleaf (*Ballads and Sea Songs from Newfoundland,* 1933, p. 359), Jackson (*Spiritual Folk-Songs of Early America,* 1937, pp. 37-38), and Eddy (*Ballads and Songs from Ohio,* 1939, pp. 286-287). Thomas and Leeder (*Singin' Gatherin',* 1939, pp. 28-29) print a Kentucky variant entitled "The Dying Knight's Farewell" with the headnote: "It is said that Queen Elizabeth forbade the singing of this ballad as it is claimed to have been written about her." Belden (*Ballads and Songs,* 1940, pp. 350-351) reports a good seven-stanza text from Missouri, and remarks that the song was printed in the 1859 edition of the *Sacred Harp,* where it is attributed to Ball and Drinkard. The song is also mentioned in McCollum and Porter's description of riddles, games, and songs in Iowa, 1873-1880 (*JAFL* 56, 1943, p. 106).

Sung by Mrs. L. A. Thomas, Anderson, Mo., Dec. 14, 1926.

I am dy-in', bro-ther, dy-in', Soon you'll miss me in your berth, For my frame will soon be ly------in' 'Neath th' o-cean's bri-ny surf.

Lay up nearer, brother, nearer,
For my limbs are growin' cold,
An' thy presence seemeth dearer
When thy arms about me fold.

Hearken to me, brother, hearken,
I have something I could say,
E'er the veil my vision darkens
An' I go from hence away.

I am goin', surely goin',
But my hope in God is strong,
I am willin' brother, knowin'
That He doeth nothin' wrong.

Tell my father when you greet him
That in death I prayed for him,
Prayed that one day I might meet him
In a world that's freed from sin.

Tell my mother, God assist her,
Now that she is growin' old,
Say her child would glad have kissed her
When his lips grew pale an' cold.

Listen, brother, catch each whisper,
It's my wife I speak of now,
Tell, oh tell her how I missed her
When the fever burned my brow.

Tell her, brother, closely listen,
Don't forget a single word,
That in death my eyes did glisten
When the tears her memory stirred.

Tell her she must kiss my children,
Like the kiss I last impressed,
Hold 'em close as when I held 'em
Folded closely to my breast.

Give 'em early to their Maker,
Puttin' all her trust in God,
An' He never will forsake her
For He's said so in His Word.

Oh my children, Heaven bless 'em,
They was all my life to me,
Wish I could once more caress 'em,
E'er I sink beneath the sea.

'Twas for them I crossed the ocean,
What my hopes was I'll not tell,
But I've gained an orphan's portion,
Yet He doeth all things well.

Tell my sister I remember
Every kindly partin' word,
An' my heart has been left tender
At the thoughts thy memory stirred.

Tell my sister that I never
Found the store of precious dust,
But I found a place called Heaven
Where the gold will never rust.

Urge all to secure an entrance,
For they'll find their brother there,
|Faith in Jesus an' repentance
Will secure for each a share.

Hark I hear my Savior callin',
Yes, I know His voice so well,
When I'm gone don't be a-weepin',
Brother, here's my last farewell.

184

OH BURY ME NOT ON THE LONE PRAIRIE

Most collectors regard this piece as an adaptation of "The Ocean Burial," an old song still current in rural West Virginia, according to Cox (*Folk-Songs of the South*, 1925, p. 250). The words of "The Ocean Burial" were written by W. H. Saunders (Pound, *Poetic Origins and the Ballad*, 1921, p. 207, *n.* 11), and the music copyrighted by George N. Allen in 1850 (*Shilling Song Book*, Boston, 1860, p. 126). Dr. H. M. Belden has left copy of his headnote to this song which will appear in the forthcoming Brown collection of North Carolina folksongs: "It now seems clear that this is the work, not of Capt. Wm. H. Saunders of the U. S. Army but, as Barry long ago suggested, of the Rev. E. H. Chapin: for it is printed under his name in the *Southern Literary Messenger* V, 615-6 (the number for September, 1839) at a date some years earlier than that assigned by Saunders' brother for Saunders' composition of it." . . . Thorp (*Songs of the Cowboys*, 1921, p. 62) claims that "Oh Bury Me Not on the Lone Prairie" was authored by H. Clemons, of Deadwood, S. D., in 1872. . . . Mr. Ed Stephens, Jane, Mo., tells me that the song was "made up" by Venice and Sam Gentry, who herded cattle for Alf Dry near Pilot Grove, Texas, in the 70's. . . Newton Gaines (*Texas Folk-Lore Society Publications* 7, 1928, p. 146) thinks that the tune is "imitative of the night noises of the prairie, the yelp of the coyote bearing the burden." . . . Other texts are reported by Belden (*Song-Ballads and Other Popular Poetry*, 1910, No. 67), Lomax (*Cowboy Songs*, 1910, p. 3), Barry (*JAFL* 25, 1912, p. 278), Pound (*American Ballads and Songs*, 1922, No. 78), Sandburg (*American Songbag*, 1927, p. 20), and Larkin (*Singing Cowboy*, 1931, pp. 21-23). For further information about the antecedents of this piece see Belden's headnote (*Ballads and Songs*, 1940, pp. 387-392). It appears also in the Brown (North Carolina Folk-Lore Society) collection.

A

Sung by Mrs. Lee Stephens, White Rock, Mo., Dec. 12, 1926.

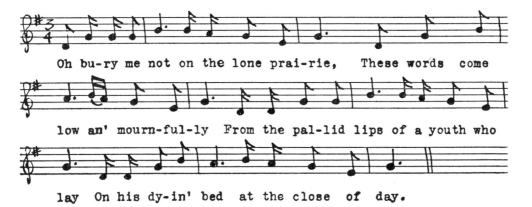

Oh bu-ry me not on the lone prai-rie, These words come
low an' mourn-ful-ly From the pal-lid lips of a youth who
lay On his dy-in' bed at the close of day.

He had wailed in pain till o'er his brow,
Death's shadows fast was gatherin' now,
He had thought of his home an' his loved ones nigh,
As the cowboys gathered to see him die.

Oh bury me not on the lone prairie,
Where the coyotes will howl over me,
In a narrow grave just six by three,
Oh bury me not on the lone prairie.

In fancy I hear the well known words
Of the free wild winds an' the song of birds,
I think of the home in the cottage bower,
An' the scenes I knew in my childhood's hour.

It matters not, I've oft been told,
Where the body lays when the heart is cold,
Yet grant, oh grant this wish to me,
An' bury me not on the lone prairie.

I've always wished to be laid when I died,
In a little church-yard on a green hillside,
By my father's grave there let mine be,
An' bury me not on the lone prairie.

There is another, whose tears may be shed
For her boy who lays in a prairie bed,
It pained me then an' it pains me now,
She has curled these locks an' kissed this brow.

These locks she has curled, shall the rattlesnake kiss?
This brow she has kissed, shall the cold grave press?
For the sake of the loved one that'll weep for me,
Oh bury me not on the lone prairie.

Oh bury me not—an' his voice failed there,
But we took no heed to his dyin' prayer,
In a narrow grave just six by three
We buried him there on the lone prairie.

Yes, we buried him there on the lone prairie,
Where the owl all night hoots mournfully,
An' the buzzard beats an' the wind blows free
O'er the lonely grave on the lone prairie.

B

Contributed by Miss Myrtle Lain, Linn Creek, Mo., Feb. 7, 1929. Miss Lain's father
learned the song in Camden County, Mo., about 1880.

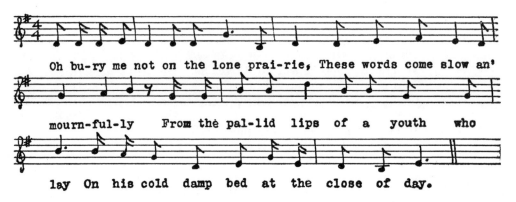

Oh bu-ry me not on the lone prai-rie, These words come slow an'
mourn-ful-ly   From the pal-lid lips of a youth who
lay On his cold damp bed at the close of day.

He had wasted an' pined till o'er his brow,
Death's shades was slowly gatherin' now,
He thought of his home an' his loved ones nigh
As the cowboys gathered to see him die.

Again he listened to the well known words,
To the wind's soft sigh an' the song of birds,
He thought of his home an' his native bowers
Where he loved to roam in his childhood hours.

I've ever wished that when I died
My grave might be on the old hillside,
Let there the place of my last rest be,
Oh bury me not on the lone prairie.

O'er my slumbers deep a mother's prayers,
An' a sister's tears will be mingled there,
Oh it's hard to know that the heart throb's o'er
An' that its fountain will gush no more.

In my dream I saw—but his voice failed there,
An' they gave no heed to his dyin' prayer,
In a shallow grave just six by three
They buried him there on the lone prairie.

May the light-winged butterfly pause to rest
O'er him who sleeps on the prairie's crest,
May the Texas rose in the breezes wave,
O'er him who sleeps in a prairie grave.

An' the cowboys now, as they roam the plain,
For they marked the spot where his bones was lain,
Fling a handful of roses o'er his grave
With a prayer to him who his soul did save.

185

ONE NIGHT AS I LAY ON THE PRAIRIE

Evidently based upon the familiar hymn "In the Sweet Bye and Bye," this piece is of comparatively recent origin. John White (*Cowboy Poet*, Westfield, N. J., 1934, p. 10) claims the authorship for D. J. O'Malley, who says it was written in the middle 80's and first published in the *Stock Grower's Journal* under the title "Sweet Bye and Bye Revised." White also quotes Will C. Barnes, who heard a half-breed Indian sing four stanzas on the Hash Knife range of northern Arizona, in 1886 or 1887. Fred Sutton (Kansas City *Journal-Post*, Feb. 2, 1930) remembers that drunken cowpokes sang a similar song in Jim East's saloon, Tacosa, Texas, as long ago as 1877. Thorp (*Songs of the Cowboys*, 1921, p. 40) thinks that the song was "written by the father of Captain Roberts, of the Texas Rangers"—presumably in the 80's. For other texts and references see Lomax (*Cowboy Songs*, 1910, p. 18), Pound (*American Ballads and Songs*, 1922, p. 166), Finger (*Frontier Ballads*, 1927, p. 101), Larkin (*Singing Cowboy*, 1931, pp. 99-102). Also the text recovered by Dobie (*Texas Folk-Lore Society Publications* 6, 1927, pp. 167-168) and reprinted by Lomax (*American Ballads and Folk Songs*, 1934, pp. 410-411). Hudson (*Folksongs of Mississippi*, 1936, p. 227) reports a Mississippi version under the title "Cowboy Meditations."

A

Sung by Mr. Ray Burleson, Camp Pike, Ark., Dec. 21, 1917.

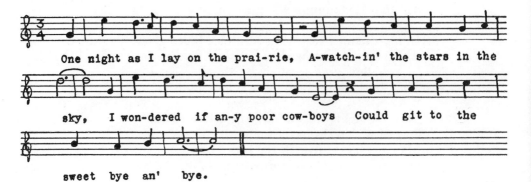

One night as I lay on the prai-rie, A-watch-in' the stars in the
sky, I won-dered if an-y poor cow-boys Could git to the
sweet bye an' bye.

The trail to that mystical country
Is a narrow dim track so they say,
But the road that goes down to perdition
It's blazed, marked an' staked all the way.

They say that there'll be a big round-up,
An' punchers like dogies will stand,
Cut out by them riders in heaven,
That's posted an' savvies each brand.

A cowboy had ought to live decent
An' fixed for that big judgment day,
So he can say to the Boss of the riders,
I'm ready to go any day.

They say that the Boss knows his business,
He watches each break that you've took,
So for safety you better git branded,
An' your name in that big Tally Book.

B

From a manuscript copy belonging to Mr. Clarence Price, Little Rock, Ark., July 12, 1938.   Mr. Price called it "The Cowboy's Dream."

Last night as I lay on the prairie
And looked at the stars in the sky,
I wondered if ever a cowboy
Would drift to that sweet bye and bye.
The road to that bright happy region
Is a dim narrow trail so they say,
But the broad one that leads to perdition
Is posted and blazed all the way.

Chorus

Roll on, roll on, roll on little dogies, roll on, roll on.
Roll on, roll on, roll on little dogies, roll on.

They tell me there'll be a great round-up,
The cowboys like dogies will stand,
To be cut by the Riders of Heaven
Who are posted and know every brand,
I'm scared that I'll be a stray yearling,
A maverick unbranded on high,
And get cut in the bunch with the rusties
When the Boss of all riders goes by.

I know there'll be many a stray cowboy
Get lost at the great final sale,
When he might have gone into green pasture
If he hadn't missed that dim narrow trail.
But then like the cows that are locoed,
Stampede at the sight of a hand,
And are dragged with a rope to the round-up,
Or get marked with some crooked man's brand.

They tell of another big owner
Who's ne'er o'er-stocked, so they say,
But always makes room for the sinner
Who drifts from the straight narrow way.
They say he will never forget you,
That he knows every action and look,
So for safety you'd better get branded,
Get your name in the Big Tally Book.

186

STARVING TO DEATH ON A GOVERNMENT CLAIM

Lomax (*Cowboy Songs*, 1910, p. 278) reports a version of this piece entitled "Greer County." Pound (*American Ballads and Songs*, 1922, p. 178) has fourteen stanzas of a similar song from South Dakota. Sandburg (*American Songbag*, 1927, p. 120) calls his text "The Lane County Bachelor." Comb's version (*Folk-Songs from the Kentucky Highlands*, 1939, pp. 32-33) is called "The Government Claim."

Sung by Mr. C. C. Bayer, Little Rock, Ark., Dec. 2, 1917. Mr. Bayer learned the song from a family named Lampson, who lived near Fayetteville, Ark.

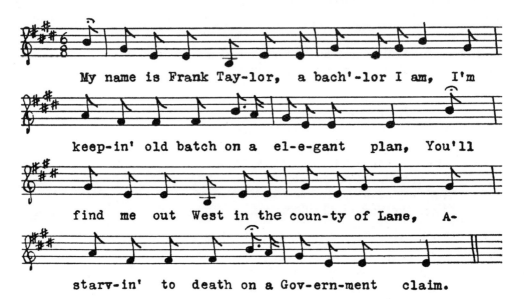

My name is Frank Tay-lor, a bach'-lor I am, I'm keep-in' old batch on a el-e-gant plan, You'll find me out West in the coun-ty of Lane, A-starv-in' to death on a Gov-ern-ment claim.

Hurrah for Lane county, the land of the free,
The home of the bedbug, grasshopper an' flea,
I'll sing of its praises an' boast of its fame
A-starvin' to death on a Government claim.

My clothes they are ragged, my language is rough,
My bread is case-hardened an' solid an' tough,
But I have a good time an' I live at my ease
On common sop-sorghum an' old bacon grease.

How happy I am when I crawl into bed,
With rattlesnakes rattlin' just under my head,
An' the gay little bedbug, so cheerful an' bright,
He keeps me a-goin' two-thirds of the night.

How happy I am on my Government claim,
I've nothin' to lose an' I've nothin' to gain,
I've nothin' to eat an' I've nothin' to wear,
An' nothin' from nothin' is honest an' fair.

Oh come to Lane county, there's room for you all
Where the wind never stops an' the rains never fall,
Oh j'ine in the chorus an' sing of her fame,
A-starvin' to death on a Government claim.

Oh don't be down-hearted, you pore hungry men,
We're all just as free as the pigs in the pen,
Just stick to your homestead an' fight with your fleas,
An' pray to your Maker to send some more breeze.

Now all you pore sinners, I hope you will stay
An' chaw on your hardtack till you're toothless an' gray,
But as for myself I don't aim to remain
An' slave like a dog on no Government claim.

Farewell to Lane county, the pride of the West,
I'm goin' back East to the gal I love best,
I'll stop in Missouri an' get me a wife,
An' live on corn dodgers the rest of my life.

187

JOE BOWERS

This piece was popular with freighters in the days of the California gold rush. There were so many verses that some bull-whackers professed to sing "Joe Bowers" all the way from Fort Leavenworth to the Rockies without a repetition, according to Sabin (*Buffalo Bill and the Overland Trail*, 1914, p. 233). The authorship of this song has been much disputed. "It has been credited," says Dolph (*"Sound Off,"* 1929, p. 314), "to Mark Twain, to a miner known as Squibob, to John Woodward, who was with a minstrel-show in Frisco in 1849, and to a man named English. . . . Then there is the story that the original ballad was written by an unknown Missourian in Colonel Doniphan's Expedition to Mexico, and carried to California by soldiers of Kearney's command." R. J. Hawkins, in 1909, (*Missouri Historical Review* 24, Oct. 1929, pp. 135-137) claimed that Joe Bowers and Sally Black really lived in Pike County, Mo., in the 40's, and that the song was written in 1849 by Frank Swift, afterwards governor of California. For further information about the origin of "Joe Bowers" see the *Life of Bret Harte*, by Henry Charles Merwin (New York, 1911, p. 59), Lomax (*American Ballads and Folk Songs*, 1934, pp. 421-423), Pound (*Southern Folklore Quarterly* 1, Sept. 1937, pp. 13-15), Belden (*Ballads and Songs*, 1940, pp. 341-343), and an article "In Honor of Joe Bowers," *Missouri Historical Review* 36, Jan. 1942, pp. 204-208.

Similar texts have been reported by Belden (*Song-Ballads and Other Popular Poetry*, 1910, No. 63), Lomax (*Cowboy Songs*, 1910, p. 15), Shearin and Combs (*Syllabus of Kentucky Folk-Songs*, 1911, p. 32), Shoemaker (*North Pennsylvania Minstrelsy*, 1919, p. 39), Pound (*American Ballads and Songs*, 1922, p. 186), Cox (*Folk-Songs of the South*, 1925, p. 234), and Shay (*Drawn from the Wood*, 1929, p. 133). The piece appears in the Brown (North Carolina Folk-Lore Society) collection.

A

Sung by Mr. H. F. Walker, Joplin, Mo., Sept. 11, 1913.

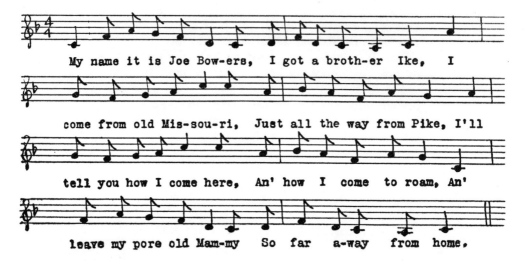

My name it is Joe Bow-ers, I got a broth-er Ike, I come from old Mis-sou-ri, Just all the way from Pike, I'll tell you how I come here, An' how I come to roam, An' leave my pore old Mam-my So far a-way from home.

I used to court a gal back home, her name was Sally Black,
I ask her if she'd marry me, she says it is a whack,
Oh Sally, dearest Sally, oh Sally, for your sake
I'll go to Californy an' try to git a stake.

When I come to this country I hadn't nary red,
I got so God damned hungry I wished that I was dead,
An' so I took to minin', put in my biggest licks,
I come down on them boulders like a hundred thousan' bricks.

One day I git a letter from my dear brother Ike,
It come from old Missouri, an' all the way from Pike,
It was the damndest letter a body ever see,
My heart it was a-bustin', an' it like to ruint me.

It said my gal had done me dirt, her love for me had went,
She married a red-head butcher an' he wasn't worth a cent,
An' more'n that, the letter says, which made me cuss an' swear,
That Sally had a baby, an' the baby had red hair.

B

Mr. J. W. Booker, Carterville, Mo., Nov. 16, 1930, showed me a similar text which contains an additional stanza:

> She says to me, Joe Bowers, before we hitch for life,
> You better get a little farm to keep your little wife,
> She says to me, Joe Bowers, you are the man to win,
> Here's a kiss to bind the bargain, and she throwed a dozen in.

C

As sung by Mr. W. F. Detherow, Batesville, Ark., June 2, 1940.

> My name it is Joe Bowers, I have a brother Ike,
> I came from old Missouri, yes, all the way from Pike,
> I'll tell you why I left there, and how I came to roam,
> To leave my dear old mammy, so far away from home.
>
> I used to love a gal there, her name was Sally Black,
> I asked her to marry me, she said it was a whack.
> Says she to me, Joe Bowers, before we hitch for life,
> You ought to have a little home to keep your little wife.
>
> Say I, my dearest Sally, oh Sally, for your sake
> I will go to California and try to raise a stake.
> Says she to me, Joe Bowers, you are the man to win,
> Give me a kiss to seal the bargain. And I throwed a dozen in.
>
> I will never forget my feelin's when I bid adieu to all,
> Sal she kotched me round the neck and I began to bawl.
> When I set in they all commenced, you never heard the like,
> The way they all took on and cried the day I left old Pike.
>
> When I got to this here country, I hadn't nary a red,
> I had such wolfish feelin's I wished myself most dead,
> At length I went to mining, put in my heaviest licks,
> Came down on them boulders just like a thousand bricks.
>
> I worked both late and early through rain, hail and snow,
> I was working for my Sally and it was all the same to Joe,
> I made a very lucky strike, as the gold itself did tell,
> For I was working for Sally, the girl I loved so well.
>
> But one day I got a letter from my kind dear brother Ike,
> It come from old Missouri, yes, all the way from Pike,
> It told me the golderndest news that ever you did hear,
> My heart it is a-bursting, so pray excuse this tear.

It said my Sally was fickle, her love for me had fled,
That she had married a butcher whose hair was awful red,
It told me more than that, it's enough to make me swear,
It said Sally had a baby and the baby had red hair.

D

Sung by Mr. Charles Ingenthron, Walnut Shade, Mo., Sept. 4, 1941. This is one of Mr. Ingenthron's favorite pieces, which he sang at entertainments in the early 1900's. He tells me that it is a *true song* written by Joe Bowers himself, and that Bowers became so famous that he had the finest tombstone in Missouri at that time! Mr. Ingenthron sings it to the same tune he uses for "Lily of the West" and "Young Caroline of Edinborough Town."

My name it is Joe Bow-ers, I have a broth-er Ike, I came from
old Mis- sour- ri, Yes, all the way from Pike, I'll tell you
why I left there And how I came to roam, And leave my
dear old moth-er So far a-way from home.

I used to court a girl there,
Her name was Sally Black,
I axed her if she'd marry me,
She said it was a whack.
But she says to me, Joe Bowers,
Before we hitch for life,
You ought to have a little home
To take your little wife.

Oh Sally, oh Sally,
Oh Sally, for your sake
I'll go to Californy
And try to raise a stake.
Says she to me, Joe Bowers,
You are the man to win,
Here's a kiss to bind the bargain,
And she hove a dozen in.

When I got to that country
I hadn't nary red,
I had such wolfish feelings
I wished myself most dead.
But the thoughts of my dear Sally
Soon made those feelings git,
And whispering hopes to Bowers,
I wish I had them yet.

At length I went to minin',
Put in my biggest licks,
Went down upon the boulders
Just like a thousand bricks.
I worked both late and early
In rain and sleet and snow,
I was working for my Sally,
'Twas all the same to Joe.

At length I got a letter
From my dear brother Ike,
It come from old Missouri,
Yes, all the way from Pike.
It brought to me the darndest news
That ever you did hear,
My heart was almost busted,
So please excuse this tear.

It said that Sal was false to me,
Her love for me had fled,
Said she'd got married to a butcher,
And the butcher's hair was red.
And more than that the letter said,
'Twas enough to make me swear,
Said Sally had a baby
And the baby had red hair.

188

THE DYING COWBOY

Apparently a Western adaptation of another old song called "The Dying Soldier," the chief difference being that the central figure here is a Texan instead of a New Englander, who leaves home to fight Indians instead of the "traitors"—which doubtless means Confederates in the original song. Lomax (*Cowboy Songs*, 1910, p. 214) reports a very similar piece from the Southwest. See also the "Dying Woodsman" song copyrighted by W. D. Patton (*The Sunny South Quartet Book*, Dalton, Ga., 1912, No. 25). Cox (*Folk-Songs of the South*, 1925, p. 263) prints an incomplete text from West Virginia, and Finger (*Frontier Ballads*, 1927, p. 170) has one called "The Dying Ranger." Compare the "Dying Cowboy" song reported by Belden (*Ballads and Songs*, 1940, pp. 397-398). See also the Brown (North Carolina Folk-Lore Society) collection.

A

Sung by Mr. Willie C. Underwood, Jane, Mo., July 23, 1928.

The sun was set-tin' in the West, it fell with a ling'-rin' ray, Be-neath the shade of the for-est where a dy-in' cow-boy lay, Be-neath the tall palm-et-to, be-neath the sul-try sky, A-way from his loved old Tex-as we laid him down to die.

A group had gathered round him, all comrades in a fright,
The tears rolled down each manly cheek as he said his last goodnight,
Up spoke the dyin' cowboy, sayin' do not weep for me,
I'm crossin' a dark deep river to a country that is free.

Draw nearer to me, comrades, an' listen to what I say,
I'm goin' to tell a story before I pass away,
Way up in northwest Texas, that good old Lone Star state,
There's one who for my comin' with a weary heart will wait.

I have a darlin' sister, she's all my joy an' pride,
I loved her from her childhood for I had none else beside,
I've loved her as a brother, an' with a brother's care
I've tried through grief an' sorrow her gentle heart to cheer.

Our country was invaded, they called for volunteers,
She throwed her arms around my neck, regardless of all fears,
Sayin' go my darlin' brother, drive them Indians from our doors,
Our hearthstone needs your presence but our country needs it more.

'Tis true I loved my country, I've give to it my all,
If it was not for my sister I would be content to fall,
Oh comrades, I am dyin', she'll never see me more,
She vainly waits my comin' at the little cottage door.

My mother she lies sleepin' beneath the church-yard sod,
An' many a day has passed away since her spirit fled to God,
My father lies a-sleepin' beneath the dark blue sea,
I have no other kindred, there's none but Nell an' me.

Draw nearer to me, comrades, an' listen to my dyin' prayer,
Who'll be to her a brother, an' shield her with his care?
Up spoke the brave young cowboys, in chorus one an' all,
We'll be to her a brother, till the strongest one shall fall.

Then one bright smile of pleasure on the pore boy's face was spread,
One quick convulsive shudder, an' the cowboy he was dead.
Far away from his darlin' sister they laid him down to rest
With a saddle for his pillow an' his rifle on his breast.

B

Sung by Mr. J. E. Dethrow, Springfield, Mo., Apr. 27, 1938. Mr. Dethrow says that the cowboy in this song was killed in Geronimo's uprising [1885], and that he himself heard the song only a few months later.

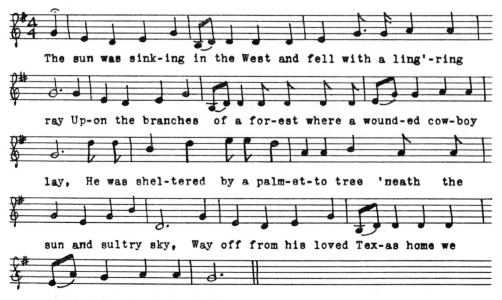

The sun was sink-ing in the West and fell with a ling'-ring ray Up-on the branches of a for-est where a wound-ed cow-boy lay, He was shel-tered by a palm-et-to tree 'neath the sun and sultry sky, Way off from his loved Tex-as home we laid him down to die.

A troop was gathered round him, his comrades in the fight,
The tears come trinking down his cheeks, as he bade his last goodnight,
One friend and loved companion was kneeling by his side,
Trying to stop his life's blood flowing, but alas in vain he tried.

His heart was filled with anguish when he found it was in vain,
Upon his loved companion the tears poured down like rain,
Up spoke the dying cowboy, oh weep no more for me,
For I am crossing a valley where all have passage free.

Oh comrades, gather round me and listen to what I say,
I'll tell you a sad story as my spirit passes away,
Way off in loved old Texas, that good old Lone Star State,
There's one that will wait my coming, with a heavy heart she'll wait.

A fair young girl is my sister she is my joy and pride,
I've loved her through her childhood, I've loved none else beside,
I've loved her as a brother, and with a brother's care
I've tried through grief and sorrow her gentle heart to cheer.

When our country was in danger and called for volunteers,
She threw her arms around me, regardless of all fears,
Saying oh my darling brother, drive the Indians from our door,
My heart may need your presence but our country needs you more.

Oh Nellie, darling sister, I'll see you here no more,
But I'll wait for you in heaven, over on the golden shore,
With a saddle for a pillow and a gun across his breast,
Way off from his loved old Texas home we laid him down to rest.

189

A FAIR LADY OF THE PLAINS

A similar song appears in B. E. Denton's novel *A Two-Gun Cyclone* (Dallas, Tex., 1927, p. 142), and Henry (*JAFL* 45, 1932, p. 153) reports a variant from Georgia. One of my Missouri texts, published in the *Arcadian Magazine* (Eminence, Mo., June 1930, p. 30), is reprinted in Margaret Larkin's *Singing Cowboy* (1931, pp. 147-149). Compare also "The Death of a Maiden Fair" reported by Henry (*Folk-Songs from the Southern Highlands*, 1938, pp. 358-359).

A

Contributed by Miss Myrtle Lain, Linn Creek, Mo., June 4, 1929. Miss Lain says that the song was introduced into her section of the Ozarks by members of the Thomas and Waisnor families, and was supposedly an old song in 1893.

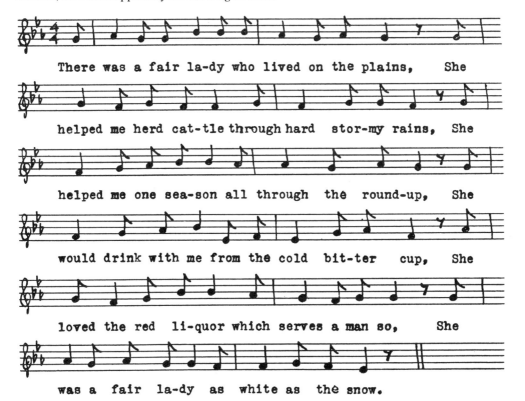

There was a fair la-dy who lived on the plains,   She
helped me herd cat-tle through hard stor-my rains,   She
helped me one sea-son all through the round-up,   She
would drink with me from the cold bit-ter cup,   She
loved the red li-quor which serves a man so,   She
was a fair la-dy as white as the snow.

She loved the red liquor which serves a man so,
She was a fair lady as white as the snow,
I taught her as a cowboy when the rangers come round,
To use a six-shooter in both of her hands,
To use a six-shooter an' never to run
As long as the loads lasted in either gun.

We was goin' down the canyon in the Spring one year,
To camp there a season with a herd of wild steers,
The Injuns charged on us at the dead hour of the night,
We rose from our slumber the battle for to fight.
Mid lightnin' an' thunder an' the downpour of rain,
It's in come a bullet an' dashed out her brains!

Mid lightnin' an' thunder an' the downpour of rain,
It's in come a bullet an' dashed out her brains.
I sprung to my saddle with a gun in each hand,
Sayin' come all you cowboys, let's fight for our band,
Sayin' come all you cowboys, let's fight for out life,
These redskins has murdered my darlin' young wife.

B

Sung by Miss Pauline McCullough, Blue Eye, Mo., Apr. 19, 1934. Miss McCullough
learned the song from her grandmother, who called it "The Cowgirl."

I come to this country to tarry a while,
Leaving all of my people, ten thousand long miles.
It's raining and hailing and the stars give no light,
Oh how can I travel this dark lonesome night.

Go put up your horses and feed them some hay,
And come and sit by me, as long as you may.
My horses aint hungry, they won't eat your hay,
I'm goin' to old Georgia, and I'll feed on my way.

I once knew a maiden who lived on the plains,
She helped me herd cattle through hard stormy rains,
She helped me herd cattle one whole year's round-up,
And drank the red liquor from a forbidding cup.

I taught her the cow trails and the Union command,
To use a six-shooter in each of her hands,
To use a six-shooter and never to run
While she had a bullet and the use of her gun.

She helped me herd cattle through hard beating rains,
Till in come a bullet and flushed out her brains,
One more word I'll tell you as I bid you goodbye,
Come all you brave cowboys, I'm here till I die.

C

Miss Miriam Lynch, Notch, Mo., Sept. 12, 1934, showed me a manuscript book containing the following text under the title "The Fair Maid." Miss Lynch told me that she had borrowed the book from Mrs. Linnie Boraker Stevens, a neighbor.

There was a fair maiden, she lived on the plain,
She helped me herd cattle through many a hard rain,
She drinked the red liquor of a ficty man's woe,
She was fair as a lily and sweet as a rose.

I learnt her the trade of a ranger command,
To shoot a six-shooter from either hand,
To shoot a six-shooter and never to run
As long as she had a bullet in either gun.

We went to the mountains in the fall of one year,
To stay there that winter with a herd of steers,
The Indians broke on us in the midst of the night,
We rose from our blankets the battle to fight.

It was thunder and lightning and down come the rain,
In come a strange bullet which dashed out her brains,
I jumped in my saddle with a gun in each hand,
Come all you brave cowboys, we'll fight for our land.

We'll fight for our country, we'll fight for our life,
For the Indians has murdered my dear darling wife,
Bring on your bright rifles, we'll give them hot lead,
Till many a brave Indian around us lies dead.

D

Sung by Mrs. Gladys McCarty, Farmington, Ark., Oct. 24, 1941. She calls it "Old Georgy."

I camped in old Geor-gy, With a herd of thin steers, In-tend-ed to stay here With a herd of thin steers.

The Indians broke in on us
At the dead hours of night,
And she rolled out of her warm bed
Sayin' a battle to fight.

She helt up a six-shooter,
One of each hand,
Clean claps of thunder,
Down fell the rain.

Long come a stray bullet,
Dashed out of her brains,
And he hopped in his saddle
With all of his command.

She fought for her pleasure,
And she fought for her fun,
But she never sees a danger
With a load in her gun.

She holp us herd cattle
One whole round-up,
And she drank that sad liquor
From a cold bitter cup.

E

Sung by Mr. Fred Woodruff, Lincoln, Ark., Dec. 12, 1941.

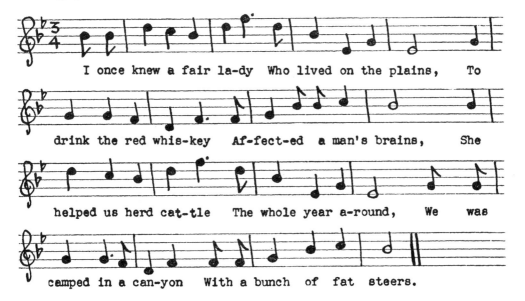

I once knew a fair la-dy Who lived on the plains, To
drink the red whis-key Af-fect-ed a man's brains, She
helped us herd cat-tle The whole year a-round, We was
camped in a can-yon With a bunch of fat steers.

The Indians broke on us
At the dead hours of night,
She arose out of her warm bed
A battle to fight.
She arose out of her warm bed
With a gun in each hand,
Says come on, you brave cowboys,
Let's win this fair land.

Come on you brave cowboys,
Let's do a small part,
For the Indians has murdered
My darling sweetheart.

190

THE WANDERING COWBOY

Dobie (*Texas Folk-Lore Society Publications* 6, 1927, pp. 165-166) reports a very similar piece entitled "Home, Sweet Home." Margaret Larkin (*Singing Cowboy*, 1931, pp. 143-146) prints this item with the remark that "in Texas, the locale of the murderer's confession is Slaughter's Ranch instead of French Ranch." The song is also given by Lomax (*Cowboy Songs*, 1938, pp. 124-125).

A

Sung by Mrs. Lee Stephens, White Rock, Mo., Aug. 4, 1928. Mrs. Stephens learned the song in McDonald County, Mo., about 1899.

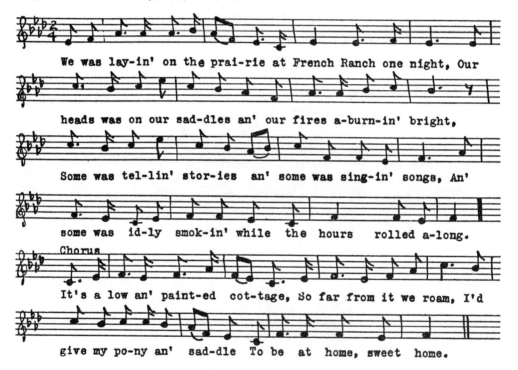

We was lay-in' on the prai-rie at French Ranch one night, Our

heads was on our sad-dles an' our fires a-burn-in' bright,

Some was tel-lin' stor-ies an' some was sing-in' songs, An'

some was id-ly smok-in' while the hours rolled a-long.

Chorus

It's a low an' paint-ed cot-tage, So far from it we roam, I'd

give my po-ny an' sad-dle To be at home, sweet home.

The boy was young an' handsome,
Though his face wore a look of care,
His eyes was the color of heavenly blue
An' he had light wavy hair.
We ask him why he left his home,
If it was so dear to him,
He looked at the ground for a moment,
His eyes with tears was dim.

Then raisin' his head, brushed away a tear,
An' looked the rough crowd o'er,
He says, well boys, I'll tell you
Why I left the Kansas shore.
I fell in love with a neighbor girl.
Her cheeks was soft an' white,
Another feller loved her too,
So it ended in a fight.

But oh, it makes me shudder
For to think of that sad night
When Tom an' me first quarreled
An' I struck him with my knife.
In dreams I still can hear Tom's voice
When he fell to the ground an' said,
Bob, old boy, you'll be sorry
When you see me layin' here dead.

I fell to the ground beside him
An' tried for to stop the blood,
Which was so fastly flowin'
From his side in a crimson flood.
So now you know the reason why
I am compelled to roam,
A murderer of the deepest dye,
So far away from home.

B

Contributed by Miss Maudeva McCord, Springfield, Mo., May 16, 1938. Miss McCord's
text is entitled "The Lone Star Ranger."

We were lying on the prairie
At Frank's low ranch one night,

· · · · · ·

I fell in love with a neighbor girl,
Her cheeks were soft and white,
Another fellow loved her too,
So it ended in a fight.
The other fellow's name was Tommy Smith,
We had been friends since boys,
We'd shared each other's trials in life,
Each other's trials and joys.

I never shall forget that night
When Tommy and I first quarreled,
It was a sad and awful sight,
I stabbed him with my knife.
I went and knelt beside him
And tried to stop the blood,
The blood that flowed from Tommy's side
In a silvery cleansing flood.

Now in my dreams I see Tommy
As he fell to the ground and said:
Bob, old boy, you'll be sorry
When you see me lying dead.
So boys, you know the reason why
I am compelled to roam,
For the murdering of Tommy Smith
I left my home sweet home.

C

Sung by Mrs. Dorothy Freeman, Natural Dam, Ark., Dec. 14, 1941.

While ly-ing on the prai-rie   In a for-eign ranch one night,

Our sad-dles for our pil-lows   The fire was burn-ing bright.

Some were telling stories,
And some were singing songs,
And some were idle smoking
As the hours rolled along.

At last they fell to talking
Of distant friends so dear,
One boy raised his head from his saddle
And brushed away a tear.

Says boys, there's a peaceful cottage,
And far from it I've roamed.
I'd give my pony and saddle
To be this night at home.

This boy was young and handsome
Though he wore bad looks of care,
His eyes were the color of heaven
And he had dark curly hair.

They asked him why he left it
If it was so dear to him,
He raised his head from his saddle,
With tears his eyes grew dim.

He raised his head, brushed back a tear,
And looked the rough crowd o'er,
Says boys, I'll tell you the reason
I've left my native shore.

I fell in love with a neighbor girl
Whose cheeks were soft and white,
Another fellow loved her too
So it ended in a fight.

This fellow's name was Thomas Brown,
We'd been good friends from boys,
Together we had shared alike
Each other's trials and joys.

And oh it makes me shudder
When I think of that sad night,
When Tom and I were quarrelling
And I struck him in the side.

And in my dreams I can hear Tom's voice
As he fell to the ground and said,
Old boy, you will be sorry
When you see me lying dead.

I dropped on my knees beside him
And tried to stop the blood
That was so swiftly flowing
From his side in a crimson flood.

Now boys, you know the reason
That I'm compelled to roam,
I'm a sinner of the deepest,
And far from home, sweet home.

191

TO THE WEST AWHILE TO STAY

The fifth stanza is very much like the seventh verse of "The Texas Rangers" as reported by Lomax (*Cowboy Songs*, New York, 1910, p. 45), but the rest of the song has little in common with the Lomax text.

Sung by Mrs. Isabel Spradley, Van Buren, Ark., May 4, 1929.

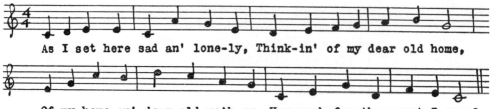

As I set here sad an' lone-ly, Think-in' of my dear old home,

Of my home an' dear old moth-er, How much fur-ther must I roam?

I was once at home an' happy,
Just as happy as could be,
But I took a foolish notion
That a rambler I would be.

Mother was down in her garden
Bendin' o'er her flowers so gay,
When I told her I was goin'
To the West awhile to stay.

Then she throwed her arms around me,
Drawed me closer as she says:
My dear boy, how can you leave me,
Leave the one that loves you best?

Though I thought she was old an' childish,
An' perhaps she did not know,
An' my mind was bent on ramblin',
To the West I was bound to go.

T'other day there come a letter,
It was from my sister May,
An' it told me they had laid her
In the cold an' silent grave.

192

SWEET BETSY FROM PIKE

Lomax (*Cowboy Songs*, 1910, pp. 258-260) has a ten-stanza text which he describes as "a California immigrant song of the fifties." Another Missouri variant is quoted by L. L. McCoy (*Missouri Historical Review* 22, 1928, pp. 363-364). Archer Hulbert (*Forty-Niners*, 1931, p. 790) prints a similar version of this piece, sung to the air of "Vilikens and His Dinah." Compare the fragment reported by Stout (*Folklore from Iowa*, 1936, p. 106). Robertson (*Check List of California Songs*, 1940, p. 48) found it in Put's *Golden Songster*, Appleton and Co., San Francisco, 1858, and Black and Robertson reprinted this text in *The Gold Rush Song Book*, Colt Press, San Francisco, 1940, pp. ix, 10-11, with a tune which Robertson recorded from the singing of John McCready, Groveland, Calif. For more texts and references see Belden (*Ballads and Songs*, 1940, pp. 343-345).

A

Sung by Mrs. May Kennedy McCord, Springfield, Mo., Apr. 27, 1938. Mrs. McCord obtained this particular version from some people in West Plains, Mo.

Oh don't you re-mem-ber sweet Bet-sy from Pike? She crossed the White Moun-tains with her lov-er Ike, With two yoke of cat-tle, a old yal-ler dog, A tall shang-hai roos-ter an' a old spot-ted hog. Sing too-ra-lay, too-ra-lay, too-ra-lay lay, Sing too-ra-lay, too-ra-lay, too-ra-lay lay, Sing too-ra-lay, too-ra-lay, too-ra-lay lay, Sing too-ra-lay, too-ra-lay, too-ra-lay lay.

One evening plumb early they camped on the Platte,
'Twas near by the road on a green shady flat,
When Betsy got tired an' lay down to repose
While Ike stood an' looked at his Pike county rose.

They travelled an' travelled till Betsy give out,
An' down on the ground she was rollin' about,
Then Ike he looked at her with lots of surprise,
Sayin' git up from there, you'll git sand in your eyes.

Sweet Betsy got up with a good deal of pain,
Sayin' she would go back to Pike county again,
But Ike heaved a sigh an' they fondly embraced,
An' they travelled along with his arm round her waist.

The wagon it fell with a mighty loud crash,
An' rolled out some bundles of all sorts of trash,
A little kid's fixin's all wrapped up with care,
You needn't to laugh, for it's all on the square.

                                         B

    Contributed by Mrs. Rose Wilder Lane, Mansfield, Mo., May 26, 1930. Mrs. Lane says
that the song is still well known in Wright and Douglas counties, Mo.

Did you ever hear tell of sweet Bessie from Pike?
She crossed the high mountains with her lover Ike,
With a tall yoke of oxen, and an old yellow dog,
A big shanghai rooster, and an old spotted hog.

They stopped at Salt Lake to enquire the way,
Old Brigham he swore that sweet Bessie should stay,
Sweet Bessie got scared, run away like a deer,
Old Brigham he pawed up the ground like a steer.

                                        193

                          HOME ON THE RANGE

    This piece, under various titles, was known all over the Southwest in the 80's and 90's.
It was printed in many newspapers and cheap songbooks, and one version was copyrighted
by Balmer and Weber in 1905, credited to William and Mary Goodwin. Almost forgotten by
1930, "Home on the Range" was suddenly revived in 1932, and some of the revivers made a
great deal of money. In 1934 Mr. and Mrs. Goodwin filed suit in New York against music
publishers, movie companies and broadcasting chains, claiming half a million dollars damages.
Mr. Samuel Moanfeldt, a defense attorney, established the fact that the verses were written
by Dr. Brewster Higley, of Smith Center, Kan., in 1873. The words have been set to several
different melodies, but the original tune was supplied by Dan Kelley, one of Dr. Higley's
neighbors.

A different story was backed by Sigmund Spaeth, who wrote (*Life* 102, June 1935, p. 23) "it seems to have been proved that the original 'Home on the Range' was . . . written in 1885 by C. O. Swartz, Bill McCabe, Bingham Graves and other prospectors in a cabin near Leadville, Colorado. . . . Swartz probably wrote the tune." The controversy was reviewed in *Frontier Times*, Bandera, Tex., 13, Apr. 1936, pp. 367-368, and has recently been revived: Spaeth (*Rotarian* 67, Nov. 1945, p. 27) gives credit to the late Kenneth S. Clark of Princeton for digging up the story, and prints a page from a letter written by Swartz to his sister, giving the circumstances of composition and the words of the song. The Higley supporters rise up in protest in the January 1946 issue of the *Rotarian*, to which Spaeth retaliates in the February number that he will change his story if documentary evidence of Higley's composition can be produced (either the original or a photostat of the words as they appeared in the *Smith Center Pioneer* in 1874). Homer Croy (*Corn Country*, 1947, pp. 164-180) devotes a whole chapter to the story of "Home on the Range." He interviewed Dr. Higley's son at Shawnee, Okla., where the doctor died in 1911.

"Home on the Range" has been recorded from oral tradition by Cook (*The Border and the Buffalo*, 1907, pp. 292-293), G. F. Will (*JAFL* 22, 1909, pp. 257-258), Lomax (*Cowboy Songs*, 1910, pp. 39-43), Larkin (*Singing Cowboy*, 1931, pp. 171-173). A. B. Macdonald (Kansas City *Star*, Oct. 25, 1936, p. 4) prints seven stanzas of the original text ascribed to Dr. Higley. Spaeth concludes his article (*Rotarian* 67, Nov. 1945, p. 27) by setting down two verses new to him, from a contributor in Huron, South Dakota.

A

Here is a text printed in the *Smith County Pioneer*, Smith Center, Kan., Feb. 19, 1914. The editor, Mr. W. H. Nelson, who had known Dr. Higley in the early days, wrote a brief description of him. The poem was written by Higley in 1873 and published in the *Pioneer* soon after it was written, according to the editor. Dr. Higley called the poem "The Western Home."

> Oh give me a home where the buffalo roam,
> Where the deer and the antelope play,
> Where never is heard a discouraging word
> And the sky is not clouded all day.
>
>> A home, a home,
>> Where the deer and the antelope play,
>> Where never is heard a discouraging word
>> And the sky is not clouded all day.
>
> Oh give me the gale of the Solomon vale,
> Where light streams with buoyancy flow,
> On the banks of the Beaver, where seldom if ever
> Any poisonous herbage doth grow.
>
> Oh, give me a land where the bright diamond sand
> Throws light from its glittering stream,
> Where glideth along the graceful white swan
> Like a maid in her heavenly dream.

I love these wild flowers in this bright land of ours,
I love, too, the curlew's wild scream,
The bluffs of white rocks and antelope flocks
That graze on our hillsides so green.

How often at night when the heavens are bright
By the light of the glittering stars,
Have I stood there amazed and asked as I gazed
If their beauty exceeds this of ours.

The air is so pure, the breezes so light,
The zephyrs so balmy at night,
I would not exchange my home here to range
Forever in azure so bright.

B

From Mrs. May Kennedy McCord, Springfield, Mo., Apr. 26, 1938. Mrs. McCord learned the song in Galena, Mo., in 1899.

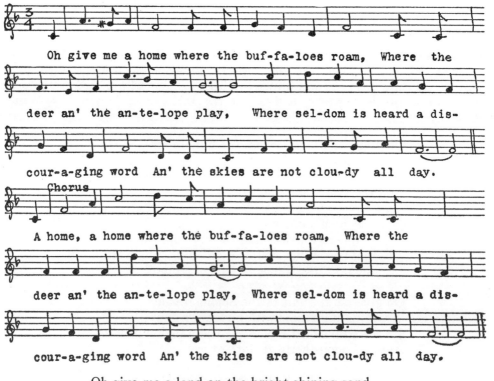

Oh give me a home where the buf-fa-loes roam, Where the deer an' the an-te-lope play, Where sel-dom is heard a dis-cour-a-ging word An' the skies are not clou-dy all day.

Chorus

A home, a home where the buf-fa-loes roam, Where the deer an' the an-te-lope play, Where sel-dom is heard a dis-cour-a-ging word An' the skies are not clou-dy all day.

Oh give me a land on the bright shining sand,
Where the buffalo roams on the plain,
I'll bridle my roan, I'll find me a home,
An' I'll ride in my saddle again.

Oh give me a jail where I can get bail,
Out under the hot shining sun,
I'll wake with the dawn, I'll chase the wild fawn,
I'll ride with my saddle an' gun.

194

THE ROLLING STONE

Similar items have been recorded by Belden (*Song-Ballads and Other Popular Poetry*, 1910, No. 66), Hamlin Garland (*A Son of the Middle Border*, 1917, pp. 43-45, 466), and Tolman and Eddy (*JAFL* 35, 1922, pp. 408-410). Miss Eddy found a manuscript copy in Ohio dated 1852. Compare Belden's headnote (*Ballads and Songs*, 1940, pp. 351-352).

A

Sung by Mr. Ben Rice, Springfield, Mo., Dec. 16, 1936. The melody is supplied by Mrs. Sidney Robertson, who made a phonograph record from Mr. Rice's singing. Mr. Rice called the piece "The Stone That Goes Rolling Will Gather No Moss."

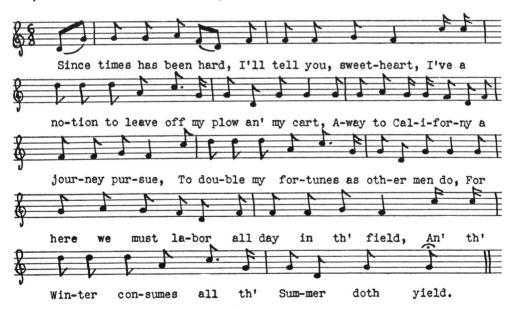

Since times has been hard, I'll tell you, sweet-heart, I've a no-tion to leave off my plow an' my cart, A-way to Cal-i-for-ny a jour-ney pur-sue, To dou-ble my for-tunes as oth-er men do, For here we must la-bor all day in th' field, An' th' Win-ter con-sumes all th' Sum-mer doth yield.

Oh husband, I'll tell you with a sorrowful heart,
You've too long neglected your plow an' your cart,
Your horses, sheep, cattle are scattered around,
An' you use Sunday's jacket most every day on,
But stick to your farm an' you'll suffer no loss,
While the stone that goes rolling will gather no moss.

Oh wife, let's be going, oh don't let us wait,
I long to get there, I long to be great,
. . . .
. . . .
An' you some rich lady, an' who knows but I
May be some great governor before that I die?

Oh husband, remember your land is to clear,
It'll cost you the labor of many a long year,
Your horses, sheep, cattle are all for to buy,
An' you'll hardly get settled before you must die.
So stick to your farm an' you'll suffer no loss,
But the stone that goes rolling will gather no moss.

Oh wife, let's be going, oh don't let us wait,
. . . .
I'll purchase a farm all clear to our hand,
. . . .
Where horses, sheep, cattle are not very dear,
An' we'll feed on fat buffalo one half of the year.

Oh husband, remember your land of delight
Is surrounded by Injuns who murder by night,
Your house they will plunder an' burn to the ground
While your wife an' dear children lay bleedin' around.
Just stick to your farm an' you'll suffer no loss,
While the stone that goes rolling will gather no moss.

Oh wife, you've convinced me, I'll argue no more,
I never once thought of dyin' before,
I love my little children although they're but small,
But you, my dear wife, I love better than all.
I'll stick to my farm an' suffer no loss,
An' the stone that goes rolling will gather no moss.

B

Mrs. Margaret Sharpe, Pineville, Mo., Aug. 7, 1928, sings a variant with the following
lines:

Dear Collins, I've seen with a sorrowful heart,
Long time you've neglected your plow an' your cart,
. . . .
. . . .
Stick close to your home an' prevent every loss,
For a stone while it's rolling can gather no moss.

C

From Mrs. Lillian Short, Cabool, Mo., Aug. 15, 1940.

> Since times are so hard I will tell you, sweetheart,
> I've a mind to lay by my plow and my cart,
> And away to Wisconsin a journey I'd go
> To better my fortune as other folks do.
> While here I might labor each day in the field
> And the winter consume all the summer does yield.
>
> Oh husband, I've noticed with sorrowful heart
> You long have neglected your plow and your cart,
> Your horses, sheep, cattle do everywhere roam,
> And your neat Sunday jacket goes every day on.
> Oh stick to your farming, you'll suffer no loss,
> For the stone that keeps rolling will not gather moss.
>
> Oh wife, let us go! Oh don't let us wait,
> I long to be there, I long to be great.
> Where horses, sheep, cattle are not very dear,
> Where we may lay up ten thousand a year,
> Where we could get rich, and who knows but I
> Might be some great governor before I shall die!
>
> Oh husband, remember your lands of delight
> Are surrounded by Indians that murder by night,
> Your house may be plundered and burnt to the ground,
> And your wife and dear children lay mangled around.
> And then you would think of all of your loss,
> And wish you'd not rolled to gather some moss.
>
> Oh wife, you've convinced me, I will argue no more,
> I never once thought of your dying before,
> I love my dear children, although they are small,
> But I love my dear wifie much more than them all.
> I will stick to my farming, and suffer no loss,
> For the stone that stops rolling will soon gather moss.

D

A fragmentary text from Mrs. Bessie Stutsman, Strafford, Mo., Jan. 7, 1941.

> Oh wife, let us go, don't let us stand,
> I long to go there and I long to be grand,
> And horses, sheep, cattle will not be so dear,
> We'll feast on fat buffalo nine months in the year.
> For here we must labor each day in the field
> And the winters consume all the summers doth yield.

Oh husband, remember that land of delight
Is surrounded by Indians that murder by night,
Your house they will plunder and burn to the ground,
Your wife and your children lay murdered around,
Let us stay on our farm, there we'll suffer no loss,
For the stone that keeps rolling will gather no moss.

Oh wife, you've convinced me, I'll argue no more,
I never once thought of you dying before,
I love my dear children although they are small,
But you, my dear wife, I love best of 'em all.
With me at my plow and you at your wheel,
Let the winters consume all the summers doth yield.

195

THE INDIAN FIGHTERS

Lomax (*Cowboy Songs*, 1938, pp. 344-346) has a text and tune sent him by a student from Waco, Texas.

Sung by Mr. Arthur Trail, Farmington, Ark., Oct. 3, 1941. Learned near Fayetteville about 1906.

I'll sing you a song, it may be the sad one, I've tri-als and trou-bles since I first be-gun, A-leav-in' my coun-try, my friends and my home   To cross old Mis-sou-ri, Wy-o-min' to roam.

Oft-times in our crossing we joined in great trains,
We talk of Sioux Indians on the wide plains,
They'll shoot the poor driver with an arrow and bow,
Them captured by Indians no mercy was shown.

We pitched our tents down on the green grassy ground,
Our mules and our horses was grazing around,
While cooking our rations we heard a low hail,
A band of Sioux Indians come down on our trail.

We had a little band of about twenty-four,
And of the Sioux Indians a hundred or more,
We jumped to our rifles with a flash in each eye,
Says a brave boy to the leader, let's fight till we die.

We fought them with courage and spoke not a word,
And in our last battle all was heard,
Jumped on our horses and mounted our train,
We had three bloody battles, what a trip on the plains.

And in our last battle there was two boys fell,
We laid them to rest in a cool shady dell.

196

HELL AND TEXAS

George E. Hastings (*Texas Folk-Lore Society Publications* 9, 1931, pp. 175-180) gives a text and tune which he learned about 1908, and discusses the background of his version, to which he added sixteen lines when he discovered the piece in Lomax's *Cowboy Songs* (1910, pp. 222-223). Lomax says that when the proprietor of the Buckhorn Saloon in San Antonio gave him a printed broadside of "Hell in Texas" in 1909, he stated that he had given away more than 100,000 copies. See Lomax (*American Ballads and Folk Songs*, 1934, pp. 397-401; *Cowboy Songs*, 1938, pp. 317-319).

In a postscript to the Hastings article (*Texas Folk-Lore Society Publications* 9, 1931, pp 180-182), J. Frank Dobie gives similar descriptive verses about Arizona, as published in 1928 and reported to have been written some fifty-odd years previously. Dobie recalled a Texas version printed in a Texas newspaper many years ago "with a note ascribing the authorship to General Sherman, who is often credited with saying that if he owned Hell and Texas, he would rent out Texas and live in the other place." To which might be added the classic Texan retort that a man should stand up for his own country. Later (*Country Gentleman* 106, June 1936, p. 80), Dobie quotes twelve lines of the song, which he says is well known, containing "forty other absurdities half based on truth."

Sung by Dr. George E. Hastings, Fayetteville, Ark., Dec. 16, 1941. Hastings tells me that he sang this in Dallas once, and the Governor of Texas was so pleased that he made him an honorary member of the Texas Rangers.

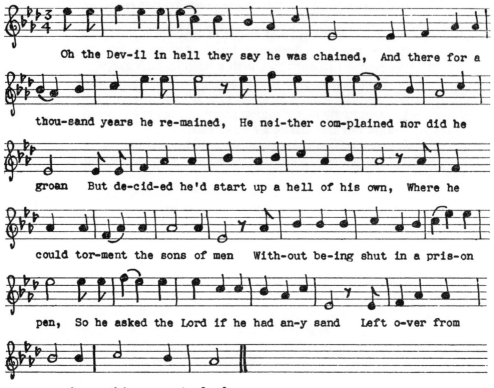

Oh the Dev-il in hell they say he was chained, And there for a thou-sand years he re-mained, He nei-ther com-plained nor did he groan But de-cid-ed he'd start up a hell of his own, Where he could tor-ment the sons of men With-out be-ing shut in a pris-on pen, So he asked the Lord if he had an-y sand Left o-ver from mak-ing this great land.

The Lord he said yes, I have plenty on hand,
But it's way down South on the Rio Grande,
And to tell you the truth the stuff is so pore
I doubt it will do for hell any more.
The Devil went down and looked over the truck
He said if it came as a gift he was stuck,
For when he'd examined it carefully and well
He decided the place was too dry for a hell.

But the Lord, just to get the stuff off his hands
He promised the Devil he'd water the land,
For he had some old water that wasn't no use,
A regular bog-hole that stunk like the deuce.
So the grant it was made and the deed it was given,
And the Lord he returned to his place up in heaven,
The Devil soon saw he had everything needed
To make up a hell, and so he proceeded.

He scattered tarantulas over the road,
Put thorns on the cactus and horns on the toads,
He sprinkled the sands with millions of ants
So the man who sits down will need soles on his pants.
He lengthened the horns of the Texas steer,
He added an inch to the jackrabbit's ear,
He put water-puppies in all of the lakes,
And under the rocks he put rattlesnakes.

He hung thorns and brambles on all of the trees,
He mixed up the dust with chiggers and fleas,
The rattlesnake bites you, the scorpion stings,
The muskeeter delights you by buzzing his wings.
The heat in the summer's a hundred and ten,
Too hot for the Devil and too hot for men,
And all who could stay in that climate soon bore
Of bites and of scratches and blisters galore.

He quickened the buck of the bronco steed,
He poisoned the feet of the centipede,
The wild boar roams in the black chaparral,
It's a hell of a place that we've got here for hell.
He planted red peppers beside of the brooks,
The Mexicans use them in all that they cook,
Just dine with a greaser and this you will shout:
I've hell on the inside as well as the out!

197

THE LITTLE OLD SOD SHANTY ON THE CLAIM

Lomax gives a text of this song (*Cowboy Songs*, 1910, pp. 187-189), to which in the 1938 edition (p. 405) he adds a tune and the note "Sung to the tune of 'The Little Old Log Cabin in the Lane.'" Sandburg (*American Songbag*, 1927, pp. 89-91) prints a fine text and tune, apparently from Nebraska. "The Little Old Log Cabin in the Lane," from which this perhaps derives, was written by Will S. Hays, copyright by J. L. Peters in 1871.

A

Sung by Mr. Jimmy Denoon, Bradleyville, Mo., Nov. 12, 1941. Learned from his grand-father at Springfield, Mo.

I'm look-in' rath-er seed-y while hold-ing down my claim, My vic-tuals are not al-ways of the best, And the mice play shy-ly round me as I nes-tle down to rest In that lit-tle old sod shan-ty on the claim. The hin-ges are of leath-er and the win-dows have no glass, The board roof lets the high-land bliz-zard in, And I hear the hun-gry coy-ote as he slinks up through the grass, Round that lit-tle old sod shan-ty on the claim.

When I left my Eastern home, a bachelor oh so gay,
To win my way up in this world to fame,
Whoever thought I'd fall so low as to burnin' twisted hay
In that little old sod shanty on the claim.

I wish that some kind-heart' girl would pity on me take
And relieve me from this mess that I am in,
The angel, how I'd bless her if this her home she'd make
In that little old sod shanty on the claim.

And if kind fate should bless us with now and then a heir
To cheer our hearts in honest pride and fame,
Oh then we'd be contented for the toil that we have spent
In that little old sod shanty on the claim.

B

Sung by Mr. Doney Hammontree, Farmington, Ark., Dec. 28, 1941.

When I left my Eastern home so happy and so gay,
To try and mine myself to wealth and fame,
Little did I think that I'd come down to burning twisted hay
In my little old sod shanty on the claim.

How I wish some kindly hearted miss would pity on me take
And come and aid me in my labors here,
How the angels they would bless her if this her home she'd make
In my little old sod shanty on the claim.

198

THE DAYS OF FORTY-NINE

A similar piece is found in *The Great Emerson New Popular Songster*, San Francisco, 1874. See Lomax (*Cowboy Songs*, 1910, pp. 9-14) and Robertson (*Check List of California Songs*, 1940, p. 14). Black and Robertson (*The Gold Rush Song Book*, 1940, pp. viii, 53-55) reprint a text from Nicholas Ball's *Pioneers of '49* (Lee & Shepard, Boston, 1891) with a tune recorded by Robertson from the singing of Leon Ponce of Tuolumne County, Calif., who learned it from a real Forty-Niner.

Sung by Mr. Wythe Bishop, Fayetteville, Ark., Dec. 9, 1941. He says he "learned it from a feller who died drunk on a ten-pin alley in Eureka Springs, Arkansas."

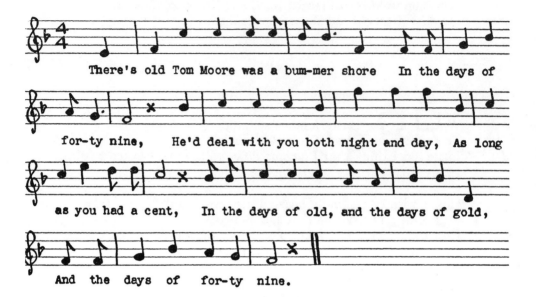

There's old Tom Moore was a bum-mer shore   In the days of for-ty nine, He'd deal with you both night and day, As long as you had a cent, In the days of old, and the days of gold, And the days of for-ty nine.

There's New York Jake, the butcher's son,
The one you all know well,
He never missed a single meal, nor never paid a cent,
He stood the kicks like good old bricks,
In the days of forty-nine.

199

BILL VANERO

The modern radio cowboys usually call this piece "The Ride of Billy Venero." Edwin Ford Piper (see Pound, *Poetic Origins and the Ballad*, 1921, p. 229n.) was the first to point out that "The Ride of Billy Venero" is derived from "The Ride of Paul Venarez," a poem by Eben E. Rexford, once well known as a writer of hymns and dime novels. The verses were published years ago in *The Youth's Companion*, and were adopted by some cowboy singers, later collected as folksong by Lomax (*Cowboy Songs*, 1910, pp. 299-302), who includes a tune in his 1938 edition (pp. 197-200). The original verses as they appeared in *The Youth's Companion* have been elsewhere reprinted, as in *One Hundred Choice Selections No. 21*, edited by Phineas Garrett (Philadelphia, c.1910, pp. 99-101). Most of the recent phonograph and radio versions apparently stem from the Lomax text. Compare the record (*Victor* 21487) by Harry McClintock. Larkin (*Singing Cowboy*, 1931, pp. 25-29) prints a very fine version from Reva Cordell, a trick rider who sang it after a Las Vegas rodeo.

A

Sung by Mr. and Mrs. Virgil Penrod, Natural Dam, Ark., Dec. 14, 1941.   The Penrods
pronounce the name "Van-err-o," accenting the second syllable.

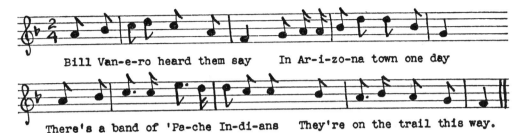

Bill Van-e-ro heard them say   In Ar-i-zo-na town one day

There's a band of 'Pa-che In-di-ans   They're on the trail this way.

Bill had heard of a murder done,
Two men killed on Rocky Run,
Though his thoughts were with the cow ranch
On the borders of Rocky Run.

Bill stood gazing all around,
Picked his lasso from the ground,
Caught his little brown champion
Not many steps away.

Now Bill, you hold your breath
For you're riding straight to death,
There's a band of approaching Indians,
They are on the trail this way.

Soon with bridle and hissing . . . .
And jingling of the spurs,
The little brown champion bore the cowboy
Away from friends and home.

Over oakey spots he sped
As his thoughts drift on ahead
To little Bess at the cow ranch
And the boys on Rocky Run.

Just then a rifle shot
Woke the echoes of the spot,
Bill Venero said I'm wounded
As he reeled from side to side.

As long as there's life there's hope,
Swiftly onward I will lope,
Suddenly Bill Venero halted
In the shadow of the hills.

From his pocket then he took
With weak hands a little book,
He tore a blank leaf from it
Saying this will be my will.

From a tree a twig he broke,
Then he dipped his pen of oak
Into the life-blood that was flowing
From the wound above his heart.

This message he wrote fast,
His first love letter and his last,
Tied it safely to the saddle
And his lips grew white with pain.

Take this message, Champ, he said,
To little Bessie if not me,
And if I never reach the cow ranch
Little Bess will know I tried.

Cow ranch forty miles away
In a lonely spot that lay,
In a green and shady valley
In a mighty wilderness.

Just at dusk a horse of brown
Covered with sweat come panting down
From the lane into the cow ranch
And stopped at Bessie's door.

The cowboy was asleep
And his slumber was so deep,
Little Bessie tried to wake him,
She tried it o'er and o'er.

Now you've heard the story told
By the young and by the old,
How the Indians killed Bill Vanero
On the trail of Rocky Run.

Many years have passed away,
And this maiden's hair turned gray,
But she still puts a wreath of roses
On Bill Vanero's grave.

B

Text from Mrs. C. P. Mahnkey, Oasis, Mo., Dec. 17, 1927. She spells the name "Venerez,"
but writes me that it is pronounced "Vanray."

Paul Venerez heard them say
In the frontier town that day,
That a band of Apache warriors
Were upon the trail of death.
Heard them tell of murder done,
Three men killed at Rocky Run,
They're in danger at the cow ranch,
Said Venerez under breath.

The cow ranch forty miles away
Was a little place that lay
In a deep and shady valley
Of the mighty wilderness.
Half a score of homes were there
And in one a maiden fair,
Held the heart of Paul Venerez,
Paul Venerez' little Bess.

So no wonder he grew pale
When he heard the awful tale
Of the men that had been murdered
That day at Rocky Run.
Sure as there's a God above
I will save the girl I love,
By my love for little Bessie
I will see that something's done.

Not a moment he delayed
When his brave resolve was made,
Why man, his comrades told him
When they heard his daring plan,
You are riding straight to death!
But he answered save your breath,
I may never reach the cow ranch
But I'll do the best I can.

Low and lower sank the sun,
He drew rein at Rocky Run,
Here three men met death, my Chapo,
And he stroked his glossy mane.
So shall those we go to warn
Ere the coming of the morn,
If we fail, God help my Bessie,
And he started on again.

Sharp and clear a rifle shot
Woke the echoes of the spot,
I am wounded, cried Venerez
As he swayed from side to side.
While there's life there's always hope,
Slowly onward I shall lope,
If I fail to reach the cow ranch
Bessie Lee shall know I tried.

I will save them yet, he cried,
Bessie Lee shall know I tried,
And he checked the flying pony
In the shadow of a hill.
And with trembling hand he took
From his chaps a little book,
Tore a blank leaf from its pages,
Saying this shall be my will.

From a limb a twig he broke,
And he dipped his pen of oak
In the warm blood that was gushing
From a wound above his heart.
Rouse, he wrote, before too late,
Redskin wariors lie in wait,
Goodbye, God bless you darling,
And he felt the cold tears start.

Then he made his message fast,
Love's first message and the last,
To the saddle horn he tied it,
And his lips were white with pain.
Take this message if not me
Straight to little Bessie Lee,
He tied himself to the saddle
And he gave his horse the rein.

Just at dusk a horse of brown
Wet with sweat, came panting down
The little lane at the cow ranch
And stopped at Bessie's door.
But the rider was asleep
And his slumber was so deep,
Little Bess could never wake him
Though she tried forever more.

Still the story they repeat,
How the redskins met defeat,
And the ranch was saved by Venerez,
Saved by Venerez though he died.
On that little strip between
They keep her flowers so green,
That little Bess had planted
Ere they laid her by his side.

C

Mrs. Lee Stephens, Jane, Mo., May 4, 1928, sings a similar variant called "Bill Vanerow" —the last syllable rhyming with "how." The text is very much like Mrs. Mahnkey's, except for the last two stanzas:

Now you've heard the story told
By the young and by the old,
Away down at the cow ranch
The night the Apaches came.
Heard them tell of the bloody fight,
How the chief fell in the flight
Of his panic-stricken warriors,
And they speak Vanerow's name.

You have heard the story told
By the young and by the old,
How the Indians killed Vanerow
On the trail at Rocky Run.
But those days have passed away,
Little Bess is getting gray,
But she still plays 'mong the roses
On Bill Vanerow's grave.

200

THE BUCKING BRONCO

Three stanzas of this piece are quoted in Stewart Edward White's story "The Rawhide" (*McClure's Magazine* 24, Dec. 1904, pp. 175-176). The entire song, also known as "The Cowboy's Hat," was printed by Thorp (*Songs of the Cowboys*, 1921, pp. 14-15) with the claim that it was written by Belle Starr, famous woman outlaw of the Indian Territory. Thorp adds this note: "Written about 1878. Song has been expurgated by me. The author was a member of a notorious gang of outlaws, but a very big-hearted woman. I know her well." Some twenty years later (*Atlantic Monthly* 66, Aug. 1940, p. 200) Thorp says that he learned the song from an anonymous "swamp angel" near Gainesville, Texas, and that this man *told* him that Belle Starr was the author! There seems to be no evidence that Belle ever even heard the song. Thorp admits (pp. 202-203) that some of the items he published as "cow-boy songs" were fakes—he says that he wrote five of them himself. John J. Niles (*The Mentor* 18, Mar. 1930, p. 70) prints two songs *about* Belle Starr (one said to have been written by her lover Blue Duck) but does not mention "The Bucking Bronco" or intimate that Belle was a writer of songs. Dobie (*Texas Folk-Lore Society Publications* 7, 1928, pp. 170-172) mentions one James Hatch of San Antonio, Texas, as claiming the authorship of this piece. "While I was at Platte City, Nebraska, in 1882 with a trail herd," says Mr. Hatch, "I composed 'The Bucking Bronco'. . . . Billie Davis, . . . also a wrangler, . . . made up the tune." Dobie tells us also that Charlie Johnson, Charco, Texas, "claims a hand" in this song, but it is not clear whether Johnson is supposed to have written the whole thing, or merely to have added stanzas to a piece already in oral circulation. Dobie prints both the Hatch and Johnson texts, with a tune for the Johnson version. Compare the items reported by Lomax (*Cowboy Songs*, 1938, pp. 267-268; *American Ballads and Folk Songs*, 1934, pp. 417-418). Margaret Larkin (*Singing Cowboy*, 1931, pp. 45-47) has recorded a good five-stanza text and tune, and follows Thorp in ascribing the song to Belle Starr. "It would have been just like her," says Miss Larkin, "to make these revelations 'from a young maiden's heart' one day, and to hold up a poker game and make off with the jackpot the next." Compare the "Broncho Buster" song reported in the Aurora (Mo.) *Advertiser*, June 17, 1937.

A

Sung by Mr. E. J. Ferris, Little Rock, Ark., Dec. 9, 1927.

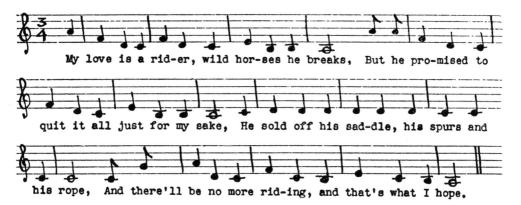

My love is a rid-er, wild hor-ses he breaks, But he pro-mised to
quit it all just for my sake, He sold off his sad-dle, his spurs and
his rope, And there'll be no more rid-ing, and that's what I hope.

The first time I saw him was early last spring,
A-riding a bronco, a high-headed thing,
He laughed and he talked as they danced to and fro,
He promised he'd not ride no other bronco.

My love has a gun that has gone to the bad
Which makes all the ladies to feel very sad,
He give me some presents, among them a ring,
But the return I gave him was a far better thing.

Now all you young ladies that live on the Platte,
Don't marry the cowboy who wears a white hat,
He'll pet you and court you and then he will go.
And ride up the trail on another bronco.

B

Mrs. Marie Wilbur, Pineville, Mo., Apr. 6, 1930, sang a similar piece with a different
ending:

Now all you young maidens, wherever you reside,
Beware of the cowboy who swings the raw-hide,
He'll court you and pet you, then leave you and go
A-riding the trail on his bucking bronco.

C

Mr. W. B. Leach, Joplin, Mo., July 5, 1933, recalls a fragment of the song as he heard it in Oklahoma in the 90's.

> One foot he ties up an' the saddle throws on,
> With a jump an' a holler he's mounted an' gone!

D

Fragment recalled by Mr. Lew Beardon, Branson, Mo., Sept. 4, 1939. He heard it near Forsyth, Mo., about 1900.

> My boy has a gun that has gone to the bad,
> It makes Uncle Sam feel mighty damn sad,
> His gun it shoots high, his gun it shoots low,
> An' squanders his lead like a buckin' broncho.

201

THE BRAZOS RIVER

Sung by Mrs. Irene Carlisle, Fayetteville, Ark., Jan. 30, 1942. Mrs. Carlisle learned it in 1921 from a hired man who had lived in Texas.

We crossed the broad Pe-cos, we ford-ed the Nu-e-ces, We swum the Gua-da-lu-pe, we fol-lowed the Bra-zos, Red Riv-er runs rust-y, the Wich-i-ta clear, But down by the Bra-zos I court-ed my dear.

Chorus

Then la la la lee lee lee, give me your hand, La la la lee lee lee give me your hand, La la la lee lee lee, give me your hand, There's a man-y a riv-er that wat-ers the land.

The fair Angelina runs glossy and gliding,
The crooked Colorado runs weaving and winding,
And the slow San Antonio it courses the plain,
But I never will walk by the Brazos again.

Then la la la lee lee lee, pole the boat on,
La la la lee lee lee pole the boat on,
La la la lee lee lee, pole the boat on,
My Brazos River sweetheart has left me and gone.

She kissed me, she hugged me, she called me her dandy,
The Trinty's muddy, the Brazos quick-sandy,
She hugged me, she kissed me, she called me her own,
But down by the Brazos she left me alone.

Then la la la lee lee lee, give me your hand,
La la la lee lee lee give me your hand,
La la la lee lee lee, give me your hand,
The Trinity's muddy but the Brazos' quicksand.

The girls of Little River they're plump and they're pretty,
The Sabine and the Sulphur have many a beauty,
On the banks of the Natchez there's girls by the score,
And down by the Brazos I'll wander no more.

Then la la la lee lee lee, give me your hand,
La la la lee lee lee give me your hand,
La la la lee lee lee, give me your hand,
There's a many a river that waters the land.

202

STRAWBERRY ROAN

Lomax (*American Ballads and Folk Songs*, 1934, pp. 392-395) has a good Arizona text, which he publishes again (*Cowboy Songs*, 1938, pp. 99-102) with another tune and this note: "Curley W. Fletcher informed me later that he himself composed the poem. His version is published in his *Songs of the Sage* (Los Angeles: Frontier Publishing Co., 1931)."

Contributed by Miss Lucile Morris, Springfield, Mo., Oct. 28, 1934. Miss Morris obtained a manuscript copy from Mrs. Ella Robertson, also of Springfield, and a similar text was printed in the Springfield *News and Leader*, Oct. 21, 1934.

I was layin' round town just spendin' my time,
Out of a job an' not makin' a dime,
When up steps a fellow an' says I suppose
You're a bronco rider by the looks of your clothes.

Well you guessed me right, an' a good one, I claim,
Do you happen to have any bad ones to tame?
He says he's got one that's a good one to buck,
An' at throwin' good riders he's had lots of luck.

He says this old bronco has never been rode,
The guy that gets on him is sure to get throwed,
I get all excited an' ask what he pays
To ride this here bronco a couple of days.

He offers a ten-spot, I says I'm your man,
The bronc never lived that I can't fan,
The bronc never tried nor he never drawed breath
That I can't ride till he starves plumb to death.

He says get your saddle, I'll give you a change,
We got in the buckboard an' went to the range,
We waited till morning and right after chuck
I went out to see if that outlaw could buck.

Down in the horse corral standing alone
Was this old cowboy's strawberry roan,
He had little pin ears that tucked at the tip,
And a big HH brand on his left hip.

He was spavined all round an' he had pigeon toes,
Little pig eyes an' a big Roman nose,
He was yew-necked an' old with a long lower jaw,
You could tell at a glance that he was an outlaw.

I buckled on my spurs an' was feelin' plumb fine,
Pulled down my hat an' curled up my twine,
I throwed the loop on him, an' well I knew then
Before I had rode him I'd sure earn my ten.

I got the blind on him with a terrible fight,
Next come the saddle, an' I screwed it down tight,
Then I stepped on him an' pulled up the blind,
I'm settin' in his middle to see him unwind.

He bowed his old neck an' I'll say he unwound,
He seemed to quit livin' down there on the ground,
He went up to the east and came down to the west,
An' me settin' on him a-doin' my best.

He sure was a frog walker, I heaved a big sigh,
He only lacked wings for to be on the fly,
He turned his old belly right up to the sun,
For he was a sun-fishin' son-of-a-gun.

He was the worst bronco I seen on the range,
He could turn on a nickel an' leave you some change,
While he was a-buckin' he squealed like a shote,
The sound of his voice was sure not no sweet note.

I tell all the people that outlaw could step,
But I was still on him a-buildin' a rep,
He come down on all fours an' turned up his sides,
I don't know how he kept from losin' his hide.

Well, I lost my stirrup an' also my hat,
I was clawin' that leather an' blind as a bat,
With one hell of a jump he made a high dive
An' sent me a-whizzin' up there through the sky.

I turned forty flips an' come down to the earth,
I set there a-cussin' the day of his birth,
I know now there's some ponies that I can't ride,
Some of them still livin' — they haven't all died.

But I bet all my money there's no man alive,
Can ride Strawberry Roan when he makes a high dive.

203

LITTLE JOE THE WRANGLER

Lomax found several versions of this piece in Texas 1907-1910, and gives a text (*Cowboy Songs*, 1910, pp. 167-171). Later, he says he discovered the song in a small collection of cowboy verse published in Estancia, N. M., by Thorp, who claims that he wrote these songs in 1898. See Thorp (*Songs of the Cowboys*, 1921, p. 96; *Atlantic Monthly* 166, Aug. 1940, pp. 202-203). The 1938 edition of Lomax (pp. 91-93) includes a tune also.

From Mrs. Lillian Short, Cabool, Mo., July 27, 1941.

Little Joe the wrangler,
He will wrangle never more;
His days a-wrangling herds are done.
Just a year ago last April
When he rode into our camp
On a little Texas pony all alone.

It was late in the evening
When he rode up to our herd,
On his little pony he called Chaw.
A ragged hat and overalls,
A tougher looking lad you
Never in hour life before had saw.

He said he had to leave his home,
His pa had been married twice
And his new ma whipped him every day or two,
So he saddled up old Chaw one night
And lit a shuck out West
And ever since he's tried to paddle his own canoe.

His saddle was a Texas style,
Made many years ago;
And an old case spur on one foot idly swung,
His old pack rolled in a cotton sack
And loosely tied behind,
And his canteen from his saddle horn was slung.

He said that if we'd give him work
He'd do the best he could
Tho he didn't know straight up about a cow,
So the boss he cut him out a mount
And kindly put him on
For he sorta liked that little stray somehow.

We taught him to wrangle horses
And try to know them all
And get them in by daylight if he could
And follow the chuck wagon,
Always help to hitch the team
And help the cook Lorena rustle wood.

We had camped down by the river,
The weather being fine.
They had bedded on the South side in the bend
When a northern started blowing
And we doubled out on guard
For it took all hands to hold the cattle in.

Between the streaks of lightning
We could see a horse ahead.
It was Little Joe the wrangler in the lead.
He was riding old Blue Rocket
With a slicker o'er his head
A-trying to check the cattle in their speed.

At last we got them milling
And they kind of quieted down,
And the extra gang back to the camp did go,
But we saw that one was missing
And we all knew at a glance
It was that little Texas stray, poor wrangling Joe.

Next morning just at daybreak
We saw where Rocket fell
In a washout about twenty feet below,
And beneath Blue Rocket, mashed to pulp,
His spurs had rung the knell,
Was that little Texas stray, poor Wranglin' Joe.

204

LITTLE JOE THE WRANGLER'S SISTER NELL

Evidently a sequel to the well-known "Little Joe the Wrangler" song.

Contributed by Mrs. Lillian Short, Cabool, Mo., Feb. 23, 1941. She had it from Mrs. A.
L. Estes, Lee's Summit, Mo.

She rode up to the wagon as the sun was getting low,
A slender little figure dressed in gray.
We told her to get down, of course, and pull up to the fire,
And red hot chuck would soon be on its way.

An old slouch hat with a hole in the top was perched upon her head,
A pair of bullhide chaps well greased and worn;
An old stock saddle scratched and scarred from working in the brush
And her slick maguey tied to her saddle horn.

She said she'd rode from Lyano, four hundred miles away
Her pony was so tired he couldn't go;
She asked to stop a day or two and kind of rest him up,
Then maybe she could find her brother, Joe.

We could see that she'd been crying, her little face was sad.
When she talked her upper lip would tremble so.
She was a living image we all saw at a glance
Of our little lost horse herder, Wrangler Joe.

We asked where Joe was working, if she knew the outfits brand,
Yes, his letter said it was a Circle Bar;
It was mailed at Amarillo about three months ago
From a trail herd headed north to Cinnabar.

I looked at Jim, he looked at Tom, and then looked back at me,
There was something in our hearts, we couldn't speak.
She said she'd got kind of worried when she never heard no more
And things at home got tougher every week.

"You see my mother died," she said, "when Joe and I were born,
And Joe and I were twins," her story ran;
"Then Dad ups and marries and gets another wife,
And then it was our troubles sure began.

"She beat us, she abused us, and starved us most the time,
You see, she had no children of her own;
Nothing Joe or I could do ever seemed just right,
Then when Joe pulled out that left me all alone."

I gave the kid my bedroll, while I bunked in with Jim,
We talked and planned and schemed the whole night through,
As to which of us would tell her the way that Joe got killed,
And break the news as gently as we knew.

"I'll wrangle in the morning, boys," she said as she turned in,
"I'll have the horses at the wagon before day."
As the morning star was rising I saw the kid roll out,
Saddle up the gray night horse and ride away.

Soon we heard the horses coming headed into camp,
It wasn't light but we plainly heard the bell,
And then someone crying coming on behind,
It was little Joe the wrangler's sister Nell.

We couldn't quite console her; she'd seen the horses' brands
As she drove them from the river bank below;
From the looks on our faces she seemed to realize
That she never again would see poor Wrangler Joe.

205

COWBOY SONG

From Mr. Whittier Burnett, Seymour, Mo., Aug. 14, 1939. He writes: "Russell Hester,
then a student at the A. & M. college at Stillwater, Okla., gave it to me some twelve years
ago. His people were large land holders around Vinita, Okla., and he got the song from the
cowboys there. I do not think it is printed in any book of collected cowboy songs."

Though your backs they are weak,
An' your legs they aint strong,
Don't be skairt, little dogies,
We'll git there 'fore long.

Hi yi yip, git along!

Though from dawn until midnight
We strike down the trail,
Jest foller your leaders
An' hold up your tail.

Though we foller the trail
That sometimes caint be found,
Jest like that durned river
That hides underground.

Yet we'll pick it up further
Somewhere in the land,
Where cactus an' mesquite
Stand thick on the sand.

Though there aint nary grass blade
This side of the sky,
An' there aint nary river
That hasn't run dry—

For there's sure water somewhere,
An' there's grass growing too,
So jest keep your tails up,
Don't never git blue—

Hi yi yip, git along!

206

UTAH CARL

Lomax includes this in his 1910 edition of *Cowboy Songs*, pp. 66-68. The 1938 edition, pp. 125-128, adds a tune and the note: "Part of this song was given to the compiler by F. C. Thorne of Fort Worth, Texas. J. T. Shirley of San Angelo, Texas, says that a cowboy on the Curve T Ranch in Schleicher County wrote this song."

Sung by Miss Reba McDonald, Farmington, Ark., Feb. 6, 1942.

My friend, you ask the question
Why I'm so sad and still,
Why my brow is always darkened
Like a cloud upon the hill.

Mid the cactus and the thistles
Of New Mexico's fine land,
Where the cattle roam by thousands
With many a mark and brand.

There's a grave without a headstone,
Without a date or name,
In silence sleeps my comrade
In the land from which I came.

Long we had ridden together,
We had ridden side by side,
I loved him as a brother,
I wept when Utah died.

Oh long we had ridden together,
Through cutouts and burned the brand,
Through dark and stormy weather
We gained that night-herd stand.

We had rounded up one morning,
Our work was almost done,
When to the right the cattle
Started in a maddened run.

Our boss's little daughter
Was herding on this side,
Started out to stop the cattle,
It was there that Utah died.

As Lenore rushed her pony
To turn them to the right,
The red blanket slipped beneath her,
She caught fast and held on tight.

When the cattle saw the blanket
Almost dragging on the ground,
They were maddened in a minute
And charged with a bound.

When the cattle saw the blanket
Every cowboy held his breath,
For they knew if her pony failed her
None could save the girl from death.

When Lenore saw the danger
She lightened the pony's pace,
And leaning in her saddle
Tried the blanket to replace.

But leaning, she lost her balance,
Fell in front of that wild tide,
Lie still, Lenore, I'm coming,
Are the words that Utah cried.

Twas in just about one moment
Utah Carl came riding past,
Little did he think that moment,
That ride would be his last.

Many times from out his saddle
He had caught the trailing rope,
But to catch her now at full speed
He saw his only hope.

The horse approached the danger,
Sure and fast at every bound,
And he swung from out his saddle
To raise her from the ground.

He leaned from out his saddle
To raise her in his arms,
He thought he'd been successful
And had saved the girl from harm.

But the weight upon the cinches
Had never been felt before,
His front cinch burst asunder
And he fell beside Lenore.

As Lenore fell from her pony
She dragged the red blanket down,
And it lay there close beside her,
As she lay upon the ground.

Utah Carl picked up the blanket
And waved it o'er his head,
And running across the prairie,
Lie still, Lenore, he said.

Soon he had turned the stampede
From Lenore his little friend,
But the cattle rushed upon him
And he stopped to meet his end.

He fought them with brave courage,
Never shrieked or grieved with fear,
The cattle rushed upon him
And he knew his end was near.

Then quickly from his holster
Utah Carl his pistol drew,
He was willing to fight while dying
As a cowboy brave and true.

His pistol flashed like lightning,
The reports rang loud and clear,
The cattle rushed upon him,
But he dropped the leading steer,

I rode into the circle,
I knew his life was o'er,
And bending I heard him whisper,
Lie still, I'm coming, Lenore.

Somewhere there is a future,
I've heard the preachers say,
I don't think that our friend Utah
Will be lost on that great day.

207

PATTONIA, THE PRIDE OF THE PLAINS

Larkin (*Singing Cowboy*, 1931, pp. 111-113) prints a version entitled "Plantonio," from a girl at Taos, N. M. Lomax (*Cowboy Songs*, 1938, pp. 356-358) has a text and tune "from the singing of the Gant family, Austin, Texas, and of Eddie Murphy, Crowley, Louisiana."

Manuscript copy from Miss Lucile Morris, Springfield, Mo., Nov. 11, 1934. She had it from Mrs. Bertha M. Naylor, Mountain Grove, Mo.

You look at that picture with a wondering eye,
And then to the arrow that hangs by its side,
You say tell the story, for I know there is one
For the name of Pattonia is a story I know.

I will tell you a story, it will thrill you I know,
Of a horse that I owned out in New Mexico,
He was swift as an antelope, black as a crow,
With a star in his forhead as white as the snow.

His hair like a lady's was glossy and fine,
He was restless and proud, yet gentle and kind,
His arched neck was hid by a thick flowing mane,
And I called him Pattonia, the pride of the plain.

The country was new and the settlers were scarce,
And the Indians on the warpath were savage and fierce,
And many a poor traveler in the distant land fell
A victim to the arrows of a murderous band.

Scouts were sent out every day from their posts,
But they never came back and we knew they were lost,
Our captain stepped up saying someone must go
For help to the border of New Mexico.

A dozen brave fellows straightway answered here,
The captain he saw me, I was standing quite near,
Pattonia was by me, with his nose in my hand,
Says the captain, your horse is the best in the land.

You're good for the rider, you're the lightest one here,
On the back of that mustang you've nothing to fear,
And if there is one in the camp can go through
And outride the Indians, my boy, it is you.

Then proud of my horse I answered I know,
Pattonia and I are both ready to go,
Then they all shook my hand and I mounted my horse
Rode down the dark trailway and turned his head north.

Full eighty long miles o'er the sand we must go,
For help to the border of New Mexico,
The black took a trot and he kept it all night
And just as the east was beginning to light,

Not a great ways behind us there rose up a yell,
And I knew that the Indians were hot on my trail,
The race now for life was only too plain,
The arrows fell around us in showers like rain.

The blood reddened forth, dashed from the black side
But he didn't once shorten his powerful speed,
So gently I jerked the bells on my rein
And stroked his neck softly and called him by name.

He answered the touch with a toss of his head
And his dark body lengthened as faster he sped,
We were leaving the Indians now, that was plain,
When suddenly I felt in my foot a sharp pain.

I knew that Pattonia, poor fellow, was hurt,
But still he dashed onward and on to the port,
I gave them the message and I went to dismount
But the pain in my foot was so sharp I could not.

The arrow you see there hanging on the wall
Was driven through stirrup, my foot and all,
. . . .
. . . .

With care Pattonia and I were soon well,
Of his death long years after I'll not stop to tell,
Over many fine horses I've since helt the rein,
But none like Pattonia, the pride of the plain.

208

ZEBRA DUN

Lomax (*Cowboy Songs*, 1910, pp. 154-157) published a text of this song, in his later edition (1938, pp. 78-81) giving two versions, each with a tune, and the note: "This song is said to have been composed by Jake, the Negro camp cook for a ranch on the Pecos River belonging to George W. Evans and John Z. Means." See also Larkin (*Singing Cowboy*, 1931, pp. 35-38) for another version. There is an almost identical piece in Loesser's *Humor in American Song*, 1942, pp. 202-203.

Manuscript copy from Miss Lucile Morris, Springfield, Mo., Nov. 11, 1934. She had it from Miss Irene Ruhle, also of Springfield.

We were camped on the plains at the head of the Cimarron
When along come a stranger and stopped to argue some,
He looked so very foolish, we began to look around,
We thought he was a greenhorn that has just escaped from town.
We asked if he'd been to breakfast, he hadn't had a smear
So we opened up the chuck box and bade him eat his share.
He took a cup of coffee and some biscuits and some beans
And then begun to talk and tell about foreign kings and queens,
And all about the Spanish War, and fighting on the seas
With torpedoes as big as steers, and guns as big as trees.
And about old Paul Jones, a mean fighting son-of-a-gun
He said he was the grittiest cuss that ever pulled a gun.
Such an educated fellow, his thoughts just come in words,
. . . .
He just kept on a-talking till he made the boys all sick
And they began to look around just how to play a trick,
He said that he had lost his job upon the Santa Fe
And he was going across the plains to strike the old F. D.
He didn't say how come it, some trouble with the boss,
But said he'd like to borrow a nice fat saddle-hoss.
This tickled all the boys to death, they laughed way down their sleeves,
We will lend you a hoss, they said, as fresh and fat as you please,
And turned . . . . , Zebra Dun,
. . . . and waited for the fun.
Old Dunny was a Rocky outlaw that had grown so awful wild,
That he could paw the white out of the moon every jump for a mile,
Old Dunny stood right still—as if he didn't know
Until they had him saddled, and ready for to go,
When the stranger hit the saddle, old Dunny quit the earth
And traveled right straight up for all that he was worth.
A-pitching and a-squealing, a-having wall-eyed fits,
His hind feet perpendicular, his front ones in the bits,
We could see the tops of mountains under Dunny every jump,

But the stranger he was growed there just like the camel's hump.
The stranger he just set there and curled his black mustache
Just like a summer boarder a-waiting for his hash,
He thumped him in the shoulders and spurred him when he whirled,
To show them flunky punchers that he was a wolf of the world,
When the stranger had dismounted once more upon the ground
We knowed he was a thoroughbred, not a gent from town.
The boss he was standing round a-watching of the show
Walked right up to the stranger and said he needn't go,
If you can use the lasso like you rode the Zebra Dun
You're the man I have been looking for ever since the year one.
Oh he could twirl the lariat, he didn't do it slow,
He could catch them forefeet nine out of ten for any kind of dough,
And when the herd stampeded he was always on the spot
To set them . . . . like the boiling pot,
There's one thing, and a sure thing, that I've learned since I've been born,
Every educated fellow aint a plumb green horn.

Chapter VI

SONGS OF THE CIVIL WAR

At the beginning of the Civil War period the Ozark hillmen were nominally Southern in their sympathies and traditions, but the truth is that most of them took very little interest in the rumors of war which reached their isolated settlements. The typical Ozarker in those days was concerned solely with local affairs. He was always ready to fight for his personal liberty, and was intensely loyal to the interests of his family and his clan, but he knew little and cared less about matters of national policy. The shadowy "Guv'mint" in far-off Washington touched him very lightly, so why should he be disturbed by this talk of secession? And the slavery question was of even less consequence, for the pioneers had neither slaves nor prejudices against them. Even today there are grown men and women in the Ozarks who have never seen a Negro. There were some red-hot secessionists in the hills, of course, and a few men who openly sympathized with the Union cause, but the great majority of the hillmen went about their affairs quite unconcerned, and paid no attention to the gathering war-clouds.

When the first armed troops appeared in the Ozarks, however, the whole situation changed at once. Some of the young men enlisted in the regular fashion, but large numbers simply "took to the hills" and made savage war on Federals and Confederates alike. Ancient feuds broke out anew, and under cover of this military excitement men shot down their old neighbors, burned their cabins, stole their cattle and other property. Re-enforced by deserters from both armies, these bushwhackers kept the hill country in constant terror all through the war period, and bitter hatreds were engendered between certain families and neighborhood groups which persist even to the present day.

But even in those parlous times there were some backwoods families so isolated that neither troops nor bushwhackers disturbed them very much. My grandfather, who fought at the battle of Pea Ridge, Ark., in 1862, met men almost within hearing of the cannon who had never even heard of the war.

When I first came to the Ozark country there were many singers who remembered the Civil War quite distinctly. I met a number of old men who were regularly enlisted in the Confederate Army, and many more who had been unofficially active in the guerilla warfare of the period. Most of the latter, however, were reluctant to discuss their exploits. In some neighborhoods there seems to be a general desire to avoid all reference to the war, as a subject uncomfortably close to the still existing feuds and family hatreds which grew out of it. It may be that this feeling explains the average Ozarker's lack of interest in the rousing old Civil War ballads. At any rate, it is certainly true that songs of this type are not very popular among the hill-folk of my acquaintance, and those recorded in the following pages have been obtained with no small measure of difficulty.

246

209

THE PEA RIDGE BATTLE

The fight at Pea Ridge, Ark., March 7, 1862, involved some 25,000 men, and was the most important battle which occurred in the Ozark region. Generals Curtis and Sigel commanded the Federal troops, while Price, Van Dorn and McCulloch led the Confederates—McCulloch being mortally wounded as the song relates. Several men who fought at Pea Ridge still lived near the battlefield in 1928, and recalled fragments of this song, said to have been written by a colonel of Confederate cavalry. Stockard (*History of Lawrence, Jackson, Independence and Stone Counties, Arkansas*, 1904, pp. 79-80) prints four verses under the title "General Price," adding that it was "often sung in Arkansas during the War." Compare the "Battle of Pea Ridge" song quoted by Stewart (*Missouri Historical Review* 22, Jan. 1928, pp. 187-188), said to have been written by A. M. House of Poosey, Mo. Allsopp (*Folklore of Romantic Arkansas*, 1931, II, p. 227) mentions the piece as "very popular . . . although the verses were the purest doggerel," but quotes only two stanzas, corresponding to those numbered 19 and 20 in the text which follows. See also "The Pea Ridge Battle" ballad in the Aurora (Mo.) *Advertiser*, Mar. 30, 1939. Belden (*Ballads and Songs*, 1940, pp. 368-369) prints a Northern version of this piece entitled "The Battle of Elkhorn Tavern."

A

Sung by Mrs. W. A. Patton, Jane, Mo., Nov. 7, 1928. Mrs. Patton lives just across the line from the Pea Ridge battlefield, and says that the song has been known in her neighborhood for many years.

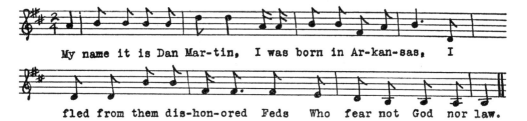

My name it is Dan Martin, I was born in Arkansas, I fled from them dis-hon-ored Feds Who fear not God nor law.

I left my aged parents,
I left my lovin' wife,
I was forced to go to Raleigh*
To try an' save my life.

I j'ined in Phelps' regiment,
I'm not ashamed to tell,
The colonel an' his officers
They used me mighty well.

There was a young lieutenant,
His name was Charley Moss,
An' o'er the whole creation
We looked on him as boss.

*Rolla, Mo., was a Federal military post.

An' when on beds of sickness,
Charley was always near,
To see we was provided for
An' nursed with tender care.

It was the sixth of March
That we did march away,
To fight the Feds an' the flop-eared Dutch
An' hear what they did say.

Oh who is Price a-fightin'?
He's fightin', I do know,
Surely it's General Curtis,
I can hear his cannons roar.

They marched us up the Bentonville road,
They marched us all that night,
An' about eleven o'clock next day
They led us into the fight.

They marched us down to the Widow Scott's,
They counter-marched us back,
We knew that Price was fightin' then
An' so was General Slack.*

It was done by brave McCulloch,
Led on by brave Van Dorn,
At Pea Ridge found us waitin'
At the tavern called Elk Horn.

They threw themselves around us
In the dark shade of the night,
They planted all their batteries
An' waited till day light.

Next mornin' soon we all marched out
Eager to meet the strife,
I never shall forget that day
As long as I have life.

An' with that dread confusion
We was forced to leave the ground,
The rollin' storms of iron balls
Was cuttin' thousands down.

*Gen. William Yarnel Slack, mortally wounded at Pea Ridge, Mar. 7, 1862.

To see our friends a-fallin'
It did us so provoke,
The sun was dim, the sky was hid
With clouds of rollin' smoke.

Some took up the left-hand road,
An' some took up the right,
McCulloch took the straightest shoot
An' led us into the fight.

It was at the Pea Ridge fight
That McManus acted queer,
Instead of shootin' at the Dutch
He knelt in silent prayer.

We seen a man a-comin',
His voice was loud an' shrill,
He hollered to the privates,
Our General McCulloch's killed.

Van Dorn was taken very sick
An' here he could not stay,
He says boys, make a swift retreat,
An' I will lead the way.

It was at the Pea Ridge fight
That Van Dorn lost his hat,
An' for about a half a mile
He laid the bushes flat.

Jumped over stumps an' scattered tents,
All this he did not dread.
The most that lay upon his mind
It was a lump of lead.

Plumb to White River he did go,
He travelled a many a ways,
He knowed that he was badly licked
An' Price would get the praise.

Old General Price rode down the line,
His horse in swiftest pace,
An' as he told us to retreat
The tears rolled down his face.

B

The following stanza is contributed by Mr. C. V. Wheat, Aurora, Mo., Mar. 5, 1939. Mr. Wheat was born on the Pea Ridge battlefield, and remembers this fragment as sung by his grandmother.

> Oh who is Price a-fightin'?
> He's fightin' now I know,
> It surely must be Sigel,
> Cause I hear the cannons roar!

210

MANASSA JUNCTION

The name "Manassa Junction" refers to a place near the Bull Run battlefield; many Southerners today speak of "the Manassa Junction victory" rather than "the battle of Bull Run." W. H. Strong (*Ozark Life*, Kingston, Ark., Nov. 3, 1928, p. 1) prints a similar text under the title "The Bull Run Battle," describing it as "one of the earliest camp songs, widely used in the Confederate army . . . brought back to the hills by my father, C. S. A., Parsons' Regiment, Co. A, Pindall's Battalion, Sharpshooters . . . I have never noted this song in any of the War Song collections, and have often wondered why."

A

Sung by Mrs. Judy Jane Whittaker, Anderson, Mo., May 4, 1928.

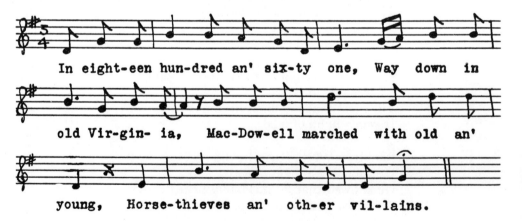

> There was Tories there an' dirty Dutch,
> An' Hessians an' Yankees bloody,
> With the regular troops from Tennessee
> United in one body.

To crush the traitor was their plan,
An' then march on to Richmond,
An' handcuff every Rebel man
As fast as they could catch 'em.

But never was a ditch they dug
More ready for the diggers,
Nor did they by their false humbug
Succeed in stealin' niggers.

Then General Scott from Chesterville
Delivered his dispatches,
While Beauregard on the battle field
Cried boys, pull down your hatches.

Then down they went on German Gulf
An' stopped their blood and thunder,
While Kirby with the Southern boys
Put all their men asunder.

An' then the race for life begun,
The Yankees seen us comin',
An' every individual man
Displayed his skill a-runnin'.

The ladies who came out to see
The rebel host defeated,
They was themselves compelled to flee
When all their men retreated.

They lost, poor souls, their crimson fine,
An' all their ball equipage
Was scattered o'er the battle line
Like common soldiers' baggage.

They left upon the battle ground
Their wounded, sick an' dyin',
They never turned their faces round
So swiftly was they flyin'.

Their ammunition, stores an' guns,
Provisions, mess an' horses,
The cowards left behind an' run
Before our Southern forces.

No men on earth did fight more brave
Than did our Southern soldiers,
But many found a soldier's grave,
An' there his body moulders.

But still they will on memory's page
Live on in song an' story,
An' honored both by youth an' age,
They fill their graves with glory.

B

The following text entitled "The Battle of Bull Run" is contributed by Dr. George E.
Hastings, Fayetteville, Ark., Nov. 14, 1938. Dr. Hastings had it from Mrs. Cora Bragg
Powell, 78 years old, Camden, Ark.

In eighteen hundred and sixty-one,
Near Bull Run in Virginia,
McDowell mustered old and young
Horse-thieves and villains many.

To crush the rebels was their plan,
And then march on to Richmond,
To handcuff every rebel man
As soon as they could catch him.

Old General Scott from Centerville
Delivered his dispatches,
While Beauregard on the battlefield
Cried boys, put down those hatches.

'Twas down they went on Sherman's guns
To stop their blood and thunder,
While Kirby and his southern sons
Cut all their men asunder.

Then helter skelter through the woods
Went wagons, teams and drivers,
They lost their chattels and their goods
While making for the river.

The ladies too who came to see
The rebel host defeated,
Were they themselves compelled to flee
When all their men retreated.

They lost, poor souls, their crinolines
And all their Fall equipage
Lay scattered o'er the battlefield
Like common soldiers' baggage.

Oh never did men fight more brave
Than did those southern soldiers,
But many fill a soldier's grave,
And there his body moulders.

But yet they live on memory's page,
They live in future story,
They're reverenced both by youths and age,
And fill their graves with glory.

211

BROTHER GREEN

This "Yankee ballet" is said to have been very popular in central Missouri about 1866, and several variants are still remembered in the Ozark country. I have heard one which had been altered to fit the mouth of a Confederate trooper, shot down by the "Northern foe." Several old-timers insist that the song was written by a Federal officer named Sutton, wounded at the Battle of Wilson's Creek, near Springfield, Mo. Pound (*Folk-Song of Nebraska and the Central West*, 1915, p. 21) mentions a Nebraska variant called "Go Tell Little Mary Not to Weep." Wyman and Brockway (*Lonesome Tunes*, 1916, p. 18) have reported a version of this piece from Kentucky; Cox (*Folk-Songs of the South*, 1925, p. 273) prints a West Virginia text; Sherman and Henry (*Hollow Folk*, 1933, pp. 145-146) found the song still popular in the Blue Ridge Mountains. Eddy (*Ballads and Songs from Ohio*, 1939, pp. 253-254) gives a text, tune and references. Belden (*Ballads and Songs*, 1940, p. 377) remarks in a footnote that it "is said to have been composed by Rev. L. J. Simpson, late chaplain in the army . . . on the death of a brother who was killed at Fort Donelson, February, 1862." See also Brewster (*Ballads and Songs of Indiana*, 1940, pp. 253-254). The piece appears in the Brown (North Carolina Folk-Lore Society) collection.

A

Sung by Mrs. Judy Jane Whittaker, Anderson, Mo., May 4, 1928. Mrs. Whittaker
learned the song about 1870.

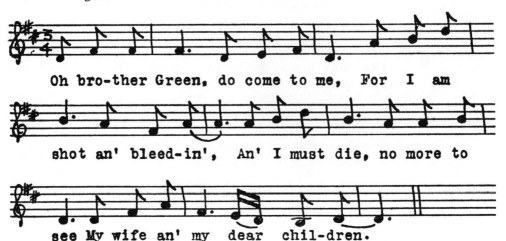

Oh bro-ther Green, do come to me, For I am

shot an' bleed-in', An' I must die, no more to

see My wife an' my dear chil-dren.

The Southern foe has laid me low
On this cold ground to suffer,
Dear brother stay, an' lay me away,
An' write my wife a letter.

Tell her that I'm prepared to die
An' go with Christ to heaven,
Dear Mary, treat my children well,
An' teach them up for heaven.

Tell sister Nancy not to grieve
The loss of her dear brother,
I'm goin' to a better world
An' meet my dear old mother.

I have one brother in this wide world,
He's fightin' for the Union,
But oh dear wife, I've lost my life
To put down this rebellion.

Dear father, you have prayed for me,
That I might seek salvation,
But I will beat you home at last,
An' say farewell, temptation.

My little babes, I love them well,
Oh could I once more see them,
That I might bid a long farewell
An' meet them all in heaven.

B

Mrs. Lee Stephens, White Rock, Mo., June 24, 1928, supplies the following text from a manuscript copy in her "friendship book."

Oh brother Green, do come to me,
For I am shot and bleeding,
Now I must die and no more see
My wife and little children.

The Southern foe has laid me low
On this cold ground to suffer,
Stay, brother, stay, lay me away,
And write my wife a letter.

Tell her that I'm prepared to die,
And hope we'll meet in heaven,
Since I believe in Jesus Christ
My sins are all forgiven.

I know that she has prayed for me,
And now her prayers are answered,
That I might be prepared to die
If I should fall in battle.

My little babes I love so well,
Oh if I could once more see them,
To bid them both a last farewell
Till we might meet in heaven.

But here I am in Tennessee
And they're in Illinois,
I am too far away from them
To hear their gentle voice.

Dear Molly, you must treat them well,
And train them up for heaven,
Teach them to love and serve the Lord
And they will be respected.

Oh sister Mamie, do not weep
For the loss of your dear brother,
I'm going to go with Christ above
And see my blessed mother.

Dear father, you have suffered long,
And prayed for my salvation,
Now I must leave you all at last
And say farewell temptation.

Two brothers yet I can't forget
Are fighting for their Union,
For which, dear wife, I lost my life
To put down this rebellion.

Oh I am dying, brother Green,
I die so very easy,
I think that death has lost its sting,
Because I love my Jesus.

So tell my wife she must not grieve,
Go kiss my little children,
I know they'll call for Pa in vain
When I am gone to heaven.

212

WE HAVE THE NAVY

It is said that this was written in reply to a Federal battle-song entitled "On To Richmond" (W. H. Strong, *Ozark Life*, Kingston, Ark., Nov. 3, 1928, p. 5). The lines "Off from Richmond, sooner in de mornin' " occur in a fragment of Negro song recorded by Talley (*Negro Folk Rhymes*, 1922, p. 15).

Sung by Mrs. Judy Jane Whittaker, Anderson, Mo., May 4, 1928. Mrs. Whittaker showed me a faded manuscript copy dated 1866, obtained from Mrs. Linnie Bullard, Pineville, Mo.

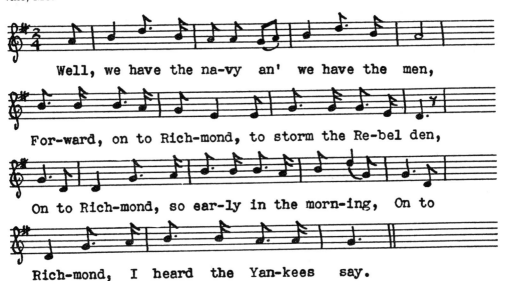

Well, we have the na-vy an' we have the men,

For-ward, on to Rich-mond, to storm the Re-bel den,

On to Rich-mond, so ear-ly in the morn-ing, On to

Rich-mond, I heard the Yan-kees say.

We'll flank it on the North an' we'll shell it on the South,
We'll storm it in the East an' we'll run the rebels out,
On to Richmond, so early in the mornin',
On to Richmond, I heard the Yankees say.

Lee was in the center an' Jackson in the rear,
An' on the right an' left sides the noble hills appear,
Longstreet he had to travel, an' branches had to cross,
An' old McGruder was about to give the Yankees grass.

It was about the first of June when the balls begun to fly,
The Yankees took an' wheeled about an' changed their battle-cry,
Off from Richmond, so early in the mornin',
Down to the gunboats, run, boys, run.

Florida is a-huntin' an' a-huntin' through the brush,
The rebels are in earnest, push, boys, push,
The Louisiana Legion, Butler was the cry,
The Texas Rangers comin' fly, boys, fly.

Virginia is a-comin' with her death-defyin' steel,
Georgia is a-chargin' across the swamps an' fields,
Off from Richmond, so early in the mornin',
Down to the gunboats, run, boys, run.

The Palmetto rebels is now upon the trail,
An' the Arkansas devils want to ride us on a rail,
Never mind your knapsacks, never mind your guns,
A-fightin' these rebels it aint no fun.

McClellan is a humbug an' Lincoln is a fool,
All of them is liars of the highest greeting school,
A home was the promise, an' every man a slave,
You better run North or you'll all find a grave.

213

A SOLDIER FROM MISSOURI

This piece is widely known in the Ozark country. It is sometimes called "The Kansas Line," and there have been numerous attempts to turn the central figure into a dying and repentant Yankee, instead of a dying and repentant Confederate. Professor Belden writes me (Feb. 9, 1930) that there are several similar texts in his collection at the University of Missouri.

A

Sung by Mrs. Judy Jane Whittaker, Anderson, Mo., May 4, 1928.

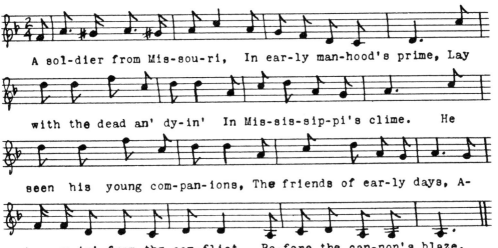

A sol-dier from Mis-sou-ri,   In ear-ly man-hood's prime, Lay

with the dead an' dy-in'   In Mis-sis-sip-pi's clime.   He

seen his young com-pan-ions, The friends of ear-ly days, A-

hur-ry-in' from the con-flict,   Be-fore the can-non's blaze.

They bore along a standard,
The starred an' barred design,
A flag that he had carried
From near the Kansas line.
Farewell, my friends an' comrades,
A long an' last adieu,
Though you may shortly follow me
I'll ne'er return to you.

A comrade stopped beside him
An' raised his droopin' head,
With me this war is over,
The youthful soldier said.
With me this war is over,
My marchin's at an end,
An' now a dyin' message
I want by you to send.

Oh bear it to my kindred
An' distant friends of mine,
For I have friends and kinfolks
Up near the Kansas line,
. . . .
. . . .
. . . .
. . . .

I have an aged mother,
You know that mother well,
Oh bear to her the tidin's
How I in battle fell.
Tell her I well remember
She give me good advice,
To stay at home in quietness.
Not j'ine the rebel Price.

I have some brothers also,
Tell them the mournful tale,
An' while in death I'm sleepin'
They will my fate bewail.
I have some wealthy neighbors
Who preached secession loud,
They counseled me an' others
To swell the rebel crowd.

There was a dark-eyed beauty,
Her name I will not call,
Who swerved me from my duty,
To throng the rebel thrall.
Her words I well remember,
No hand with mine unites
Unless I find them boldly
Defendin' Southern rights.

B

Mr. Charles Mosier, Sulphur Springs, Ark., Sept. 4, 1928, says that the first part of the
final stanza should read:

There is that dark-eyed beauty,
I need not call her name,
Who swerved me from my duty,
An' fanned the Rebel flame.

214

THE BONNIE BLUE FLAG

With the single exception of "Dixie," this was the most popular of the Confederate battle-songs. It was "composed, arranged and sung by Harry Macarthy, the Arkansas Comedian . . . dedicated to Albert G. Pike, Esq., the Poet Lawyer of Arkansas," first published by A. E. Blackmar and Bro., New Orleans, 1861. S. J. A. Fitz-Gerald (*Stories of Famous Songs*, 1898, p. 106) credits the words to Annie Chambers Ketchum. The melody, according to Dolph ("*Sound Off*," 1929, p. 245) derives from an old Irish tune called "The Jaunting Car." Macarthy and his sister sang it all over the South. After the fall of New Orleans, General Ben Butler fined the publisher $500, while anybody caught singing it was subject to a fine of $25. This same Macarthy was the author of "Missouri," another stirring Southern war song, calling upon Missouri to secede and "add your bright Star to our Flag of Eleven." The stand-ard text of the "Bonnie Blue Flag" has been printed in many songbooks; see Chapple (*Heart Songs*, Boston, 1909, p. 60), W. H. Strong (*Ozark Life*, Kingston, Ark., April, 1928, p. 6), Dolph (*Sound Off*, 1929, p. 245). Belden (*Ballads and Songs*, 1940, pp. 357-359) reports the piece from an Arkansas scrapbook of the 60's. See also the Brown (North Carolina Folk-Lore Society) collection.

Sung by Mr. Harvey Ross, Batesville, Ark., Aug. 21, 1914. Mr. Ross learned the song from his father, who rode with General J. E. B. Stuart.

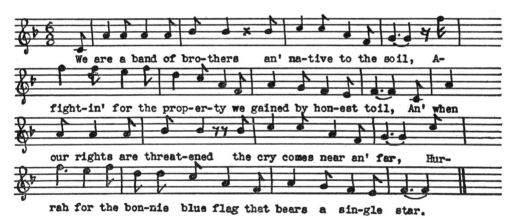

We are a band of bro-thers   an' na-tive to the soil,   A-
fight-in' for the prop-er-ty we gained by hon-est toil,   An' when
our rights are threat-ened   the cry comes near an' far,   Hurrah for the bon-nie blue flag that bears a sin-gle star.

First gallant South Carolina nobly made the stand,
Then come Alabama an' took her by the hand,
Next quickly Mississippi, Georgia an' Florida,
All raised the bonnie blue flag that bears a single star.

As long as the Union was faithful to her trust,
Like friends an' like brothers, we was kind an' just,
But now when Northern treachery attempts our rights to mar,
Hurrah for the bonnie blue flag that bears a single star.

An' here's to brave Virginia, the Old Dominion state,
Texas an' Louisiana with her have linked their fate,
Impelled by her example, now other states prepare
To raise the bonnie blue flag that bears a single star.

Then cheer, boys, cheer, an' raise a royal shout,
For Arkansas an' North Carolina now have both went out,
An' let another royal cheer for Tennessee be given,
The bonnie blue flag's single star has grown to be eleven.

215

THE HOMESPUN DRESS

   W. H. Strong (*Ozark Life*, Kingston, Ark., May 1928, p. 7) says that this piece was written by a Lieutenant Harrington who rode into Lexington, Ky., with Morgan's cavalry, and was much impressed by the ladies' homespun gowns. Harrington was killed at the battle of Perryville, Oct. 9, 1862, but his song became very popular, and was printed in many of the Civil War songbooks. Williams (*JAFL* 5, 1892, pp. 281-282) prints a text from oral sources under the title "The Southern Girl's Song." Stockard (*History of Lawrence, Jackson, Independence and Stone Counties, Arkansas*, 1904, p. 83) says that "it was written at Stringtown on the Pike, in Kentucky." A book entitled *The Confederate Woman of Arkansas*, published by the United Confederate Veterans, Little Rock, Ark., 1907, p. 192, prints the song with the following note: "This ballad was written by Miss Carrie Belle Sinclair, Augusta, Ga., in the midsummer of 1862." Hudson (*Folksongs of Mississippi*, 1936, pp. 265-266) reports a very similar piece, which he credits to "Lieutenant Harrington, an Alabaman belonging to Forrest's cavalry." Belden (*Ballads and Songs*, 1940, p. 360) recovered a text from a scrapbook compiled in Carroll County, Arkansas, during the Civil War. The piece appears in the Brown (North Carolina Folk-Lore Society) collection.

Sung by Mrs. Linnie Bullard, Pineville, Mo., July 7, 1928. The melody is identical with that of the "Bonnie Blue Flag" song.

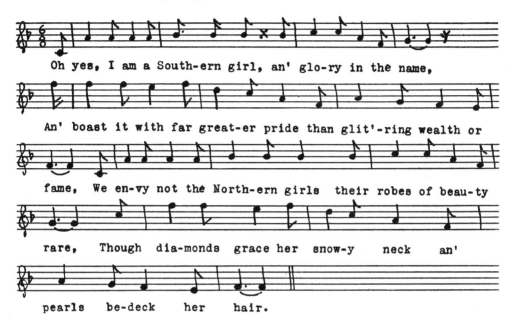

Oh yes, I am a South-ern girl, an' glo-ry in the name, An' boast it with far great-er pride than glit'-ring wealth or fame, We en-vy not the North-ern girls their robes of beau-ty rare, Though dia-monds grace her snow-y neck an' pearls be-deck her hair.

Now Northern goods are out of date, an' since old Abe's blockade,
We southern girls will be content with goods that's southern made,
We send the bravest of our land to battle with the foe,
An' we will lend a helpin' hand, we love the South, you know.

The homespun dress is plain, I know, my hat's palmetto too,
But still it shows what southern girls for southern rights will do,
We scorn to wear a bit of silk, a bit of northern lace,
We make our homespun dresses an' we wear 'em with a grace.

The southern land's a glorious land, an' has a glorious cause,
Let's give three cheers for southern rights, an' for our southern boys,
We sent our sweethearts to the war, but dear girls, don't you cry,
Your gallant soldier won't forget the girl he left behind.

An' now young men, a word with you, if you would win the fair
Go to the field where honor calls, an' win your lady there,
Remember that our brightest smiles are for the brave an' true,
An' that our hearts are all for him that fills a soldier's grave.

216

THE DYING SOLDIER

There are several of these "the sun was setting in the West" songs—perhaps they are all adaptations from some older piece. Compare "The Dying Cowboy" as reported elsewhere in this book. Another one called "The Dying Woodsman," about a Texan who was killed in the Spanish-American War, was copyrighted by J. D. Patton in 1904 and published in *The Sunny South Quartet Book* (Dalton, Ga., 1912, No. 25). See also the "Dying Ranger" song published by Lomax (*Cowboy Songs*, 1910, p. 214), Cox (*Folk-Songs of the South*, 1925, p. 263) and Finger (*Frontier Ballads*, 1927, p. 170).

Sung by Mrs. Lee Stephens, White Rock, Mo., June 24, 1928.

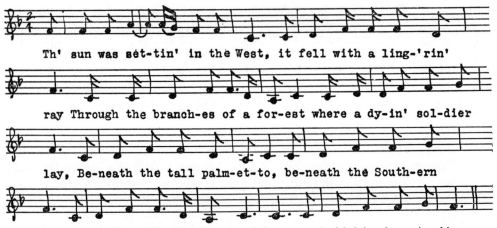

Th' sun was set-tin' in the West, it fell with a ling-'rin' ray Through the branch-es of a for-est where a dy-in' sol-dier lay, Be-neath the tall palm-et-to, be-neath the South-ern sky, A-way from his New Eng-land home we laid him down to die.

A group has gathered round him, his comrades in the fight,
But their hearts sunk deep within them as he breathed his last goodnight,
One dear friend an' companion had knelt down by his side,
Tryin' for to stay the life-blood, it was all in vain, he sighed.

But their hearts sunk deep within them as they seen it was in vain,
An' on his dear companion's cheeks the tears fell down like rain,
Harry, spoke the dyin' soldier, Harry weep no more for me,
I'm a-crossin' a dark river, but all beyond is free.

Stand up comrades, gather round me, listen to the words I say,
There is somethin' I would tell you, e'er my soul will pass away,
Far away in old New England, in that dear old Pine Tree state,
There is one who for my comin' with a saddened heart will wait.

A fair young girl, my sister, my blessin' an' my pride,
My care an' joy from boyhood, for I had none beside,
I've no mother, she lies sleepin' beneath the church-yard sod,
It is many many years ago her spirit went to God.

I've no father, he lies sleepin' beneath the cold dark sea,
I've no brother, I've no kindred, there was only Nell an' me,
But I sorrow for the future of that loved one brave an' true,
When her only friend an' brother sleeps in this here soldier's grave.

When our country was invaded an' had called for volunteers,
She threw her arms around me as she bursted into tears,
Sayin' go, my darlin' brother, drive the traitors from our shore,
My heart will need thy presence, but thy country needs you more.

An' although my heart seems burstin' I will not bid you stay,
But here in our old homestead I will wait thee day by day,
But my comrades, I'm a-dyin', an' shall never see her more,
All in vain she'll wait my comin' by that little cottage door.

I have loved my country truly, I have given it my all,
An' but for my darlin' sister I would be content to fall,
I've loved her as a brother should, an' with a father's care,
I have strove from grief an' sorrow her tender heart to spare.

Stand up comrades, closely listen, listen to my dyin' prayer,
Who will be to her a brother, shield her with a father's care?
The soldiers spoke together, like one voice it seemed to fall,
She shall be to us a sister, we'll protect her one an' all.

A smile of radiant brightness a halo o'er him shed,
One quick convulsive shudder an' the soldier boy was dead.
On the banks of the old Potomac we laid him down to rest,
With his knapsack for his pillow an' his musket on his breast.

217

I FIGHT MIT SIGEL

This is one of the "Dutch" dialect songs, which were sung by both armies during the Civil War, inspired by the fact that many of the Union soldiers in the West were Germans. Williams (*JAFL* 5, 1892, p. 271) published one stanza of this piece under the title "I'm Going to Fight Mit Sigel." W. H. Strong (*Ozark Life*, Kingston, Ark., July 1927, p. 12) prints several stanzas of a similar text; he spells the name *Seigle*, but since he makes it rhyme with *eagle* there can be no doubt that he is referring to General Franz Sigel, one of the German officers who led Federal troops into the Ozarks. See also Allsopp (*Folklore of Romantic Arkansas*, 1931, II, p. 222), and Stout (*Folklore from Iowa*, 1936, p. 100). Several of these "jump-up Dutch" songs were set to the tune of "The Girl I Left Behind Me." For a more serious "I Fight Mit Sigel" see the Aurora (Mo.) *Advertiser*, Oct. 14, 1937. Rayburn (*Ozark Country*, 1941, pp. 235-236) prints three verses and a chorus of "I Fight Mit Sigel" which he obtained from the late A. M. Haswell of Joplin, Mo.

A

Sung by Mr. Charles Morris, Columbia, Mo., July 28, 1916. Mr. Morris said that he heard the song in Taney County, Mo., in 1864.

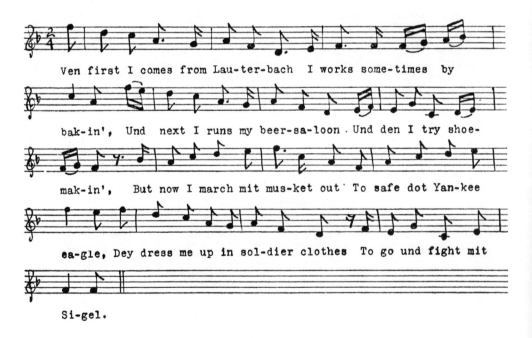

Ven first I comes from Lau-ter-bach I works some-times by bak-in', Und next I runs my beer-sa-loon. Und den I try shoe-mak-in', But now I march mit mus-ket out To safe dot Yan-kee ea-gle, Dey dress me up in sol-dier clothes To go und fight mit Si-gel.

B

Mr. J. F. Gould, Pittsburg, Kansas, June 7, 1913, remembered a similar piece as sung by Union soldiers at Pea Ridge, Ark. Each stanza of Mr. Gould's version was followed by a sort of bugle-call chorus:

We'll toot an' toot an' toot an' fight mit Si-gel,

Zwei glass o' beer, Zwei glass o' beer,

We'll toot an' toot an' toot an' fight mit Si-gel,

Zwei glass o' beer, Zwei glass o' beer.

218

THE YANKEE DUTCHMAN

Sung by Mr. Booth Campbell, Cane Hill, Ark., Feb. 5, 1942. He heard it in the 80's.
"There was lots of Dutch in the Yankee army," he remarked.

My heart is bro-ken in vun lit-tle bit, I'll tell you

all what for, My sweet-heart was a ver-y pa-tri-ot-ic girl,

She drive me off mit de war. I fight for her de bat-tle of

de flag Just brave as ev-er I can, But a long time a-go

she nix re-mem-bered me And ran off mit an-ud-der man!

Chorus.

Oh Flo-rie! What makes you so ver-y un-kind, As to go

mit Hans in Ger-man-y to dwell And left poor Schnapps be-

hind, And left poor Schnapps be-hind.

We travelled all day when de rain come down
So fast like Moses' flood,
I slept at night mit my head upon a stump
And I sunk down in de mud.
De nightmare come and I catch him mighty bad,
I dreampt I slept mit a ghost,
I woke in de morning frozen in de mud
Just stiff like one stone post.

They gave me hardtack for to eat
Vot like to broke my jaw,
Sometimes I split it mit a iron wedge
And sometimes mit a saw.
De beef it was so very very salt
Vot Adam's wife might know,
I really did believe they put it in de brine
One hundred years ago.

At length we took one city in de South,
We held it one whole year,
I got plenty of sauerkraut
And lots of lager beer.
I met one rebel lady in de street
Just pretty as ever can be,
I made one very gallant bow unto her,
And ach, she spit on me!

219

JOE STINER

Belden (*Ballads and Songs*, 1940, pp. 362-363) has a text entitled "Joe Slinsworth," which he recovered from a Civil War scrapbook compiled in Carroll County, Ark. "Presumably a camp song of the Confederates in Missouri. I have not found it elsewhere," says Belden's headnote.

Mr. M. I. Anthis, Springfield, Mo., recalled the following as a song that his father, a Civil War veteran, sang many years ago. Mr. Anthis' text was printed in the Springfield, Mo., *Leader*, Oct. 16, 1933. The references are to the Battle of Wilson's Creek, which occurred near Springfield, Aug. 10, 1861.

My name is Joe Stiner
I came from Amsterdam;
I am a full-blooded Dutchman
From that there is no sham.
I came off to this country—
They say the land is free,
Oh, there I makes much money
Oh, that's the land for me.

One day as I was drinking
Mine glass of lager beer,
And thinking of no danger
In this great country here,
They all cries out "This Union,"
"This Union!" very loud.
And they makes us walk together
In one very big Dutch crowd.

Now they say we got to fight
This Union for to save,
Mine God and Himmel did I think
Such a country we should have.
The first thing that we done
Was to take old General Frost
And shoot the women on our way
Through Camp Jackson as we crossed.

Then next we came to Rolla
Oh, how the secessionists flew
We made them get in every style
It was such glorious fun.
Then next we came to Springfield,
And there we stopped and stayed
Until our General Lyon
Had got his plans well laid.

They say that Price has got
Most all his secessionists
Camped way down on Crane creek
'Twas in a pretty fix.
And so we goes down there
Within about four miles,
When our batteries they did crack
And our rifles they did play.

What I seen there
I never shall forget,
Seemed like the ground was all alive
With secessionists.
Their blamed old rifles shot so true,
I can not tell you why.
They strike us in our stomachs
And they hit us in our eyes.

They kills our General Lyon
And they makes our Siegel run
Solomon hid in the college,
I'll tell you it was no fun.
They kills our men, they took our guns,
They knocked us into fits.
And many a prisoner, too, they took
But I gets up and gets.

Now I am in Springfield,
My legs were almost broke,
And for the want of lager beer
I was so nearly choked.
This blamed old secessionist country,
Will never do for me,
I vamish runs, I gets away,
For the city of St. Louis.

When I gets there
May I be roasted done,
If ever I shoot secessionist again
For money, love or fun.
I sits myself down by my frau,
I hears my children cry,
And this shall be my Dutch prayer—
I bid you all goodby!

220

THE BATTLE ON SHILOH'S HILL

"Shiloh" was the name of a log meeting-house on a ridge, about three miles out from Pittsburg Landing, Tenn. Confederate troops under Generals Johnston and Beauregard attacked Grant's forces here on April 6, 1862, and were repulsed after two days of desperate fighting. The author of the song exaggerates a bit when he says that "ten thousand men was killed" on the second day, since the official reports show only about 3,500 killed altogether, but the rest of the description is doubtless accurate enough. Compare Brown (*Ballad-Literature in North Carolina*, 1914, p. 10), also the three-stanza text reported by Hudson (*Folksongs of Mississippi*, 1936, pp. 260-261). Dichter and Shapiro (*Early American Sheet Music*, New York, 1941, p. 115) list a publication of "The Battle of Shiloh, or Pittsburg Landing" by Oliver Ditson and Co., Boston, 1862. The piece appears in the Brown (North Carolina Folk-Lore Society) collection.

Sung by Mrs. Judy Jane Whittaker, Anderson, Mo., May 4, 1928.

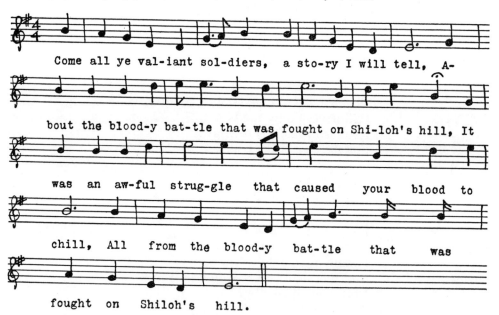

Come all ye val-iant sol-diers, a sto-ry I will tell, A-bout the blood-y bat-tle that was fought on Shi-loh's hill, It was an aw-ful strug-gle that caused your blood to chill, All from the blood-y bat-tle that was fought on Shiloh's hill.

'Twas on the sixth of April, about the break of day,
The drums an' fifes was playin' for us to march away,
My feelin's at that moment I do remember still,
When first my feet was trompin' on the top of Shiloh's hill.

About the hour of sunrise the battle first began,
Before the day was ended we fought 'em hand to hand,
The horrors of that battle did my soul with anguish fill,
The wounded men an' dyin' all laid on Shiloh's hill.

They was men from every nation laid on them bloody plains,
They was fathers, sons an' brothers all numbered with the slain,
The wounded men was cryin' for help from everywhere,
An' others was a-dyin' an' offerin' God their prayer.

Very early then next mornin' we was called to arms again,
Unmindful of the wounded, unuseful to the slain,
The battle was renewed again, ten thousand men was killed,
An' from their deadly wounds the blood run like a rill.

An' now my song is ended about them bloody plains,
I hope the sight to mortal man may ne'er be seen again,
I'll pray to God my Savior, consistent with his will,
To save the souls of them brave men who fell on Shiloh's hill.

221

THE BRASS-MOUNTED ARMY

It seems very odd that a song of this type should have escaped the wartime anthologists, but such seems to have been the case. Dr. Belden writes me (Apr. 25, 1938) that it does not occur in his collection at the University of Missouri, and that he has found no reference to it in the literature. The "Kerby's army" is probably that commanded by General Edmund Kirby-Smith, the last Confederate general to surrender in the Civil War.

Sung by Mrs. Judy Jane Whittaker, Anderson, Mo., May 4, 1928. Mrs. Whittaker says that it was well known in southwest Missouri shortly after the Civil War.

Oh whis-key is the mon-ster That ru-ins great an' small, But
in old Ker-by's ar-my Head-quar-ters gets it all.
Chorus Oh how do you like the ar-my? The brass-moun-ted ar-my, The
high-fal-lu-tin' ar-my, Where ea-gle but-tons rule?

They drink it when it's plenty,
Although they think it hard,
But if a private touches it
They put him under guard.

Our army is more richer
Than when the war begun,
Furnishes three tables,
An' then they set but one.

The first is richly laden
Of chicken, goose an' duck,
The next is pork an' mutton,
The third is pore old buck.

Our generals eat the poultry,
They git it very cheap,
Our colonels an' our captains
Devours the hogs an' sheep.

Our soldiers git so hungry
They're bound to press a pig,
The biggest stump in Dixie
They're sure to have to dig.

But when we are a-marchin',
The order number blank,
It makes the private soldier
Forever stay in rank.

On every big plantation
Or a nigger-holder's yard,
Just to save his property,
Our generals place a guard.

An' now my song is ended,
It's beautiful an' true,
The pore men an' the widders
Must have a line or two.

But there no guard is stationed,
Their fence is often burned,
Their property's molested,
As long ago we learned.

222

PRAIRIE GROVE

This is a fragmentary story of the battle at Prairie Grove, some ten miles south of Fayetteville, Ark., Dec. 7, 1862. The Confederate General Hindman attacked a Federal force under General Herron, who was driven from the field despite the artillery fire of Blount's division, which arrived during the fight. It was a barren victory, since Hindman's troops had no supplies and were forced to retire, upon which the Federals returned to their original position. Several Confederate veterans have told me that they heard this "Yankee ballet" as early as 1864.

Sung by Mrs. Judy Jane Whittaker, Anderson, Mo., May 4, 1928.

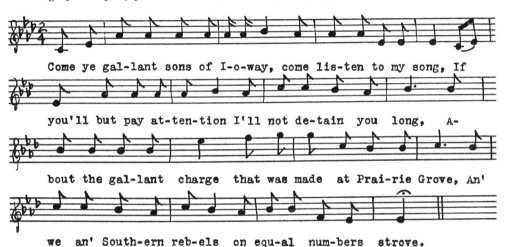

Come ye gal-lant sons of I-o-way, come lis-ten to my song, If you'll but pay at-ten-tion I'll not de-tain you long, A-bout the gal-lant charge that was made at Prai-rie Grove, An' we an' South-ern reb-els on equ-al num-bers strove.

Through fields of blood we waded, was about to gain the day,
Until old Blount's artillery had then began to play,
The cannons loud did roar an' put 'em all to flight,
An' they all had to retreat by the dead hours of the night.

I was sorry the next mornin' to see the rebels' wives
A-huntin' their dead husbands, with melancholy cries,
As we put 'em all in order, just like on dress parade,
An' we put a board at each man's head, to mark where he was laid.

223

THE SOUTHERN ENCAMPMENT

It appears that this piece was well known in McDonald, Barry and Newton counties, Mo., in the late 60's, but I have been unable to find any reference to it in the folksong literature.

Sung by Mrs. Linnie Bullard, Pineville, Mo., July 7, 1926. Mrs. Bullard said that she first heard the song near White Rock, Mo., in 1863.

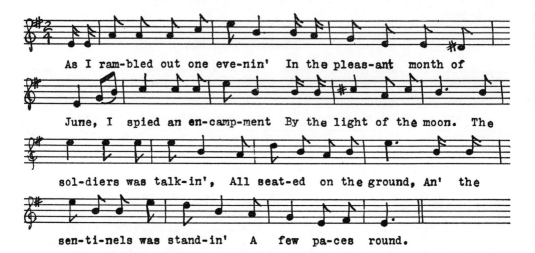

As I ram-bled out one eve-nin' In the pleas-ant month of June, I spied an en-camp-ment By the light of the moon. The sol-diers was talk-in', All seat-ed on the ground, An' the sen-ti-nels was stand-in' A few pa-ces round.

I stepped up to one of 'em
An' unto him did say,
Pray tell to me what meaneth this
An' the order of the day.
These are brave Southerners
Encamped here tonight,
Their country is invaded,
An' they intend to fight.

They are young, brave an' hardy,
An' not easy put to flight,
An' if Lincoln should assail 'em
He sure will have to fight.
They have left their wives an' children
An' every thing that's dear,
An' have encamped here
Their hardships for to share.

Their rations they are scanty,
An' their beds are very hard,
But when they whip the Linconites
They'll get their reward.

. . . .
. . . .
. . . .
. . . .

I give to you my feelings
On paper with my pen,
I bein' a female
My help I cannot lend.
But may the God of Battles
By the Southern Army stand,
An' help to drive the Lincolnites
Away from our land.

224

OLD GENERAL PRICE

The "hard times" refrain is common to several songs popular in the early 60's. See Belden (*Song-Ballads and Other Popular Poetry*, 1910, No. 108), Lomax (*Cowboy Songs*, 1910, p. 103), Hudson (*JAFL* 39, 1926, pp. 183-184), Cox (*Folk-Songs of the South*, 1925, p. 511) and Lomax (*American Ballads and Folk-Songs*, 1934, pp. 332-334). Add the "Song of the Times" reported from Missouri by Belden (*Ballads and Songs*, 1940, pp. 433-434).

Sung by Mr. J. H. Story, Pineville, Mo., July 14, 1922. Mr. Story heard the song shortly after the battle of Pea Ridge, which was fought near his home. Mr. Story visited the Confederate camp as a boy, and saw "Pappy" Price many times.

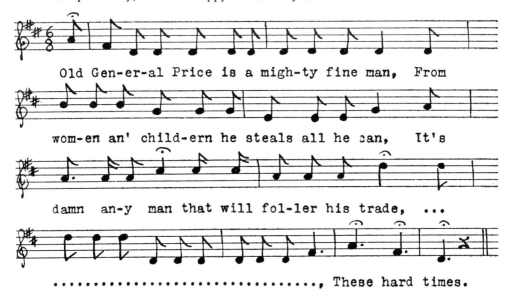

Old Gen-er-al Price is a migh-ty fine man, From
wom-en an' child-ern he steals all he can, It's
damn an-y man that will fol-ler his trade, ...
. . . . , These hard times.

225

THE BATTLE OF VICKSBURG

This piece is adapted from an older song "On Buena Vista's Battlefield," which was written by Colonel Henry Petriken, set to music by Albert G. Emerick, and printed in Emerick's *Songs for the People* (Philadelphia, 1848, I, pp. 112-116). See Lomax (*Cowboy Songs*, 1910, p. 34), Tolman and Eddy (*JAFL* 35, 1922, pp. 359-360), and Pound (*American Ballads and Songs*, 1922, No. 40). Hudson (*Folksongs of Mississippi*, 1936, p. 261) reports a similar text, and points out that both this piece and the "Buena Vista" song are reminiscent of "Bingen on the Rhine," written about the middle of the 19th century by Mrs. E. S. Norton.

A

Sung by Mr. J. P. Cleveland, Jane, Mo., July 17, 1928.

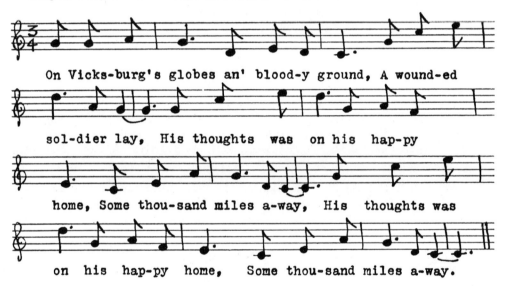

On Vicks-burg's globes an' blood-y ground, A wound-ed sol-dier lay, His thoughts was on his hap-py home, Some thou-sand miles a-way, His thoughts was on his hap-py home, Some thou-sand miles a-way.

Oh comrades dear, come close to me,
My heart's with you today,
Come hear the word I have to send
Some thousand miles away,
Come hear the word I have to send
Some thousand miles away.

An' when you meet my mother dear,
Be careful how you speak,
The cords of life are almost run,
Her heart may be too weak,
The cords of life are almost run,
Her heart may be too weak.

An' there's another so dear to me,
She's gentle as a fawn,
She lives behind yon distant glow,
Down by the murmurin' stream,
She lives behind yon distant glow,
Down by the murmurin' stream.

An' when I'm dead take this here ring—
An' bear it to yon shore,
Tell Molly 'tis the gift of one
Who sleeps to wake no more,
Tell Molly 'tis the gift of one
Who sleeps to wake no more.

An' here's a tress her own hand gave,
With it I never shall part,
An' when I'm dead don't you forget
To press it to my heart,
An' when I'm dead don't you forget
To press it to my heart.

The blood fast trickled down his side,
A tear stood in his eye,
He sighed, I ne'er shall see thee more,
Sweet maid, before I die.
He sighed, I ne'er shall see thee more,
Sweet maid before I die.

Oh comrades dear, come close my eyes,
An' make my last cold bed,
Before the mornin' sun shall rise
I shall be numbered dead.
Before the mornin' sun shall rise
I shall be numbered dead.

B

Mrs. Rosie Lattin, Pineville, Mo., Sept. 14, 1932, recalls a fragment of "On Buena Vista's Battlefield," from which the "Battle of Vicksburg" song was derived.

On Buena Vista's battlefield
A dying soldier lay,
His thoughts was on his mountain home
Some thousand miles away.

. . . . . .

Speak not to her in hurried words
The blighting news you bear,
The cords of life might snap too soon,
So comrades, have a care.

. . . . .

Tell her when death was on my brow,
An' life recedin' fast,
Her voice, her form, her partin' words
Was with me to the last.

. . . . .

On Buena Vista's battlefield,
Tell her I dyin' lay,
An' that I knew she thought of me,
Some thousand miles away.

226

THE HAPPY LAND OF CANAAN

Cox (*Folk-Songs of the South*, 1925, p. 270) prints a fragment of a similar Civil War song from Kentucky. Sharp (*English Folk Songs from the Southern Appalachians*, 1932, II, p. 201) has a Federal version with the more or less cryptic lines: "It takes forty yards of alapac to cover up the hoops, and to cover up the happy land of money." See also the "Happy Land of Canaan" which Belden (*Ballads and Songs*, 1940, pp. 363-364) recovered in Miller County, Missouri. "Evidently a minstrel-stage song," says Belden, "remade to catch the favor of Confederate sympathisers; though the refrain suggests that it was made on the basis of some hymn or religious song—a 'spiritual,' perhaps." According to *Missouri: A Guide to the 'Show Me' State* (New York, 1941, p. 159) a Howard County Negro sang during the Civil War: "God bless the whole kepoodle, Hail Columbia, Yankee Doodle, We're fightin' for the happy land of Cannan."

A

Sung by Mr. J. F. Gould, Pittsburg, Kan., June 4, 1930. Mr. Gould first heard the song at Batesville, Ark., in 1862.

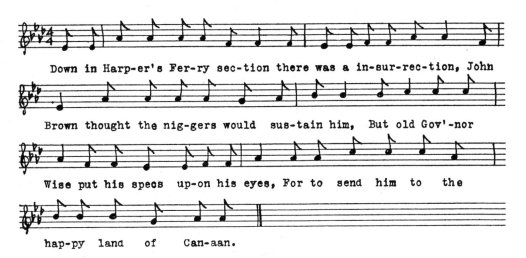

Down in Harp-er's Fer-ry sec-tion there was a in-sur-rec-tion, John

Brown thought the nig-gers would sus-tain him, But old Gov'-nor

Wise put his specs up-on his eyes, For to send him to the

hap-py land of Can-aan.

> The up-country volunteers have left their little dears
> To go to Camp Cowskin for trainin',
> To prepare to meet the Dutch, that they love so very much,
> When they meet 'em in the happy land of Canaan.

B

Contributed by Mr. Otto Ernest Rayburn, Kingston, Ark., Oct. 23, 1933. Mr. Rayburn obtained this text from Mr. J. S. Ripley, in the Ouachita River country. Mr. Ripley said that it was "made up" by John A. Kelley, who was a member of the "Rust Guards" mentioned in the song, perhaps named in honor of Brig. Gen. Albert Rust, C.S.A.

> At the Harper's Ferry section
> There was an insurrection,
> Old Brown thought the niggers would sustain him, ha ha,
> But old Governor Wise put the specs upon his eyes,
> For to show him to the Happy Land of Canaan.
>
> Governor Wise shakes his fist
> At the Abolition list,
> How he would like for to train 'em, ha ha,
> He'd hang 'em all genteely,
> Garate Smith and Horace Greeley,
> If he caught 'em in the Happy Land of Canaan.

The Rust Guard boys
Don't fear none of Lincoln's noise,
They are on the way to Richmond for to train him, ha ha,
They are bound to have their rights
Or there'll be some awful fights,
When they get to the Happy Land of Canaan.

We're commanded by a man
Who from no one ever ran,
And he always treats the boys genteely, ha ha,
He will lead us to the fight
And we'll lick the Yankees right,
When we get to the Happy Land of Canaan.

We were presented with a flag,
On what we can brag,
The name of the lady was Miss Akins, ha ha,
She told us for to go
And to let the Yankees know,
That we come from the Happy Land of Canaan.

I will mention in my song
Though it may be very wrong,
About a couple of old misers in Ashley, ha ha,
When we went to protect their bread,
They gave us nary red,
For to take us to the Happy Land of Canaan.

Fountain Hill is a place
Where they met us face to face,
And they treated us as soldiers should be treated, ha ha,
And we will our voices raise
Evermore to sing their praise,
As we march to the Happy Land of Canaan.

Troy is all right,
They helped us with all their might,
And treated us like their our darling children, ha, ha,
They divided with us their bread,
And they give us their last red
For to take us to the Happy Land of Canaan.

Hamburg is a town
On which our volunteers are down,
They treated us mighty rough while marching, ha ha,
Somebody stole our corn,
And they helped us—in a horn,
For to get us to the Happy Land of Canaan.

Next at Collins's we stopped
And a good plan did adopt,
Which was to keep us orderly and genteely, ha ha,
The general give us our fill,
And advised us how to drill,
Which will help us in the Happy Land of Cannan.

We had a very early start
Which made all the boys smart,
They were on to Gaines' Landing for breakfast, ha ha,
They gave us the very fits,
For they charged each one six bits,
As we went to the Happy Land of Canaan.

Now all you volunteers,
I hope you have no fears,
When you see the Yankees a-coming, ha, ha,
For you know very well
That we can blow them all to hell,
When you get to the Happy Land of Canaan.

C

Professor A. W. Breeden, Manhattan, Kan., Apr. 12, 1935, sings a Northern version of this piece, which he learned in Stone County, Mo., in the early 90's.

Oh the Ioway First are the boys they fear the worst,
And on the Johnny Rebs we are gainin',
If they fight instead of run, we'll show 'em lots of fun,
And they'll never see the Happy Land of Canaan.

Oh ho, oh ho, oh ho! Ah ha, ah ha, ah ha!
On the Johnny Rebs we are gainin',
And with bayonet and shell we will give the Johnnies hell
An they'll never see the Happy Land of Canaan.

227

IN EIGHTEEN HUNDRED AND SIXTY-ONE

There is a similar refrain in the sailors' chantey "Johnny, Fill Up the Bowl" which Eckstorm and Smyth (*Minstrelsy of Maine*, 1937, pp. 241-242) heard on the Maine coast. The tune is that of "When Johnny Comes Marching Home," which was written by Patrick S. Gilmore (pseudonym Louis Lambert) in 1863, and revived at the time of the Spanish-American War. Jean Thomas (*Ballad Makin'*, 1939, p. 54) reports three stanzas from Kentucky with the line "we'll all drink stone *wine*" instead of "stone *blind*" as in the Ozark text. The piece is in the Brown (North Carolina Folk-Lore Society) collection.

A

Contributed by Dr. George E. Hastings, Fayetteville, Ark., Nov. 14, 1938. Dr. Hastings obtained it from one of his students at the University of Arkansas.

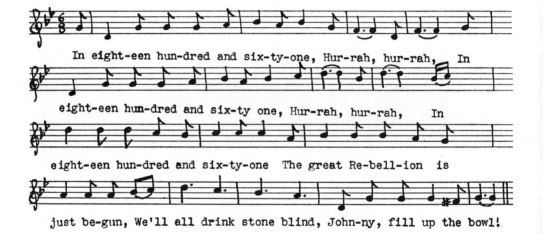

In eight-een hun-dred and six-ty-one, Hur-rah, hur-rah, In eight-een hun-dred and six-ty one, Hur-rah, hur-rah, In eight-een hun-dred and six-ty-one The great Re-bell-ion is just be-gun, We'll all drink stone blind, John-ny, fill up the bowl!

In eighteen hundred and sixty-two,
Hurrah, hurrah,
In eighteen hundred and sixty-two
Hurrah, hurrah,
In eighteen hundred and sixty-two
The rebels put the Yankees through,
We'll all drink stone blind,
Johnny, fill up the bowl!

In eighteen hundred and sixty-three,
Hurrah, hurrah,
In eighteen hundred and sixty-three
Hurrah, hurrah,
In eighteen hundred and sixty-three
Abe Lincoln set the niggers free,
We'll all drink stone blind,
Johnny, fill up the bowl!

In eighteen hundred and sixty-four,
Hurrah, hurrah,
In eighteen hundred and sixty-four
Hurrah, hurrah,
In eighteen hundred and sixty-four
We'll elect Jeff Davis for four years more,
We'll all drink stone blind,
Johnny, fill up the bowl!

In eighteen hundred and sixty-five,
Hurrah, hurrah,
In eighteen hundred and sixty-five
Hurrah, hurrah,
In eighteen hundred and sixty-five
We'll git Abe Lincoln dead or alive,
We'll all drink stone blind,
Johnny, fill up the bowl!

In eighteen hundred and sixty-six,
Hurrah, hurrah,
In eighteen hundred and sixty-six
Hurrah, hurrah,
In eighteen hundred and sixty-six
This country'll be in a pretty fix,
We'll all drink stone blind,
Johnny, fill up the bowl!

B

A curious variant is sung by Mr. Booth Campbell, Cane Hill, Ark., Feb. 5, 1942. He insists that this piece has been well known at Cane Hill since the 80's to his personal knowledge, and was never called by any other name than "Football" or "The Football Song."

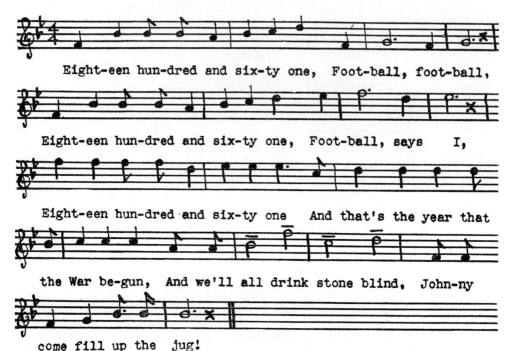

Eight-een hun-dred and six-ty one, Foot-ball, foot-ball,

Eight-een hun-dred and six-ty one, Foot-ball, says   I,

Eight-een hun-dred and six-ty one   And that's the year that

the War be-gun, And we'll all drink stone blind, John-ny

come fill up the   jug!

Eighteen hundred and sixty-two,
Football, football,
Eighteen hundred and sixty-two,
Football, says I,
Eighteen hundred and sixty-two
And the rebels was puttin' the Yankees through,
And we'll all drink stone blind,
Johnny come fill up the jug.

Eighteen hundred and sixty-three,
Football, football,
Eighteen hundred and sixty-three,
Football, says I,
Eighteen hundred and sixty-three,
And Lincoln set our niggers free,
And we'll all drink stone blind,
Johnny come fill up the jug.

. . . . . .

Eighteen hundred and sixty-five,
Football, football,
Eighteen hundred and sixty-five,
Football, says I,
Eighteen hundred and sixty-five,
And there wasn't a ninety-day Yankee alive,
And we'll all drink stone blind,
Johnny come fill up the jug.

Eighteen hundred and sixty-six,
Football, football,
Eighteen hundred and sixty-six,
Football, says I,
Eighteen hundred and sixty-six,
And the Southern States in a hell of a fix,
And we'll all drink stone blind,
Johnny come fill up the jug.

228

THE CAPTAIN WITH HIS WHISKERS

This must be pretty old; it was mentioned, together with other old-time song titles, in
"The Song of All Songs," words of uncertain authorship, tune by Stephen Foster, published
by Ditson in 1863 (see Morneweck, *Chronicles of Stephen Foster's Family*, 1944, II, pp. 555-
556). See also the *Bella Union Melodeon Songster No. 1* (D. E. Appleton & Co., San Francisco, 1860) and the *Marching Through Georgia Songster* (D. E. Appleton & Co., San Francisco,
1867). Mrs. Violet Savory Justis, Clinton, Mo., once showed me a manuscript copy of a
"popular gag song" dated 1889, to be sung to the tune of "The Captain and His Whiskers."

Sung by Mrs. Marie Wilbur, Pineville, Mo., Jan. 21, 1926.

When we met at the ball I of course thought 'twas right
To pretend that we never had met before that night,
He knew me at once, I perceived by his glance,
And I hung down my head when he asked me to dance.
He sat by my side at the end of the set,
And the sweet words he spoke I never shall forget.
My heart was enlisted and could not get free
When the captain with his whiskers took a sly glance at me.

But he marched from the town and I seen him no more,
Yet I often think of him and the whiskers that he wore,
I dream all the night and I talk all the day
Of the love of a captain who has gone far away.
I remember with superabundant delight
How we met in the street, and we danced all the night,
And I keep in my mind how my heart jumped with glee
When the captain with his whiskers took a sly glance at me!

229

BABYLON IS FALLING

This piece is credited to Henry C. Work, author of "Marching Through Georgia" and other wartime favorites, according to White (*American Negro Folk-Songs*, 1928, p. 170).

Sung by Mr. J. F. Gould, Pittsburg, Kansas, Sept. 3, 1926. Mr. Gould heard it sung by Federal troops in Arkansas, in 1864.

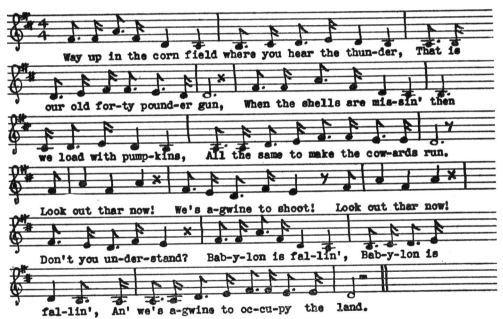

Way up in the corn field where you hear the thun-der, That is
our old for-ty pound-er gun, When the shells are mis-sin' then
we load with pump-kins, All the same to make the cow-ards run.
Look out thar now! We's a-gwine to shoot! Look out thar now!
Don't you un-der-stand? Bab-y-lon is fal-lin', Bab-y-lon is
fal-lin', An' we's a-gwine to oc-cu-py the land.

Old Massa was a colonel in the rebel army,
Jest before he come to run away,
But his darlin' darkies didn't like his doin's
So they up an' tuck him prisoner t'other day.
Look out thar, now! We's a-gwine to shoot!
Look out thar, now! Don't you understand?
Babylon is fallin', Babylon is fallin',
An' we's a-gwine to occupy the land.

230

THE YEAR OF JUBELO

This is the "Kingdom Coming" song written by Henry Clay Work during the Civil War. It was copyrighted in 1861, according to White (*American Negro Folk-Songs*, 1928, p. 170) and published by Root and Cady in 1862, according to Dichter and Shapiro (*Early American Sheet Music*, 1941, p. 116). Eggleston (*American War Ballads and Lyrics*, 1889, pp. 200-202) says that the song was sung by Negro troops as they marched into Richmond, and later became quite popular among Southern whites, "being sung with great applause by young men and maidens in well-nigh every house in Virginia." For other texts see White (*Poetry of the Civil War*, 1866, p. 254), Chapple (*Heart Songs*, 1909, pp. 152-153), and Talley (*Negro Folk Rhymes*, 1922, p. 58). The piece appears in the Brown (North Carolina Folk-Lore Society) collection. Compare also the phonograph record by Frank Crumit (*Victor* 21108).

Sung by Mr. J. F. Gould, Pittsburg, Kans, Sept. 3, 1926. Mr. Gould served in the Illinois cavalry at Pea Ridge, and heard the song in Arkansas military camps in 1862 or 1863.

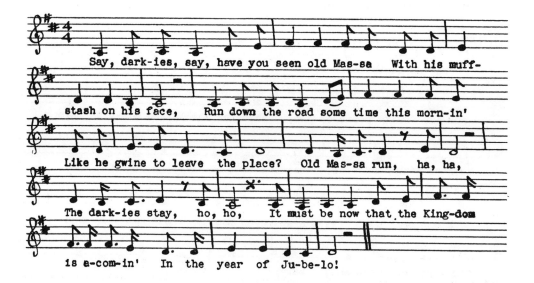

The overseer he make us trouble,
He drive us round a spell,
We lock him up in the smoke-house cellar
With the key throwed in the well.

He was six foot one way an' two foot the other,
An' he weighed three hundred pounds,
His coat was so big that he couldn't pay the tailor
An' it wouldn't go half-way round.

He seen some smoke way up the river
Where the Linkum gunboats lay,
He picks up his hat an' he left mighty sudden,
I 'spect he's run away.

There's plenty o' wine an' cider in the cellar
An' the darkies they'll have some,
For I expect we'll all be cornfiscated
When the Linkum soldiers come.

The whip is lost an' the handcuffs busted,
Old Massa's got his pay,
He's big 'nough an' old 'nough, he orter know better
Than to went an' run away.

231

I'M A GOOD OLD REBEL

Herbert Quick (*Colliers' Weekly* 53, Apr. 4, 1914, p. 20) says that this song was written shortly after the Civil War by Major Innes Randolph, a Virginian who served on J. E. B. Stuart's staff. It was described as "a bit of fun, not supposed to reflect Major Randolph's own sentiments, but to illustrate the irreconcilable spirit of the illiterate element in some sections." The Duchess of Manchester sang it before the Prince of Wales, who repeatedly asked for "that fine American song with the cuss words in it." Queen Victoria herself, according to Cora Brown Potter (*Cosmopolitan Magazine*, Mar. 1933, pp. 18-19) "was quite fascinated by it." Similar texts from oral tradition are reported by Cox (*Folk-Songs of the South*, 1925, pp. 281-282), Lomax (*American Ballads and Folk Songs*, 1934, pp. 535-540), and Brown (North Carolina Folk-Lore Society) collection.

Reed Smith (*South Carolina Ballads*, 1928, pp. 45-47) prints the song as written by Innes Randolph, also a text recovered from oral tradition in Texas by Lomax. For the original text see *Poems by Innes Randolph, Compiled by His Son Harold Randolph from the Original Manuscript*, Baltimore, Williams and Wilkin Co., 1898. Dichter and Shapiro (*Early American Sheet Music*, 1941, p. 123) list this item, "supposed to have been issued by Blackmar, New Orleans, ca. 1866."

A

Text and tune supplied by Mrs. May Kennedy McCord, Springfield, Mo., July 30, 1940. Mrs. McCord obtained the text in manuscript from one of her neighbors, but it probably goes back to recent print.

Oh I'm a good old reb-el, Now that's just what I am, For
this fair land of free-dom I do not care a damn.

I'm glad I fit against it,
I only wish we'd won,
An' I don't want no pardon
For anything I done.

I hates the Constitution,
This great Republic too,
I hates the Freedman's Bureau
In uniforms of blue.

I hates the nasty eagle
With all her brags an' fuss,
The lyin' thievin' Yankees,
I hates 'em wuss an' wuss.

I hates the Yankee nation
An' everything they do,
I hates the Declaration
Of Independence, too.

I hates the glorious Union
A-dripping with our blood,
I hates their striped banners,
I fit it all I could.

I follered old Marse Robert
For four year, near about.
Got wounded in three places,
An' starved at Point Lookout.

I kotch the rheumatism
A-campin' in the snow,
But I killed a chance o' Yankees,
An' I'd like to kill some more.

Three hundred thousand Yankees
Lies stiff in southern dust,
We got three hundred thousand
Before they conquered us.

They died of southern fever
An' southern steel an' shot,
I wisht they was three million
Instead of what we got.

I caint take up my musket
An' fight 'em any more,
But I aint a-goin' to love 'em,
An' that is sartin shore.

An' I don't want no pardon
For what I was an' am,
I won't be reconstructed,
An' I do not give a damn.

B

Sung by Mr. Wythe Bishop, Fayetteville, Ark., Dec. 9, 1941. Bishop told me solemnly that this "little parody" was written by the same man who wrote "The Days of '49!"

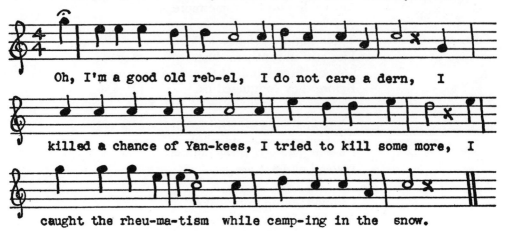

Oh, I'm a good old reb-el, I do not care a dern, I killed a chance of Yan-kees, I tried to kill some more, I caught the rheu-ma-tism while camp-ing in the snow.

> I hate the nasty eagle,
> I hate the pardon too,
> I hate the . . . .
> In uniforms of blue.
> I follered old Tom Roberts
> Ten thousand miles or more,
> I caught the rheumatism
> While campin' in the snow.

C

Sung by Mr. Booth Campbell, Cane Hill, Ark., Feb. 5, 1942. Learned at Cane Hill in the 80's. Mr. Campbell was a little afraid to sing this at first. "The country's at war right now," said he, "and it aint no time for a feller to be singin' songs ag'in the Flag and the Government."

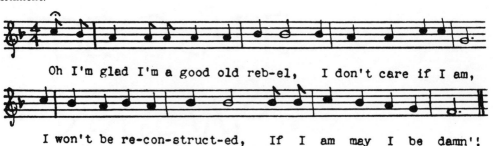

Oh I'm glad I'm a good old reb-el, I don't care if I am, I won't be re-con-struct-ed, If I am may I be damn'!

> Oh I follered old Marse Robert
> For four years near about,
> Got wounded in three places
> And starved at Camp Lookout.

I hate that Yankee nation,
And all they say and do,
I hate the Declaration
Of Independence too.

I hate that striped banner
With all it's r'ar and fuss,
Them lyin', thievin' Yankees,
I hate 'em worse and worse.

I caint take up my musket
And fight 'em any more,
But I aint a-goin' to love 'em,
Now that am certain shore!

Yes, I'm glad I'm a good old rebel,
Hat, boots, coat and all,
I won't be reconstructed,
No sir, not at all.

232

BENJY HAVENS

Part of an old Regular Army song, all about one Bennie Havens who served as a lieutenant in the War of 1812, and spent the rest of his life selling whiskey to the cadets at West Point (Dolph,"*Sound Off*," 1929, p. 563). Edgar Allan Poe, expelled from the Academy after six months of drunken roystering, often said that Bennie was "the only congenial soul in the entire God-forsaken place." The original song was written by Lieutenant O'Brien of the Eighth Infantry in 1838, but many verses have been added since, and the song has become traditional at West Point. It was sung by both Union and Confederate troops in the Civil War.

Sung by Mr. Bert Hawes, Sylamore, Ark., Sept. 20, 1919. He learned it from Yankee soldiers—St. Louis Dutch, he called them—in 1865.

Oh   Ben-jy Hav-ens   oh,   Oh   Ben-jy Hav-ens   oh,   We'll

sing   some rem-in-is-cen-ces   Of   Ben-jy   Hav-ens   oh.

233

THE UNION VOLUNTEER

The Ozark singers regard this as a Civil War song. It seems to be an adaptation of "The Bold Privateer," printed in many old songbooks (*Trifet's Budget of Music No. 15*, 1892, p. 158), the words practically unchanged except that "Union volunteer" is substituted for "Bold Privateer"—the name of the ship on which Johnny was about to sail. Compare the "Yankee Man of War" piece reported by Belden (*Ballads and Songs*, 1940, pp. 379-380) from a Missouri manuscript dated 1876.

Contributed by Mr. Lewis Kelley, Cyclone, Mo., Aug. 2, 1931. Mr. Kelley has a manuscript copy dated 1897.

It's oh my dear-est Mol-ly   you and I must part,   I am go-ing
a-cross the sea, love,   I leave to you my heart,   My ship she
lies in wait-ing, so fare you well, my dear,   I am just a-go-ing on
board as a Un-ion vol-un-teer,   My ship she lies in wait-ing, so
fare you well, my dear,   I am just a-go-ing on board   as a
Un-ion vol-un-teer.

Oh my dearest Johnny, great dangers has been crossed,
And many a sweet life in this here war's been lost,
You had better stay at home with the girl that loves you dear,
And forever bid adieu to this Union volunteer,
To this Union volunteer, love, to this Union volunteer.

Oh my dearest Molly, your friends do me dislike,
Besides you have two brothers who would quickly take my life,
So change your ring with me, love, come change your ring with me,
An' it shall be a token when I am far away,
When I am far away, love, when I am far away.

An' when this war is over, if heaven spares my life,
So soon I will come back to my sweet lovin' wife,
So soon I will get married to the girl that loves me dear,
An' forever bid adieu to this Union volunteer,
To this Union volunteer, love, this Union volunteer.

234

THAT LAST FIERCE FIGHT

This piece is usually called "The Battle of Fredericksburg" in the Ozarks, though a text printed in the Aurora (Mo.) *Advertiser*, Jan. 5, 1939, is described as "a poem about the Custer massacre, June 25, 1876." Barry (*JAFL* 27, 1914, p. 70) has a tune from Massachusetts, and texts from oral tradition have been reported by Dean (*The Flying Cloud*, 1922, pp. 14-16), Mackenzie (*Ballads and Sea Songs from Nova Scotia*, 1928, pp. 298-300), Fuson (*Ballads of the Kentucky Highlands*, 1935, pp. 94-95), Henry (*Folk-Songs from the Southern Highlands*, 1938, pp. 363-364), Eddy (*Ballads and Songs from Ohio*, 1939, pp. 301-304), Belden (*Ballads and Songs*, 1940, pp. 383-387), and Brown (North Carolina Folk-Lore Society) collection.

A

Sung by Mr. Doney Hammontree, Farmington, Ark., Dec. 28, 1941. He learned it in
the 90's, near Fayetteville, Ark., and sings it to the same tune he uses for "Young Charlotte."

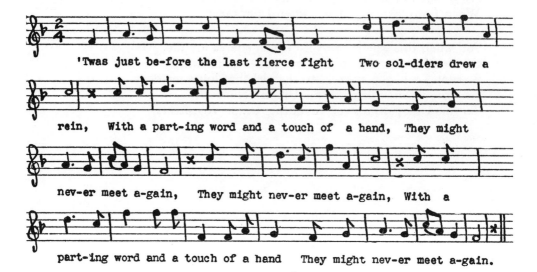

'Twas just be-fore the last fierce fight   Two sol-diers drew a

rein,   With a part-ing word and a touch of a hand, They might

nev-er meet a-gain,   They might nev-er meet a-gain,   With a

part-ing word and a touch of a hand   They might nev-er meet a-gain.

One had blue eyes and curly hair,
Eighteen scarce a month ago,
And down his cheeks there rolled a tear
For he was but a boy, you know.
For he was but a boy, you know,
And down his cheeks there rolled a tear
For he was but a boy, you know.

The other was tall, dark, stern and proud,
And his faith in the world was dim,
For he only trusted the girl he loved,
She was all the world to him,
She was all the world to him,
For he only trusted the girl that he loved,
She was all the world to him.

The tall dark man was the first to speak,
Saying Charley, the hour has come,
Oh promise this letter you'll send to her
For me if I am gone.
For me if I am gone,
Oh promise this letter you'll send to her
For me if I am gone.

Tears filled the eyes of the blue-eyed boy
As he answered faint and low,
Saying I'll do your bidding, comrade mine,
If I ever write home any more.
If I ever write home any more,
Saying I'll do your bidding, comrade mine,
If I ever write home any more.

If you write home to the loved ones there,
You'll do as much for me,
For I've a mother that would hear the news,
Tell her most tenderly.
Tell her most tenderly,
For I've a mother that would hear the news,
Tell her most tenderly.

They rode along to the crest of the hill
While the cannon shot and shell,
While volley after volley came
To cheer them as they fell.
And cheered them as they fell,
While volley after volley came
And cheered them as they fell.

Among the dead and dying lay
The boy with the curly hair,
And close by his side lay the tall dark man,
He was dead beside him there.
He was dead beside him there,
And close by his side lay the tall dark man,
He was dead beside him there.

Oh who will write to that dear little girl,
These words which hath been said,
And who will tell that mother at home
That her own dear boy is dead?
That her own dear boy is dead,
And who will tell that mother at home
That her own dear boy is dead?

B

Text from Mrs. Violet Savory Justis, Clinton, Mo., Dec. 20, 1929. She calls it "The Comrades' Last Brave Charge."

Just before the last brave charge
Two soldiers drew a rein,
With a parting word and a touch of the hand
That they might not meet again.
One had blue eyes and curly hair,
Nineteen but a month ago,
With rosy cheeks and a beardless chin,
He's only a lad, you know.

The other one was a tall dark man
Whose faith in the world was dim,
He only trusted the more in one
Who was all this world to him.
They'd fought together against many a foe,
Marched forth in many a mile,
But never before had they met the foe
Like here with a helpless smile.

The tall dark man was the first to speak,
Saying Charley, my hour has come,
We'll ride together up this here hill
But you'll ride back alone.
It's promise me a little trouble to take
For me when I am gone.

There is a face upon my breast,
I wear it into the fight,
With clustering curls and soft blue eyes
That gleams like morning light.
Like morning light was her love to me,
That glided along my life,
But little did I care for the forms of earth
Till she promised to be my wife.

Tears dimmed the eyes of the blue-eyed boy,
And he lowered his voice with pain,
I'll do your bidding, comrade mine,
If I ride back again.
But if you ride back and I am gone
You must do as much for me,
I have a mother who must know the news,
Write to her tenderly.

. . . . one after the other
She's buried both husband and son,
I was the last, my country called,
She kissed me and sent me on.

Just then the order came to march,
With an instant touch of the hand,
They answered back we are on our way
In a brave devoted band.
On they rode to the crest of the hill
That leads upon the plain,
Then those that were wounded but able to ride
Rode slowly back again.

But amongst the dead that was left behind
Was the boy with the curly hair,
And the tall dark man that rode by his side
Lay dead beside him there.

There's no one to write to the blue-eyed girl
The words her lover had said,
There's a mother at home who waits for her son,
Not knowing that he is dead.
She never will know the last fond thought,
The thought that would soften her pain,
Until she crosses the river of death
And stands by his side again.

235

COME RAISE ME IN YOUR ARMS, DEAR BROTHER

Sung by Mr. Doney Hammontree, Farmington, Ark., Dec. 28, 1941. He learned it near
Fayetteville, Ark., in the early 90's.

Come raise me in your arms, dear broth-er, And let me
see that glo-ri-ous sun, For I am wea-ry, faint and dy-ing,
How could that bat-tle lost or won.

I remember you, my brother,
Sent to me that fatal dart,
Brothers fighting against brothers,
Well, 'tis well that thus they part.

Father fighting for the Union,
You will meet him on the field,
How could you raise your hand to smite him,
How could you bid our father yield?

He who loved us in our childhood,
Taught us infant prayers we said,
Brother, I am surely dying,
Shall soon be numbered with the dead.

Do you ever think of mother
In that home far in the land?
Watching, praying for her children,
If I could see that home again!

Write a letter to my mother,
Send it when her boy is dead.
That he perished by his brother,
Not one word of that be said.

Brother, take from me a warning,
Keep that secret you have won,
For it would kill our aged old mother
If she knew what you have done.

236

JOHN MARSHALL

Sung by Mrs. Lessie Stringfellow Read, Fayetteville, Ark., Dec. 23, 1941. She learned it from her father, Captain H. M. Stringfellow, C.S.A., who told her it was written by Innes Randolph, a relative of the Stringfellows, in 1866, when Virginia was ruled by Federal authorities and known as District Number One. The tune is adapted from a Confederate bugle-call.

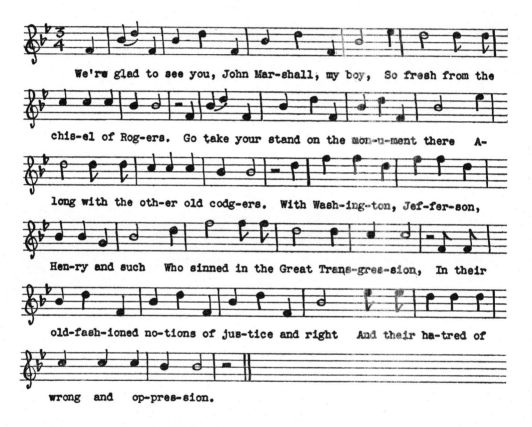

We're glad to see you, John Mar-shall, my boy, So fresh from the chis-el of Rog-ers. Go take your stand on the mon-u-ment there A-long with the oth-er old codg-ers. With Wash-ing-ton, Jef-fer-son, Hen-ry and such Who sinned in the Great Trans-gres-sion, In their old-fash-ioned no-tions of jus-tice and right And their ha-tred of wrong and op-pres-sion.

You come rather late to your pedestal, John,
For sooner you ought to have been there,
The volume you hold is no longer the law,
And this is no longer Virginia.
The old Marshall law you expounded of yore
Is not now at all to the purpose,
For the martial law of the new brigadier
Is stronger than habeas corpus.

Then keep you your law-volume shut up with care,
For the days of the law are all over,
And it takes all your brass to be holding it there
With JUSTICE inscribed on its cover.

Could life awaken those limbs of bronze
And blaze in the burnished eye,
What would ye do with your moment of life,
Ye men of these days now gone by?
Would ye chide us, or pity us, or blame us, or weep,
Ye men of the days gone by?
Would Jefferson throw down the scroll that he holds
And which times since have sought to belie?

Would Marshall shut up his volume of law
And stand there in dignified silence
While this Military District Number One
Became a grim victim of violence?
Would Mason tear up the old Bill of Rights
From a "Nation" unworthy to scan it?
Would Pat Henry dash down his eloquent sword
And clang it against his granite?

And Washington — — riding there in massy state
On a charger that paws the air—
Could he see his sons in their deep disgrace,
Would he ride so proudly there?

No, he would get him down from his big brass horse
And cover his face at our shame,
For the land that he loved is now District One,
Virginia was once its name.

We are glad to see you, John Marshall, my boy,
So fresh from the chisel of Rogers,
Go take your stand on the monument there
Along with the other old codgers.

237

ANDERSONVILLE PRISON

Manuscript copy from Mrs. Violet Savory Justis, Clinton, Mo., Dec. 20, 1929.

On western Georgia's sandy soil
Within a lonesome prison pen,
Lay many a thousand shattered forms
Who once was brave and loyal men.

They lay uncovered on the ground
Beneath the burning southern sun,
And out into the great unknown
They passed unheeded one by one.

A creek of filth run through that pen
From which each one was forced to take
What little water he could get
His paltry gill of meal to bake.

He left his happy home and friends
All for the sake of his dear land,
And ever in the battle front
Wielded his sword with steady hand.

One evening as the sun sank low
Behind the western horizon,
A lad walked down toward the creek,
He was a widow's only son.

Slowly he hobbled on the ground,
Thinking of his far distant home,
But suddenly he stopped, stepped back,
He on that fatal line had come.

At once a savage shot rung out,
Fired by some heartless villain's hand,
And with a cry his form sank down,
His life blood streaming on the sand.

One of his chums, a noble lad
Whose once bright face looked pale and sad,
Knelt by his dying friend to pray,
And hear the last words he might say.

Tell mother she was not disgraced by me,
The dying soldier gasped,
Around his weeping comrade's neck
His weakened trembling arms were clasped.

Ask Mary to forgive me, Tom,
If I have ever done her wrong,
I never meant it if I did,
You know she loved me true and long.

The day we started to the front
I kissed her on her snow white brow,
I told her that she'd soon be mine,
But I shall never see her now.

Tell her I — — but his voice was gone,
He sank into his comrade's arms,
And in one moment passed away
Where sin and sorrow never harms.

Just as the sun sank out of sight,
That ragged faded suit of blue,
Dyed with a noble heart's best blood,
Was changed for that of spotless hue.

238

BARBRO BUCK

Sharp (*English Folk Songs from the Southern Appalachians*, II, 1932, p. 274) prints the first four lines of this piece just as I record them here, except that he spells the soldier's name "Barbara."

Contributed by Mrs. A. J. Forgy, Center Point, Ark., Mar. 27, 1930. Mrs. Forgy learned the song from her mother, Mrs. E. E. Briggs, Little Rock, Ark. Mrs. Briggs says that it is frequently known as "The Southern Soldier Boy."

Barbro Buck is my sweetheart's name,
He's off to the wars and gone,
He's fighting for his Nannie dear,
His sword is buckled on.

He's fighting for his own true love,
He is my only joy,
He is the darling of my heart,
My Southern soldier boy.

239

THE DRUMMER BOY OF SHILOH

See Belden (*Song-Ballads and Other Popular Poetry Known in Missouri*, 1910, No. 123), also an excellent text reported by Henry (*JAFL* 45, 1932, p. 163), and the Brown (North Carolina Folk-Lore Society) collection. In the Aurora (Mo.) *Advertiser*, July 22, 1937, it is intimated that the late Major-General John L. Clem had some connection with the authorship of this piece. As a piece of sheet music written and composed by Will S. Hays and published by D. P. Faulds, Louisville, Ky., 1862, this song is listed by Dichter and Shapiro (*Early American Sheet Music*, 1941, p. 115).

Contributed by Mrs. Ollie Smith, Neosho, Mo., Apr. 11, 1927. Mrs. Smith says that the text was "found in a tablet of old time songs which my grandmother had over fifty years ago."

> On Shiloh's dark and bloody ground
> The dead and wounded lay,
> Amongst them was a drummer boy
> Who beat the drum that day.
> A wounded soldier held him up,
> His drum was by his side,
> He clasped his hands, then raised his eyes
> And prayed before he died.
>
> Look down upon the battlefield,
> Oh thou, our heavenly friend,
> Have mercy on our sinful souls,
> The soldiers cry amen.
> For gathered round a little group
> Each brave man knelt and cried,
> They listened to the drummer boy
> Who prayed before he died.
>
> Oh mother, said the dying boy,
> Looking down from heaven on me,
> Receive me to thy fond embrace,
> Oh take me home to thee,
> I've loved my country and my God,
> To save them both I've tried,
> He smiled, shook hands, death seized the boy
> Who prayed before he died.

Each soldier wept then like a child,
Stout hearts were they and brave,
The flag his winding sheet, God took
The key into his grave.
They wrote upon a simple board
These words: This is a guide
To those who mourned the drummer boy
Who prayed before he died.

Ye angels round the throne of grace
Look down upon the brave,
Who fought and died on Shiloh's plains,
. . . .
. . . .
How many hearts have sighed,
How many like the drummer boy
Who prayed before he died.

240

I WISH I WAS AT HOME

Two very similar stanzas were printed in the Springfield (Mo.) *News and Leader* (July 6, 1939) by May Kennedy McCord, who had them from Mrs. Margaret Safrona Massey, Bolivar, Mo.

Sung by Mr. J. H. Story, Pineville, Mo., May 4, 1925. Mr. Story learned the song in Arkansas in the 70's.

I'm marchin' down to Washington
With a heavy load an' a rusty gun,
An' I wish I was at home,
An' I wish I was at home.

They carried me down to the navy yard,
An' round me they place a mounted guard,
An' I wish I was at home,
An' I wish I was at home.

241

IT'S TIME I WAS A BRIDE

This piece was published in sheet-music form by Blackmar & Bro., New Orleans, in 1862, "composed by Theod. von LaHache, author of 'Near the Banks of That Lone River,' 'Carrie Bell,' etc."

Sung by Miss Leila Morse, Joplin, Mo., Feb. 17, 1925. Miss Morse had it from an old lady near Siloam Springs, Ark., about 1910.

I'd like mighty well to change my name
And share another's home,
A man that's true and kind to me
And who will not care to roam.

My school days they are over,
My books are throwed aside,
I've oft-times been a bridesmaid,
It's time I was a bride.

And so I'd like to change my name,
And settle down in life,
Here is a chance for some young man
That's looking for a wife.

Old maids has oft-times told me
There's cares in married life,
I let 'em talk but heed 'em not
For I'm bound to be a wife.

Perhaps you think I'm jesting
But I mean just what I say,
And if some young man asks me
He'll find I'll not say nay.

But he must be a soldier,
A veteran of the wars,
One who has fought for Southern rights
Beneath the Stars and Bars.

242

THE JOLLY UNION BOYS

Mrs. Belle Smith Estey (*Missouri Historical Review*, Apr. 22, 1928, pp. 364-365) reports four stanzas of this piece with the following note: "Song composed by Lieut. B. T. Locke and sung by volunteers on the eve of their leaving for the Union Army in the Spring of '62."

Gerard Schultz (*History of Miller County, Mo.*, Jefferson City, Mo., 1933, pp. 127-128) prints 23 stanzas of a text entitled "Come On, My Jolly Union Boys." He says it was "made up" by Benjamin F. Locke of Saline Creek, and written down by one of his neighbors.

Belden (*Ballads and Songs*, 1940, pp. 366-367) has a good text entitled "The War in Missouri in '61." He repeats the story that it was written by B. F. Locke of Miller Co., Mo., who was "killed in a fight with Jim and Bill Matthews . . . shortly after the war."

Contributed by Miss Lucile Morris, Springfield, Mo., Oct. 28, 1934, from an old manuscript copy.

Come all you jolly Union boys,
To you the truth I'll tell,
Concerning Governor Jackson[1]
Who I know very well.

There was a man in Jefferson,
His name was Thomas Price,[2]
He come to see the governor
And give him good advice.

Then up comes the governor
Who thought he was so wise,
His . . . . violations
Made the Harney Compromise.[3]

They sent men to St. Louis,
I suppose it was to drill,
They had not been there very long
Till they all got their fill.

They had a great commander,
His name was Billy Frost,[4]
But in come a lion
And not a man was lost.

---

[1]Claiborne F. Jackson, Governor of Missouri in 1861; he tried to align Missouri with the Confederacy.

[2]Thomas Lawson Price, Congressman in 1861, opposed Governor Jackson.

[3]General William S. Harney, who commanded United States troops in St. Louis in 1861. He was replaced by General Lyon.

[4]General Daniel M. Frost commanded the Missouri Militia at Camp Jackson, surrendered to Lyon May 10, 1861.

Old Jackson walked out on the key
And swore he'd cut a dash,
He walked into the treasure store
And stole away the cash.

They seen the lion marching in,
The flank bear by his side,
The sesesh boys they says right now
It's time for us to slide.

McCulla[5] brought up artillery,
Some figuring was done,
Before they fired the third round
They wished he hadn't begun.

Next come the battle at Carthage,
They thought they'd see some fun,
But they run afoul of Sigels[6]
And everybody run.

In a little old creek bottom
Three hundred yards around,
Was thirteen hundred of the bravest men
A-laying on the ground.

Then old McCulla says to Price,[7]
He's mighty hard to beat,
That Dutchman could whip the Devil
And all the time retreat!

The ball from a rebel cannon
Sent the lion to his den,
But the bursting of a bomb
It done for old Ben.

[5]General Ben McCullough fought at Wilson Creek, was killed at Pea Ridge, Ark.
[6]General Franz Sigel. It was really Sigel who "run" at Carthage, July 5, 1861.
[7]General Sterling Price, C.S.A., who fought under General Van Dorn at Pea Ridge.

243

MOTHER, IS THE BATTLE OVER?

This song, composed by Henry Werner, was published by Balmer and Weber, St. Louis, 1863. A copy is available in the Music Collection of the State Historical Society of Missouri.

Sung by Charles M. Curtis, Picher, Okla., Dec. 24, 1919. Mr. Curtis learned the song from his mother in southwestern Missouri about 1890.

Oh mother dear, is the battle over?
Ten thousand have been slain, they say.
Is my father coming? Tell me,
Have the rebels gained the day?

Is he well, or is he wounded?
Mother, do you think he's slain?
If you know, I pray you tell me,
Will my father come home again?

Mother dear, you are always sighing,
Since you last the paper read,
Tell me why you're always crying,
Why that cap is on your head?

Oh I see you cannot tell me,
Father is among the slain,
And although he loved us dearly
He will never come home again.

Yes, my boy, your father is dead,
He is numbered among the slain,
We'll never see him more on earth
But in heaven we'll meet again.

He died for the union's glory,
Our day may not be . . . .
But I hope at the last trumpet sound
We will all meet together again.

244

THE SOLDIER'S LETTER

I have seen an almost identical manuscript copy in the possession of Mrs. Margaret Sharp, Pittsburg, Kansas, in May, 1925; she obtained it from her grandfather, Mr. Elisha Mills, Independence, Kan., in the 90's; Mr. Mills had learned it when he was a boy in Genessee County, New York.

Sung by Dr. H. Vanderventer, Washington County, Ark., July 3, 1921.

Dear Madam I am a soldier,
And my speech is rough and plain,
I'm not much used to writing,
And I hate to give my name.
But I promised that I'd do it,
I thought it might be so,
If it came from one who loved you
Perhaps 'twould ease the woe.

The time has come, you can surely guess,
The truth I fain would hide,
You will pardon a poor soldier boy
When I tell you how he died.
'Twas the night before the battle
When in our crowded tent,
More than one brave boy was sobbing there,
While many a knee was bent.

For we knew not on the morrow,
When this bloody fray was done,
How many that were seated there
Would see the setting sun.
It was not ourselves we cared for
As for the loved at home,
It was always worse to think of them
Than to hear the cannon's boom.

It was then we left our crowded tent,
Your soldier boy and I,
We both marched out together
Underneath the bright blue sky.
I am more than ten years older,
Yet he liked to talk to me,
And oftener than the younger
He sought my company.

He seemed to like to talk of home,
And those he loved most dear,
Although I've none to talk about
I always liked to hear.
He told me on that very night
Of the time he came away,
How you would surely grieve for him,
But they would not let him stay.

And how high his fond hopes had been,
When the cruel war was through,
He might go back with honor
To his friends at home and you.
He named his sisters one by one,
And then a deep blush came,
He told me of another one
But he could not speak her name.

And then he said: Dear Robert,
It might be that I shall fall,
Will you write to them at home
And tell how I loved them all?
I promised but I did not think
The time would come so soon,
The fight was just three days ago,
And he died today at noon.

It seems so hard that one so loved
As he, should now be gone,
While I am still a-living here
And have no friends or home.
It was on the morrow's battle,
Fast rained the shot and shell,
I was fighting close beside him
And I saw him as he fell.

I ran and took him in my arms,
And laid him on the grass,
It was going against the orders
But I thought they'd let it pass.
'Twas a minie-ball that struck him,
But it entered in the side,
We did not think it fatal,
Till the morning that he died.

And when he found that he must die
He called me to his side,
And said: You won't forget to write
When you learn that I have died.
Tell them all how I loved them,
And bid them all goodbye,
Tell them I did the best I could
And was'nt afraid to die.

And underneath my pillow
You'll find a lock of hair,
And the name that's on the paper—
Send it in my mother's care.
Last night I wanted so to live,
It seemed so hard to go,
Last week I passed my birthday,
I was nineteen years, you know.

He talked of all he had planned to do,
It seemed so hard to die,
He prayed to God and He gave him grace,
And then his cares passed by.
And then his voice grew weaker,
He merely raised his head,
And whispered: Goodbye, Mother,
And your boy was dead.

We wrapped his cloak around him,
And bore him out that night,
We laid him on a pile of brush
Where the moon was shining bright.
I carved him out a headstone
As skillful as I could,
And if you want to see it
I could tell you where it stood.

I send you his hymn-book,
And the cap he used to wear,
And the lock I clipped the night before
Of his bright and curly hair.
I send to you his Bible;
The night before he died,
We turned its leaves together,
And read them side by side.

I keep the belt he used to wear,
He told me so to do.
It has a hole in the side of it
'Tis where the ball went through.
So now I've done my bidding,
I've nothing more to tell,
But I always mean to mourn with you
For the boy I loved so well.

245

OLD ABE'S ELECTED

Judge John Turner White, Jefferson City, Feb. 7, 1938, told me that he heard this at Springfield about the beginning of the Civil War, sung to the tune of Yankee Doodle:

Old Abe's elected so they say
Along with Darkey Hamlin,
The Yankees think they'll gain the day
By nigger votes and gamblin'.

246

THE REBEL SOLDIER

Kittredge (*JAFL* 30, 1917, p. 345) noted that this piece is an adaptation of "The Forsaken Girl," resembling also "The Poor Stranger." Cox (*Folk-Songs of the South*, 1925, pp. 279-280) gives references and two texts. A somewhat similar piece entitled "Rabble Soldier" is given by Sandburg (*American Songbag*, 1927, pp. 284-285). See also Sharp (*English Folk Songs from the Southern Appalachians*, 1932, II, pp. 212-215), and Belden's "Roving Soldier" items under "The Guerrilla Boy" (*Ballads and Songs*, 1940, p. 376).

Manuscript from Dr. George E. Hastings, Univ. of Ark., Jan. 6, 1942. Note: "Given to Mrs. Clara Robinson, Kingston, Ark., by a Mr. Salter who lived at Higdon, Ark., and was in the rebel army, fighting in a battle at Cane Hill, known then as Boonesbury."

I'll go to Price's army, at home I can't stay
For the home quarrels and Federals have driven me away,
For home quarrels and Federals have caused me to roam,
I'm a poor rebel soldier, and far away from home.

I'll eat when I'm hungry, and I'll drink when I'm dry,
And if a tree don't fall on me, I'll live till I die.
If Miss Mollie forsakes me, and causes me to mourn,
I'm a poor rebel soldier, and far away from home.

I'll build my true love a castle upon some mountain high,
Where the wild beast and crickets can hear her lonesome cry,
Where the wild beasts and crickets can hear her lonesome mourn,
I'm a poor rebel soldier, and far away from home.

247

COLONEL SHELBY

Manuscript from Dr. George E. Hastings, Univ. of Ark., Jan. 6, 1942. As sung by Mrs.
Jane McAlister Medlin, who was born in 1848, lived and died near Dardanelle, Ark.

Colonel Shelby, Colonel Shelby,
I do not think it right,
For you to charge on Dardanelle
At such a time of night.

This old coat, I don't want it,
I guess I'll have to run,
I've not got sword or pistol,
Nor even a shot-gun.

This old coat, I don't want it,
But I don't care,
For 'twas in the rebel army
That I stole this old hat.

248

ROOT HOG OR DIE

A Civil War adaptation of the old "Root Hog or Die" song. See Belden(*Ballads and
Songs*, 1940, pp. 361-362) for a similar "Root Abe or Die" piece. Douglas Stewart (*Missouri
Historical Review* 21, Oct. 1926, p. 55) quotes a fragment:

Lyon bit the dust and Sigel ran away,
Just like he did at Carthage upon a summer's day.

Judge John Turner White, Jefferson City, Mo., Aug. 10, 1939, told me that at Springfield, Mo., during the Civil War, he heard people singing about Sigel's remarkable

. . . . run
With two Dutch guards and nary gun.

The Springfield, Mo., *Leader*, Aug. 10, 1932, prints one stanza of an old Confederate camp song:

> Old Sigel fought some on that day
> But lost his army in the fray,
> Then off to Springfield he did run
> With two Dutch guards and nary gun.

The *run* credited to Sigel occurred at the Battle of Wilson's Creek, where Lyon was killed Aug. 10, 1861. The crack about Carthage refers to the fact that at Carthage, Mo., July 5, 1861, Sigel was outnumbered and he retreated without much fighting.

Manuscript copy from Dr. George E. Hastings, Univ. of Ark., Jan. 6, 1942. He had it from Eloise Guilliams, who learned it from her grandmother in Fayetteville. The first lines are taken from "The Bonnie Blue Flag."

> We are a band of brothers
> Natives of our soil
> Fighting for the property
> We gained by honest toil.
> And all along the ranks
> They all did cry,
> Tomorrow boys, we'll make the Dutch
> Root hog or die.

> Hurrah, boys, hurrah,
> We rangers know our rights,
> And if they trample on our toes
> We'll make them see sights.
> The Lion cease to roar
> And old Segal's on the shy,
> Big Abe, little Abe,
> Root hog or die.

> If Abe isn't satisfied
> And wants to fight again
> All he has to do is
> Just muster up his men.
> To whip old Ben McCulloch
> He can always get to try,
> But he'll find the southern boys
> Won't root hog or die.

249

CONFEDERATE "YANKEE DOODLE"

From May Kennedy McCord, Springfield, Mo., Mar. 22, 1941. She calls it "The New Yankee Doodle," and says that her manuscript text was copied in 1882 from a songster entitled *The Stonewall Song Book.*

Yankee Doodle had a mind to whip the Southern traitors
Because they didn't choose to live on codfish and potatoes.
Yankee doodle doodle do, Yankee doodle dandy,
And so to keep his courage up he took a drink of brandy.

Yankee Doodle drew his sword and practiced all the passes,
Come boys, we'll take another drink when we get to Manassas.
Yankee doodle doodle do, Yankee doodle dandy,
They never reached Manassas' plain and never got the brandy.

Yankee Doodle, oh for shame, you're always intermeddling,
Let guns alone, they're dangerous things, you'd better stick to peddling
Yankee doodle doodle do, Yankee doodle dandy,
When next you go to Bully Run you'll throw away the brandy.

250

OH YOU WHO ARE ABLE . . .

From Mr. J. G. Hawarth, Joplin, Mo., July 12, 1924. Mr. Hawarth says it was sung to a bugle-call tune. It refers to General Earl Van Dorn, who commanded the Confederate troops at the battle of Pea Ridge, Ark.

Oh you who are able go out to the stable,
And throw down your horses some corn,
If you don't do it the sergeant will know it
And report you to General Van Dorn.

251

THERE WILL BE ONE VACANT CHAIR

This piece was composed at Thanksgiving, 1861, and published by Root and Cady, in Chicago (Dichter and Shapiro, *Early American Sheet Music*, 1941, p. 117). According to the *Franklin Square Song Collection* 3 (1885, p. 131), H. S. Washburn was responsible for the words and George F. Root for the music. See also *Heart Songs* (1909, p. 32).

Manuscript copy from Mrs. Laura Wasson, Elm Springs, Ark., Jan. 28, 1942.

We shall meet, but we shall miss him,
There will be one vacant chair,
We shall linger to caress him
When we breathe our evening prayer.
Just a year ago we gathered,
Joy was in his mild blue eye,
But the gold cord now is severed
And our hopes in ruins lie.

At our fireside sad and lonely,
Often will our bosoms swell
As we hear the old old story
How our noble Willie fell.
How he strove to save our banner
In the thickest of the fight,
And uphold our country's honor
In the strength of manhood's might.

Sleep today, oh bravely fallen,
In the green and narrow bed,
Dirges from the pine and cypress
Mingle with the tears we shed.
We shall meet, but we shall miss him,
There will be one vacant chair,
We shall linger to caress him
When we breathe our evening prayer.

Chapter VII

NEGRO AND PSEUDO-NEGRO SONGS

A few Negro slaves were brought into the Ozarks before the Civil War, but the majority of the early settlers came from the mountain districts of the Southern Appalachians and had made little contact with either slaves or slave-owners. There are comparatively few Negroes in the Ozarks today, and large numbers of people in the more isolated sections have never even seen a Negro. A friend of mine who used to go into the White River country for the bass-fishing told me that the natives came from miles around to see his colored cook, and children stood about his camp for hours on end, gazing at the black man in open-mouthed amazement.

It may be that some of the songs in this chapter are genuine Negro folksongs, inherited from pioneers who learned them from Negroes, but I suspect that most of them are mere echoes from the old-timer "nigger minstrels."

The craze for "nigger" music began about 1830, when such songs as "Zip Coon," "Jump Jim Crow," and "Old Virginny Nebber Tire" suddenly became popular on the vaudeville stage. The earliest of these jingles were really of Negro origin (White, *American Negro Folk-Songs*, 1928, pp. 7-9), but spurious songs soon replaced the genuine article, just as burnt cork came to be substituted for natural cutaneous pigmentation. Certainly the most popular singers, such as Dan Emmett, Charles White, T. G. Booth, "Jim Crow" Rice and Henry H. Paul, were white men, and there is no question that they wrote many of their songs. Charles White once offered a cash prize of fifty dollars to anybody who could prove that he was *not* the author of some forty "nigger songs," including many which were claimed by other celebrated minstrels of the day.

In the Ozark hill-country the old-fashioned medicine-shows are still common; most of them feature a long-haired doctor with his marvellous Indian herb remedy and several black-face singers and banjo-pickers. In the early days medicine-shows were even more numerous, and it may well be that they are, in a large measure, responsible for the persistence of these "nigger minstrel" songs.

252

JUMP JIM CROW

Dichter and Shapiro (*Early American Sheet Music*, 1941, p. 52) list the first edition of this piece as published in New York by E. Riley, circa 1829, and containing 19 verses, later editions having 44. White (*American Negro Folk-Songs*, 1928, p. 162) says that this was one of the earliest minstrel pieces, "introduced upon the stage between 1833 and 1835 by Thomas D. Rice, known thereafter as Jim Crow Rice. Rice got it from Jim Crow, an old slave in Louisville, who used to execute a queer dance to the refrain." For further information about Rice see Coad and Mims' *The American Stage* (1929, p. 150). It appears that Rice's text was soon lost. As early as 1855 the author of "Negro Minstrelsy, Ancient and Modern" (*Putnam's Monthly* 5, 1855, pp. 72-79) was unable to find the original version, although there were plenty of imitations even then. The song made a tremendous hit in London, and soon spread to many parts of the world; Bayard Taylor heard it even among the Hindoo minstrels at Delhi (White, *American Negro Folk-Songs*, p. 149). For further texts and references see Talley (*Negro Folk Rhymes*, 1922, p. 13) and Scarborough (*On the Trail of Negro Folk-Songs*, 1925, pp. 126, 217). The first line of the following fragment occurs in a Negro reel recorded by Odum (*American Mercury* 17, Aug. 1929, p. 398). The "hop light, ladies" refrain is found in a song which Harris (*Uncle Remus, His Songs and His Sayings* [1st ed. 1880] 1928, p. 191) reported from Georgia in 1856.

Sung by Mrs. Emma Baird Chambliss, Anderson, Mo., May 12, 1930. Mrs. Chambliss says that her people knew it as a game-song many years ago.

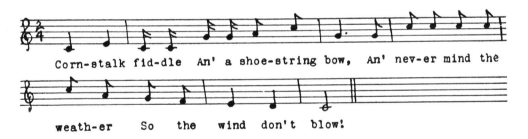

Corn-stalk fid-dle An' a shoe-string bow, An' nev-er mind the
weath-er So the wind don't blow!

Hop light, ladies!
The cake's all dough,
Never mind the weather
So the wind don't blow!

First on the heel
An' then on the toe,
Ever' time you turn around
You jump Jim Crow!

253

THE BANJO SONG

Reed Smith (*South Carolina Ballads*, 1928, p. 42) has traced this back to print as a Negro dialect poem "De Fust Banjo" from *Christmas Night in the Quarters*, by Irwin Russell, first published in 1878. Compare a song entitled "The Ark" (Talley, *Negro Folk Rhymes*, 1922, p. 44), also the "Old Noah" piece reported by Cox (*Folk-Songs of the South*, 1925, p. 508). A very similar item known as "De Fust Banjo" is reprinted in the Aurora (Mo.) *Advertiser*, Nov. 25, 1937.

A

Sung by Mrs. Ina Burnett, Anderson, Mo., Feb. 21, 1928.

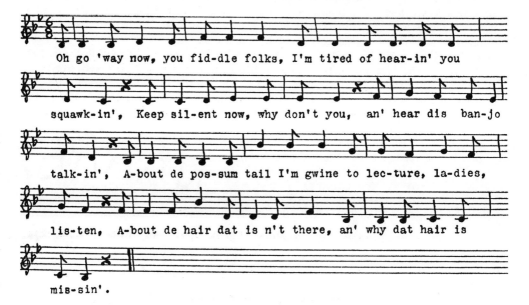

Oh go 'way now, you fid-dle folks, I'm tired of hear-in' you squawk-in', Keep sil-ent now, why don't you, an' hear dis ban-jo talk-in', A-bout de pos-sum tail I'm gwine to lec-ture, la-dies, lis-ten, A-bout de hair dat is n't there, an' why dat hair is mis-sin'.

There's goin' to be an overflow, says Noah, lookin' solemn,
Cause Noah took the Herald an' he read it, ever' column.
He done set all his men to work a-clearin' timber patches,
For Noah's gwine to build a ark that'll beat the steamer Natches.

Old Noah kept a-chippin' an' a-nailin' an' a-sawin',
An' all his wicked neighbors kept a-laughin' an' a-jawin',
But Noah didn't mind at all, he knowed what was gwine to happen,
For forty days an' forty nights the rain it kept a-drappin'.

Old Noah went an' ketched a lot of every kind of beastes,
An' them there shows that travels round, he beat 'em all to pieces,
He had a rampin' Morgan colt an' a lot of Jersey cattle,
He druv 'em all on board the ark when he heard the thunder rattle.

An' such a awful fall of rain, it was awful heavy,
The river riz up all at once an' busted through the levee.
The people all got drowned, 'cept Noah an' his critters,
A couple o' men to manage the boat, an' one to mix the bitters.

Now Ham was the only nigger that was aboard the packet,
Got lonesome in the barber shop an' couldn't stand the racket,
An' so for to amuse himself he got some wood an' bent it,
An' soon he had a banjo made, the first that was invented.

He wet some leather an' stretched it on with screw an' bridge an' apron,
An' fitted in a proper neck, but very long an' taperin',
He twisted him some tin into a thimble for to ring it,
An' then the mighty question rose, how was he gwine to string it?

Now the possum had so fine a tail, is what I have been singin',
Hair so long an' fine an' strong, just right for banjo-stringin',
An' so that nigger cut 'em off as short as bachelor's graces,
An' separated of 'em out from little E's to basses.

He tuned her up an' struck a jig, it was never mind the weather,
It sounded like a thousand bands a-playin' all together,
An' some would pat an' some would dance, while Noah called the figgers,
An' Ham he set an' knocked a tune, the happiest of niggers.

An' since that day there's never been the leastest bit of showin'
Of any hair at all upon the possum's tail a-growin',
An' strange it is the niggers' ways, the people never lost 'em,
For everywhere the nigger is, there's the banjo an' the possum.

B

Sung by Mr. Doney Hammontree, Farmington, Ark., Dec. 13, 1941. He calls it "The Possum and the Banjo," and says it was popular near Farmington in the 90's.

There's gwine to be an o-ver-flow, said Noah look-in' sol-emn, Kaze No-ah picked the pa-per up an' read the riv-er col-umn, He set his hir-ed hands to work cl'ar-in' tim-ber patch-es, Kaze he lowed he's gwine to build a boat to beat the steam-er Natch-ez.

Old Noah kept a-waiting, a-chopping and a-sawing,
And all his wicked friends kept a-laughing and a-chawing,
Old Noah didn't mind them, knowing what would happen,
For forty days and forty nights the rain would keep a-drappin'.

Old Noah had a mighty lot of every kind of beastes,
Of all the shows that comes around it beat them all to pieces,
Old Noah had a Morgan colt and several Jersey cattle,
He driv them all aboard the Ark when the thunder 'gin to rattle.

Such another rainin', it fell so thick an' heavy,
The river riz immediately an' busted through the levee,
And drownded all the people 'cept Noah and his critters,
And the man he'd hired to run the boat, and one to mix the bitters.

The Ark it kept a-glidin', a-floatin' and a-sailin',
The lion got his dander up an' like to broke the palin',
The serpent hissed, the tiger yelled, the monkeys kept a-fussin',
Till you could hardly hear the mate a-bossin' and a-cussin'.

And Ham, the only nigger ridin' on the packet,
Got lonesome in the barber-shop an' couldn't stand the racket,
An' so to kinder 'muse himself he got some wood and bent it,
An' soon he had a banjo up, the first that was invented.

He wet the leather, stretched it tight, he made bridge, screws and apron,
An' fitted it a proper neck so very long an' taperin',
He got some tin an' twisted it, made thimbles for to ring it,
An' then the mighty question riz, how was he gwine to string it?

The possum had as fine a tail as this song I am singin',
The hair was long, thick an' strong, just right for banjo-stringin',
Dat nigger shaved the hair off short as wash-day dinner graces,
An' sorted them all out to size, from little E's to basses.

He tuned it up an' struck a jig, 'twas "Never Mind the Weather,"
It sound like forty-'leven bands a-playin' all together,
Dat nigger's ways, 'tis strange to say, his people never lost 'em,
An' where you find a nigger, there's a banjo an' a possum.

254

INJY-RUBBER OVERCOAT

The chorus of this piece is taken from a jig song "What's de Matter, Susy?" written by Dan Emmett (White, *American Negro Folk-Songs*, 1928, p. 149). The last two lines of the second stanza are similar to a verse in "Old Dan Tucker," also claimed by the celebrated Emmett "and sung by him with unbounded applause in Howe's Amphitheatre of the Republic, New York" (*Marsh's Selection*, New York, 1854, p. 622). White (*American Negro Folk-Songs*, p. 332) quotes a fragment from Alabama with the line "angel rubber overcoat, patent leather shoes." Nonsense syllables similar to "hip-te-doo-den-doo" are common to several old minstrel songs; Chapple (*Heart Songs*, Boston, 1909, p. 110) has one called "Hoop de Dooden Do," credited to A. Nish.

Sung by Mrs. Marie Wilbur, Pineville, Mo., Aug. 2, 1919.

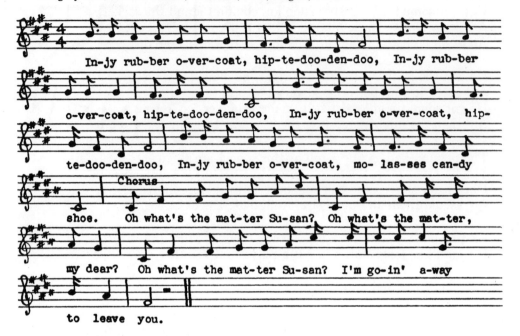

In-jy rub-ber o-ver-coat, hip-te-doo-den-doo, In-jy rub-ber o-ver-coat, hip-te-doo-den-doo, In-jy rub-ber o-ver-coat, hip-te-doo-den-doo, In-jy rub-ber o-ver-coat, mo- las-ses can-dy shoe. Oh what's the mat-ter Su-san? Oh what's the mat-ter, my dear? Oh what's the mat-ter Su-san? I'm go-in' a-way to leave you.

Nigger in the woodpile, hip-te-doo-den-doo,
Nigger in the woodpile, hip-te-doo-den-doo,
Nigger in the woodpile, couldn't count eleven,
Put him in the featherbed, thought he was in heaven.

255

SHORTENIN' BREAD

Perrow (*JAFL* 28, 1915, p. 142) found this piece among the mountain whites in Tennessee, and Talley (*Negro Folk Rhymes*, 1922, pp. 173, 187) reported several Negro variants. Scarborough (*On the Trail of Negro Folk-Songs*, 1925, pp. 149-153) has four texts from various parts of the South. Richardson (*American Mountain Songs*, 1927, p. 81) prints one from the southern Appalachians, and remarks (p. 116) that "shortenin' bread is made of water-ground meal, with lard or fat for leaven." White (*American Negro Folk-Songs*, 1928, p. 193) quotes several stanzas from Georgia and Tennessee, and "suspects that the song originated with the whites." Compare the "Wild Horse" song which Lunsford and Stringfield (*30 and 1 Folk Songs*, 1929, p. 55) report from North Carolina. See also Lomax (*American Ballads and Folk Songs*, 1934, pp. 234-236), and the Brown (North Carolina Folk-Lore Society) collection. There are phonograph records by Gid Tanner (*Columbia* 15123-D) and Dyke's Magic City Trio (*Brunswick* 125).

A

Sung by Mrs. Marie Wilbur, Pineville, Mo., Aug. 2, 1919.

Three lit-tle nig-gers, lay-in' in bed, Heels crack o-pen like short'-nin' bread. How 'bout yo-ur short'-nin', How 'bout yo-ur short'-nin' bread?

One turn white an' one turn red,
Mammy thought they shore was dead.
How 'bout your short'nin',
How 'bout your short'nin' bread?

Sent for the doctor, the doctor he said,
Feed them niggers on short'nin' bread.
How 'bout your short'nin',
How 'bout your short'nin' bread?

B

From Mrs. Lillian Short, Cabool, Mo., Apr. 25, 1941.

Put on de skillet, put on de led,
Mammy's gwine to make some shortenin' bread.
Dat aint all she's gwine to do,
She's gwine to make a lil coffee too.

Mammy's lil baby loves shortenin', shortenin',
Mammy's lil baby loves shortenin' bread.
Mammy's lil baby loves shortenin', shortenin',
Mammy's lil baby loves shortenin' bread.

Went to de kitchen, lift up de led,
Fill my pockets wid shortenin' bread.
Stole de skillet, stole de led,
Stole de gal a-makin' shortenin' bread.

Caught me wid de skillet, caught me wid de led,
Caught me wid de gal a-makin' shortenin' bread.
Paid six dollars for de skillet, six dollars for de led,
Spent six months in jail eatin' shortenin' bread.

256

WENT TO THE RIVER

This song evidently derives from one of the old minstrels, as similar lines are found in "Ole Virginny Nebber Tire," a song credited to Thomas D. Rice (*Negro Singers' Own Book*, 1846, p. 329) and occur also in "Gumbo Chaff" (*Ethiopian Glee Book*, 1848, p. 124). Compare the swapping song in Wheeler's *Mother Goose's Melodies* (1878, p. 80). The tune was popular even in Jamaica, according to Walter Jekyll (*Jamaican Song and Story*, 1907, p. 227). For other texts and references see Perrow (*JAFL* 26, 1913, p. 127), Campbell and Sharp (*English Folk Songs from the Southern Appalachians*, 1917, No. 115), Campbell (*The Southern Highlander*, 1921, p. 101), Talley (*Negro Folk Rhymes*, 1922, pp. 6, 45), Scarborough (*On the Trail of Negro Folk-Songs*, 1925, p. 185), Richardson (*American Mountain Songs*, 1927, p. 48), Bradley Kincaid (*My Favorite Mountain Ballads*, 1928, p. 39), and Ray Wood (*Mother Goose in the Ozarks*, 1938, pp. 43-47).

Sung by Mrs. Marie Wilbur, Pineville, Mo., Aug. 10, 1919.

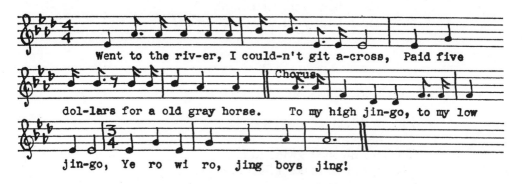

Went to the riv-er, I could-n't git a-cross, Paid five
dol-lars for a old gray horse. To my high jin-go, to my low
jin-go, Ye ro wi ro, jing boys jing!

Plunged him in an' I found he couldn't swim,
Paid five dollars for to git him out ag'in.

Sold my horse an' bought me a cow,
Never made a bargain but what I knowed how.

Sold my cow an' bought me a calf,
Never made a bargain but what I lost half.

Sold my calf an' bought me a goose,
Aint that a purty thing to set on a roost?

Sold my goose an' bought a hen,
Aint that a purty thing to put in a pen?

Sold my hen an' bought me a louse,
Jumped in my head an' made hisself a house!

257

DON'T YOU GRIEVE AFTER ME

Pound (*Folk-Song of Nebraska and the Central West*, 1915, p. 58) quotes one stanza of this piece under the title "I Told Him Not to Grieve After Me," describing it as "the adventures of a man who beats his way." The "don't grieve after me" line occurs also in the "Jacob's Ladder" song, in one of the Fisk spirituals (Marsh, *Story of the Jubilee Singers*, 1880, p. 216), and in a nameless Negro piece reported by Scarborough (*On the Trail of Negro Folk-Songs*, 1925, p. 9). The "horse-and-river" incident is mentioned in many Negro songs (*Ibid.*, pp. 184-185), and is often included in the Ozark version of "Turkey in the Straw."

Sung by Mrs. Marie Wilbur, Pineville, Mo., Oct. 1, 1926. Mrs. Wilbur heard it at a medicine-show in the 90's.

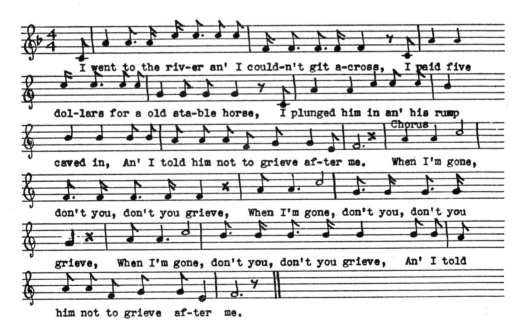

I went to the riv-er an' I could-n't git a-cross, I paid five
dol-lars for a old sta-ble horse, I plunged him in an' his rump
caved in, An' I told him not to grieve af-ter me. When I'm gone,
don't you, don't you grieve, When I'm gone, don't you, don't you
grieve, When I'm gone, don't you, don't you grieve, An' I told
him not to grieve af-ter me.

I went down town a-feelin' mighty funny,
Picked up a pocketbook chuck full of money,
Police comes along, says drop that, sonny!
An' I told him not to grieve after me.

I went to the hotel to stay all night,
He says fifty cents, an' I says all right,
I jumped in bed an' I covered up my head,
An' I told him not to grieve after me.

Got up next mornin' an' washed my feet,
Went down to the table an' you orter seen me eat,
Jumped up quick an' hollered dead beat!
An' I told him not to grieve after me.

258

EASE THAT TROUBLE IN THE MIND

Sung by Lon Jordan, Farmington, Ark., Dec. 24, 1941. It is one stanza of a very long nigger-minstrel piece, he says, that was popular in the 90's.

I went to the river an' I couldn't get across,
Ease that trouble in the mind,
I jumped on a log an' thought it was a horse,
Ease that trouble in the mind.

259

THE JAWBONE SONG

See "Sally is de Gal for Me" (*Negro Singer's Own Book*, 1846, p. 34), also Talley (*Negro Folk Rhymes*, 1922, p. 12). Scarborough (*On the Trail of Negro Folk-Songs*, 1925, pp. 102-104, 125) prints several Negro songs in which the jawbone is mentioned as a musical instrument —"the jawbone of a horse or ox or mule, with the teeth left in, which made a queer sound when a key or other piece of metal was drawn across the teeth." White (*American Negro Folk-Songs*, 1928, pp. 305, 333) refers to an old minstrel song entitled "Jawbone Walk an' Jawbone Talk." Several country dance tunes are still known as "jawbone songs," and I myself heard the jawbone played as part of a dance orchestra at Springfield, Mo., in 1934. Morris (*Southern Folklore Quarterly* 8, 1944, p. 182) says that this fiddle tune was popular in central Florida and southern Georgia around the turn of the century.

Sung by Miss Leone Duvall, Pineville, Mo., Sept. 6, 1926. Miss Duvall learned the song from her father, Dr. W. C. Duvall, who came West from Kentucky during the Civil War.

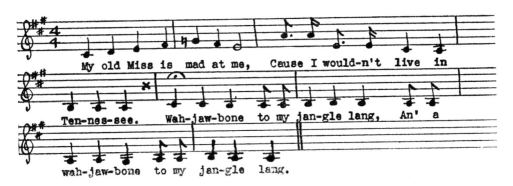

My old Miss is mad at me, Cause I would-n't live in Ten-nes-see. Wah-jaw-bone to my jan-gle lang, An' a wah-jaw-bone to my jan-gle lang.

I laid that jawbone on the fence,
An I aint never seen that jawbone since,
Wah-jawbone to my jangle lang,
An' a wah-jawbone to my jangle lang.

260

KITTY, CAINT YOU COME ALONG TOO?

This fragment derives from an antebellum minstrel hit entitled "Old Sandy Boy" (*Negro Singer's Own Book*, 1846, p. 309). For related texts and references see Kittredge (*JAFL* 35, 1922, p. 396), Scarborough (*On the Trail of Negro Folk-Songs*, 1925, p. 156), Odum (*Negro Workaday Songs*, 1926, p. 187), Richardson (*American Mountain Songs*, 1927, p. 98), and White (*American Negro Folk-Songs*, 1928, pp. 175, 243, 451). Compare Chubby Parker's phonograph record "King Kong Kitchie Ki-Me-O" (*Columbia* 15296-D), which is a variant of "The Frog's Courtship" with a nonsense-syllable refrain. See also "There Was an Old Frog" as printed elsewhere in this book.

Sung by Miss Leone Duvall, Pineville, Mo., Sept. 6, 1926.

The rac-coon got a ring-ed tail, The pos-sum's tail is bare, The rab-bit haint no tail at all, Just a lit-tle bunch of hair. *Chorus* Oh come a-long, oh San-dy boy, Oh come a-long, oh do, Oh what will Un-cle Gab-riel say? Kit-ty caint you come a-long too?

The peacock got a mighty fine tail,
It reaches to the moon,
He roll his eye down on his foot
An' his tail fall mighty soon.

261

UNCLE NED

The original "Uncle Ned" song was copyrighted by Stephen C. Foster in 1848, and is found in several antebellum minstrel books, such as White's *New Illustrated Melodion* (n.d., p. 24) and Gumbo Chaff's *Ethiopian Glee Book* (1848, p. 116). See also Perrow (*JAFL* 26, 1913, p. 125), Talley (*Negro Folk Rhymes*, 1922, p. 61); compare the phonograph records by Oscar Seagle (*Columbia* 64M) and Chubby Parker (*Supertone* 9192). White (*American Negro Folk-Songs*, 1928, pp. 164-167) says that "Uncle Ned" has long ago passed into oral tradition among the Negroes, and quotes a colored friend to the effect that it is sung in Negro schools and even in churches.

Sung by Mrs. Marie Wilbur, Pineville, Mo., Oct. 1, 1926.

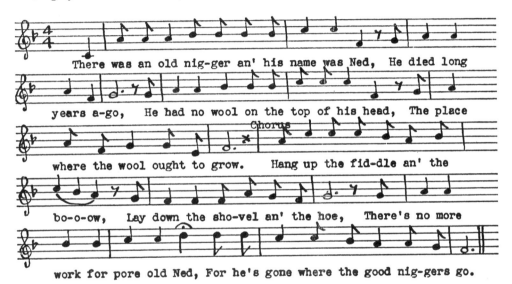

There was an old nig-ger an' his name was Ned, He died long years a-go, He had no wool on the top of his head, The place where the wool ought to grow. Hang up the fid-dle an' the bo-o-ow, Lay down the sho-vel an' the hoe, There's no more work for pore old Ned, For he's gone where the good nig-gers go.

His fingers was long like the cane in the brakes,
He had no eyes for to see,
He had no teeth for to eat the corn cakes
So he had to let the corn cakes be.

One cold frosty mornin' when everything was still,
The darkies stood round the bed,
Not a thing was done, not a thing was said,
For pore old Ned was dead.

When old Ned died Miss' took it mighty hard,
The tears poured down like rain
Old Marse turned pale an' he looked mighty sad,
Cause he'd never see the old man again.

I once heard this piece at a church entertainment in Pineville, Mo., in 1931, sung by Mr. Ranzy Bone, who came from Pea Ridge, Ark. At the conclusion he said: "Some of these educated fellers don't sing 'Uncle Ned' that way no more—this is how *they* sing it." Upon which he burst out with the parody beginning:

> There was an ancient colored individual
> Whose cognomen was Uncle Edwin . . .

I did not record the words at the time, but the song was very similar to the paraphrase in White's *Serenader's Song Book* (1851, p. 61) and in *The Ethiopian Serenader's Own Book* (1857, pp. 41-42), which is reprinted by White (*American Negro Folk-Songs*, 1928, pp. 166-167). An old lady in Benton County, Ark., once told me that she had heard a "college Uncle Ned" piece sung by a Confederate trooper during the Civil War.

262

JACOB'S LADDER

This is a fragment of an old piece which Allen (*Slave Songs of the United States*, 1867, p. vi, *n.*) found in early Methodist hymnbooks, and which has frequently been published by folk-song collectors. See Higginson (*Atlantic Monthly* 19, June 1867, p. 689) for a stanza of a funeral hymn in which appears the line "For to climb up Jacob's ladder," also Marsh (*Story of the Jubilee Singers*, 1880, p. 190), Perrow (*JAFL* 26, 1913, p. 156), Perkins (*JAFL* 35, 1922, p. 233), Odum (*Negro Workaday Songs*, 1926, p. 111), White (*American Negro Folk-Songs*, 1928, p. 59), and the Brown (North Carolina Folk-Lore Society) collection. The refrain "Don't you grieve after me" is common to several old songs (Marsh, *Story of the Jubilee Singers*, p. 216). Compare also the phonograph record of "Jacob's Ladder" by Frank and James McCravy (*Victor* 21188).

Sung by Mrs. Marie Wilbur, Pineville, Mo., Dec. 28, 1922.

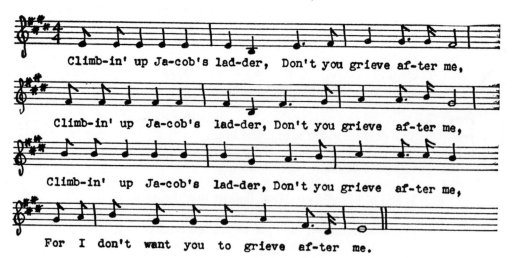

263

DINKY

Evidently a variant of the Negro reel known as "Juba," one of the most popular of the old jigs or short-step dance tunes. See Talley (*Negro Folk Rhymes*, 1922, pp. 19, 233), Scarborough (*On the Trail of Negro Folk-Songs*, 1925, p. 98) and White (*American Negro Folk-Songs*, 1928, p. 163).

Sung by Mrs. Frances Hall, Pineville, Mo., Oct. 1, 1926. Mrs. Hall learned the song many years ago in Searcy, Ark.

Din-ky pret-ty lit-tle ba-by, Din-ky pret-ty lit-tle ba-by,

Din-ky up an' din-ky down, Din-ky all a-round the town,

Din-ky up an' din-ky down, Din-ky all a-round the town.

264

RUN, NIGGER, RUN

See White's *Serenader's Song Book* (1851, p. 66), Perrow (*JAFL* 28, 1915, p. 138), Harris (*Uncle Remus and His Friends* [1st ed. 1892] 1920, p. 200), Talley (*Negro Folk Rhymes*, 1922, p. 34), Scarborough (*On the Trail of Negro Folk-Songs*, 1925, p. 23), White (*American Negro Folk-Songs*, 1928, p. 168), Lomax (*American Ballads and Folk Songs*, 1934, pp. 228-231), Botkin (*American Play-Party Song*, 1937, pp. 299-300), and the Brown (North Carolina Folk-Lore Society) collection. Another version is reprinted from Allen, Ware and Garrison (*Slave Songs of the United States*, 1867) by Botkin (*Treasury of American Folklore*, 1944, p. 906). There are phonograph records, too, by Bates (*Brunswick* 275) and Gid Tanner (*Columbia* 15158-D).

Sung by Mrs. Marie Wilbur, Pineville, Mo., Oct. 1, 1926. Mrs. Wilbur thinks that some of the stanzas were formerly used in a play-party song.

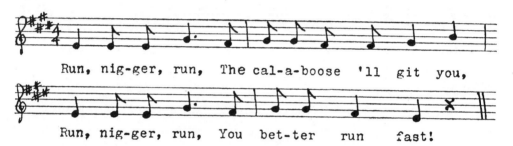

Run, nig-ger, run, The cal-a-boose 'll git you,
Run, nig-ger, run, You bet-ter run fast!

This nigger run,
He run his best,
He stuck his head
In a hornets' nest.

Jump the fence,
Run through the pasture
White man run
But the nigger run faster.

Chicken in the bread-tray
Scratchin' out the dough,
Granny, will your dog bite?
No, child, no.

265

RAT COON, RAT COON

This is a fragment of a much longer piece, evidently widely known among Negroes in the South, before the Civil War. Dr. F. X. Baynes, Worcester, Mass., Dec. 3, 1914, tells me that he heard it chanted by his grandfather, who was born a slave in Virginia.

Sung by Mrs. Marie Wilbur, Pineville, Mo., Oct. 19, 1926. She spoke or chanted the first two lines in a peculiar nasal fashion.

266

I HOPE I'LL J'INE THE BAND

Very similar to "Gwine Ride Up in the Chariot" as sung by the Fisk Singers (Marsh, *Story of the Jubilee Singers*, 1880, p. 138). Compare the "camp meeting chorus" quoted by A. M. Haswell in *A Daughter of the Ozarks* (Boston, 1921, p. 24). The "hope I'll j'ine the band" line is the refrain of a Negro hymn which Scarborough (*On the Trail of Negro Folk-Songs*, 1925, p. 16) obtained from a black janitor in Louisiana.

A

Sung by Mrs. Marie Wilbur, Pineville, Mo., Oct. 10, 1926.

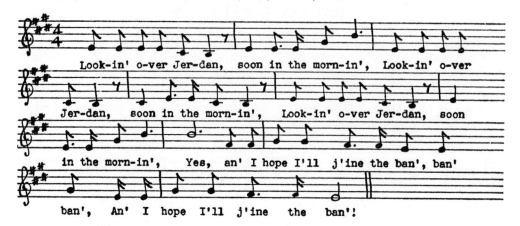

Look-in' o-ver Jer-dan, soon in the morn-in', Look-in' o-ver
Jer-dan, soon in the morn-in', Look-in' o-ver Jer-dan, soon
in the morn-in', Yes, an' I hope I'll j'ine the ban', ban'
ban', An' I hope I'll j'ine the ban'!

Goin' to see my Jesus, soon in the mornin',
Goin' to see my Jesus, soon in the mornin',
Goin' to see my Jesus, soon in the mornin',
Yes, an' I hope I'll j'ine the ban', ban', ban',
An' I hope I'll j'ine the ban'.

Goin' to walk an' talk with Jesus, soon in the mornin',
Goin' to walk an' talk with Jesus, soon in the mornin',
Goin' to walk an' talk with Jesus, soon in the mornin',
Yes, an' I hope I'll j'ine the ban', ban', ban,'
An' I hope I'll j'ine the ban'.

Goin' to see my father soon in the mornin',
Goin' to see my father, soon in the mornin',
Goin' to see my father, soon in the mornin',
Yes, an' I hope I'll j'ine the ban', ban', ban,'
An' I hope I'll j'ine the ban'.

Other verses follow, all about walking and talking with mother, sister, brother, uncle, children, teacher, preacher and so on.

B

Manuscript copy from Mrs. Effa M. Wilson, Verona, Mo., Apr. 8, 1942. "Ship Rock Ashore," she calls it.

Ships rock ashore, sooner in the morning,
Ships rock ashore, sooner in the morning,
Ships rock ashore, sooner in the morning,
Hope come join our band.

Mother took a flight, gone to heaven,
Mother took a flight, gone to heaven,
Mother took a flight, gone to heaven,
Hope come join our band.

C

Sung by Mr. Doney Hammontree, Farmington, Ark., Feb. 8, 1941. `He calls it "Chatter
With the Angels."

Chatter with de angels, soon in de mornin',
Chatter with de angels, soon in de mornin',
Chatter with de angels, soon in de mornin',
Hope I jine de band, band, band,
An' I hope I jine de band!

Walk an' talk with Jesus, soon in de mornin',
Walk an' talk with Jesus, soon in de mornin',
Walk an' talk with Jesus, soon in de mornin',
Hope I jine de band, band, band,
An' I hope I jine de band!

Meet our fathers there, soon in de mornin',
Meet our fathers there, soon in de mornin',
Meet our fathers there, soon in de mornin',
Hope I jine de band, band, band,
An' I hope I jine de band!

Meet our mothers there, soon in de mornin',
Meet our mothers there, soon in de mornin',
Meet our mothers there, soon in de mornin',
Hope I jine de band, band, band,
An' I hope I jine de band!

Meet our neighbors there, soon in de mornin',
Meet our neighbors there, soon in de mornin',
Meet our neighbors there, soon in de mornin',
Hope I jine de band, band, band,
An' I hope I jine de band!

267

I'LL MEET YOU IN THE EVENING

Talley (*Negro Folk Rhymes*, 1922, p. 29) has a fragment called "Bring on Your Hot Corn" which is similar to the chorus of this piece. He tells us in a solemn footnote that "a jimmy-john is a whiskey jug." Compare also the "Fotch along a jimmy-john" reference in an item recorded from Arkansas by Ray Wood (*Mother Goose in the Ozarks*, 1938, p. 54).

A

Sung by Miss Leone Duvall, Pineville, Mo., Sept. 7, 1926.

Don't for-git to curl your hair, Don't for-git to curl your hair,

All the la-dies will be there, Won't we have a jol-ly time

Eat-in' cake an' drink-in' wine, Ha, me yal-ler gal, I'll

meet you in the eve-nin'. Bring a-long a hotch o' corn,

Bring a-long a hotch o' corn, Bring a-long a hotch o' corn,

Fetch a-long a jim-my john, Bring a-long a hotch o' corn,

Fetch a-long a jim-my john, Ha, me yal-ler gal, I'll

meet you in the eve-nin'.

B

Sung by Mr. Booth Campbell, Cane Hill, Ark., Feb. 5, 1942. He calls it "Green Corn," and says it is related to a well-known dance-tune of the same name. He learned these words in the 90's.

Oh a rain come a wet me, sun come a dry me, Stand back,

nig-ger gal, don't you get a nigh me, Come on, my pret-ty

gal, set down by me, Good-bye, my yel-ler gal, meet you in

Chorus

the eve-nin'. Green corn, green corn, Green corn a nig-ger

corn, Green corn, green corn, Good for a nig-ger corn,

Green corn, green corn, Looks sort o' lim-ber corn, You

on the hill-side, Fetch a-long a dem-i-john!

Stand boys, stand boys, no use a-runnin',
It's look up the hill, you'll see ol' Massa comin',
Got a cowhide in one hand, horsewhip in the other,
Done kill forty niggers, goin' to kill another,
. . . .
Got a string in his pocket for to tie you' hands together,
Goodbye, my yeller gal, meet you in the evenin'.

268

MISTER BOOGER

The "Mister Booger" line comes from the chorus of an antebellum Negro reel known as "Johnny Booker" (Scarborough, *On the Trail of Negro Folk-Songs*, 1925, p. 100). Compare "Johnny Boker, or de Broken Yoke," a minstrel piece printed in *Trifet's Budget of Music No. 15*, Mar. 1892, p. 136. Hergesheimer (*Swords and Roses*, 1929, p. 268) tells us that this song was a great favorite with General J. E. B. Stuart, the famous Confederate cavalry leader, who always kept a banjo-player with him in the field. There have been many versions, and some of them were sung by "nigger minstrels" and med-show comedians as recently as 1910, usually set to a melody derived from "Turkey in the Straw." It is said that the Anthony's Mill mentioned in the following text is identical with an Anthony's Mill in Crawford County, Mo. The reference to "Wright's shop" becomes "Wright's old mill" in a stanza printed by Lomax (*American Ballads and Folk Songs*, 1934, p. 231), who assigns it to the "Run, Nigger, Run" song.

A

Sung by Mr. Ed Stephens, Jane, Mo., Sept. 20, 1928. Mr. Stephens says that it is often called "The Old Wagoner."

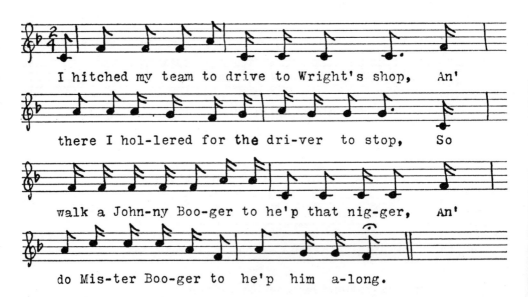

I hitched my team to drive to Wright's shop, An'
there I hol-lered for the dri-ver to stop, So
walk a John-ny Boo-ger to he'p that nig-ger, An'
do Mis-ter Boo-ger to he'p him a-long.

Says I to him, can you mend my yoke?
He stepped to the bellows an' blowed up smoke,
So walk a Johnny Booger to he'p that nigger,
An' do Mister Booger to he'p him along.

An' I drove from there to Anthony's Mill
An' there I stalled a-goin' up hill.
So I placed my shoulder ag'in the wheel,
An' on the ground I placed both heels.

An' there I shoved an' there I strained,
But all my help it proved in vain,
So I set right down an' begun to cry,
Along come a wagoner a-passin' by.

Says I to him caint you-all he'p me?
He unhitched his horses, one-two-three,
An' while I was a-wipin' the fallin' tears
He hitched his horses afore my steers.

It's now I've ended my old song,
I'll start to Arkansas a-rackin' along,
So walk a Johnny Booger to he'p that nigger,
An' do Mister Booger to he'p him along.

B

Mrs. Marie Wilbur, Pineville, Mo., Oct. 1, 1926, sings the following as part of a Negro song which she heard in Searcy, Ark., in the early 90's.

Oh do, Mis-ter Boo-ger, Won't you he'p dis nig-ger, Oh

do, Mis-ter Boo-ger, oh do!

269

BLACK SHEEP LULLABY

This song was formerly common among both whites and Negroes in many parts of the South. Scarborough (*On the Trail of Negro Folk-Songs*, 1925, pp. 145-149) reports nine variants from Negro singers in Texas, Mississippi and Virginia. There are several similar lines in another lullaby known as "Go to Sleepy," which Sandburg (*American Songbag*, 1927, p. 454) recovered in Athens, Ga. See also Lomax (*American Ballads and Folk Songs*, 1934, pp. 304-305).

A

Sung by Mrs. Marie Wilbur, Pineville, Mo., Mar. 21, 1930. Mrs. Wilbur had it from her mother's people, who came from Memphis, Tenn.

Black sheep, black sheep, where'd you leave your lamb? Left it o-ver in the med-der, The buz-zards an' the flies Kept a-peck-in' at its eyes, Lit-tle lamb cried for its moth-er. Way o-ver yon-der in that field, All them pret-ty lit-tle hors-es, Black an' bay an' dap-ple gray, All be-long to lit-tle Ma-ry.

B

This text is from an anonymous correspondent at West Plains, Mo., Oct. 30, 1935.

> Black sheepy, black sheepy,
> Where is your lambie?
> Way down yonder in the valley.
> The gnats and the flies
> Pecking out its eyes,
> Poor little lambie!
>
> Poor little black sheepy,
> Got no mammy, got no mammy,
> Poor little black sheepy got no mammy,
> Got no mammy oh!

270

GO TELL AUNT RHODY

Scarborough (*On the Trail of Negro Folk-Songs*, 1925, pp. 8, 195) reports two Texas versions, in which the owner of the goose is called "Aunt Patsy" and "Aunt Tabby"; she refers also to other texts with the names "Aunt Abby" and "Aunt Nancy," and quotes Professor Kittredge to the effect that his grandfather, born in New Hampshire in 1798, always sang it "Aunt Dinah." Jackson (*White Spirituals in the Southern Uplands*, 1933, pp. 173-174) says that the tune, usually known as "Greenville" or "Rousseau's Dream," was published as a piano solo about 1818. See also the variant reported by Lomax (*American Ballads and Folk Songs*, 1934, pp. 305-306), and the related play-party song recovered in Oklahoma by John M. Oskison (*Brothers Three*, 1935, p. 47). Chase (*Old Songs and Singing Games*, 1938, p. 4) tells us that the melody "was used in an opera written by Jean Jacques Rousseau in 1750." Linscott (*Folk Songs of Old New England*, 1939, p. 207) says that the melody of this little ditty is a variation of the "Good Shepherd" tune. See also Gardner (*Ballads and Songs of Southern Michigan*, 1939, p. 466) for references and texts, and McCollum and Porter (*JAFL* 56, 1943, p. 110) for an Iowa text. The piece appears in the Brown (North Carolina Folk-Lore Society) collection.

A

Sung by Mrs. Frances Hall, Pineville, Mo., Oct. 14, 1928. Mrs. Hall points out that an old hymn "Come Ye Sinners Poor and Needy" is sung to the same tune.

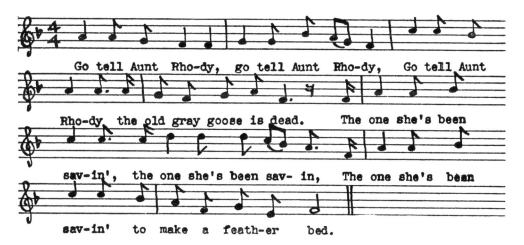

Go tell Aunt Rho-dy, go tell Aunt Rho-dy, Go tell Aunt Rho-dy, the old gray goose is dead. The one she's been sav-in', the one she's been sav-in, The one she's been sav-in' to make a feath-er bed.

Somebody killed it, somebody killed it,
Somebody killed it, knocked it in the head.
It died easy, it died easy,
It died easy, out in the old barn-yard.

B

Sung by Mrs. Stella Buchanan, Farmington, Ark., Oct. 2, 1941.

Go tell Aunt Phoebe,
Go tell Aunt Phoebe,
Go tell Aunt Phoebe,
The old gray goose is dead.

She died last Friday,
She died last Friday,
She died last Friday,
Floating on the pond.

The one she was saving,
The one she was saving,
The one she was saving,
To make a feather bed.

Poor old Aunt Phoebe,
Poor old Aunt Phoebe,
Poor old Aunt Phoebe,
She'll have no feather bed.

C

Mrs. May Kennedy McCord, Springfield, Mo., Nov. 12, 1941, sings "Aunt Rhody" with the following stanza:

She died in the manger,
She died in the manger,
She died in the manger,
With toothache in her head.

D

Mrs. Olga Trail, Farmington, Ark., Dec. 8, 1941, adds the following stanzas:

Go tell Aunt Patsy,
Go tell Aunt Patsy,
Go tell Aunt Patsy,
The old gray goose is dead.

She died with the slow fever,
She died with the slow fever,
She died with the slow fever,
Out behind the shed.

No more little goslin's,
No more little goslin's,
No more little goslin's,
To make a feather bed.

271

THE OLD GRAY HORSE

Scarborough (*On the Trail of Negro Folk-Songs*, 1925, p. 13) prints several additional stanzas from the singing of Southern Negroes, all ending in "down in Alabam'" instead of "down in Arkansas." Sandburg (*American Songbag*, 1927, p. 102) has a humorous version of a similar piece, remarking that it is derived from a Negro spiritual. A religious marching song, "Go in the Wilderness," was given by Higginson (*Atlantic Monthly* 19, June 1867, p. 690). Botkin (*Texas Folk-Lore Society Publications* 7, 1928, p. 18) found "The Old Gray Mare" used as a game-song in rural Oklahoma. The "down in Alabama" refrain occurs in the version reported by McCollum (*JAFL* 56, 1943, p. 102). The song is reported in the Brown (North Carolina Folk-Lore Society) collection. Compare also Vernon Dalhart's phonograph record (*Harmony* 552D7042, *Conqueror* 7071).

A

Sung by Miss Leone Duvall, Pineville, Mo., Sept. 7, 1926.

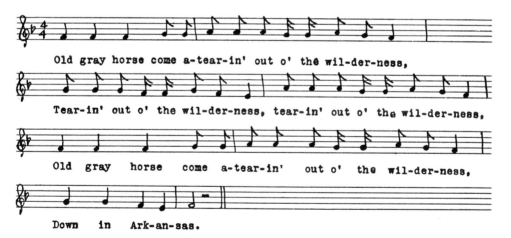

Old gray horse come a-tear-in' out o' the wil-der-ness,

Tear-in' out o' the wil-der-ness, tear-in' out o' the wil-der-ness,

Old gray horse come a-tear-in' out o' the wil-der-ness,

Down in Ark-an-sas.

B

Mr. Robert Linthicum, St. Louis, Mo., Sept. 17, 1935, sings a similar stanza to the same melody:

Little black bull come down in the wilderness,
Down in the wilderness, down in the wilderness,
Little black bull come down in the wilderness,
Long time ago.

C

Sung by Booth Campbell, Cane Hill, Ark., Feb. 5, 1942. Mr. Campbell sings it with a great deal of loud banjo-strumming and an occasional "Hey-oh, hi-whoop!"

Was an old nigger and come from Guinea,
And she come from Guinea, and she come from Guinea,
Was an old nigger and she come from Guinea,
Down in Alabam.

Old nigger swore her name was Jinny,
Her name was Jinny, her name was Jinny,
Old nigger swore her name was Jinny
Down in Alabam.

Old gray horse come tearin' out o' the wilderness,
Tearin' out o' the wilderness, tearin' out o' the wilderness,
Old gray horse come tearin' out o' the wilderness
Down in Alabam.

Was an old mule and he come from Jerusalem,
He come from Jerusalem, he come from Jerusalem,
Was an old mule and he come from Jerusalem
Down in Alabam.

Barnum caught him, put him in his museum,
Put him in his museum, put him in his museum,
Barnum caught him, put him in his museum,
Down in Alabam.

Aint you mighty glad to get out o' the wilderness,
Get out o' the wilderness, out o' the wilderness,
Aint you mighty glad to get out o' the wilderness
Down in Alabam.

Fifteen cents to get out o' the wilderness,
Get out o' the wilderness, get out o' the wilderness,
Fifteen cents to get out o' the wilderness
Down in Alabam.

272

JINNY GO ROUND AND AROUND

Several of these "I-wouldn't-marry" songs are mentioned in the literature, and many of the stanzas derive from the old minstrel routines. See Perrow (*JAFL* 28, 1915, pp. 136-137, 176), Talley (*Negro Folk Rhymes*, 1922, pp. 56, 63), Scarborough (*In the Land of Cotton*, 1923, p. 12), Odum (*The Negro and His Songs*, 1925, p. 191), Blair (*JAFL* 40, 1927, p. 98), and White (*American Negro Folk-Songs*, 1928, p. 323). The first stanza of the variant presented here is paralleled in "Cindy," a play-party song reported by Lunsford and Stringfield (*30 and 1 Folk Songs*, 1929, p. 42) from the Southern Appalachians. There are several phonograph records of related items (*Victor* 20137-B, *Challenge* 687, *Gray Gull* 552D2323, *Radiex* 1F23230). For further information see Belden's headnote (*Ballads and Songs*, 1940, pp. 262-263). The "Rockinham" mentioned is doubtless Rockingham County, Virginia.

Sung by Miss Leone Duvall, Pineville, Mo., Oct. 14, 1928.

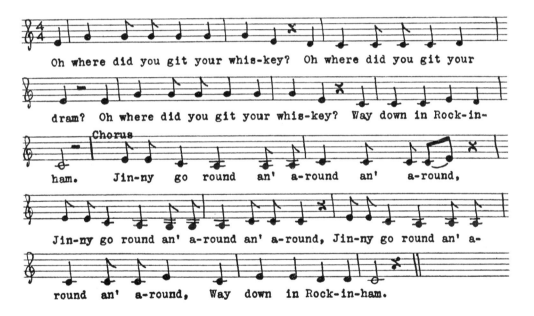

I wouldn't marry a old maid,
I'll tell you the reason why,
Her nose is always leakin'
An' her chin is never dry.

I wouldn't marry a widder,
I'll tell you the reason why,
She's got too many children
To make the biscuits fly.

I wouldn't marry a Dutch gal,
I'll tell you the reason why,
Her neck's so long and stringy
I'm afeared she'll never die.

I wouldn't marry old Joe's gal,
I'll tell you the reason why,
. . . . . . in the biscuit tray
An' called it pumpkin pie

273

SHOO FLY

One of the most popular nonsense-songs of the Civil War period, this piece was revived years later in "Captain Jinks of the Horse Marine," Ethel Barrymore's first play. It is usually credited to Thomas Brigham Bishop, who also claimed to have written the words of "John Brown's Body." Scarborough (*On the Trail of Negro Folk-Songs*, 1925, pp. 200-201, 286) refers to a "shoo-fly" piece heard among Mississippi Negroes, and quotes Professor Kittredge, who remembers the song as a minstrel hit. Spaeth (*Read 'Em and Weep*, 1927, pp. 63-64) prints the words and music as credited to Billy Reeves and Frank Campbell. A similar text is reported by Roe and Schwenck (*Bartender's Guide and Song Book*, New York, 1930, p. 73). Botkin (*American Play-Party Song*, 1937, pp. 304-308) found the song used as a play-party number in Oklahoma. A somewhat different version is printed as an old minstrel piece in Loesser's *Humor in American Song*, 1942, pp. 117-119.

Sung by Mrs. Marie Wilbur, Pineville, Mo., Apr. 2, 1926.

I feel, I feel, I feel like a morn-in' star, I feel, I feel, I feel like a morn-in' star. Shoo fly, don't both-er me, Shoo fly, don't both-er me, Shoo fly, don't both-er me, For I just been on a mer-ry spree.

274

TURKEY IN THE STRAW

"Turkey in the Straw" was originally a comic song entitled "Old Zip Coon," sung by many of the early black-face minstrels. An edition of "Zip Coon, A Popular Negro Song. As Sung by Mr. Dixon With Great Applause" was published in Baltimore about 1834, and contains 9 verses, the last about President Jackson, "for he blow up de Banks" (Dichter and Shapiro, *Early American Sheet Music*, 1941, p. 53). The song is now chiefly known as a fiddle-tune (Spaeth, *Read 'Em and Weep*, 1927, p. 17). Linscott (*Folk Songs of Old New England*, 1939, p. 101) says that the melody is derived from the ballad-tune "My Grandmother Lived on Yonder Little Green." There are words to the melody which are known by nearly any mountain singer—at least a stanza or two. Sandburg (*American Songbag*, 1927, p. 94) prints two good texts with music. Ford (*Traditional Music of America*, 1940, pp. 435-438) prints a text and tune, and three other items which he regards as parodies of "Turkey in the Straw." See also the Brown (North Carolina Folk-Lore Society) collection. There are phonograph records by Sam Jones (*Columbia* 201-D), Gid Tanner (*Columbia* 15084-D), Billy Golden (*Columbia* A-5031), Percy Grainger (*Columbia* 2002M), Kissinger Brothers (*Brunswick* 235), Hobbs Brothers (*Conqueror* 7332), and Alpheus McFayden (*Victor* 21128).

A

Sung by Mr. and Mrs. Percy Fitzhugh, Calico Rock, Ark., July 7, 1920.

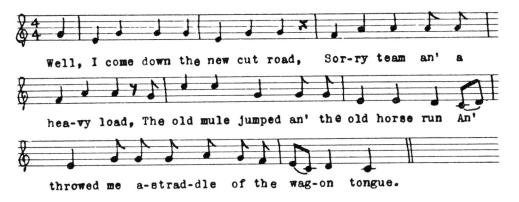

Well, I come down the new cut road, Sor-ry team an' a hea-vy load, The old mule jumped an' the old horse run An' throwed me a-strad-dle of the wag-on tongue.

Mud to the hubs an' the britchin' mighty weak,
All starved out on Still-house Creek,
Ever'body livin' on rock-an'-rye,
With bullfrog chitlins an' polecat pie.

Well, if you want to know how to milk a old yoe,
It's out in the timber you must go,
It's two at the head an' two at the hams,
An' two little devils for to knock off the lambs.

Turkey in the straw, boys, turkey in the straw,
Twist up your britches in a high tucky-haw,
An' it's do-se-do with your mother-in-law
While we hit 'em up a tune called Turkey in the Straw.

Well the cowboy takes 'em as they come,
Head full of moonshine, belly full of rum,
But the cowboy's mind don't pack no load,
An' he allus spends his money like he found it in the road.

Come to the river an' I couldn't git across,
Paid five dollars for a old stable-horse,
Jumped on his back an' his rump caved in
An' it's oh Lord God how the water rushed in!

Jaybird settin' on a hick'ry limb,
Along come a crow an' kicked him in the shin,
Jaybird holler an' old crow caw,
While we hit 'em up a tune called Turkey in the Straw.

Little red hen with a little white foot
Built her nest in a huckleberry root,
Out come a snake as long as your arm,
So another little snort won't do us any harm.

Got to git up just as shore as you're born,
Chiggers all a-bitin' an' a cheench blowed his horn,
The old coon a-coonin' an' the possum he trot,
The guinea-hen cackled an' the gander he sot.

B

Contributed by Mrs. Mabel E. Mueller, Rolla, Mo., Apr. 21, 1935.

As I come down the new-cut road
I met Mister Bullfrog and Miss Toad,
And every time Miss Toad would sing
Old Mister Bullfrog cut a pigeon-wing.

Met Mister Catfish coming down stream,
I says Mister Catfish, what do you mean?
Caught Mister Catfish by the snout
And turned Mister Catfish inside out.

Come to the river and I couldn't get across,
Paid five dollars for an old blind horse,
Wouldn't go ahead, nor he wouldn't stand still,
So he went up and down like an old sawmill.

Oh I jumped in the seat, and I give a little yell,
The horse run away, broke the wagon all to hell,
Sugar in the gourd and honey in the horn,
Never was so happy since the day I was born.

C

Sung by Mrs. Jewell Lamberson, Bentonville, Ark., Nov. 21, 1935. Mrs. Lamberson
heard it sung by some people who came from McDonald County, Mo.

Oh dip the 'taters down in grease,
An' fling the dogs a 'tater a-piece,
Run your brogans clean of tacks,
Split the splinters an' fetch me the axe.

275

THE CROW SONG

It has been suggested that this is an echo from some old minstrel piece, possibly derived
from "The Three Ravens" (Child, *English and Scottish Popular Ballads*, 1882-1898, No. 26),
a comic version of which was once popular in America. For related texts and further references see Talley (*Negro Folk Rhymes*, 1922, pp. 59, 183), Cox (*Folk-Songs of the South*, 1925,
p. 31), Sharp (*English Folk Songs from the Southern Appalachians*, 1932, II, p. 304), and Belden
(*Ballads and Songs*, 1940, p. 32). Porter (*JAFL* 54, 1941, p. 170) gives one stanza of "The Crow
Song" as sung by his grandfather, from Ohio. Compare the "Bird Song" which Loesser (*Humor
in American Song*, 1942, pp. 40-41) recorded from the Appalachians, with a remark that the
tune is very old, and "contains only five tones."

A

Sung by Miss Leone Duvall, Pineville, Mo., Oct. 14, 1928.

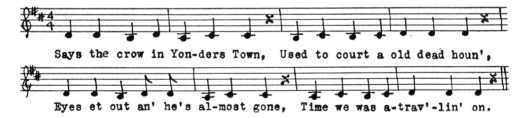

Says the crow in Yon-ders Town, Used to court a old dead houn',
Eyes et out an' he's al-most gone, Time we was a-trav'-lin' on.

Says the hawk unto the crow,
Down to the corn-patch we must go,
To pull up corn an' l'arn to scratch,
Been our trade since we was hatched.

B

Sung by Miss Laura A. Wilson, Pittsburg, Kan., Apr. 21, 1916. Miss Wilson learned it near Springfield, Mo., about 1885.

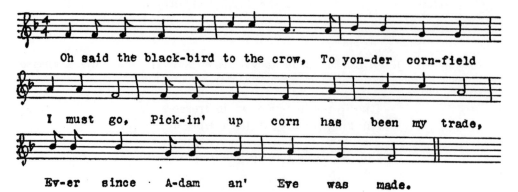

Oh said the black-bird to the crow, To yon-der corn-field I must go, Pick-in' up corn has been my trade, Ev-er since A-dam an' Eve was made.

> Well, says the redbird to the crane,
> Pray to the Lord for a little more rain,
> The ponds all muddy an' the creeks all dry,
> If it wasn't for the tadpoles we'd all die.
>
> Well, says the peckerwood as he flew,
> When I was young I courted too,
> But she grew fickle an' from me fled
> An' ever since then my head's been red.

C

Additional stanzas contributed by Professor A. W. Breeden, Manhattan, Kan., Oct. 5, 1935. Mr. Breeden learned the song near Galena, Mo., in the late 90's.

> Oh said the black bird to the crow,
> What makes the white folks hate us so?
> Stealing corn has been our trade
> Ever since the world was made.
>
> Oh said the bobwhite in the grass,
> Once I courted a fair lady lass,
> But she grew fickle and took to flight,
> Ever since then I holler bobwhite.

D

Related perhaps is a fragment of play-party song remembered by Mrs. Dorn Higgins, Sulphur Springs, Ark., Aug. 2, 1936.

> What did the blackbird say to the crow?
> It aint goin' to rain no more!

E

Dr. O. St. John, Pineville, Mo., Dec. 20, 1923, recalls a jingle which used to be sung at corn-planting time:

> One for the blackbird,
> Two for the crow,
> Three for the cutworm
> An' the rest for to grow.

276

THE POSSUM SONG

A similar piece appeared in at least one of the *Hamlin's Wizard Oil* songbooks which were common here in the 90's. A four-stanza text entitled "Carve Dat Possum" was printed in the Aurora (Mo.) *Advertiser*, Aug. 17, 1939. Versions elsewhere reported are those of Odum (*JAFL* 24, 1911, pp. 375-376), Wier (*The Book of a Thousand Songs*, 1918, p. 90), Odum and Johnson (*The Negro and His Songs*, 1925, pp. 240-241). The melody and words are accredited to Sam Lucas by Johnson (*Rolling Along in Song*, 1937, p. 149).

A

Sung by Miss Fanny Mulhollan, Pineville, Mo., Sept. 7, 1928.

Pos-sum meat is good to eat, Carve him to de heart, You'll allus find him good an' sweet, Carve him to de heart.

Chorus

Carve dat pos-sum, carve dat pos-sum, chil-dern, Carve dat pos-sum, oh it's carve him to de heart.

> Lay sweet taters in de pan,
> Carve him to de heart,
> Sweetest eatin' in de lan',
> Carve him to de heart.

B

A related fragment, sung to a different tune, is supplied by Mrs. Marie Wilbur, Pineville, Mo., Sept. 7, 1928.

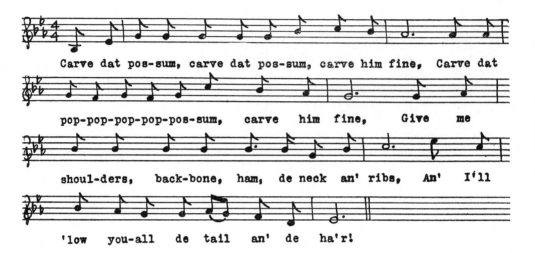

Carve dat pos-sum, carve dat pos-sum, carve him fine, Carve dat

pop-pop-pop-pop-pos-sum, carve him fine, Give me

shoul-ders, back-bone, ham, de neck an' ribs, An' I'll

'low you-all de tail an' de ha'r!

C

Contributed by Mrs. May Kennedy McCord, Springfield, Mo., Feb. 19, 1933.

My dog he barked and I went to see,
Carve him to the heart;
There was a possum up that tree,
Carve him to the heart;
I reached out for to pull him in,
That possum he begun to grin,
Carve him to the heart;
I took him home and dressed him off,
I hung him up that night in the loft,
Carve him to the heart.

The way to cook that possum down,
Carve him to the heart;
First parboil him, then bake him brown,
Carve him to the heart;
Lay sweet potatoes in the pan,
The sweetest eatin' in all the land,
Carve him to the heart.

277

OLD MOLLY HARE

Talley (*Negro Folk Rhymes*, 1922, p. 22) reports this piece at some length, and Scarborough (*On the Trail of Negro Folk-Songs*, 1925, p. 175) prints a similar song in the Gullah dialect of South Carolina. Richardson (*American Mountain Songs*, 1927, pp. 98, 118) has a "Bell Cow" piece with many related lines, and suggests that "Mother Goose might have been responsible for this nursery jingle." Harris (*Uncle Remus* [1st ed. 1880] 1928, p. 24) quotes a stanza as heard among Negro singers in Georgia. The "Old Mother Hare" song recorded by Lomax (*American Ballads and Folk Songs*, 1934, pp. 283-284) is very close to the Ozark version. Compare the "Old Mother Hare" verses reported from Arkansas by Ray Wood (*Mother Goose in the Ozarks*, 1938, p. 8). See too the Brown (North Carolina Folk-Lore Society) collection. There is also a phonograph record by Puckett and McMichen (*Columbia* 15295-D).

Sung by Mrs. Marie Wilbur, Pineville, Mo., Oct. 1, 1926. There are, she tells me, many amusing but unprintable verses, each beginning "Old Molly Ha'r, whut you doin' thar?" and ending with a reference to sexual or skatological matters.

Old Mol-ly Ha'r, whut you do-in' thar? Set-tin' in the cor-ner,

smok-in' see-gar. Rab-bit in the corn-fiel' eat-in' up the peas,

Bell cow, yell cow, kick-in' up her heels.

278

GO SLOW, BOYS

This fragment is similar to the first stanza of the "Banjo Picking" song reported by Talley (*Negro Folk Rhymes*, 1922, p. 21). Some singers end this verse with a more or less musical imitation of a cock's crowing.

Sung by Mrs. Marie Wilbur, Pineville, Mo., Sept. 11, 1928. Mrs. Wilbur learned the piece years ago from a relative who lived in Searcy, Ark.

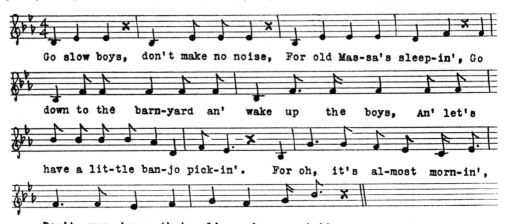

Go slow boys, don't make no noise, For old Mas-sa's sleep-in', Go down to the barn-yard an' wake up the boys, An' let's have a lit-tle ban-jo pick-in'. For oh, it's al-most morn-in', Don't you hear that old cock crow-in'?

279

IF I HAD A SCOLDING WIFE

This is part of an old minstrel song entitled "Lucy Long." See *Marsh's Selection* (New York, 1854, part 2, p. 192), Chapple (*Heart Songs*, 1909, p. 289), Perrow (*JAFL* 28, 1915, p. 188), Piper (*JAFL* 28, 1915, pp. 271-272), Tolman and Eddy (*JAFL* 35, 1922, pp. 431-432), White (*American Negro Folk-Songs*, 1928, p. 449), Botkin (*American Play-Party Song*, 1937, pp. 182-183), Ford (*Traditional Music of America*, 1940, p. 395), and the Brown (North Carolina Folk-Lore Society) collection. I heard my father, who came from South Carolina, sing this fragment about 1897, under the impression that it was a genuine Negro folksong.

Sung by Dr. Leo McKellops, Anderson, Mo., May 6, 1933.

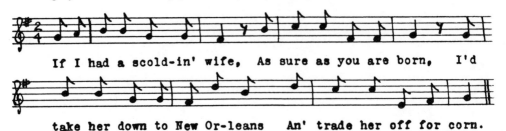

If I had a scold-in' wife, As sure as you are born, I'd take her down to New Or-leans An' trade her off for corn.

280

POSSUM UP A GUM STUMP

Similar items have been reported by Campbell and Sharp (*English Folk Songs from the Southern Appalachians*, 1917, No. 88), White (*American Negro Folk-Songs*, 1928, pp. 237-239), Combs (*Folk-Say*, 1930, p. 242), Lomax (*American Ballads and Folk Songs*, 1934, p. 238) and Botkin (*American Play-Party Song*, 1937, p. 296).

Sung by Mr. Lewis Kelley, Cyclone, Mo., Jan. 5, 1928. Mr. Kelley learned the song from his parents, about 1885.

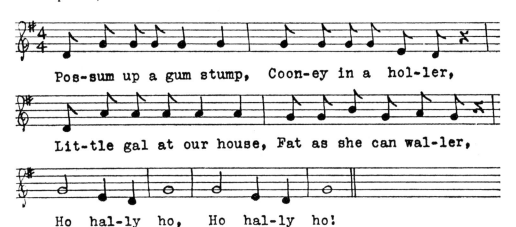

Pos-sum up a gum stump, Coon-ey in a hol-ler,

Lit-tle gal at our house, Fat as she can wal-ler,

Ho hal-ly ho, Ho hal-ly ho!

281

COULDN'T RAISE NO SUGAR CORN

Compare this with the "Dem Taters" song recovered in East Tennessee by Perrow (*JAFL* 28, 1915, p. 138). See also the "Harvest Song" which Talley (*Negro Folk Rhymes*, 1922, p. 57) heard sung by Southern Negroes, and the first stanza of a related piece reported by Scarborough (*On the Trail of Negro Folk-Songs*, 1925, p. 187). The radio hillbillies sing a similar verse as part of the "Jordan Is a Hard Road to Travel, I Believe" song.

Sung by Mr. Robert Ketterman, Pittsburg, Kan., Jan. 1, 1916. Mr. Ketterman learned the song in Joplin, Mo., about 1910.

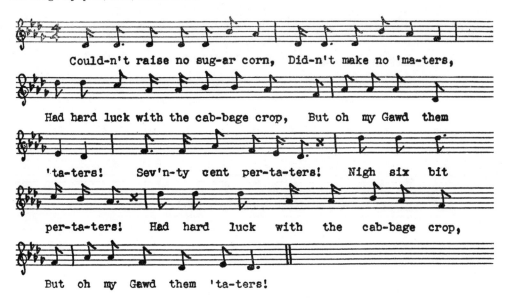

Could-n't raise no sug-ar corn, Did-n't make no 'ma-ters,

Had hard luck with the cab-bage crop, But oh my Gawd them

'ta-ters! Sev'n-ty cent per-ta-ters! Nigh six bit

per-ta-ters! Had hard luck with the cab-bage crop,

But oh my Gawd them 'ta-ters!

282

THERE WAS AN OLD FROG

This piece was sung by several of the early blackface minstrels (Christy and Wood, *New Song Book*, 1854, pp. 7-8). It is based upon an English nonsense-rhyme, according to Kittredge (*JAFL* 35, 1922, p. 396). See also Campbell and Sharp (*English Folk Songs from the Southern Appalachians*, 1917, p. 319), Scarborough (*On the Trail of Negro Folk-Songs*, 1925, pp. 156-157, 201, 285), and Odum (*Negro Workaday Songs*, 1926, p. 187). White (*American Negro Folk-Songs*, 1928, pp. 175-176) reports several variants of the song, and prints a very similar refrain which was used as a class yell at Trinity College, N. C., in 1921. Belden (*Ballads and Songs*, 1940, p. 496) reports two Missouri stanzas, which he apparently regards as part of "The Frog's Courtship." See also Ira W. Ford (*Traditional Music of America*, 1940, pp. 418-419, 450-451). Brewster (*Ballads and Songs of Indiana*, 1940, pp. 324-325) gives other references.

A

Sung by Mr. Curt Boren, Bentonville, Ark., Nov. 9, 1931.

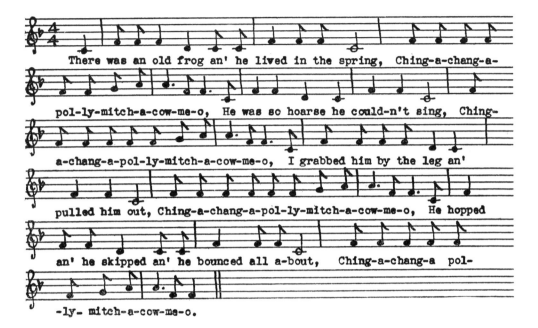

There was an old frog an' he lived in the spring, Ching-a-chang-a-pol-ly-mitch-a-cow-me-o, He was so hoarse he could-n't sing, Ching-a-chang-a-pol-ly-mitch-a-cow-me-o, I grabbed him by the leg an' pulled him out, Ching-a-chang-a-pol-ly-mitch-a-cow-me-o, He hopped an' he skipped an' he bounced all a-bout, Ching-a-chang-a pol-ly- mitch-a-cow-me-o.

Cheese in the spring house nine days old,
Ching-a-chang-a-polly-mitch-a-cow-me-o,
Rats an' skippers is a-gittin' mighty bold,
Ching-a-chang-a-polly-mitch-a-cow-me-o,
Big fat rat an' a bucket o' souse,
Ching-a-chang-a-polly-mitch-a-cow-me-o,
Take it back to the big white house,
Ching-a-chang-a-polly-mitch-a-cow-me-o.

Way down South on Cedar Street,
Ching-a-chang-a-polly-mitch-a-cow-me-o,
Them yaller niggers grow ten feet,
Ching-a-chang-a-polly-mitch-a-cow-me-o,
They go to bed but it aint no use,
Ching-a-chang-a-polly-mitch-a-cow-me-o,
Their feet stick out like a chicken roost,
Ching-a-chang-a-polly-mitch-a-cow-me-o.

B

Mrs. Marie Wilbur, Pineville, Mo., Dec. 28, 1931, sings a very similar song with the following refrain after each verse:

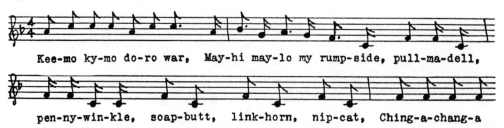

Kee-mo ky-mo do-ro war, May-hi may-lo my rump-side, pull-ma-dell,

pen-ny-win-kle, soap-butt, link-horn, nip-cat, Ching-a-chang-a

pol-ly-mitch-a-cow-me-o.

C

Mrs. Sylvia Hill, Thayer, Mo., Oct. 17, 1940, recalls the following fragments:

> Came-o came-o, do-mi-ro-ma-ho.
> Ma-he, ma-hi, rim strim Parmalee,
> Lipe on a rig-tum ri-tum,
> Put 'em in the kime-bo.

> Came-o came-o, do-mi-ro-ma-ho,
> Ma-he, ma-hi, rip back pennywinkle,
> Sing sing Sally,
> Can't you ki-me-o.

D

From Mrs. Lillian Short, Cabool, Mo., Apr. 25, 1941. She gives "Kemo Kimo" as the local title.

> Way down yonder on Beaver Creek,
> Sing song kitty caint you kimeo,
> Darkies grow to be ten feet,
> Sing song kitty caint you kimeo.

> Kemo kimo dee ro art,
> Me-he me-hi me hum drum penny winkle,
> Tit, tat, pitty pat, blue eyed pussy cat,
> Sing song kitty caint you kimeo.

> They go to bed but it aint no use,
> Sing song kitty caint you kimeo,
> Feet stick out for the chickens to roost,
> Sing song kitty caint you kimeo.

Our dog went out to get a bone,
Sing song kitty caint you kimeo,
He looked at me and I run home,
Sing song kitty caint you kimeo.

Our cow won't give milk in summer,
Sing song kitty caint you kimeo,
So we have to take it from her,
Sing song kitty caint you kimeo.

283

ON A COLD FROSTY MORNING

A Meridian, Miss., item, "Cold, Frosty Morning," played on the fiddle, was recorded by
Herbert Halpert in 1939 (*Check-List . . . Archive of American Folk Song*, 1942, p. 59). Four
lines of a similar piece are in the Brown (North Carolina Folk-Lore Society) collection.

A

Sung by Miss Louise Copeland, Springfield, Mo., Mar. 19, 1941. Learned it from her
grandmother, no local title.

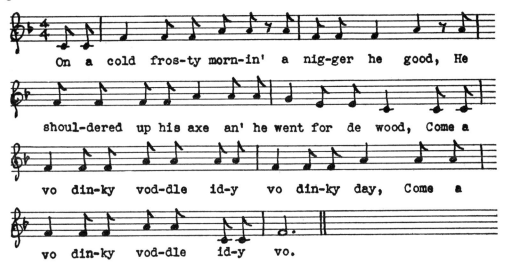

De corn am to shell an' to pack to de mill,
An' de hogs am to feed at de bottom ob de hill,
Come a vo dinky voddle idy vo dinky day,
Come a vo dinky voddle idy vo.

When a nigger goes to church an' down he sets,
He rolls back his eyes an' golly how he sweats,
Come a vo dinky voddle idy vo dinky day,
Come a vo dinky voddle idy vo.

De creek am muddy an' de ribber am a-risin',
Just a gettin' back from a nigger baptisin',
Come a vo dinky voddle idy vo dinky day,
Come a vo dinky voddle idy vo.

B

Sung by Mr. James Bitner, Joplin, Mo., Aug. 10, 1927. Mr. Bitner learned it years ago
in Hot Springs, Ark., as part of a medicine-show minstrel piece.

On a cold frosty mornin' a nigger feels good,
With his axe on his shoulder he's off for the woods,

Singin' hey hey ticky, wicky falla lalla day,
Singin' hey hey ticky, wicky falla lalla day.

In comes a nigger pretty near froze to death,
Sayin' stand aside, Massa, I got to warm myself.

There aint much to eat but a little ball o' fat,
An' the devil gets a nigger if he eat much o' that.

The corn am to shell, then I take it to the mill,
The hogs am to feed at the bottom of the hill.

The shoes am to black an' the boots am to grease,
But the devil gets the yaller gal . . . . . .!

284

THE GOLDEN AXE

Sung by Mrs. Marie Wilbur, Pineville, Mo., Jan. 1, 1922. Mrs. Wilbur heard it near
Pineville in the late 90's, as part of a "nigger" song.

Whut you goin' to do? Why, knock you in the head with a

gold-en axe!

285

WHISTLING RUFUS

Pieces with this title were recorded at Springfield, Mo., as played on the French harp in 1936, and at the migratory camp, Indio, Calif., as sung with guitar in 1939 (*Check-List* . . . *Archive of American Folk Song*, 1942, p. 428). See also the Brown (North Carolina Folk-Lore Society) collection.

Sung by Mr. Tommy Davis, Galena, Mo., Sept. 21, 1941. Asked if the last line shouldn't be "one-man band," Mr. Davis said no, that the line was "one band man," just as he sung it.

286

JONAH AND THE WHALE

Three stanzas and chorus of this piece are published under the title "Hide Away" in a *Hamlin's Wizard Oil Songbook*, n.d., c. 1897. See also the Brown (North Carolina Folk-Lore Society) collection.

William Allen White (*Autobiography*, 1946, p. 93) says that he sang a song called "The Gospel Raft" with the chorus:

> Get your baggage on the deck
> And don't forget your check,
> For you can't sneak on board and hide away!

at El Dorado, Kan., in 1883. He describes it as "a Negro minstrel imitation of the spirituals of the slaves."

Sung by Mr. Fred Woodruff, Lincoln, Ark., Dec. 12, 1941. He said it was a minstrel piece which he learned about 1908.

I am go-ing down the riv-er in a lit-tle gos-pel ray * Like

No-ah in his good old ark, Keep them can-dle lights burn-ing,

Keep them burn-ing all the while Or you'll lose your-self and

Chorus

stum-ble in the dark. If your heart aint white and pure The

devil git you sure, So git you read-y for that aw-ful judg-ment

day, Git your bag-gage on the deck and don't for-get to take your

check, for you can't steal on board, hide a-way.

raft in the *Wizard Oil* text.

Little children take the working and don't mistake the charge,
For the opposition boat's a-running too,
She's liable to bust the boiler up at any time at all
And she'll cook them niggers all in stew.

I have a little private box and a little opera glass
To see them niggers moseying by the door,
If you cannot say your prayers I will fling you down the stairs
For I don't want to see you any more.

Hide away, hide away, hide away, hide away,
There's no use a-trying to hide away,
Get your baggage on the deck and don't forget to take your check
For you can't steal on board, hide away.

I'll tell you about the army that old Pharoah did command,
As he follered poor old Moses long ago,
They got drownded in the river as the lines was pressing on,
And the fishes had a juber down below.

Old Jonah like a fool got stubborn like a mule,
The whale it made him quickly disappear,
Jonah jerked his razor out and he cut the whale in two,
And he paddled to the shore upon his ear.

288

HISTORY OF THE WORLD

An almost identical piece is "De History ob de World" in *Trifet's Budget of Music No. 15*, March 1892, p. 123. I have seen similar texts in two unidentified med-show songbooks circulated in the 90's. Compare Ford (*Traditional Music of America*, 1940, pp. 278-280). In *Songs of Yesterday* (New York, 1941, pp. 231-233), Philip D. Jordan and Lillian Kessler give the text and tune as sung "by Wm. Parker in the Popular Extravaganza of the Buffalo Gals at the Adelphi," copyrighted 1847 by C. H. Keith.

Sung by Mr. Booth Campbell, Cane Hill, Ark., Dec. 25, 1941. He calls it "The Creation," and says that it was a popular nigger-minstrel piece in the early 90's, and perhaps earlier.

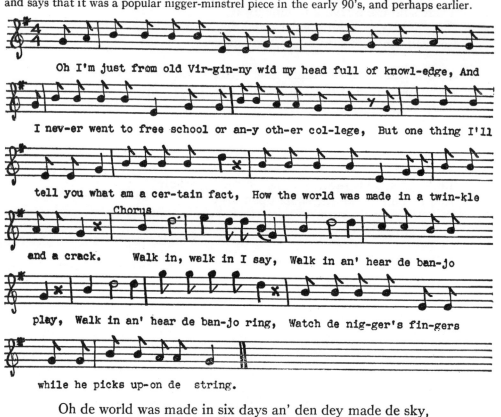

Oh I'm just from old Vir-gin-ny wid my head full of knowl-edge, And
I nev-er went to free school or an-y oth-er col-lege, But one thing I'll
tell you what am a cer-tain fact, How the world was made in a twin-kle
and a crack. Walk in, walk in I say, Walk in an' hear de ban-jo
play, Walk in an' hear de ban-jo ring, Watch de nig-ger's fin-gers
while he picks up-on de string.

Oh de world was made in six days an' den dey made de sky,
An' den dey hung it over head an' left it dar to dry,
An' den dey made de stars out o' nigger-wenches' eyes,
For to give a little light when de moon don't rise.

Adam was de first man, Eve she was de other,
Cain . . . . .* because he killed his brother,
Old mother Eve couldn't sleep without she had a piller,
An' de greatest man dat ever lived was Jack de Giant-killer.

---

*"Cain walked on de tread-mill," according to an unidentified med-show songbook.

Oh lightnin' is a yeller gal, she lives in de clouds,
Thunder is a black man, 'cause he holler loud,
When he kiss de lightnin' she dodge an' wonder,
Run away an' tear her clothes, an' dat makes de thunder.

Wind began to blow an' de rain began to fall,
De water come so high dat it drownd de niggers all,
It rain forty days an' nights, exactly by de countin',
An' it landed Noah's Ark in de Alleghany Mountains.

289

SONG AND DANCE

Sung by Mr. Wythe Bishop, Fayetteville, Ark., Dec. 13, 1941. He says that there used to be a dance to go with it, but that he is seventy-five years old and doesn't feel quite up to dancing nowadays.

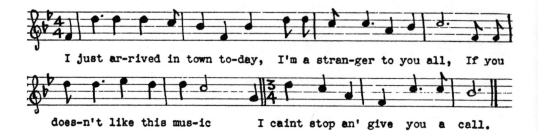

I just ar-rived in town to-day, I'm a stran-ger to you all, If you

does-n't like this mus-ic   I caint stop an' give you a call.

As I go down the street it's every girl I meet,
There's a twinkle in their eyes at me,
Great big legs and mighty small feet,
Oh my, don't we look so neat.

Here I am from old Louisiana,
Do, do, my huckleberry do,
The only girl I ever loved,
And I called her my turtle-dove.

I hugged her an' I kissed her,
An' on her lips I raised a blister,
But I'll never raise no more,
Kaze I'm fur away . . .

290

OLD MOSES SMOTE DE WATERS

See the Brown (North Carolina Folk-Lore Society) collection.

Sung by Mr. Doney Hammontree, Farmington, Ark., Dec. 28, 1941. He says it is a nigger-minstrel song, a sort of burlesque of a Negro spiritual. He learned it at Fayetteville, Ark., about 1895.

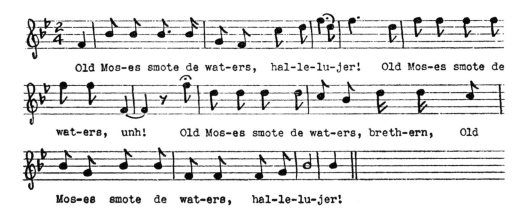

Old Mos-es smote de wat-ers, hal-le-lu-jer! Old Mos-es smote de

wat-ers, unh! Old Mos-es smote de wat-ers, breth-ern, Old

Mos-es smote de wat-ers, hal-le-lu-jer!

De waters they divided, hallelujer!
De waters they divided *unh*!
De waters they divided, brethren,
An' de waters they divided, hallelujer!

De children pass-ed over, hallelujer!
De children pass-ed over *unh*!
De children pass-ed over, brethren,
An' de children pass-ed over, hallelujer!

Old Pharoah's host got drownded, hallelujer!
Old Pharoah's host got drownded *unh*!
Old Pharoah's host got drownded, brethren,
Old Pharoah's host got drownded, hallelujer!

I see dat ship a-comin', hallelujer!
I see dat ship a-comin' *unh*!
I see dat ship a-comin', brethren,
An' I see dat ship a-comin', hallelujer!

She runs as steady as a die-er, hallelujer!
She runs as steady as a die-er *unh*!
She runs as steady as a die-er, brethren,
She runs as steady as a die-er, hallelujer!

She'll take us home to glory, hallelujer!
She'll take us home to glory *unh*!
She'll take us home to glory, brethren,
She'll take us home to glory, hallelujer!

Dar'll be shoutin' with de angels, hallelujer,
Dar'll be shoutin' with de angels *unh*!
Dar'll be shoutin' with de angels, brethren,
An' dar'll be shoutin' with de angels, hallelujer!

291

METHODIST PIE

A similar text was reported by C. V. Wheat (Aurora, Mo., *Advertiser*, July 25, 1940) from Lawrence County, Mo.

A

Sung by Mrs. Laura Wasson, Elm Springs, Ark., Jan. 28, 1942. Sometimes she sings this with an exaggerated nigger-minstrel pronunciation, using *de* for *the*, *udder* for *other*, etc.

I went to the camp-meet-in' t'oth-er aft-er-noon, To hear

them shout and sing, And tell each oth-er how they love one

an-oth-er And to make hal-le-lu-jah ring. They all went

there to have a good time, And eat the grub so sly, Ap-ple

sauce, but-ter, sug-ar in the gourd, And a great big Meth-od-ist

Chorus

pie. Oh lit-tle chil-lens, I be-lieve, Oh lit-tle chil-lens,

I be-lieve, Oh lit-tle chil-lens, I be-lieve, I'm a Meth-od-

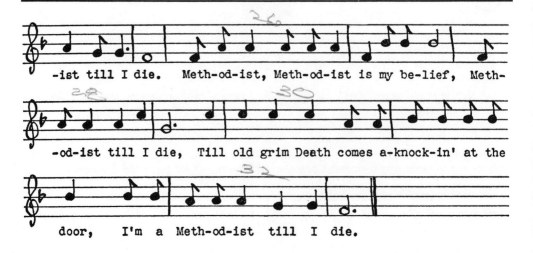

-ist till I die.   Meth-od-ist, Meth-od-ist is my be-lief, Meth-

-od-ist till I die,   Till old grim Death comes a-knock-in' at the

door,   I'm a Meth-od-ist till I die.

There was old Uncle Daniel and Brother Ebeneezer,
Uncle Rufus and his lame gal Sue,
Polly and Malindy and old Brother Bendy,
You never saw a happier crew.
You ought to hear the ringin' when they all got to singin'
That good old Bye and Bye,
And see Jim Magee in the top of a tree
Sayin' how is this for high?

They all took hands and walloped round the ring,
Kept singin' all the while,
You'd have thought it was a cyclone comin' through the air,
You could hear them shout half a mile.

B

From Mrs. Lillian Short, Galena, Mo., Feb. 23, 1941. She had it from Mrs. A. L. Estes, Lee's Summit, Mo.

> Then they all catch hands and march around the ring,
> Keep a-singin' all the while,
> You'd think it was a cyclone coming through the air,
> You could hear them shout a half a mile.
>
> Then the bell rings loud and a great big crowd
> Breaks ranks and up they fly,
> While I took the board on the sugar in the gourd
> And cleaned up the Methodist pie.

292

THE MIDNIGHT SPECIAL

See Sandburg (*American Songbag*, 1927, pp. 26-27, 217) for two "Midnight Special" texts, also a version in J. Rosamond Johnson's *Rolling Along in Song* (1937, pp. 176-177). Botkin (*Treasury of American Folklore*, 1944, pp. 908-909) gives five stanzas and a chorus as sung by Huddie ("Lead Belly") Ledbetter and transcribed by Peter Seeger.

Sung by Robert Pounds, Farmington, Mo., Feb. 2, 1942. Learned from some Texas Negroes. The first stanza serves as a refrain, being repeated after each of the subsequent verses.

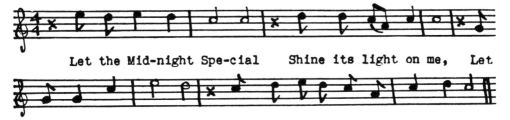

Let the Mid-night Spe-cial   Shine its light on me,   Let the Mid-night Spe-cial   Shine its ev-er lov-in' light on me.

> If you ever get to Dallas,
> Well you better walk right,
> Well you better not gamble,
> Well you better not fight.
>
> That sheriff will get you
> And he tuck you in,
> The judge will sentence you,
> And you're penitentiary bound.

Yonder come a little Rosy,
How in the world do you know?
I can tell her by her apron
And the dress she wore.

Umbrella round her shoulder,
Piece of paper in her hand,
Look a here, Mister Warden,
I wants my ever-lovin' man.

293

OLD ZIP COON

This piece is reported in the Brown (North Carolina Folk-Lore Society) collection.

Sung by Mr. Booth Campbell, Cane Hill, Ark., Feb. 5, 1942. He heard it sung at Cane Hill in the 80's.

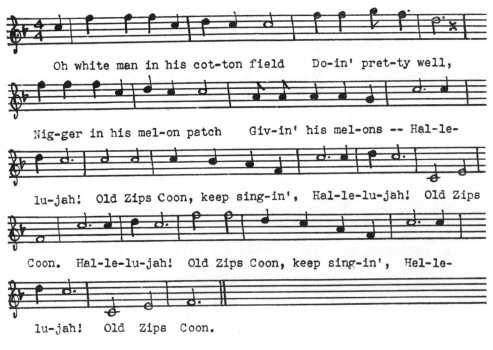

Oh white man in his cot-ton field   Do-in' pret-ty well,

Nig-ger in his mel-on patch   Giv-in' his mel-ons -- Hal-le-

lu-jah! Old Zips Coon, keep sing-in', Hal-le-lu-jah! Old Zips

Coon. Hal-le-lu-jah! Old Zips Coon, keep sing-in', Hel-le-

lu-jah! Old Zips Coon.

Lord made Adam an' Eve,
An' they done pretty well,
Soon as he turned his back on Eve
She give them apples — —

294

ONE MORE RIVER

Higginson (*Atlantic Monthly* 19, June 1867, p. 687) gives a stanza with the line "Dere ain't but one more river." A similar piece entitled "Pull the String and Let It Go" was printed in *St. Joseph's Liver Regulator Songbook*, circa 1897. C. V. Wheat (Aurora, Mo., *Advertiser*, Oct. 24, 1940) prints a text from Shell Knob, Mo., said to date from the 80's. I heard my father sing many verses in Noel, Mo., in 1899; he said it was a Negro song, and that he had learned it in South Carolina during the Civil War. Compare the "Noah's Ark" song in Loesser's *Humor in American Song*, 1942, pp. 120-121.

A

Sung by Mrs. Hugo Blair, Joplin, Mo., Sept. 8, 1929. She describes it as a "nigger minstrel piece" which she heard at a medicine-show near Joplin in 1890.

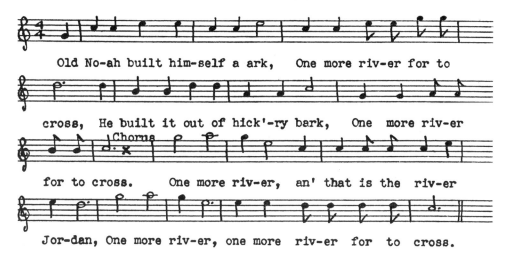

Old No-ah built him-self a ark, One more riv-er for to cross, He built it out of hick'-ry bark, One more riv-er for to cross. One more riv-er, an' that is the riv-er Jor-dan, One more riv-er, one more riv-er for to cross.

The animals went in two by two,
One more river for to cross,
The elephant a-leanin' on the kangaroo,
One more river for to cross.

The animals went in three by three,
One more river for to cross,
Polecat a-talkin' to the bumblebee,
One more river for to cross.

The animals went in four by four,
One more river for to cross,
Old Noah got mad and hollered for more,
One more river for to cross.

The animals went in five by five,
One more river for to cross,
Old Noah hollered you look alive,
One more river for to cross.

The animals went in six by six,
One more river for to cross,
The hyena laughin' at the monkey's tricks,
One more river for to cross.

The animals went in eight by eight,
One more river for to cross,
Old Noah hollered don't you shut that gate,
One more river for to cross.

The animals went in ten by ten,
One more river for to cross,
Old Noah blowed his whistle then,
One more river for to cross.

B

Manuscript copy from Mrs. Maggie Morgan, Springdale, Ark., Feb. 1, 1942. She heard it sung about 1890.

Now ladies, give this ark a tow,
There's one more river to cross,
Just pull the string and let it go,
There's one more river to cross.

One more river, and that's the river of Jordan,
One more river, there's one more river to cross.

Old Noah he did build an ark,
There's one more river to cross,
He built it out of hickory bark,
There's one more river to cross.

Old Noah had to load his stock,
There's one more river to cross,
He anchored to a great big rock,
There's one more river to cross.

The animals went in one by one,
There's one more river to cross,
The elephant chewin' a caraway bun,
There's one more river to cross.

The animals went in two by two,
There's one more river to cross,
The rhinoceros and the kangaroo,
There's one more river to cross.

The animals went in three by three,
There's one more river to cross,
The bat, the bear and the bumblebee,
There's one more river to cross,

The animals went in four by four,
There's one more river to cross,
Old Noah got mad and hollered for more,
There's one more river to cross.

The animals went in five by five,
There's one more river to cross,
With Saratoga trunks they did arrive,
There's one more river to cross.

The animals went in six by six,
There's one more river to cross,
The hyena laughed at the monkey's tricks,
There's one more river to cross.

The animals went in seven by seven,
There's one more river to cross,
Says the ant to the elephant who are you shovin'?
There's one more river to cross.

The animals went in eight by eight,
There's one more river to cross,
Old Noah hollered it's a-getting mighty late,
There's one more river to cross.

The animals went in nine by nine,
There's one more river to cross,
Old Noah hollered for to cut that line,
There's one more river to cross.

The animals went in ten by ten,
There's one more river to cross,
Old Noah blowed his whistle then,
There's one more river to cross.

Then the voyage did begin,
There's one more river to cross,
Old Noah pulled his gang-plank in,
There's one more river to cross.

They never knowed where they was at,
There's one more river to cross
Till the old ark bumped on Ararat,
There's one more river to cross.

295

OLD BLUE

This item is similar to the work-song reported by White (*American Negro Folk-Songs*, 1928, pp. 207-208) as sung by a Negro construction gang in Alabama. White thinks that it "has too much form and unity to be quite convincing" as a Negro folksong. It may be derived from some of the old-time "nigger minstrel" pieces. Compare the "Come On, Blue" song of which Perrow (*JAFL* 26, 1913, p. 128) remarks "it was said to have been composed by an old Negro in honor of his dog." Hudson (*JAFL* 39, 1926, p. 177) prints a similar text from Mississippi. The verse about the "silver spade an' . . . golden chain" is found also in "The Cholly Blues" reported by Lomax (*American Ballads and Folk Songs*, 1934, p. 202).

A

Contributed by Mrs. Cora Pinkley Call, Eureka Springs, Ark., Dec. 18, 1932.

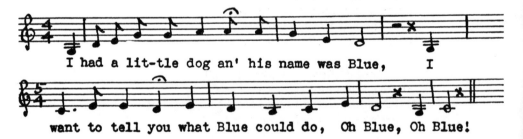

I had a lit-tle dog an' his name was Blue,   I

want to tell you what Blue could do, Oh Blue, Oh Blue!

Every night, just about dark,
You'll hear old Blue begin to bark,
Oh Blue, oh Blue!

I lights my lantern an' goes to see,
He's got a possum up a 'simmon tree,
Oh Blue, oh Blue!

I climb right up an' fotch him down,
I take him home an' bake him brown,
Oh Blue, oh Blue!

Early one mornin' old Blue took sick,
I sent for the doctor to come right quick,
Oh Blue, oh Blue!

When the doctor come he come on a run,
He says old Blue, your huntin' is done,
Oh Blue, oh Blue!

When old Blue died he died so hard,
He dug little holes all over th' yard,
Oh Blue, oh Blue!

I dug his grave with a silver spade,
An' let him down with a golden chain,
Oh Blue, oh Blue.

I put a snow white dove at the foot of his grave,
An' at his head put a possum face,
Oh Blue, oh Blue.

I'll clasp my heart an' cross my hands,
An' pray to meet Blue in the promised land,
Oh Blue, oh Blue!

B

From Miss Reba McDonald, Farmington, Ark., Feb. 6, 1942.

They dug his grave with a silver spade
And covered him over with a possum's face.

They let him down with a golden chain
. . . .
As every link passed through his hand,
Old Blue has gone to the promised land.

296

WALK ALONG JOHN

Doubtless related to the old fiddle-tune of the same name, still popular at the country dances. The "Walk Along John" chorus as given below by Mr. Campbell is the first stanza of a game-song of the same name reported by Wolford (*Play-Party in Indiana*, 1916, pp. 100-101). A minstrel song called "Walk Along John" is often credited to Dan Emmett. Compare a piece with a somewhat similar chorus given by Brewster (*JAFL* 57, 1944, pp. 283-284).

Sung by Mr. Booth Campbell, Cane Hill, Ark., Feb. 5, 1942. Says he heard it in the late 80's, at Cane Hill.

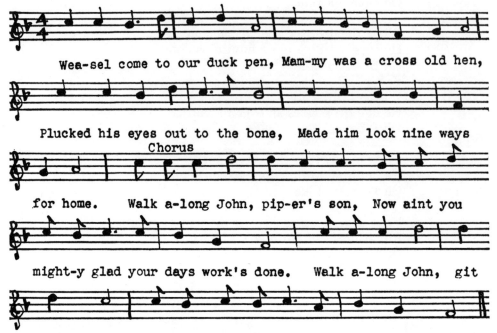

Wea-sel come to our duck pen, Mam-my was a cross old hen,

Plucked his eyes out to the bone, Made him look nine ways

for home. Walk a-long John, pip-er's son, Now aint you

might-y glad your days work's done. Walk a-long John, git

towards home, Aint you might-y glad your days work's done.

> Milk in the dairy nine days old,
> Skippers and the mice is a-gittin' mighty bold,
> Long-tailed rats from way down South
> Just come down to the white folks' house.
>
> Black Sam come to our smoke house,
> Walked in the door as still as a mouse,
> He stole our Lizzie's hoecake meal,
> Then he run across our cornfield.

297

CHICKEN RUN FAST

Sung by Miss Leone Duvall, Pineville, Mo., Sept. 7, 1926.

> Chicken run fast, chicken run slow,
> Chicken run by the Methodist preacher
> Chicken never run no more.

Water run fast, water run slow,
Water run by the Campbellite preacher
Water never run no more.

Turkey run fast, turkey run slow,
Turkey run by the Baptist preacher
Turkey never run no more.

298

GINGER BLUE

Ginger Blue is mentioned in many Negro songs. See *Negro Singer's Own Book* (1846, pp. 12, 348), White (*American Negro Folk-Songs*, 1928, pp. 380-381). White (380) says that "Ginger Blue was apparently a dangerous character whose history belongs to pre-minstrel obscurity." A roadhouse near Lanagan, Mo., is called the Ginger Blue Hotel, and a grave on the front lawn is said to contain the body of the original Ginger Blue, described as "a big chief of the Osage Indians." Compare the lengthy "Ginger Blue" song in *Richard Marsh's Selection, or Singing for the Million* (New York, 1854, part 2, p. 157) quoted by White (*American Negro Folk-Songs*, 1928, p. 448). See also the Brown (North Carolina Folk-Lore Society) collection. Charles Morrow Wilson published a boys' book about treasure-hunting in the Ozarks entitled *Ginger Blue* (Caxton Printers, Caldwell, Idaho, 1940). Ford (*Traditional Music of America*, 1940, p. 34) gives "Ginger Blue" as a traditional fiddle-tune. They tell me that the part of Fayetteville, Ark., in which Negroes live is called "Ginger Blue," but I have never been able to learn anything about the origin of the name.

Sung by Mrs. Marie Wilbur, Pineville, Mo., Nov. 11, 1926.

Walky, talky, Ginger Blue,
White man run, but the nigger he flew!

299

I KNOW A LITTLE FELLER

This is a fragment of a Texas Negro song entitled "I Went Down to New Orleans," reported by Bales (*Texas Folk-Lore Society Publications* 7, 1928, p. 100). May Kennedy McCord published one stanza in the Springfield (Mo.) *News and Leader*, May 6, 1934.

Sung by Mrs. May Kennedy McCord, Springfield, Mo., May 14, 1934.

I know a little feller, an' he's got the money too,
Oh don't I love my honey?
An' can't I spend his money?
I'm happy as a flower that sips the morning dew,
For I've got a little feller
And he's got the money, too!

300

OH YOU CAINT GO TO HEAVEN

Similar text under the title "I Aint Gonna Grieve My Lord No More" in the Aurora (Mo.) *Advertiser*, Nov. 28, 1940.

Sung by Mr. Charles McMahon, Joplin, Mo., Apr. 3, 1928.

Oh you caint go to heaven
In a rockin' chair,
Get down on your knees
An' say a prayer.

Oh you caint go to heaven
In them dancin' shoes,
An' you caint go to heaven
With your belly full of booze.

An' you caint go to heaven
On them roller skates,
You'll roll right by
The golden gates.

If you get there
Before I do
Just tell the Lord
I'm a-comin' too.

If you get there,
Before I do,
Just bore a hole
An' pull me through.

Oh the devil's mad
An' I am glad,
He lost a soul
That he thought he had.

301

CLIMBIN' UP THE GOLDEN STAIRS

See Ira W. Ford (*Traditional Music of America*, 1940, pp. 283-284). I heard this myself in Pittsburg, Kansas, about 1900.

From Miss Katherine Ollinger, Fayetteville, Ark., Dec. 21, 1941.

Come all you little niggers
Now watch your cues and figgers
Climbing up the golden stairs,
If they think you are a dude
They will treat you rather rude,
When you're climbing up the golden stairs.

Then hear them bells a-ringing,
'Tis sweet, I do declare,
To hear them darkies singing
Climbing up them golden stairs.

Old Peter looked so wicked
When I asked him for a ticket
Climbing up the golden stairs,
If I give him half a dollar
He will grab me by the collar
And fire me up the golden stairs.

Old Satan he's a dandy
He won't feed you on mixed candy
When you're climbing up the golden stairs,
Brimstone is plenty good enough,
No tobacco, beer or snuff
When you're climbing up the golden stairs.

They'll lock you in a stable
Make you fight for Cain and Abel
Climbing up the golden stairs,
Old Adam and his wife
They will play the drum and fife
To greet you on the golden stairs.

Go tell the Jersey Lily
That the sights would knock her silly
Climbing up the golden stairs,
And tell John L. Sullivan
That he can't be a Gulliver
If he tries to climb the golden stairs.

Bob Ingersoll is respected
But I think he'll be rejected
Climbing up the golden stairs,
Oh won't he kick and yell
When they fire him into—well,
Climbing up the golden stairs.

302

THE DEVIL'S MAD AND I AM GLAD

A similar stanza occurs in a religious song, "My Sins Are All Taken Away" (Chappell, *Folk-Songs of Roanoke and the Albemarle*, 1939, p. 151).

From Dr. J. H. Young, Galena, Mo., Nov. 14, 1941. He learned it at Ozark, Mo., in the 90's.

The devil's mad an' I am glad,
Oh hally hallelujah!
He lost one soul that he thought he had,
Oh hally hallelujah!
I run through the thickets
An' I dodged all the pickets
An' my soul's goin' home to glory!

303

ROLL, JORDAN, ROLL

A similar song is reported in the Brown (North Carolina Folk-Lore Society) collection.

Sung by Mrs. Maggie Morgan, Springdale, Ark., Feb. 21, 1942.

Away down South on Cedar Street
Roll sweet Jordan roll,
Where every nigger grows eleven feet
Roll sweet Jordan roll.

Roll, Jordan, roll,
Roll, Jordon, roll,
I want to go to heaven when I die
To hear sweet Jordan roll.

The monkey climb the telegraph pole
Roll sweet Jordan roll,
He couldn't get down to save his soul,
Roll sweet Jordan roll.

Kate went a-fishing de udder night,
Roll sweet Jordan roll,
She broke eleven hooks and never got a bite,
Roll sweet Jordan roll.

She gave her hook a right quick flip,
Roll sweet Jordan roll,
She caught dat nigger by the under lip,
Roll sweet Jordan roll.

Behind the chicken-coop on my knees,
Roll sweet Jordan roll,
I thought I heard a chicken sneeze,
Roll sweet Jordan roll.

It sneezed so hard with the whooping-cough,
Roll sweet Jordan roll,
It sneezed its head and tail both off,
Roll sweet Jordan roll.

Beefsteak, ham and mutton chop,
Roll sweet Jordan roll,
Makes dat nigger's lip go flipper-flop,
Roll sweet Jordan roll,

The Debil am a liar and conjurer too,
Roll sweet Jordan roll,
If you don't watch he'll conjure you,
Roll sweet Jordan roll.

304

IN THE MORNING BY THE BRIGHT LIGHT

In *Dr. M. A. Simmons' Song, Fortune, Dream & Cook Book* (St. Louis, Mo., n.d.) this piece is credited to James Bland, and printed "by permission Oliver Ditson Co., Boston."

Sung by Mrs. Maggie Morgan, Springdale, Ark., Feb. 21, 1942.

I'se gwine away by the light of the moon,
Want all the children to follow me,
I hope I'll meet you darkies soon,
Oh hally, hally hallelujah!
So tell the brothers that you meet,
Want all the children to follow me,
That I will travel on my feet,
Oh hally, hally hallelujah!

In the morning, morning by the bright **light**,
Hear Gabriel blow his trumpet in the **morning**.

Go get a match and light that lamp,
Want all the children for to follow me,
And show me the way to the Baptist camp,
Oh hally, hally hallelujah!
We'll have beefsteak and spare-rib stew,
Want all the children for to follow me,
And nice boiled onions dipped in dew,
Oh hally, hally hallelujah!

I'll take my old banjo along,
Want all the children for to follow me,
In case the boys should sing a song,
Oh hally, hally hallelujah!
For no one has to pay any fare,
Want all the children for to follow me,
So don't forget to curl your hair,
Oh hally, hally hallelujah!

305

THE OTHER SIDE OF JORDAN

Compare "Jordan Am a Hard Road to Travel," credited to T. F. Briggs (*Heart Songs*, 1909, pp. 136-137), the music composed by Dan Emmett and published by David A. Truax, Cincinnati, 1853 (Dichter and Shapiro, *Early American Sheet Music*, 1941, p. 145). Mentioned in *Put's Golden Songster*, Appleton & Co., San Francisco, 1858, "Jordan Is a Hard Road to Travel" was parodied in "Richmond Is a Hard Road to Travel, I Believe," a Southern war-song published by A. E. Blackmar & Co., New Orleans, 1863. Sheet music of the parody is in the Music Collection of the State Historical Society, Columbia, Mo.

Sung by Dr. B. B. McKellops, Galena, Mo., June 4, 1933. Dr. McKellops says that this piece was known to her family as long ago as 1840.

Oh I look to the East an' I look to the West
An' I seen old Nick a-comin',
With four bay horses all in a-breast
Acrost on the other side of Jordan.

Off with your coats, boys, an' roll up your **sleeves**,
Jordan is a hard road to travel, I believe,
Off with your coats, boys, an' roll up your **sleeves**,
Jordan is a hard road to travel, I believe.

Jonah in the whale, forty days an' forty nights,
No way to git out for certain,
Jonah took a straw, tickled the whale under the jaw,
An' it throwed him on the other side of Jordan.

Chapter VIII

SONGS OF TEMPERANCE

The Ozark country was originally settled by men from Virginia and Kentucky and Tennessee—hard-drinking Southerners who brought their "worms" over the mountains on packhorses—and in the early days they would tolerate no talk of temperance. I quote the following from J. A. Sturges' *History of McDonald County, Missouri* (Pineville, Mo., 1897, pp. 210-212). This particular section of Sturges' book was written by Mrs. Lora S. Lamance, and she refers to conditions at Pineville, Mo., in the sixties:

> Most of the stores sold whisky, and sold it with as little concealment as they did their calicoes; every farmer brought his jug with him when he came to town to trade; every horse swapping or land sale was confirmed by treats all around; every house and barn raising was dedicated by the passing of the whisky jug from hand to hand; the guests at every wedding grew hilarious with exhilarating corn-juice, while all too often the mourners of the funeral drowned their sorrows the same day in the oblivion of drunkenness . . . There were days of general uproariousness, led by reckless characters who drank and caroused, and held high carnival, bullying quiet, respectable citizens, defying the law, and over-riding the peace officers. On such days bullets would fly upon the streets until sober men would leap upon their horses and flee for their lives.

Unlike many temperance workers, Mrs. Lamance was not given to exaggeration in these matters. I once lived in the village of which she wrote, and have talked with dozens of the old-timers, who tell me that conditions such as she describes were common not only at Pineville but in many other Ozark settlements.

The late 70's saw a marked increase in the religious element in the hill country, and many itinerant evangelists began to preach temperance and even total abstinence. Then came several temperance societies, such as the "Blue Ribbon Club," the "Murphy Temperance Union," the "Good Templars," the "Sons of Temperance" and finally the "Woman's Christian Temperance Union." These people held meetings in the churches and schoolhouses, pledged themselves never to touch intoxicants, wore conspicuous badges and distributed temperance literature. Some of the more fanatical even went with song and exhortation to the homes of the local drunkards, and women followed these unfortunates about the streets, crying up the advantages of temperance and sobriety and so on. As one old man told me, "some of them women went plumb hawg-wild 'bout this here temperance—jest made a plumb damn fool out'n theirself!"

It was during this period of temperance agitation that the songs in this chapter came into use in the Ozarks. They were sung in the churches, in street parades, at the meetings of the temperance organizations, and even by school children in the public schools. Although I have been unable to identify some of these songs, or to find any reference to them in the literature of the subject, I have no doubt that they all go back to print, and probably appeared in the temperance songbooks of the time, or in the leaflets distributed by the various temperance societies.

306

THE DRUNKARD

Cox (*Folk-Songs of the South*, 1925, p. 403) prints a West Virginia variant of this song. Sandburg (*American Songbag*, 1927, p. 104) records seven verses from Ohio under the title "The Drunkard's Doom," with a very effective harmonization by H. L. Mencken. One of my Ozark texts (*The Ozarks*, 1931, p. 210) is reprinted by Lomax (*American Ballads and Folk Songs*, 1934, pp. 174-175). Compare the North Carolina version recorded by Matteson and Henry (*Beech Mountain Folk-Songs and Ballads*, New York, 1936, pp. 34-35), the Ohio version given by Eddy (*Ballads and Songs from Ohio*, 1939, p. 308), and that from Indiana given by Brewster (*Southern Folklore Quarterly* 4, 1940, pp. 183-184). Belden (*Ballads and Songs*, 1940, pp. 468-469) prints six stanzas and a chorus from Missouri, and gives several references to the literature.

Sung by Mrs. James Cleveland, Jane, Mo., Apr. 16, 1928.

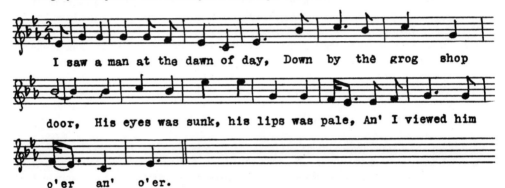

I saw a man at the dawn of day, Down by the grog shop door, His eyes was sunk, his lips was pale, An' I viewed him o'er an' o'er.

His oldest son stood by his side,
An' weepin', murmurin' said:
Father, mother is sick at home,
An' sister cries for bread.

The drunkard rose an' staggered in
As he had done before,
An' to the landlord falterin' said,
Oh give me one glass more!

He took the glass in his tremblin' hand,
An' drunk the liquor foul,
He drunk while wife an' children starved,
An' he ruined his pore soul.

Oh God forgive my husband dear,
The dyin' woman said,
Although he's been unkind to me
An' his children has cried for bread.

In just one year I passed that way,
The hearse stood at the door,
I ask the cause, an' they told me
That the drunkard was no more.

I seen the funeral passin' by,
No wife nor children there,
For they had gone on long before
An' left this world of care.

307

THE DRUNKARD'S DREAM

The English version of this piece is known as "The Husband's Dream." I have seen a printed copy, probably clipped from some old farm magazine, with the prefatory comment: "An English song, as sung by Fred Hill, an English sailor and ordinary seaman on board the United States sloop-of-war Portsmouth, West Coast of Africa, 1850." Miss Lucile Morris, Springfield, Mo., Jan. 16, 1935, showed me a manuscript copy dated 1857, which began: "Why, DeMont, you are healthy now!" For other American texts and references see Shearin and Combs (*Syllabus of Kentucky Folk-Songs*, 1911, p. 33), Cox (*Folk-Songs of the South*, 1925, p. 398), Richardson (*American Mountain Songs*, 1927, p. 41), Spaeth (*Weep Some More, My Lady*, 1927, p. 193), Greenleaf (*Ballads and Sea Songs from Newfoundland*, 1933, pp. 151-152), Eddy (*Ballads and Songs from Ohio*, 1939, pp. 225-227), Belden (*Ballads and Songs*, 1940, pp. 469-470), Brewster (*Southern Folklore Quarterly* 4, 1940, pp. 188-191), Henry and Matteson (*Southern Folklore Quarterly* 5, 1941, p. 144), and the Brown (North Carolina Folk-Lore Society) collection.

A

Sung by Mrs. Judy Jane Whittaker, Anderson, Mo., Apr. 16, 1928. "This certainly is an old song," says Mrs. Whittaker. "I learned it from my mother when I was just about knee-high, an' I'm nearly eighty now."

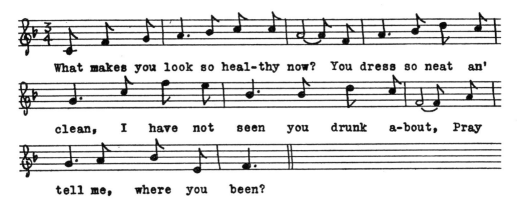

An' is your wife an' children well?
You once did use them strange,
Or have you to them kinder grown,
What makes this happy change?

It was a dream, a warnin' one,
That Heaven sent to me,
That snatched me from a drunkard's curse,
Great wants an' misery.

My wages was all spent in drink,
Oh what a wretched view,
I almost broke my Mary's heart
An' starved my children, too.

Oh Mary's form did waste away,
I seen her sunken eyes,
I starved my children night an' day,
I heard their wailin' cries.

I thought once more I staggered home,
I seen a silent gloom,
I missed my wife—where could she be?
An' strangers in the room.

I heard them say: Pore thing, she's dead,
She's lived a turrible life,
Grief an' sorrow has broke her heart,
Who'd be a drunkard's wife!

My children stood a-cryin' round,
They scarcely drawed their breath,
I knelt an' kissed her lifeless form
Forever cold in death.

Oh father, father, wake her up,
The folks all say she's dead,
An' make her speak an' smile once more,
An' we won't cry for bread.

She is not dead, I frantic cried,
I run to where she lay,
I knelt an' kissed her once warm lips
Which now was cold as clay.

Oh Mary, speak once more for me,
I'll never give you pain,
I'll never grieve your lovin' heart,
I'll never drink again!

Oh Mary, speak, it's Edward's call,
I says. I know, she cried,
An' when I woke my Mary dear
Was weepin' by my side.

I pressed her to my throbbin' heart,
An' joy an' tears did stream,
I ever since have Heaven blessed
For sendin' me that dream.

B

Mrs. Marie Wilbur, Pineville, Mo., June 7, 1929, sings a variant in which the dream is introduced by the following stanza:

I laughed an' sang in drunken joy,
While Mary's tears did stream,
An' like a wretch I fell asleep,
An' had this warnin' dream.

C

Sung by Mrs. Sula Hudson, Crane, Mo., Sept. 15, 1941. She learned it about 1905.

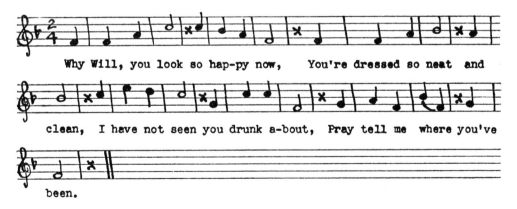

Why Will, you look so hap-py now, You're dressed so neat and clean, I have not seen you drunk a-bout, Pray tell me where you've been.

And is your wife and children well?
You once did treat them strange,
Or have you to them better grown?
How come this happy change?

It was a dream, a warning dream,
Oh which was sent to me,
To snatch me from a drunkard's grave
Of want and misery.

My children they have often woke,
Oh papa, they would say,
Poor mother has been growing weaker
Because we have no bread.

Oh papa, come and wake her up,
The people say she's dead,
And make her speak to us once more,
We will never cry for bread.

Oh speak to me, was William's call,
I will never give you pain,
I will not grieve your feeling heart
By getting drunk again.

308

FATHER, DEAR FATHER, COME HOME WITH ME NOW

Written by Henry Clay Work, author of "Marching Through Georgia" and other Civil War songs, and copyrighted by him in 1864, the original title was simply "Come Home, Father," but the song is better known by its opening and most quotable line. It was featured in the play "Ten Nights in a Bar-Room," credited to W. W. Pratt. Chapple (*Heart Songs*, 1909, p. 230) publishes one of the better-known versions. Spaeth (*Read 'Em and Weep*, 1927, p. 65) reprints the whole piece as originally published. See also the words and music in Frank Shay's *Drawn from the Wood* (1929, p. 27), and the text printed by Roe and Schwenck (*Bartender's Guide and Song Book*, New York, 1930, p. 48). This piece appears in the Brown (North Carolina Folk-Lore Society) collection. The original song had a chorus which has been lost in the Ozark variant, and the dying child was a boy named Benny, instead of the "Jenny" of the present text. There are several phonograph records (*Victor* 19716, *Gray Gull* 552D4122, *Radiex* 1F41220). There have been many parodies of this piece, such as "Father, Dear Father, Come Down with the Stamps," by Frank Wilde, published in 1867, and reprinted in Loesser's *Humor in American Song*, 1942, pp. 287-289.

Sung by Mr. R. K. Robinson, Siloam Springs, Ark., Dec. 4, 1913.

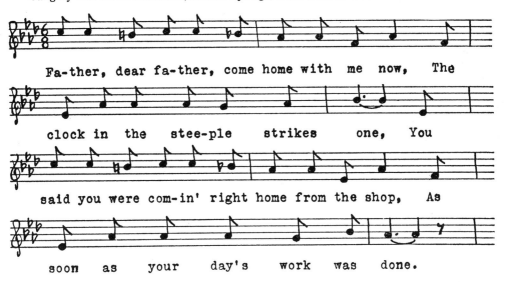

Fa-ther, dear fa-ther, come home with me now, The
clock in the stee-ple strikes one, You
said you were com-in' right home from the shop, As
soon as your day's work was done.

Our fire has went out, our home is all dark,
An' mother's a-watchin' for thee,
With pore little Jenny so sick in her arms
An' no one to help her but me.

Father, dear father, come home with me now,
The clock in the steeple strikes two,
The weather is colder an' Jenny is worse,
An' always a-callin' for you.

Jenny is worse an' maw says she will die
Perhaps before mornin' shall dawn,
An' this is the word that she sent me to bring,
Come home quick or she will be gone.

Father, dear father, come home with me now,
The clock in the steeple strikes three,
The house is so lonesome an' time is so long
For pore weepin' mother an' me.

We're all alone now, for Jenny is gone,
She went with the angels so bright,
An' those was the very last words that she said,
I want to kiss papa goodnight.

309

THE DRUNKARD'S LONE CHILD

A slightly different version is found in Spaeth (*Weep Some More, My Lady*, 1927, p. 191), who remarks feelingly that "there are some lines in this song that should be framed in every saloon in America today!' Spaeth includes a creditable chorus, which is lacking from the song as it is sung in the Ozarks. Mrs. Lora S. Lamance, Pineville, Mo., one of the pioneer temperance workers in southwestern Missouri, tells me that this song was a great favorite in the 60's. Henry (*JAFL* 45, 1932, pp. 58-59) reports an excellent text from oral tradition in the southern mountains. Compare the variant printed by C. V. Wheat in the Aurora (Mo.) *Advertiser*, Feb. 28, 1935. See also two related items noted by Stout (*Folklore from Iowa*, 1936, pp. 122-124), a piece from the Kentucky mountains reported by Campbell (*Southern Folklore Quarterly* 2, 1938, p. 163), the text and tune recorded by Ford (*Traditional Music of America*, 1940, pp. 370-371), and the piece in the Brown (North Carolina Folk-Lore Society) collection. There are phonograph records by Smith (*Columbia* 15137-D) and by the indefatigable Dalhart (*Edison* 51749).

A

Sung by Mrs. L. A. Thomas, Anderson, Mo., Aug. 29, 1928.

Out in the gloom-y night, sad-ly I roam, No one to love me, no
friends an' no home, No-bo-dy cares for me, no one would cry
Ev-en if poor lit-tle Bes-sie should die.

Mother, oh why did you leave me alone,
With no one to love me, no friends an' no home?
Dark is the night an' the storm rages wild,
God pity poor Bessie, the drunkard's lone child.

We was so happy till father drank rum,
Then all our troubles an' sorrows begun,
Mother grew paler an' wept every day,
Baby an' I was too hungry to play.

Hungry an' tired I've wandered all day
Askin' for work, but I'm too small, they say,
All day long I've been beggin' for bread,
Father's a drunkard an' mother is dead.

Oh if some temperance men only could find
Poor wretched father an' speak very kind,
An' if they could stop him from drinkin', why then,
I should be very soon happy again.

Is it too late? Men of temperance, please try,
For poor little Bessie will soon starve an' die.
On the damp ground I must now lay my head,
For father's a drunkard an' mother is dead.

B

Here is a text from Mrs. Ena Gregory, Hutton Valley, Mo., Feb. 4, 1930.

I'm alone, all alone, my friends has all fled,
My father's a drunkard and mother is dead,
I'm a poor little child, I wander and weep
For the voice of my mother to sing me to sleep.

I'm lonely and sad in this cold world so wild,
God look down and pity the drunkard's lone child,
In pity look down, oh hasten to me
And take me to dwell with my mother and Thee.

It's springtime on earth and the birds are so glad,
I listen and wonder my heart is so sad,
Sweet flowers around and the strangers pass by,
But the form of my mother no longer is nigh.

Last night in my dreams she seemed to draw nigh,
She kissed me as sweet as when she was here,
She smiled on me too and she fondled my brow,
And whispered sleep on, I'm a-watching you now.

C

Sung by Mr. Herschel Haworth, Springfield, Mo., Apr. 16, 1938.

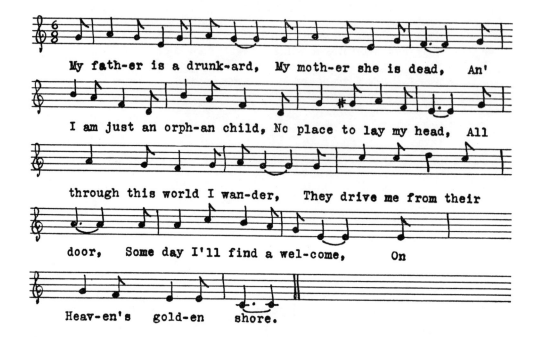

My fath-er is a drunk-ard, My moth-er she is dead,   An'

I am just an orph-an child, No place to lay my head,   All

through this world I wan-der,   They drive me from their

door,   Some day I'll find a wel-come,   On

Heav-en's   gold-en   shore.

Now if to me you'll listen
I'll tell my story sad,
How drinking rum and gambling
Have stolen away my dad;
My mother is in heaven
Where God and the angels smile,
And now I know she's watching
Her lonely orphan child.

We all were once so happy,
And had a happy home,
Till dad he went to drinking rum
And then he gambled some.
He left my darling mother,
She died of a broken heart,
And as I tell my story
I see your tear drops start.

Don't weep for me and mother,
Although I know it's sad,
But try to get some one to cheer
And save my poor lonely dad.
I'm awful cold and hungry,
She closed her eyes and sighed,
Then those who heard her story
Knew the orphan child had died.

D

The last stanza of "The Drunkard's Lone Child" as sung by Mrs. J. H. Trail, Farmington,
Ark., Nov. 2, 1941.

Oh men of triumph why don't you all try,
Poor little Bessie will soon starve an' die
No one cares for me, no one will cry,
Even if poor little Bessie should die.

E

Sung by Miss Wilma McDonald, Farmington, Ark., Feb. 10, 1942.

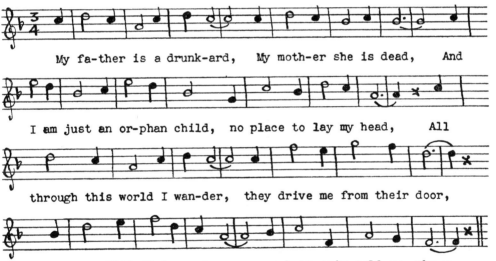

My fa-ther is a drunk-ard, My moth-er she is dead, And
I am just an or-phan child, no place to lay my head, All
through this world I wan-der, they drive me from their door,
Some say I'll find a wel-come on heav-en's gold-en shore.

Now if to me you'll listen I'll tell a story sad,
How drinking rum and a gambling hall have stolen away my dad,
My mother is in heaven, where God and the angels smile,
And now I know she's watching her lonely orphan child.

We all were so happy once, and had a happy home,
Till dad he went to drinking rum and then he gambled some,
He left my darling mother, she died of a broken heart,
And as I tell my story I see your tear-drops start.

Don't weep for me and mother, although I know 'tis sad,
But try to get someone to cheer and save my poor old dad,
I'm awful cold and hungry, she closed her eyes and sighed,
And those who heard her story knew the orphan child had died.

310

THE TWIN BALLOTS

Several Ozark temperance workers tell me that this song was popular in the 90's. The text appeared in *One Hundred Choice Selections No. 36*, edited by Phineas Garrett (Philadelphia, c. 1897, pp. 15-16). It is not represented in Belden's *Ballads and Songs*. Some very similar lines are found in *The Life of Carry A. Nation* (Topeka, Kans., 1908, p. 169), perhaps indicating that Mrs. Nation was familiar with the song.

Sung by Miss Leone Duvall, Pineville, Mo., Feb. 7, 1925.

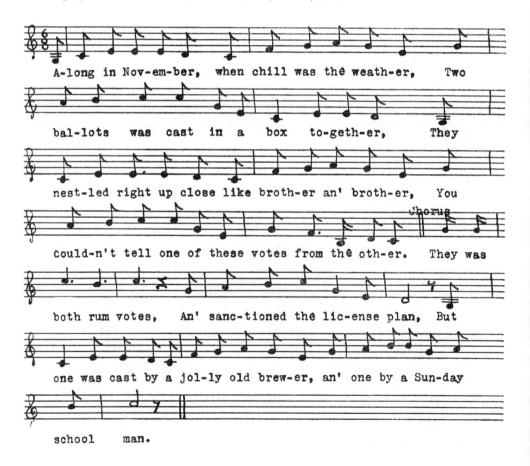

The Sunday School man—no man could be truer,
Kept busy all summer denouncin' the brewer,
But his temper cooled off with the change in the weather,
An' late in the Fall they both voted together.

The Sunday School man has allus been noted
For fightin' saloons—except when he voted.
He piled up his prayers with a holy perfection,
But he knocked 'em all down on the day of election.

The cunnin' old brewer was cheerful an' meller,
Says he, I admire this Sunday School feller,
He's true to his church, to his party he's truer,
He talks for the Lord, but he votes for the brewer!

311

LITTLE BLOSSOM

Another of the old favorites, popular in southwest Missouri in the 90's, and perhaps earlier. Little girls in starched white dresses used to sing it in front of the courthouse at election time. And the grown folk listened in all seriousness, it is said. Compare the text and tune in my *The Ozarks* (1931, pp. 211-214). Lucile Morris published ten stanzas of a similar piece under the title "Little Blossom," in the Springfield (Mo.) *News and Leader* (Oct. 14, 1934). For another Ozark text see C. V. Wheat in the Aurora (Mo.) *Advertiser* (Aug. 8, 1935). A Kentucky version is reported by Campbell (*Southern Folklore Quarterly* 2, 1938, pp. 163-164). Slim Wilson, a radio singer (KWTO, Springfield, Mo., May 28, 1941), sang "Little Blossom" to a different and much more sprightly tune.

A

Sung by Mrs. Bertha Combs, Kansas City, Mo., Dec. 25, 1923. Mrs. Combs learned the song from Mr. Columbus Bible, Rocky Comfort, Mo., about 1904.

Oh dear, I'm so tired an' lone-some, I won-der why
mam-ma don't come, She told me to shut up my blue
eyes, An' 'fore I'd wake up she'd come home.

I think I'll go down an' meet papa,
I reckon he stopped at the store,
It's a pretty big store full of bottles,
I wish he wouldn't go there no more.

Sometimes he is sick when he comes home,
An' stumbles an' falls on the stair,
An' one time he come in the parlor,
An' kicked at my pore little chair.

An' I 'member how papa was angry,
His face was so red an' so wild,
An' I 'member he struck at pore mamma,
A-smilin' so meek an' so mild.

But I reckon I better go find him,
Perhaps he'll come home with me soon,
An' then it won't be dark an' lonesome
A-waitin' for mamma to come.

Out into the night went the baby,
Her little heart beatin' with fright,
Till her tired feet reached the gin-palace,
All radiant with music an' light.

The little hand pushed the door open,
Though her touch was a light as a breath,
The little feet entered the portal
That leads but to ruin an' death.

Oh papa, she cried as she reached him,
An' her voice rippled out sweet an' clear,
I thought if I come here I'd find you,
I knowed that you'd surely be here!

A moment the bleared eyes gazed wildly
Down into the face sweet an' fair,
An' then as the demon possessed him
He grabbed at the back of a chair.

One moment, one second, 'twas over,
The work of the fiend was complete.
An' his pore little innocent baby
Lay quiverin' an' crushed at his feet.

Then swift as the light come his reason
An' showed him the deed he had done,
With a groan that the devil might pity
He knelt by her quiverin' form.

He pressed the pale face to his bosom,
He lifted the fair golden head,
A moment the baby lips quivered,
Then pore little Phoebe was dead.

Then in come the law so majestic
An' says with his life he must pay,
That only a fiend or a madman
Would murder a child that-a-way.

But the man that had sold him the pizen
That made him a demon of hell,
Why, he must be loved an' respected
Because he was licensed to sell.

He may rob you of friends an' of money,
Send you down to perdition an' woe,
But so long as he pays for the license,
The law must protect him, you know.

God pity the women an' children
Who live under the juggernaut rum.
God hasten the day when against it
Neither heart, voice nor pen shall be dumb!

B

Mr. J. H. Story, Pineville, Mo., July 14, 1922, showed me a text clipped from some old newspaper, with the final stanza as follows:

God pity the women and children
Who rail at the *jugomint* rum,
And hasten the day when against it
Every heart, voice and pen shall be won!

C

Sung by Mrs. Roy Oxford, Fayetteville, Ark., Dec. 13, 1941.

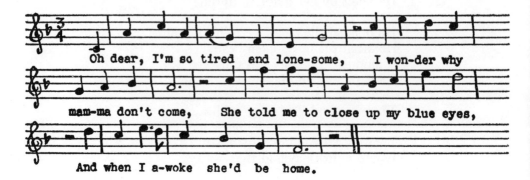

Oh dear, I'm so tired and lone-some,   I won-der why

mam-ma don't come,   She told me to close up my blue eyes,

And when I a-woke she'd be home.

She said she was going to see Grandma
Who lives by the river so bright,
But I guess that poor mamma fell in there,
I 'spose she won't be home tonight.

So I guess I'll go down and meet papa,
I 'spose he stopped down at the store,
It's a great big old store full of bottles,
And I hope he don't go there no more.

'Cause sometimes he's sick when he comes home,
He stumbles and falls at the stair,
And once when he came through the parlor
He kicked my poor little chair.

But I love him and guess I'll go find him,
And I hope he'll come home with me soon,
For then it won't be so lonesome
A-waiting for mamma to come.

So out in the dark went the baby
Her little heart beating with fright,
With a . . . . as the morning
And a . . . . of golden brown hair.

Out in the dark went the baby
Her little heart beating with fright,
Until she entered the portal
All radiant with music and light.

Her little hand pushed the door open,
Her touch was as light as her breath,
Until she reached the portal
That leads to both ruin and death.

Way down the . . . hall she pattered,
Her pretty blue eyes opened wide,
Till she spied in a corner her father
Her little feet crept to his side.

Oh papa, she cried as he saw her,
Her little voice . . . . . . clear,
I knew if I come I would find you
And I is so glad you is here.

A moment the . . . . . gazed wildly
Down into her face . . . .
A moment the demon pressed on him
And he grabbed at the back of a chair.

A moment, a second, 'twas over,
The work of a fiend was complete,
And poor little innocent Blossom
Lay quivering and crushed at his feet.

He pressed her fair face to his bosom,
He lifted her golden brown head,
A moment the baby lips quivered
And then little Blossom was dead.

In came the law and the justice
To show him the price he must pay,
For only a fiend or a madman
Could murder a child in that way.

But the man who had sold him the poison
And made him a demon to kill,
He must be loved and respected
For he has a license to sell.

312

THE WHISKEY SELLER

The early temperance workers had a trick of setting their propaganda to music already popular—a method used later by the Salvation Army, the Industrial Workers of the World, and various other reformers. It was with singular appropriateness and a humorous appreciation of values that they sang this "Whiskey Seller" song to the air of "The Little Brown Jug" (*The Ozarks*, 1931, pp. 214-215). I first heard this piece sung by a preacher at Camp Pike, Ark., in 1917. This man claimed to have "made up" the song himself when he lived near Siloam Springs, Ark., about 1900. Later on I discovered that it had been known and sung in Missouri long before the turn of the century. Recently I have seen a text from Mrs. Violet Savory Justis, Clinton, Mo., which may go back to the late 80's. Mrs. Justis found it, together with some manuscript copies of other old songs, in a chest belonging to her grandmother. "These songs was so old," she writes (July 13, 1930) "that the paper has turn brown and had to be peced to gather as they would brake and crumble all up."

Sung by Mr. Clint Maxwell, Joplin, Mo., Dec. 23, 1922.

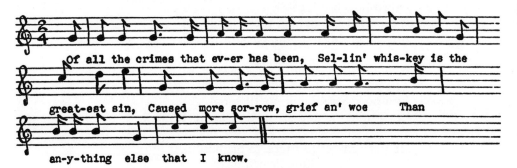

Of all the crimes that ev-er has been, Sel-lin' whis-key is the great-est sin, Caused more sor-row, grief an' woe Than an-y-thing else that I know.

> The old distiller an' the whiskey seller
> Has ruined many a clever feller,
> Caused more sorrow, grief an' woe
> Than anything else that I know.
>
> You rob the rich man of his store
> An' cause him to beg from door to door,
> You cause his wife an' children to mourn
> Because they have no home of their own.
>
> You rob the strong man of his stren'th,
> An' throw him in the mud full len'th,
> Leave him there for to curse an' roll.
> An' don't care nothin' for the pore man's soul.
>
> You rob the statesman of his brains,
> An' fill his head with achin' pains,
> He's often in the gullies found
> A-feelin' upwards for the ground.

You rob the children of their bread,
An' they are hungry sent to bed,
It causes them such bitter cries,
An' makes tears flow from the mother's eyes.

313

THE DRUNKARD'S HELL

Lomax (*Cowboy Songs*, 1910, p. 395) has a somewhat longer version of this piece, and I have seen a still more complete manuscript copy belonging to Mr. W. I. Wells of Paint Rock, Ala. Several Ozark singers tell me that the song was known in Arkansas as long ago as 1887.

A

Contributed by Mrs. J. C. Clanton, Washburn, Mo., Mar. 23, 1930.

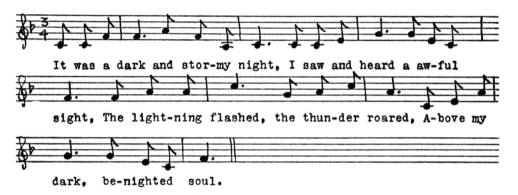

It was a dark and stor-my night, I saw and heard a aw-ful sight, The light-ning flashed, the thun-der roared, A-bove my dark, be-nighted soul.

I thought I saw that gulf below,
Where all poor dying drunkards go,
My feeling there no tongue can tell,
In this sure place of a drunkard's hell.

I went on and got there at last,
And thought I'd take a social glass,
But every time I'd stir it well,
I'd think about the drunkard's hell.

I dashed it out and left the place,
And went to seek redeeming grace,
Down on my knees to Jesus there
Poured out my soul in humble prayer.

I went on home to change my life,
And to my lone neglected wife,
I found her kneeling by the bed,
Because our infant babe lay dead.

I told her not to cry and weep
Because our babe had went to sleep,
Its precious soul has fled away
To live with Christ in endless day.

I took her by her lily white hand,
She was so weak she could not stand,
Down on our knees to Jesus there
Poured out our souls in humble prayer.

B

Contributed by an anonymous correspondent in Fort Smith, Ark., Aug. 12, 1932, who wrote: "I am now 62 year old and my grandmother knowed these songs, so I figure they must be anyhow a hundred year old by now."

I thought I seen a wicked crowd,
With voices strong they cried aloud,
Come on, young man, we'll find you room,
This is the whiskey-seller's doom.

I dashed it out all over the place,
And went to seek redeeming grace,
I felt like Paul when he did pray,
Because his sins was washed away.

. . . . . .

I taken her by her small white hand,
She was so weak she could not stand,
I bowed my head and breathed a prayer
That God might guide and save us there.

Seven long years has passed away
Since I first bowed my head to pray,
But still I live a Christian life
With a happy home and a Christian wife.

314

PUT THE TRAFFIC DOWN

This piece was favored by some of the temperance crusaders who whooped it up in the Ozarks about 1897 or 1898. Whether or not it was known earlier I have been unable to find out. A Holy Roller evangelist near Van Buren, Ark., once told me that the song was originally entitled "The Yorktown Rum Seller." Pound (*Folk-Song of Nebraska and the Central West*, 1915, p. 55) quotes four lines of this piece under the title "Old Jones."

A

Sung by Miss Elizabeth Waddell, Ash Grove, Mo., June 11, 1930. Miss Waddell learned
the song from her parents.

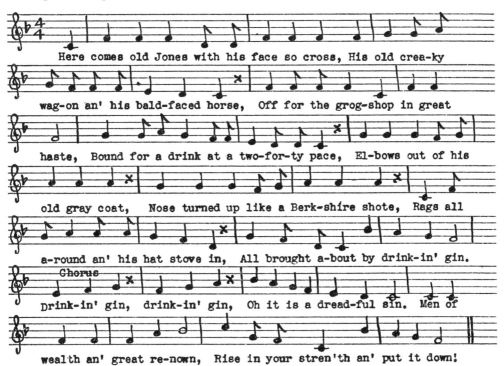

Here comes old Jones with his face so cross, His old crea-ky
wag-on an' his bald-faced horse, Off for the grog-shop in great
haste, Bound for a drink at a two-for-ty pace, El-bows out of his
old gray coat, Nose turned up like a Berk-shire shote, Rags all
a-round an' his hat stove in, All brought a-bout by drink-in' gin.
Chorus
Drink-in' gin, drink-in' gin, Oh it is a dread-ful sin. Men of
wealth an' great re-nown, Rise in your stren'th an' put it down!

Here comes Squire Brown with his rig so neat,
His wife an' his daughter an' his dairy-man Pete.
Dressed like a king from top to toe,
Off for a drive an' to make a fine show!
Neighbors bow as he passes by,
All are anxious to catch his eye.
He is rich, he's got the "tin,"
All brought about by sellin' gin.

Chorus

Sellin' gin, sellin' gin,
Oh it is a dreadful sin.
Men of wealth an' great renown,
Rise in your stren'th an' put it down!

Put it down, put it down,
Put the unholy traffic down!
Men of wealth an' great renown,
Rise in your stren'th an' put it down!

B

Mr. P. E. Bain, Picher, Okla., May 7, 1924, contributes a similar text with an additional
stanza:

You think it strange from my song, no doubt,
But wait till I tell you what it's all about,
An' don't get excited when I say
Squire Brown is the man we're after today.
Though he rides in his carriage neat,
Driven out by his dairy-man Pete,
He doth sell for the sake of gain,
Rum, gin an' brandy without shame.

Chorus

Without shame, without shame,
Quite regardless of his fame.
He doth sell for the sake of gain,
Rum, gin an' brandy without shame.

315

GONE LONG AGO

An adaptation of the well-known "Long, Long Ago" piece of the old songbooks, credited
to Thomas H. Bayly. Cf. *Heart Songs* (Boston, 1909, p. 435).

Sung by Mrs. May Kennedy McCord, Springfield, Mo., Apr. 29, 1938. Mrs. McCord's
sister, Miss Maudeva Kennedy, used to sing this piece at temperance rallies in Stone County,
Mo., about 1901 or 1902.

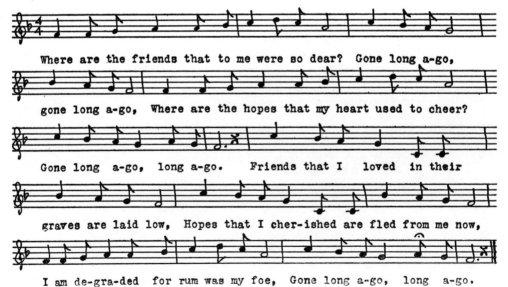

Where are the friends that to me were so dear? Gone long a-go,
gone long a-go, Where are the hopes that my heart used to cheer?
Gone long a-go, long a-go. Friends that I loved in their
graves are laid low, Hopes that I cher-ished are fled from me now,
I am de-gra-ded for rum was my foe, Gone long a-go, long a-go.

Sadly my wife bowed her beautiful head,
Gone long ago, gone long ago,
Oh how I wept when I knew she was dead,
Gone long ago, long ago.
Vainly to save me from ruin she tried,
Vainly she sought me to cherish and guide,
Poor broken heart, it was well that she died,
Gone long ago, long ago.

Let me look back on the days of my youth,
Gone long ago, gone long ago,
I was no stranger to virtue and truth,
Gone long ago, long ago.
Where are the hopes that were bright as the day?
Where are the friends that were happy and gay?
Where are the years that I squandered away?
Gone long ago, long ago.

316

OH, ONCE I HAD A FORTUNE

The first stanza is part of the "Eliza Jane" song reported from North Carolina by Henry (*Folk-Songs from the Southern Highlands*, 1938, p. 431). Compare also the first stanza of "Locked in the Walls of Prison," found elsewhere in this book.

Sung by Mr. Charles Ingenthron, Walnut Shade, Mo., June 30, 1940.

Oh once I had a for-tune, All locked up in a trunk, I lost
it all in a gam-bling hall One night when I got drunk. I'll
nev-er get drunk an-y more, I'll nev-er get drunk an-y more, I'll
keep my-self from the bar-room door, And I'll nev-er get
drunk an-y more.

Oh once I had a plenty
And friends all around me did stand,
But now my pockets are empty,
Not a friend have I in this land.

My sweetheart has a new fellow,
And me she has turned aside,
Farewell, farewell, my dearest little darling,
I'll go where the world is wide.

317

TEMPERANCE SONG

Sung by Miss Rose O'Neill, Day, Mo., Sept. 2, 1941. Learned about forty years ago.

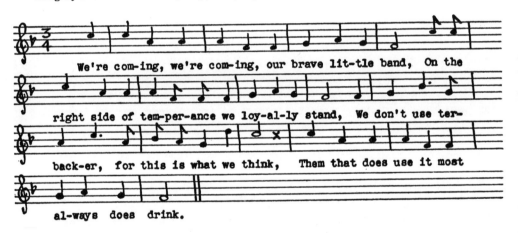

We're com-ing, we're com-ing, our brave lit-tle band, On the
right side of tem-per-ance we loy-al-ly stand, We don't use ter-
back-er, for this is what we think, Them that does use it most
al-ways does drink.

318

THE DRUNKARD'S HORSE

Sharp (*English Folk Songs from the Southern Appalachians*, II, 1932, p. 220) reports four stanzas of a related piece from Virginia, entitled "The Horse's Complaint." Compare the "Old Gray" song which Dobie (*Texas Folk-Lore Society Publications* 6, 1927, pp. 123-124) found in Texas.

A

Sung by Mr. Fred Woodruff, Lincoln, Ark., Dec. 12, 1941. He learned it in Washington County, Ark., about 1910.

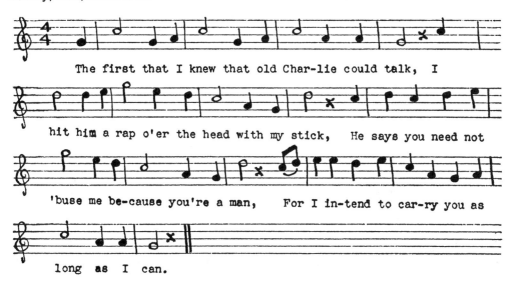

The first that I knew that old Charlie could talk, I hit him a rap o'er the head with my stick, He says you need not 'buse me because you're a man, For I intend to carry you as long as I can.

Last Monday morning you gave me my dues,
You rode me to London without any shoes,
All over the mountain and all over the rough ground,
The end of your journey I yet haven't found.

B

Text from Mr. James Bitner, Joplin, Mo., Aug. 10, 1927. Mr. Bitner could not remember where he first heard the song, but believed it was "a nigger minstrel parody" of some other old piece.

On one Sunday morning it come to my mind,
I'll saddle old Charley, some pleasure to find.
I never once thought that old Charley could speak
Till I give him a rap on the head with my stick.

He says do not bruise me, just to prove you're a man,
You know I will carry you as far as I can,
But last Monday morning, to bid me adieu
You rode me clear to Northburg without ary shoe.

There's hills and there's hollers and rocks in the ground,
And my revolution has never been found,
I stopped at each tavern to rest up my seat,
And fed you more corn than you really can eat.

It's when you are sober it's well for to know,
You feed very well and you ride very slow,
But when you're a-drinking you bawl and you squall,
You ride like the devil and feed none at all.

. . . .
. . . .

You crawl to the hitch-rack just about break of day,
And depend on old Charley to carry you away.

C

Sung by Mr. Wiley Hembree, Farmington, Ark., Dec. 29, 1941.

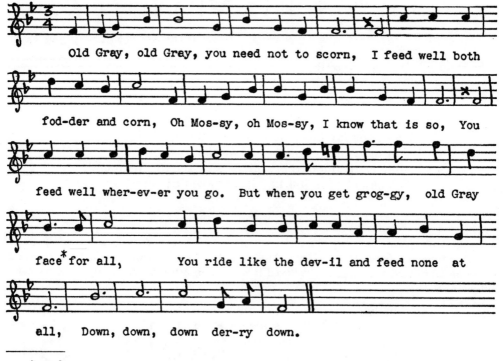

*pays?

320

RAG PAT

Sung by Mrs. Ray Oxford, Fayetteville, Ark., Dec. 13, 1941.

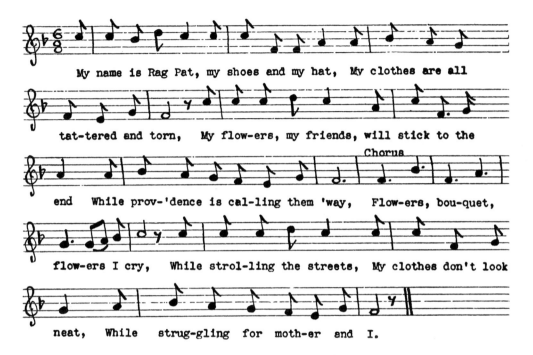

My name is Rag Pat, my shoes and my hat, My clothes are all
tat-tered and torn, My flow-ers, my friends, will stick to the
end While prov-'dence is cal-ling them 'way, Flow-ers, bou-quet,
flow-ers I cry, While strol-ling the streets, My clothes don't look
neat, While strug-gling for moth-er and I.

When I was a lad I had a bad dad
Although he was good in his way,
But the very last cent for whiskey he spent
While providence is calling them away.

One morning I rose and put on my clothes,
To try and sell flowers for bread,
When I returned my poor heart did burn
To find my poor mother was dead.

321

WE'LL GET THERE ALL THE SAME

Sung by Mrs. Maggie Morgan, Springdale, Ark., Feb. 9, 1942. She says it was popular in temperance circles in the early 90's.

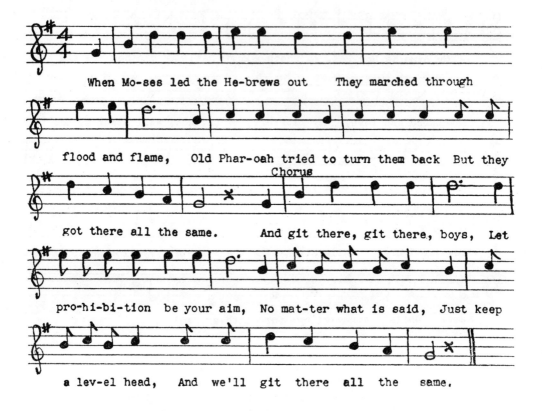

When Mo-ses led the He-brews out   They marched through flood and flame,   Old Phar-oah tried to turn them back But they got there all the same.   And git there, git there, boys,   Let pro-hi-bi-tion be your aim, No mat-ter what is said,   Just keep a lev-el head,   And we'll git there all the same.

Good Noah working on the Ark
Was put to open shame,
The people laughed and hooted him
But he got there all the same.

Our fathers brave in seventy-six
Our freedom did proclaim,
King George pronounced them rebel cranks,
But they got there all the same.

Some people call us temperance cranks
And we accept the name,
A crank is what you run things with,
And it gets there all the same.

322

DON'T SELL HIM ANY MORE RUM

Sung by Mrs. Maggie Morgan, Springdale, Ark., Feb. 9, 1942.

Don't sell him an-y more rum, He's reel-ing al-read-y, you see, I know when he comes home to-night He'll beat poor mam-ma and me. She's wait-ing in dark-ness and cold, and dread-ing to hear him come home, He treats her so bad when he's drunk, Don't sell him an-y more rum. Don't sell him an-y more rum, He's reel-ing al-read-y, you see, I know when he comes home to-night, He'll beat poor mam-ma and me.

I heard Mamma praying last night,
She thought I was quite sound asleep,
She prayed God her husband to save,
His soul from temptation to keep.
She cried like her poor heart would break,
And I tried to comfort her some,
I told her I'd beg you today
Not to sell Father any more rum.

Why don't you keep something to sell
That won't make people so sad?
That won't make happy mothers weep,
Kind fathers cruel and bad?
I know 'tis hard, I can see,
You are angry because I have come,
But forgive a poor little girl,
And don't sell Father any more rum.

323

THESE TEMPERANCE FOLKS

Sung by Mrs. Maggie Morgan, Springdale, Ark., Feb. 9, 1942. She learned it in the late 80's.

These temp-'rance folks do crowd us aw-ful-ly, Crowd us

aw-ful-ly, crowd us aw-ful-ly, These temp-'rance folks do

crowd us aw-ful-ly, They need not think I care. I'm not the

man to lose my lib-er-ty, lose my lib-er-ty, I'm not the man to

lose my lib-er-ty, I've not a bit to spare. I'd like to know

what's all this fuss a-bout, Some-thing's smash-ing through,

They hold their meet-ings round e-ter-nal-ly, I won-der what

Chorus

they do. Then for-ward, boys, hur-rah! We'll join the glo-

ri-ous fray, We'll hoist our flags and on to vic-to-ry,

The right shall gain the day.

They stick the pledge, these blue teetotalers,
Blue teetotalers, blue teetotalers,
They stick the pledge, these blue teetotalers,
Beneath each ruby nose.
They talk of woe and want and poverty,
Want and poverty, want and poverty,
They talk of woe and want and poverty,
There's truth in that, I s'pose.
I know my coat is rather seedy
And my pants are tattered too,
My right foot goes but poorly booted
And my left one wears a shoe.

I wish these chaps would cease to pity me,
Cease to pity me, cease to pity me,
I wish these chaps would cease to pity me,
I'm not yet quite bereft.
Though come to search my once fat pocketbook,
Once fat pocketbook, once fat pocketbook,
Though come to search my once fat pocketbook,
I've nary sixpence left.
I've a wife down town that would smile like Venus
If I'd sign the pledge today,
And a bright-haired boy that would jump and caper,
You may pass the pledge this way.

324

THE DRUNKARD'S STORY

Sung by Mrs. Ethel Robinett, Springfield, Mo., Sept. 3, 1940. She learned it from her father, Mr. John Crone, of Stone County, Mo.

Come all you young fellows and listen unto me,
And listen to the story I will relate to thee,
'Tis all about myself while in my wild career
When I was drinking whiskey, wine and lager beer.

I was a very good fellow, my parents worshipped me,
They set me up in business as soon as I was free,
And being young and handsome while in the prime of life,
I courted a fair lady and took her for a wife.

We settled in a little town far out in the west,
Where the people were all lively, myself among the rest,
Of course I took to drinking and staying out so late,
My wife would get uneasy and meet me at the gate.

She'd throw her arms around me and talk to me so kind,
I'd promise her to quit it but yet I would not mind,
So on and on I went till at last I had gone through
With the little home in which we lived and all our money too.

Starvation stared us in the face, I knew not what to do,
My darling wife and little ones were almost naked too,
My friends had left me one by one, I knew not where to go
To get a sack of flour or a yard of calico.

Cold and hungry as they were although a helper came,
And took them all away from me and left me in my shame,
I rambled around for several days without a bite to eat,
When night would overtake me my bed was on the street.

The saloon keepers would kick me out as they will always do,
For boys, when all your money's gone they've got no use for you,
And now my life is ended, my days on earth are o'er,
I say to all good fellows, don't never drink no more.

325

FATHER IS DRINKING AGAIN

Contributed by Miss Leone Duvall, Pineville, Mo., Aug. 22, 1927. Miss Duvall first
sang this at a temperance party in Pineville, about 1896.

I've been wandering all day in the cold and the rain,
To try my poor father to see,
He's been gone since last night, and mother's been told,
In the bar-room unconscious is he.

She sent me to find him and bring him to her,
All alone in the cold and the rain,
Oh God in thy mercy come help the poor child
Whose father is drinking again.

326

FRIENDS OF TEMPERANCE

This song was sung in Ozark churches as lately as 1910. I have seen a printed version in an unidentified shape-note songbook, credited to Arthur Bittenger, with the date 1875. A somewhat similar piece, "Song of Temperance," (*Franklin Square Song Collection* 7, 1890, p. 86) begins "Friends of freedom, swell the song."

Sung by Mr. Luther White, Joplin, Mo., Feb. 21, 1919.

> Friends of temperance, lift your banners,
> Wave them in the air,
> Sing ye now your glad hosannahs,
> Sing them loud and clear!
>
> Lo, the hour of victory cometh,
> See the dawning day,
> Rouse ye, drunkards, break your bondage,
> Dash your cups away!

327

SHIVERING IN THE COLD

Five stanzas of this piece are printed in the *Harvest Bells Songbook* (Eureka Springs, Ark., 1887, No. 271), both words and music credited to Mrs. Knowles Shaw. For a similar piece from oral sources, see the Aurora (Mo.) *Advertiser*, Apr. 29, 1937.

A

Sung by Mr. Lewis Kelley, Cyclone, Mo., Aug. 3, 1932. Mr. Kelley heard it often in McDonald County, Mo., in the late 80's.

> Far back in my childhood I remember today,
> I was happy and beloved e'er I wandered away,
> I was taught by my father, who sleeps 'neath the stone,
> And caressed by my mother, yet I wandered alone.
>
> > Yes alone, all alone,
> > And I feel I'm growing old,
> > Yet I wander, oh how lonely
> > And I'm shivering in the cold.
>
> I remember the maiden, and my heart bleeds to tell
> How I loved her devotion, but on this I cannot dwell,
> We were wed, our path was pleasant, and the sun of fortune shone,
> But alas, I took to drinking, now I wander alone.

I remember too my children, how they climbed upon my knee,
When I kissed my little darlings in the days when I was free,
But I squandered all my fortune, I'm now without a home,
And I know it's all from drinking, that I wander alone.

Oh can I break this bondage, and bust this hateful chain?
Can I escape these shackles? Can I be free again?
Oh help me, men of temperance, my bondage is untold,
While I wander sad and lonely, and shivering in the cold.

B

Sung by Mr. J. E. Dethrow, Springfield, Mo., Aug. 18, 1938.

Far back in my childhood, I remember today,
I was happy an' beloved, e'er I wandered away,
I was taught by my mother, who sleeps 'neath the stone,
An' caressed by my father, but I wander alone.

Yes alone, all alone,
An' I feel I'm growin' old,
Yet I wander, oh how lonely,
An' I'm shiverin' in the cold.

But why do I stand trembling and blighted by this curse?
I know I am not mending, I'm only growing worse,
I wander lone and friendless, I know I'm growing old,
No home, no food, no shelter, I am shivering in the cold.

328

SIGNING THE PLEDGE

Contributed by Mr. Ambrose L. Gates, Hot Springs, Ark., Jan. 16, 1920.

The old folks would be happy
If they knew I'd signed the pledge,
For my feet have long been straying
On the brink of ruin's edge.

But now I've quit my drinking,
No more shame upon my brow,
And the old folks would be happy
Could they see their boy just now.

Often they have pleaded with me
That I should try myself to save,
It was them kind words that kept me
From a drunkard's shameful grave.

They are growing old and feeble,
Swiftly passing down life's hill,
I must live to help and cheer them,
And God helping me, I will!

329

STAY, FATHER, STAY!

Perhaps this is related to the "Don't Go Out Tonight, Dear Father" song by Will L. Thompson (pub. by the W. L. Thompson Co., East Liverpool, Ohio, Feb. 15, 1877).

Sung by Mr. Luther White, Joplin, Mo., Feb. 21, 1919.

Stay, father, stay! the night is wild,
Oh leave not your dying child,
I feel the icy hand of death,
Shorter and shorter grows my breath.

Stay, father, stay, ere morning's light
My soul may wing its upward flight,
And oh I cannot, cannot die
While thou, my father, art not by.

Stay, father, stay, my mother's gone
And thou and I are left alone,
And from her starlit home on high
She'll weep that I alone should die.

Stay father, stay, oh leave alone this night
The maddening bowl whose withering blight
Has cast so dark a shade around
The home where joy alone was found.

Stay, father, stay, alone, alone,
With none to cheer and none to mourn
How can I leave this world of woe
And to the land of spirits go?

Stay, father, stay, once more I ask,
Oh count it not a heavy task
To stay with me till life shall end,
My last, my only earthly friend.

330

TOUCH NOT THE CUP

The words of this song are by J. H. Aikman and the music is by T. H. Bayly; see the *Franklin Square Song Collection* 3, 1885, p. 78.

Text from Miss Elizabeth Waddell, Ash Grove, Mo., June 17, 1927.

Touch not the cup—it is death to thy soul,
Touch not the cup, touch not the cup.
Many I know who have quaffed from the bowl,
Touch not the cup, touch it not.
Little they thought that the Demon was there,
Blindly they drank and were caught in its snare,
Then of that death-dealing bowl, oh beware,
Touch not the cup—touch it not.

Touch not the cup where the wine glistens bright,
Touch not the cup, touch not the cup,
Though like a ruby it shines in the light,
Touch not the cup, touch it not.
Fangs of the serpent lie hid in the bowl,
Deeply the poison will enter thy soul,
Soon it will plunge thee beyond thy control,
Touch not the cup—touch it not.

331

THE DRUNKARD'S CHILD

A Kentucky piece entitled "The Drunkard's Child" was recorded in 1937 by Alan Lomax (*Check-List . . . Archive of American Folk Song*, 1942, p. 87).

From Mrs. Joseph Pointer, Cabool, Mo., Aug. 8, 1940.

Oh, father, do not ask me why the tears roll down my cheek,
Nor think it strange indeed that I should own a grief or speak;
But, oh, my grief is very great, my brain is almost wild;
It breaks my heart to think that I must be a drunkard's child.

A drunkard's child, oh Lord, how sad! For mother was so mild;
But now she's sleeping in the tomb and I'm an orphan child.
My father never stays at home, he's drinking all the while;
It breaks my heart to think that I should be a drunkard's child.

Oh, father, once you loved your child, and we had much to eat;
Mother and I were nicely clad, and life it seemed so sweet;
You never spoke unkindly then nor dealt an angry blow;
Oh father, dear, 'tis hard to think that rum has changed you so.

My playmates they all shun me now or pass me by in scorn,
Because my dress is ragged, my shoes are old and worn;
And if I heed them not, "there goes the drunkard's child," they cry;
Oh then how much I wish that God would let this orphan die.

Oh father, don't be angry now, because I tell you this;
But let me feel upon my brow your warm and loving kiss;
And promise me those lips no more with drink shall be defiled,
And from a life of want and woe to save your weeping child.

Oh father, look to God through faith; His love can make you whole;
His power can break that appetite and save your sin-sick soul;
Oh, will you heed His patient call, His tender voice of love,
And follow in dear mother's steps to mansions bright above.

332

THE DRUNKARD'S WIFE

I have seen this piece in an unidentified songbook, copyright 1894 by L. L. Pickett. The tune of this piece was Pickett's, the words credited to M. W. Knapp. Compare also the Brown (North Carolina Folk-Lore Society) collection.

From Mrs. Sylvia Hill, Thayer, Mo., Aug. 25, 1940.

In the midst of a meeting a woman arose
And a warning she uttered there,
For the girls in the bloom of their beautiful youth
Who were happy and free and fair.

Oh, I married a drunkard, dear girls, she exclaimed,
And was giddy and young and gay,
But like mist in the morning my joys took their flight
And thus swiftly they passed away.

Oh girls, she then pleaded, oh heed me well,
And listen while I my story tell,
Too late I had learned of my wasted life
The terrible fate of a drunkard's wife.

I have learned that the crown of all sorrow below
Which will crush and will blight the heart,
The poor wife of a drunkard is destined to know
And to writhe and to suffer the smart.
Though young, yet behold my hair is white
Made so by the scenes of one sad night.

Oh the sight, oh the sight of that terrible night,
She exclaimed in an anguished tone,
And the scenes of the past seemed to rush o'er her sight
As if reason they would dethrone.
With hands that were pale she hid her face
As if to conceal her deep disgrace.

The delirium tremens, oh girls, have you seen?
May God spare you the fearful sight
Of a husband insane by the demon drink
As he staggers toward home at night.
Oh take them away! I heard him scream,
It seems like a sad and awful dream.

On that night I was sitting beside my sick boy
And my two little girls at rest.
With a feeling of fear, that they both were unsafe,
Of my soul possessed.
I rushed to their room, and on the bed
I found they were mangled, cold and dead.

By the hands of their father they both had been slain
And the knife with their blood still red,
In the frenzy of drink and madness of shame
He still raved with his reason fled.
On me he then glared, his wretched wife
And then with a thrust he took his life.

Then I fell to the floor and was borne from the room,
A wreck since that night I've been,
And the boy that was left had a passion for drink,
The sad mark of his father's sin.
It chained him, though young, a hopeless slave,
And early he filled a drunkard's grave.

I beg of you girls, as you value your lives
From the drinker to turn aside,
And give heed to no plea, whatever it be
Of a drinker to be the bride.
To save from such sorrow as wrecked my life,
Oh never become a drunkard's wife.

333

THE RUM SALOON SHALL GO

An unidentified songbook, from which the title page is lacking, credits the words to Jno. O. Foster and the music to Jno. R. Sweeney, adding that the song was copyrighted in 1888. See also a shape-note songbook *Tears and Triumphs*, published by L. L. Pickett, Louisville, Ky., 1894.

From Mrs. Sylvia Hill, Thayer, Mo., Aug. 25, 1940.

A wave is rolling o'er the land
With heavy undertow,
And voices sounding on the strand
The rum saloon shall go.

Shall go, shall go,
We know, we know,
A cry is sounding o'er the land,
The rum saloon shall go.

Its doom is written on the sky
Above the shining bow,
For indignation now is high
The rum saloon shall go.

We've stood the wretched bitter moans
Full long enough, you know.
And soon we'll speak in thunder tones
Unless they close and go.

The land is tired of the curse,
The people have said so,
And if it halts we'll make it worse
And help them soon to go.

334

WE'LL CROWN THEM WITH ROSES

From Miss Elizabeth Waddell, Ash Grove, Mo., June 17, 1927.

We'll take up our stand for the youth of our land
And weave them a garland to wear,
Though no leaves of the vine in our wreath we'll entwine
For we'll crown them with roses so fair.

We'll crown them, we'll crown them,
We'll crown them with roses so fair,
We'll crown them we'll crown them,
We'll crown them with roses to wear.

We'll tempt not their youth from its fountain of truth
Whose waters are pure and divine,
But will banish fore'er from our homes that are dear
The chalice that sparkles with wine.

Our sweet household joys, the girls and the boys,
We'll shield from the tempter so bold,
And we'll bind their white brows that with innocence glow
With a crown that is richer than gold.

335

DOWN IN A LICENSED SALOON

The words and music of this song by W. A. Williams, who copyrighted it in 1892, appeared in *Prohibition Songs*, edited by Charles M. and J. H. Fillmore (Cincinnati, 1903, No. 15), under the caption "An answer to, 'Where is My Wandering Boy To-night?'" The words of the second verse differ from the text given here.

From Mrs. Lillian Short, Cabool, Mo., Dec. 30, 1940.

Where is my wandering boy tonight,
Down in a licensed saloon.
Down in a room all cozy and bright,
Filled with the glare of many a light.
Ruined and wrecked by the drink appetite,
Down in the licensed saloon.

Down, down, down, down in a licensed saloon.

Once he was pure as morning dew,
As he knelt at his mother's knee,
No face was more fair,
No heart more true,
And none were as sweet as he.

Little arms were once thrown around my neck,
Look at him now! My poor heart will break.
Think of my boy tonight.
A sad wreck!
Down in a licensed saloon.

Brother, I guess you'd enter the fight
If it were your own
Down there tonight.
Ruined and wrecked by the drink appetite
Down in a licensed saloon.

336

NOR WILL I SIN

This fragment was published in the Pineville (Mo.) *Democrat*, Oct. 30, 1903. I have not seen it elsewhere. A somewhat similar song called "The Drink I'll Use," by A. W. Orwig and J. H. Kurzenknabe, is No. 215 in *American School Songs*, edited by Kurzenknabe (Chicago, 1904).

Sung by Mrs. Marie Wilbur, Pineville, Mo., Apr. 14, 1930.

Nor will I sin by drinking gin,
And cider, too, will never do,
Nor brewers' beer my heart shall cheer,
Nor sparkling ale my face to pale.

To quench my thirst I'll always bring
Clear water from the well or spring,
So here I pledge perpetual hate
To all that can intoxicate.

337

DON'T NEVER MARRY A DRUNKARD

C. V. Wheat (Aurora, Mo., *Advertiser*, Nov. 21, 1940) has a very similar text entitled "Seven Long Years," collected in Lawrence County, Mo. "I'm Going to Georgia" as reported by Henry (*Folk-Songs from the Southern Highlands*, 1938, p. 278) has the same theme and several similar lines, but it is not the same song.

From Mr. Elmo Playter, Joplin, Mo., Sept. 4, 1926. Mr. Playter learned it from his mother, who was a native of eastern Tennessee.

Seven long years I've done been married,
I wish to God I was a old maid,
For I aint seen nothin' but trouble,
My man he won't work at his trade.

He promised me before we was married
He'd dress me up in silks so gay,
And every night when work was over
He'd take me to a ball or play.

But now I get up in the morning
And work and toil the livelong day,
And then I got to get his supper
And wash the dishes and put them away.

Then he goes down to the bar room,
Go bring him home now if you can,
Oh girls, you never know no trouble
Until you're tied to a drunken man.

I wash the children's little faces,
And try to put them both to bed,
And then in comes their drunken father,
He says he wishes they was dead.

When I was livin' at my father's
I was always treated very well,
But now I'm married to a drunkard
Sometimes I wish I was in hell.

Come all you pretty nice young girls
And listen to my good advice,
Don't never marry with a drunkard,
It's better to live a single life.

338

MOLLY AND THE BABY

C. V. Wheat printed a similar text in the Aurora, Mo., *Advertiser*, Aug. 22, 1935.

Sung by Mrs. Maggie Morgan, Springdale, Ark., Feb. 21, 1942.

There's a patient little woman here below,
And a little kid that ought to have a show,
Now I'll give the whiskey up and I'll take a coffee cup
With Mollie and the baby don't you know.

Don't you know, don't you know,
What a fellow ought to do
When he's got a little family
Depending on him so,
He should try to be a man
And to do the best he can
For Mollie and the baby, don't you know.

You may tell the liquor sellers not to crow,
They will never get a nickel from me now,
They may keep their poison trash and I'll put away my cash
For Mollie and the baby, don't you know.

You may tell the politicians they may go,
I am in for Prohibition head and toe,
For at last I've turned my coat and I'll cast a temperance vote,
For Mollie and the baby, don't you know.

339

DON'T GO OUT TONIGHT, MY DARLING

Sung by Mrs. Maggie Morgan, Springdale, Ark., Feb. 21, 1942. She showed me a manuscript copy apparently written in 1889, headed "Don't Go Out Tonight, My Darling—a faithful wife's pleadings to her drunken husband."

Don't go out tonight, my darling,
Do not leave me here alone,
Stay at home with me, my darling,
I am lonely when you're gone.
Though the wine-cup may be tempting,
And your friends are full of glee,
I will do my best to cheer you,
Darling won't you stay with me?

Don't go out tonight, my darling,
Do not leave me here alone,
Stay at home tonight, my darling,
I am lonely when you're gone.

Oh my darling, do not leave me,
For my heart is filled with fear,
Stay at home tonight, my darling,
Let me feel your presence near.
Oh my God, he's gone and left me,
With a curse upon his lips,
Who can tell how much I suffer
From the accurs'd cup he drinks.

Hear the tread of heavy foot-steps,
Hear the rap upon the door,
They have brought me home my husband,
There he lays upon the floor.
No caress of mine can wake him,
All he craves is rum, more rum,
And the fondest hopes I cherished
All have faded one by one.

340

I'M STICKING TO THE MURPHYS

"The Old-Timer," reminiscing in the Springfield, Mo., *News and Leader*, Jan. 24, 1936, says that the Murphy movement came to Springfield some sixty years ago. Hundreds signed the pledge:

> I, the undersigned, do pledge my word and sacred honor, God helping me, to abstain from all intoxicating liquors as a beverage and I will, by all honorable means, encourage others to abstain.

"When one signed," says Old-Timer, "a blue badge was given and this was to be worn. The blue ribbon was especially attractive to the young boys of the day and they signed up in large numbers so as to get the decoration. That is about as far as the interest of many went. A few men in Springfield wore yellow badges, which meant that they were opposed to the prohibition movement." The Old-Timer reprints a song from the Mount Vernon, Mo., *Chieftain*, printed 58 years ago:

> I'm sticking to the Murphys,
> I'll fight 'em till I die;
> I can't help spitting cotton
> Because I am so dry.
>
> You'd bust your ribs with laughter,
> Stick to the pledge I must,
> But the more I drink cold water
> The more I'm belching dust.

341

LIPS THAT TOUCH LIQUOR SHALL NEVER TOUCH MINE

I have seen an old newspaper clipping, probably dating to 1901, in which this poem is credited to George W. Young. As of Young's composition it appears in *One Hundred Choice Selections No. 16*, edited by Phineas Garrett (Philadelphia, c. 1906, pp. 88-89).

Manuscript copy from Mrs. Maggie Morgan, Springdale, Ark., Feb. 1, 1942. She heard it sung at temperance meetings some time prior to 1917.

> You are coming to court me, but not as of yore
> When I hastened to answer your ring at my door,
> For I trusted that he who stood waiting me then
> Was the brightest and truest and noblest of men.
> When your lips on mine imprinted farewell
> They had never been soiled by the beverage of hell,
> But they come to me now with that terrible sign,
> And the lips that touch liquor shall never touch mine.

I think of that night in the garden alone
When in whispers you told me your heart was my own,
That your love in the future should faithfully be
Never shared by no other, kept faithfully for me.
Oh sweet to my soul is that memory still
Of the lips that met mine when I murmered I will,
But now to that pressure no more I incline,
For the lips that touch liquor shall never touch mine.

Oh John, how it crushed me when first in your face
The pen of the Demon had written disgrace,
And turned me in silence and tears from the breath
All poisoned and fouled with the perfume of death.
It scattered the hopes I had treasured to last,
It ruined the future and darkened the past,
It shattered my idle and sullied the shrine,
For the lips that touch liquor shall never touch mine.

I loved you dearer than language can tell,
You saw it, you knew it, you proved it too well,
But the man whom I loved was far other than he
Who now from the barroom comes reeling to me.
In manhood and honor so noble and right,
Your heart was so true and your genius so bright,
Your soul was unstained, unpolluted by wine,
But the lips that touch liquor shall never touch mine.

You promised reform, but I trusted in vain,
The pledge was but made to be broken again,
And the lover so false to his promises now
Would not as my husband be true to his vow.
The word must be spoken that bids you depart,
Though the effort to speak it will shatter my heart,
In silence, with blighted affection I'll pine,
But the lips that touch liquor shall never touch mine.

If one spark of virtue within you remains,
Go fan it with prayers till it kindles again,
Resolve with God's help you in future will be
From wine, beer and whiskey unshackled and free,
And if you can conquer this foe of the soul,
In manhood and honor beyond its control,
This heart will again beat responsive to thine,
And your lips free from liquor be welcome to mine.